CANADA 1911

THE DECISIVE ELECTION
THAT SHAPED THE COUNTRY

— PATRICE DUTIL AND DAVID MacKENZIE —

DUNDURN
TORONTO

Editor: Allison Hirst
Design: Jesse Hooper
Printer: Webcom

Library and Archives Canada Cataloguing in Publication

Dutil, Patrice A., 1960-
    Canada 1911 : the decisive election that shaped the country / Patrice Dutil and David MacKenzie.

Includes bibliographical references and index.
Issued also in electronic formats.
ISBN 978-1-55488-947-1

    1. Canada--Politics and government--1896-1911. 2. Canada--Politics and government--1911-1921. 3. Canada--History--1867-1914. I. MacKenzie, David (David Clark), 1953- II. Title.

FC550.D88 2011   971.05'6   C2011-901153-0

1   2   3   4   5   15   14   13   12   11

 Conseil des Arts
du Canada   Canada Council
for the Arts   Canada   ONTARIO ARTS COUNCIL
CONSEIL DES ARTS DE L'ONTARIO

We acknowledge the support of the **Canada Council for the Arts** and the **Ontario Arts Council** for our publishing program. We also acknowledge the financial support of the **Government of Canada** through the **Canada Book Fund** and **Livres Canada Books**, and the **Government of Ontario** through the **Ontario Book Publishing Tax Credit** and the **Ontario Media Development Corporation**.

Care has been taken to trace the ownership of copyright material used in this book. The author and the publisher welcome any information enabling them to rectify any references or credits in subsequent editions.

J. Kirk Howard, President

Printed and bound in Canada.
www.dundurn.com

Dundurn Press
3 Church Street, Suite 500
Toronto, Ontario, Canada
M5E 1M2

Gazelle Book Services Limited
White Cross Mills
High Town, Lancaster, England
LA1 4XS

Dundurn Press
2250 Military Road
Tonawanda, NY
U.S.A. 14150

 MIX
Paper from
responsible sources
FSC
www.fsc.org   FSC® C004071

For Maha Dutil and Teresa Lemieux

CONTENTS

PREFACE

One hundred years ago, Canadians witnessed one of the most dramatic political events in their history. During the election of 1911, they fiercely debated issues vital to national independence and global in scale as they considered their country's place in the British Empire, its attitude toward the arms race that raged between Germany and England, and its relations with the United States. It involved great personalities, important issues, regional tensions, and passionate arguments. It was Canada's first great modern contest, and the issues presented to Canadians a century ago are still with us today. The decisions they made still have an effect on us in 2011.

It was a contest of political giants. In July 1911, Sir Wilfrid Laurier, the widely popular and charismatic leader of the Liberal Party, unexpectedly launched a fourth bid for re-election. Almost seventy, he counted on his legendary charm to sell Canadians on his bold ideas for reciprocity with the United States and a modest but independent Canadian navy. "Sir John was the Moses of Reciprocity who failed to reach the Promised Land," he announced. "I will be the Joshua who will lead the people of Canada to the goal." He took the ultimate risk by calling an election a year earlier than expected (the first time this had ever been done), even though his Liberal Party was divided. In Quebec he was condemned as an imperialist for choosing to build a navy and for doing the British Empire's bidding at a time when it was actively engaged in an arms race with Germany; in Ontario he was labelled anti-British for not doing enough and for choosing instead to promote closer ties with the United States. In both provinces he lost many supporters. Laurier also underestimated his opposition, not so much the Conservatives as much as former prominent Liberals, who denounced him and actively worked to defeat him.

Laurier faced Robert Borden, fifty-seven, the Conservative leader of the Opposition since 1901. Borden had already lost to Laurier twice, and his leadership of his own party was often in doubt, but in 1911 he was ready for battle. Canada had changed, he thought, and the old charm of Laurier would be no match for his cold political calculations. Borden won the contest and woke up to find himself prime minister; the government elected that day in 1911 went on to lead the nation through the cataclysm of the First World War. Canadian history from that moment unfolded as it did because of the decisions made by Canadians in September 1911.

Beyond the limits of charisma that can be recognized easily today, the 1911 election was also important for the issues it illuminated. It revealed, with uncommon clarity, the muscles that flex Canada's political body. It showed the unique political aspects of the West, Quebec, and the Maritimes, and the strength of the business class in Toronto and Montreal. It showed that in the minds of the people of Canada there were many different ideas of what it meant to be "Canadian," and that in Quebec the principles of Canadian autonomy were core values. It revealed the uneasiness of Canadians toward their neighbour to the south and the growing sense of attachment, at the time, to the British Empire. Finally, the 1911 election showed how major issues can be decided by a relatively small and concentrated number of electors who make a decision to switch their voting allegiance.

Success in Canadian politics is often measured as an ability to compromise and balance competing languages, provinces, and groups, and our traditional understanding of Laurier and Borden is that the former was flexible and able to compromise whereas the latter was stiff and inflexible and, ultimately, less successful. These traditional views retain considerable insight, but the election of 1911 forces us to reconsider some of these basic premises. Laurier's defeat in 1911 was less the result of his failure to compromise and more the shifting mood of the country that increasingly found his efforts at compromise unacceptable. The picture of Laurier that emerges here is not one of a desperate and fading politician grasping for one more term in office after his star had declined, but rather one of an assertive and determined leader with a platform — founded on the twin pillars of a Canadian navy and reciprocity with the United States — that pointed optimistically to a new future for Canadians. It was the Canadian public (including many Liberals) who would no longer tolerate Laurier's compromises — and their views were expressed effectively, not only by Borden and the Conservatives, but also by the likes of Clifford Sifton, Henri Bourassa, Frederick Monk, Armand Lavergne, Sir Edmund Walker, Zebulon Lash, and many others.

For his part, Borden was less the stolid and earnest politician and ultimate benefactor of Laurier's folly and more a skilled and driven leader who pursued his victory in a determined, thorough, and methodical way. Perhaps more than Laurier, Borden sensed how Canada had changed — the country was more mature, self-confident, and economically prosperous than ever before, but unsure of how to expend its energies — and he was able to capitalize on this new reality. Victory did not simply drop into his lap as a result of the failure of a weak, dispirited, and tired Liberal Party; it was won thanks to his party's exhaustive campaigning, a strong Conservative organization, a clear and straightforward message that was repeated endlessly across the country, and to some of the most daring political bargaining that this country has ever seen.

It was all a gamble and each leader risked his political future. Laurier chose to run on a platform of reciprocity, his navy, and an undeniable record of prosperity, hoping that he could convince enough Canadians of the benefits of his policies without alienating the support the Liberal Party already could count on, especially in Ontario and Quebec. Borden also gambled that he could convince enough Canadians to look beyond the immediate economic benefits of reciprocity by focusing on nationalism and the question of loyalty to the Empire. Turning his back on the economic arguments that favoured reciprocity, he based his campaign on nationalism, loyalty, country, and Empire. For both leaders and their parties it was a daring leap of faith.

The election of 1911 was unusual in a number of other ways. With its clear issues of reciprocity and the navy, it was one of the few elections that revolved around international questions. Canadians understood that the vote was essentially a referendum on the future direction of the country and its relationships with Great Britain and the United States. In the process of the campaign, however, the stakes were raised so high that both sides claimed that, depending on how Canadians voted, the ultimate survival of the country hung in the balance. With stakes so high, the politics of fear emerged. Both sides were quick to portray the issues of the campaign as matters of life and death and to paint their opponents variously as warmongers, traitors, cowards, fools, sell-outs, and the harbingers of economic disaster.

The 1911 election was also a unique juncture in Canadian history that brought together an extraordinary cast of characters from the world of politics and business, including three future prime ministers (Bennett, Meighen, and King) and a host of others who made important appearances, including Sir William Van Horne, J.W. Dafoe, Stephen Leacock, Sir Sandford Fleming, Joseph Flavelle, J.S. Willison, Rodolphe Lemieux, Sam Hughes, Max Aitken (the future Lord Beaverbrook), William Howard Taft, the president of the United States, and Rudyard Kipling. Women were also active in this campaign — the last one in which they did not vote — as they manifested their interest in the issues, were present at the mass rallies, and organized for both sides. Their leadership in this campaign was mostly anonymous, but contributed to reinforcing the view that their absence at the ballot box was an absurdity.

The central questions raised in 1911 were not resolved for good in the general election, but the way they were discussed shaped the country's politics for the rest of the century. Canadians ultimately returned to free trade in 1988 and continue to wrestle with the ramifications of the agreement; the place of Quebec in Canada remains a question today, and we live with the uncertainty of Quebec nationalism; our political contests continue to focus on the leaders as much as the issues; and the use of fear first deployed in 1911 is still a common political tool. Looking back to 1911, then, is not only to open a door on the past but also a way to broaden our understanding of the present.

The centennial of the 1911 election, therefore, offers an extraordinary opportunity to revisit, remember, and re-examine this momentous turn in Canadian history, when Canadians truly found themselves forced to make fundamental decisions about the future of their country. American president Taft said that Canada had come to a "parting of the ways," while the novelist Rudyard Kipling wrote at the time that this federal election was nothing less than a fight for Canada's soul. This book explains why.

Our goal has been to write as comprehensive an account of the 1911 election as possible and in the course of our work we have examined the personal papers of all the key players, along with others who played smaller but important roles. We also made great use of material originally written or published in French and have assumed the task of translating this material ourselves. We have also tried to expand and deepen our understanding of the election by conducting research in the national archives of both the United States and Great Britain. In addition to this primary material, we surveyed most of the important newspapers to get a flavour of how the issues were played out across the country.

We have had the good fortune of being able to count on a number of people for support. The first thanks go to our research assistants, Daniel Quintal, Jeff Jenkins, and Josh McLarnon, who helped us scour libraries, scroll through newspaper reels, collect electoral data, and track down parliamentary debates and documents. Josh McLarnon's special contribution was in drawing the maps, based in part on detective work, clever interpretations of smudged newspaper charts, and some educated guesswork. We are thankful for their energy and dedication.

We are grateful to John Ward, Senior Conservation Architect at Public Works and Government Services Canada, for taking the time to interpret the political architecture of the East Block. His insights came in handy in situating where the government politicians had their offices. At Library and Archives Canada, Catherine Hobbs and Risë Segall went out of their way to help us find material. Sophie Tellier and Gaya Déri were especially generous in helping track down pictures.

As well, our thanks go to the many staff at the Archives of Ontario, the Nova Scotia Archives, the Toronto Reference Library (including its dedicated staff in the Baldwin Room), the Ryerson University Library, the Fisher Rare Book Library at the University of Toronto, and the Law Library of the University of Toronto.

A number of colleagues were very kind in reading the manuscript and in gently pointing out errors, and we thank Terry Copp, Herb Emory, John English, and Paul Litt for their help. Naturally, we acknowledge responsibility for any mistakes that would have escaped their watchful attention. We also acknowledge the institutional support that we received from Ryerson University that helped make this book a possibility. Our thanks for support go to Carla Cassidy, the former Dean of Arts; Mark Lovewell, the interim Dean of Arts; Philip Coppack, the Associate Dean of Arts; Carl Benn, Chair of the History Department; Neil Thomlinson, Chair of the Department of Politics and Public Administration; and our colleague Ron Stagg.

We gratefully acknowledge the commitment of the staff at Dundurn Press for their support. The enthusiasm shown by Michael Carroll for every dimension of this project was always a lift that promised that good ideas would see the light of day. Thank you also to Allison Hirst, who copyedited our text and ensured that our styles were as consistent as possible. Finally, we are grateful for the support of our families over the long period of time that it has taken to write this book. We dedicate this book to them.

CHAPTER 1

LAURIER'S DARE

On or about December 1910 human nature changed.
— VIRGINIA WOOLF, "MR. BENNETT AND MRS. BROWN" (1924)

Were it not for the politics, July 29, 1911, was a pretty ordinary summer day. The weather in Ottawa was pleasant, but the summer's heat was getting under the collars of many people in the nation's capital. It was a Saturday, and Sir Wilfrid Laurier had a quiet breakfast on his shady verandah at home, at the corner of Theodore[1] and Chapel Streets.

The political crisis that had practically paralyzed his government since the spring had now come to a climax. The papers were again full of the stormy commentary on his government that only added to the shouted criticism he heard from the Borden Conservatives. Since his return on July 10 from a visit to London to discuss and debate the matters of the British Empire and to celebrate the coronation of King George V, the political winds seemed to offer a direction for his government. Two weeks before, ten thousand people had greeted his landing in Quebec City, boisterously confirming his popularity. There was opposition, of course, but surely, he thought, the old charm could work its magic one more time.

Laurier's nine-week absence embittered his adversaries, and with the resumption of Parliament in a rare summer session, tempers flared. For ten consecutive days, the Conservative Party opposition had hammered the Laurier government in Parliament for its proposed Reciprocity Agreement to lower and eliminate trade barriers with the United States and for not sufficiently supporting the British government in its arms race with the Germans. At the same time, Laurier was condemned in the *nationaliste* newspapers, such as Henri Bourassa's *Le Devoir*, for recklessly making promises to the British that Canada would be a willing ally in the foreseeable conflict with Germany.

Laurier considered the possibilities as his patience wore thin. He could, of course, withdraw the bill on reciprocity, but that option was easily dismissed. He could introduce closure and put a stop to the endless debate so that the Liberal majority could simply use its heft and pass the proposal into law, but this measure was not popular and would easily expose the government to accusations of being undemocratic. The third possibility was to take the battle to both the Conservatives, who insisted on "no truck or trade" with the United States, and the dissident Liberals, who wanted to do more for the Empire (they were called the "imperialists"), and the *nationalistes* in Quebec, who wanted nothing of it. Surely, they could never work together against him, for their positions were based on mutually irreconcilable grounds. The die was cast that Saturday morning: he would meet with the cabinet and then send a request to the governor general that the legislature be dissolved, even though his four-year mandate was not finished. This was unprecedented in Canada, but Laurier convinced himself that he had no recourse. The Opposition was arrogant in holding up the debate on reciprocity, and needed to be taught a lesson by him and by the electorate. The election would be in seven weeks, on September 21.

Laurier was four months away from his seventieth birthday, but he felt strong and relaxed from his trip to Europe. The Opposition did not scare him. As he cast his mind back, he could remember the adversities he had faced over his long career. He had been prime minister since 1896, and had seen crises come and go; but always he had survived. Could things be so different now? If his critics were insistent about his failings, the people of Canada who had returned him to power with great majorities in 1900, 1904, and 1908 were surely still with him. He was, after all, by far the most popular man in the country.

———•◦•———

Wilfrid Laurier was born in the small town of St. Lin, about fifty kilometres northeast of Montreal, in 1841.[2] His father, Carolus, was a surveyor and a farmer of modest means. Laurier's first brush with adversity was a respiratory ailment that would nag him all his life. Long trapped in the house, he developed a taste for reading at an early age. His mother died when he was seven, but his father quickly remarried. Adeline Ethier, his stepmother, proved to be very kind, sharing with the young boy both her affections and her love of literature. After a few years of schooling in French, the boy Wilfrid was sent to New Glasgow, the town down the road, where he attended school in English and boarded with a Scottish-Presbyterian family. Young Wilfrid did well in school, and ambitions for him ran high. He learned to speak and write English and gained insight into the "others." A very bright student, he finished school at L'Assomption College and graduated first in his class.

It could be said that Laurier first experienced opposition by being in opposition. At age nineteen, he enrolled at McGill University to study law. He excelled in his studies in English by day, but gravitated in the more radical *rouges* nationalist circles by night. The early 1860s were a heady time for a young, self-styled radical such as Laurier. Led by Antoine-Aimé Dorion, the *Parti rouge* challenged the idea proposed by the likes of John A. Macdonald and George-Étienne Cartier that the only way Canada could prosper was through integration with other British North American provinces. The fear was that French Canada would lose clout in a Confederation arrangement, overwhelmed by an intolerant English majority that would undoubtedly engineer every possible scheme to ensure the assimilation of francophones.

Laurier was sympathetic to the *rouge* cause, and imbibed it while clerking with Rodolphe Laflamme, one of its most ardent proponents and one of Montreal's leading lawyers. He did not share all its beliefs, however. While he might be opposed to the role of the Church in politics, Laurier never contested its influence in society, and he lived as a good church-going Catholic. Nevertheless, there was a certain ethos about *rouge* thinking that he liked to defend, and when asked to lead a newspaper dedicated to the cause of fighting the Macdonald-Cartier-Brown idea of Confederation, Laurier gave himself entirely to the task. *Rouge* philosophy was an odd blend of ideas, reflexes, and

Courtesy LAC, C-003930.

Wilfrid Laurier giving his last speech of the campaign, Ste-Anne-de-Beaupré, September 20, 1911.

attitudes. In part, it was a clear statement that authority had to be challenged, and that government belonged rightfully to the people. It was against privilege, against received wisdom, and it was in favour of what was modern. Its program was vague at best, but it had the merit of attracting various shades of romantics, free thinkers, annexationists, and establishment figures that had no patience for the Macdonald Conservatives.

Laurier, however, had no real gift for journalism. People ignored him and his newspaper and soon it had to shut down. It was during this period, in 1868, that Wilfrid courted and then married Zoë Lafontaine, a young lady from Montreal. He soon allied himself with Joseph Lavergne, a school chum, and started a small law practice in the village of Arthabaska, on the south shore of the St. Lawrence near Victoriaville, about midway between Montreal and Quebec City.

Laurier was about as gifted in the law as he was in journalism, however, and never excelled. There were few clients, but while the law seemed to spurn him, politics beckoned. Laurier jumped at the invitation to run for the Liberals in the provincial election of 1871, and he was elected in the riding of Drummond-Arthabaska. If life was good it was because his partner, Joseph Lavergne, attracted enough clients for the both of them, and Wilfrid and Zoë (they never would have children) had a spacious home built across the street from his law practice.[3] The duties of a young member of the provincial parliament were not onerous, and while he enjoyed the trips to Quebec City he quickly recognized that the Conservative stronghold in Quebec was not likely to give him opportunities soon. His gaze turned to Ottawa, now that the Liberals under Alexander Mackenzie had broken John A. Macdonald's firm grip on power. In 1874, he was elected to the House of Commons, and settled in the backbenches. A golden opportunity presented itself in early 1877 to leap forward, and Laurier did not let it pass.

The occasion was a visit of a Vatican envoy sent to Quebec to investigate the degree of hostility between the Church and the Liberal politicians. It was, for the moderate *rouges* like Laurier, an opportunity to show that they really were part of the mainstream and to convince the Church in Quebec to accept Liberalism. In a public speech that was well promoted in advance and then widely distributed in pamphlet form, he argued that Liberals aspired not to a "social" liberalism (a sort of libertine habit), or even a "catholic" liberalism, but to a political liberalism fashioned after the British model. The Catholic Church had nothing to fear. According to Laurier, French-Canadian Liberals were not like European Liberals, who in fact were not "liberals" but "revolutionaries" who "in their principles" were "so extravagant that they aim at nothing less than the destruction of modern society....

"With these men," Laurier announced, "we have nothing in common."[4]

Laurier showed that the Liberal Party in Quebec was able to live with the Church on condition that the Church respected a certain degree of distance from the State. "I am a Liberal of the English school," he said. He was not an anticlerical, he argued, nor was the Liberal Party. The speech worked reassuringly well, and Laurier, now thirty-six, was courted to join the cabinet. In those days, cabinet members had to be confirmed in ridings. This time Laurier was defeated — the handiwork of an organizational wizard who went by the inimitable, unforgettable name of Israel Tarte. Another seat was found for Laurier in Quebec East, and he was finally re-elected to the House of Commons in late 1877 and sworn into the Mackenzie cabinet as minister of national revenue. Within three years he had risen in the public eye from an obscure backbencher to Minister of the Crown. He was not the great success people expected, let alone a contributing presence. Laurier's pulmonary ailment kept him to his bed for much of his tenure as a young cabinet member.

Within a year he was out of office, swept aside by the returning Macdonald juggernaut in the election of November 1878. Mackenzie soon retired as leader, leaving Edward Blake to take the helm. Blake, forty-five, was an extraordinarily well-read and reflective Ontario lawyer who was passionate for all things British, and proved something of an intoxicant for the impressionable Laurier. Laurier watched Blake with intense curiosity: the style, the turns of phrase, the understanding of the people, the country, and the issues. Blake was a good speaker, but against a John A. Macdonald in full rhetorical and administrative flight, he was no match. Opposition was boring, with the

Liberals making rare inroads only when the Conservatives literally offered up scandals on silver platters. Laurier, for his part, did very little, idling mostly in the splendid legislative library, doing what he liked to do best: reading. In this pursuit, he was among accomplished and cherished friends — Laurier's personal circle counted some of the leading lights of French-Canadian literature, such as Louis-Honoré Fréchette and Louis-Olivier David.

One issue, however, brought Laurier to full attention. Louis Riel, the leader of the Métis people who had rebelled against the creation of Manitoba in 1870, had returned in 1884 to Canada with the idea of seizing land for the Métis and the Cree in Saskatchewan. The government in Ottawa considered the act an insurrection and in 1885 dispatched a militia to the west. After confrontations at Batoche and Duck Lake, Riel was taken prisoner and eventually hanged in Regina. Quebec's pleas for mercy and understanding were brutally rejected and Laurier signalled himself again as an eloquent speaker in Riel's defence: "Had I been born on the banks of the Saskatchewan," he famously told the enormous crowds gathered in Montreal's Champ de Mars, "I myself would have shouldered a musket."[5]

Discouraged by losing yet another campaign to Macdonald in 1887, Edward Blake retired and recommended to the Liberals that Laurier become leader. (Blake soon left for Britain where he was elected to the House of Commons. He died in London in 1912.) Laurier, now forty-six, could shine in his own light, although he had little confidence in himself or in the prospects before him. When he assumed the leadership of the Liberal Party, the Montreal *Gazette* opined that he was "wanting in training, the knowledge and the industry indispensable in the occupant of such a position."[6]

He was, after all, facing the same John A. he had read about since he was a teenager. The contrast could not have been greater. Against a theatrical Macdonald, Laurier cut a fastidious figure. He did not smoke, drink, or play; his gestures were restrained. He could not win on personality so Laurier fell back on what he understood to be Liberal principles. He hardened the party's position in favour of open trade with the United States and argued for an end to privilege and more openness in government affairs; but his approach made no difference. Macdonald won the 1891 election handily, even increasing the Conservative share of the popular vote. But "Old Tomorrow" would not reap much of that election's rewards, as he died that June, leaving the government to a succession of leaders: John Abbott from 1891–92, John Thompson from 1892–94, and Mackenzie Bowell from 1894–96. But it would be the last who would be a formidable opponent for the Liberals as the election approached: seventy-five-year-old doctor Charles Tupper, one of the Nova Scotia fathers of Confederation and the lion of the Conservative Party.

Laurier worked on his style to shed the general impression that, while he had some style and ability, he was "lazy." He cultivated the anglophone elite, worked on his English (he always spoke with something of a French accent)[7] and refined his manner. His wardrobe improved and a diamond-studded lucky horseshoe stickpin appeared in his perfectly folded cravat, signalling him easily as one of the best-dressed men in Canada. The awkward late-bloomer gained credibility through the 1890s and Canadians recognized in him a potential prime minister, even though he had precious little experience at anything. But he could smile, and whether it was priests or priest-hating Orangemen, Laurier found a way to address them with authority and with a disarming charm. "Never one with such mellifluous music in voice, such easy grace in his style, such a cardinal's hauteur when he wanted to be alone and such a fascinating urbanity when he wanted to impress a company, or caucus or a crowd," remembered Augustus Bridle, a journalist with a felicitous turn of phrase. Laurier was "the kaleidoscopic enigma of Canadian public life":

> Laurier was nearly all things to all men …. He was a human solar system, in which many kinds of people wanted to gravitate, even to the ragged little girl on the prairies who picked the wildflowers he wore in his coat as far as she could see him on the train platform…. Laurier could perform obvious tricks with consummate grace. And he performed many. There was never a moment of his waking life when he could not have been lifted from a play. His movements, his

words, his accent, his clothes, his facial lineaments
were never commonplace, even when his motives
often may have been. He was Debussy's *Afternoon of
a Faun*.[8]

Undaunted and unimpressed (and clearly unaware of Debussy's
popularity), Tupper called an election for June 23, 1896, soon after
assuming the prime minister's office. This time Laurier was ready
for a strong campaign. He was better known across the country; his
speeches were invigorating, but at the same time were reassuring. Gone
were the old positions on "reciprocity" that alienated people in Ontario
and the demands for "the freedom of thought" that tended to whip up
the clergy against the damnable *rouges*. Laurier's tenuous peace with
the Church, his appeals for moderation on trade and language issues,
his promise of good government, and the disarray of the Conservative
campaign combined in a rousing victory for the Liberals. Laurier, who
at age fifty-five had no clear accomplishment of which he could be
proud, who had never travelled, managed an organization, or written
more than two memorable speeches, ran a great campaign to become
prime minister of Canada.

The country was ready for a change. The economy had been in
an economic depression since the early 1890s, although some would
say that it had never recovered from the downturn of the 1870s. The
settlements in the western half of the country were languishing, and a
nagging issue of language rights in Manitoba for francophone schools
seemed unsolvable. Laurier promised competent government, a solution for the Manitoba schools question, and to work hard to bring
prosperity back. Suddenly, Canada was willing to take a chance on
him, and he defeated the Tupper Tories with ease.

Decades later, one of the first students of his leadership reflected
on how ill-prepared Laurier was to take up government duties. "There
were many who doubted, even after his nine years of party leadership,
whether he would be more than the titular head of the government,"
wrote Oscar Skelton. "They did not think it possible that a man so
courteous could show himself firm when firmness was called for.
Could a leader who had made his fame by his oratory develop the

qualities needed to control a ministry and to guide a distracted country through difficult days?"[9]

Laurier knew this, and crafted his first cabinet to be a showcase of talent. As a new prime minister, he made sure he had reasonable geographical representation in his team, but he appointed experienced administrators to head ministries. Cabinet was composed of sixteen men, but he relied on six individuals — including three former provincial premiers (A.G. Blair from New Brunswick, Oliver Mowat from Ontario, and William Fielding from Nova Scotia) — to address the government's priorities.

Three members of the first ministry would persevere until 1911. The first was William Fielding, the forty-eight-year-old premier of Nova Scotia since 1886 (when he had campaigned to take Nova Scotia, New Brunswick, and Prince Edward Island out of Confederation), who quit his position to join Laurier. He assumed responsibility for the finance ministry and stayed in the job for the next fifteen years. The second was the eloquent, mutton-chopped Richard Cartwright of Montreal, sixty-one, who was put in charge of trade and commerce. Cartwright had been minister of finance under Alexander Mackenzie almost twenty years before and was known to be an ardent free trader. Laurier appointed forty-nine-year-old doctor Frederick W. Borden of Nova Scotia to head up a new Department of the Militia.[10] Borden, who had studied at Harvard Medical School, was also an expert in military affairs and made a secret of the fact that he wanted to professionalize the army.[11]

Laurier was also practical in addressing priorities. To direct the critically important Ministry of the Interior he sought out Clifford Sifton, the Manitoba Attorney General, who at age thirty-five became the youngest member of the cabinet in the fall of 1896. Rounding out the team was Israel Tarte — the same Tarte who had worked to defeat Laurier in the by-election after the famous 1877 speech — but who had turned against the Conservatives on account of corruption. Now forty-eight, he was put in charge of the Ministry of Public Works. Laurier was happy. "So long as I have Tarte and Sifton with me, I shall be master of Canada." In the 1911 election, Laurier had neither: Tarte was dead and Sifton had left the Liberal Party to whip the anti-Laurier campaign.[12]

Capable as it was, the first Laurier government was mostly successful because the economy recovered dramatically. Settlers were pouring in from Europe, farm products found markets more easily, and for the first time in a generation, Canadians had reason to be fairly happy. The only tension was around Laurier's foreign policy. He had made it a cornerstone of his approach that Canada's relations with the British Empire would be supportive and positive, but within limits. The issue came up in 1899 when Britain asked for help to defend settlers in South Africa against the Boer offensive. English Canada rose to the occasion as many newspapers argued that Canada had to meet its obligations to the Empire by sending its military forces to the other end of the world and help defeat the enemy. Laurier hesitated, for he knew the move would not be popular in Quebec, where the opinion-makers were concerned that any action in favour of Britain could be used as a precedent for deeper involvement in global affairs. The Laurier government conceived a compromise solution: it would equip and defray the cost of sending over a thousand Canadians to South Africa, but once there, would have no further involvement in command or in repatriation of the troops. That would be left to the British forces.

The solution — not debated in the House of Commons but issued through an Order-in-Council — appeased most in English Canada, save for the most imperialist. In Quebec, it aroused suspicion. It was Henri Bourassa, the Liberal MP for Labelle, who took the matter to heart. Bourassa was the grandson of Louis-Joseph Papineau, the leader of the *Patriotes* during the 1820s and 1830s who had articulated demands for more effective and responsible government. Like his grandfather, Bourassa wished for Canada to have more independence from the British Crown. He was smart, articulate, and sincere. Educated in part in the United States, he spoke and wrote English with as much panache and conviction as he did French. Still only thirty-one years old, yet full of self-assurance, he boldly confronted the prime minister at a reception hosted by Israel Tarte, and argued that the government's position was morally and legally wrong. Laurier dismissed Bourassa's concerns as naive.

Laurier had displayed a political golden touch: Canada's participation in the South African War did little to hurt the Liberals. Laurier was applauded as the master of compromise on this issue in the same way he had manufactured a consensus on Manitoba schools and preferential tariffs for the Empire. The prime minister, who had found ways to satisfy both sides of many disputes, however grudgingly, was re-elected handily in 1900. But there was a cost. In Quebec, his compromises stirred the embers of national identity, particularly among younger students, including a young Armand Lavergne, his old law partner's son, who now gravitated around Bourassa. In 1903, a *Ligue nationaliste* was founded to animate discussions, and within a year the movement was deemed strong enough to support a weekly, *Le Nationaliste*, edited by Olivar Asselin. In 1904, the *Association catholique de la jeunesse canadienne-française* was established across Quebec to discuss and to mix religious and political affairs, particularly where they related to the health of the French language and the place of Canada within the British Empire. These groups wanted much more of the former, and much less of the latter.

That was enough for Charles Tupper, who had to suffer the embarrassment of finishing his political career by losing his own Cape Breton seat. He announced his retirement, and Robert Borden, a forty-two-year-old Nova Scotia lawyer, was chosen as leader. Borden was of a different generation than Laurier and could not have been more different. If Laurier was grace and charm incarnate, Borden was the epitome of quiet correctness and aplomb. He suffered from insomnia much of his life, and various stomach ailments that often laid him low. The pains seemed to deepen his eyes, giving him somewhat of a tired air. From his earliest pictures, he parted his hair in the middle, an uncommon fashion at that time. He did sport, however, a splendid moustache.

Born in Grand Pré, in the heart of Nova Scotia, in 1854, he had been unsure of what route to take in life. He became a schoolteacher, and even taught in New Jersey for a year before concluding that he had a better future in law. He learned the law through apprenticeship and by the time he was in his early thirties he was already one of the most prominent lawyers in Halifax, arguing cases before the Supreme Court of Canada and the Judicial Committee of the Privy Council in London (which in those days was the final court of appeal). He grew prosperous through his law firm as he represented some of the largest companies in the province, such as the Bank of Nova Scotia,

Moirs (the confectioners), and the Nova Scotia Telephone Company. His multiple business contacts and investments made him wealthy. By the time he was forty, he had joined various corporate boards, including Nova Scotia Telephone and the Eastern Trust Company, the Bank of Nova Scotia, and the Crown Life Insurance Company.

In 1889, at the age of thirty-five, he married the elegant Laura Bond. They were well matched, enjoying travelling to Europe, Britain, and New England. Childless, they eventually settled into one of the most beautiful homes in Halifax. Politically, Borden took a long time to decide whether he was a Liberal or a Conservative (he once even spoke in favour of his cousin Frederick and even supported Fielding in his election in 1888), but finally chose to enter public life at the national level and to represent the Conservative Party led by fellow Nova Scotian Charles Tupper. He was elected to the House of Commons in the Laurier sweep of 1896 and promptly made no impression at all in the capital as a forlorn backbencher. He did discover something, however: the bicycle. Robert Borden was an early adopter of the new contraption that, unlike the old penny farthing, had wheels of equal size mounted on pneumatic tires. The bicycle was comfortable, and Borden was happiest when gliding along the streets of *belle époque* Ottawa.[13]

"My early impressions of Parliament are still vivid," Borden later wrote. "I had entered public life with a very high conception of its duties and responsibilities and with a rather lofty ideal of the dignity of Parliament as the grand inquest of the nation. My first impressions were disappointing as there seemed a singular lack of dignity in the attitude and behaviours of members as well as in the conduct of debate — methods were unbusinesslike and waste of time enormous. However, I soon realized that the House had an instinctive sense of dignity which was not at first apparent, and I quickly became convinced that in parliamentary government waste of time is quite inevitable."[14]

Borden was described as "personally upright, clean, and fair in political tactics, a serious and diligent student of the country's problems, a recognized constitutional authority, endowed with no little patience and persistence, he had the respect of all his countrymen."[15] He was not a charmer like Macdonald and displayed none of the dogged persistence and raw energy of Tupper. He was a man of "stolid worth,"[16] a man of "dignity and courtesy," "always fair and always more interested in principles than in personalities."[17]

In the late summer and early fall of 1902, Borden took his first tour of Western Canada, and it was during this trip that he first met two future prime ministers: Richard Bedford Bennett and Arthur Meighen. The two-month swing through the Prairies and the Rockies proved to be a real strain. The logistics of the voyage were confused, leaving a bad impression of Borden in the West. "We were not always a

Robert Borden, n.d.

Courtesy LAC, PA-117660.

happy 'family party,'" he later conceded. Back home, Borden turned his energies to building his party and he found a theme in administrative competence that would focus his opposition. In the words of Arthur Meighen many years later, however, Borden proved a "weighty but not a happy warrior."[18]

———·•·———

Slowly, but surely, Laurier began to lose his top cabinet ministers for reasons that had much more to do with ideological and practical differences than competence. Mowat, tired from the ten-hour days, stayed only until 1897, when he asked to be named lieutenant-governor of Ontario and return to Toronto.[19] Israel Tarte was fired from cabinet in the fall of 1902 for speaking in favour of higher tariffs to protect Canadian industry. In the summer of 1903, A.G. Blair resigned as minister for railways over a serious disagreement on the funding of the Grand Trunk Pacific. (Laurier himself would have to table the bill to support the building of that project.[20]) In 1904, the organizational whirlwind William Mulock, frustrated by his inability to get better transportation rates from the privately owned railway lines and his failure in enlisting the prime minister's support for his cause, indicated to Laurier that the time had come for him to leave. Exhausted, he left government when a judgeship opened on the Ontario Court of Appeal. Laurier lost a formidable administrator and a key Ontario organizer.

Nevertheless, the next election (in 1904) was a triumph for the Liberals.[21] The economy was in full expansion and confidence reigned across the country. The government was portrayed as incompetent by Borden Conservatives, but it had accumulated a surplus of $15 million and organized the building of a second national railway, the National Transcontinental. Laurier won big everywhere, especially in the West. It was Ontario, and particularly Toronto, that did not warm to him. The Liberals took only thirty-eight Ontario seats — ten less than the Conservatives — and all of Toronto's five seats went to Borden and the Conservatives. Laurier crushed the opposition on a national basis, taking 64.5 percent of the votes; 2 percent more than in 1900. With the exception of Ontario and Prince Edward Island, the Liberals took a plurality of seats in every province. Fifty-three ridings in

Quebec elected Liberals to the House of Commons while eleven sent Conservatives. Borden's performance had been worse than Tupper's in 1900. Adding insult to injury, the Liberals swept the eighteen seats in Borden's native Nova Scotia, including that of the Leader of the loyal Opposition. (Borden quickly found another seat elsewhere.)

Laurier could now deal with the creation of two new provinces in the growing West. They would be called Saskatchewan and Alberta, but there remained considerable debate over the issue of language rights for French-speaking children in those territories. Clifford Sifton, his minister in charge of settlement, was adamant that the deal he had worked to negotiate in Manitoba in 1896 was now unacceptable in the West. Laurier was inclined to think that it would work, judging that a solid precedent had been set and that the Manitoba settlement had been successful in striking an acceptable compromise. Henri Bourassa was also opposed to a deal. He wanted more than what had been delivered in Manitoba. He wanted the West to be fully bilingual.

Laurier could only disappoint his two lieutenants, and in February 1905, three months after the 1904 election, Clifford Sifton resigned abruptly from cabinet. His vision of Canada was that of an English-Protestant country with a large French-Catholic minority confined to the province of Quebec and he did not share with Laurier any vision of a bi-cultural nation that should be welcoming to both English and French. Sifton was under no illusion. "I was not Sir Wilfrid Laurier's colleague for eight years without finding out that he is, despite his courtesy and gracious charm, a masterful man set on having his own way, and equally resolute that his colleagues shall not have their way unless this is quite agreeable to him," he said. "I had a good many experiences of the difficulty in getting my policies accepted and acted upon when they did not make a special appeal to him; I should perhaps never have been successful in giving effect to some of the things upon which my heart was set if I had not had in the cabinet three or four associates who backed me up, and whom I in turn backed up. At that, with a smile and a laugh that was in part a chuckle, the old chief was very frequently too much for all of us."[22] Bourassa, for his part, resigned from the legislature. He would take his fight to Quebec City and run for provincial parliament. Bourassa, now twice spurned by Laurier and motivated by nothing less than hatred, vowed vengeance. By the summer of 1908, rumours were rampant that Borden had made a deal with the emerging *nationalistes* and that "the alliance with Bourassa is pretty close now."[23] A few years later these two Liberals would work with Borden and exact that revenge as the key architects of Laurier's defeat in the election of 1911.

The years between 1904 and 1908, when Laurier again sought re-election, were difficult. The Liberals were accused of maladministration, of excesses of patronage, and of misguided policies. To stanch the accusations, Laurier created royal commissions and sought to root out the excesses. One royal commission that reported in 1907 recommended that the civil service be revamped to make it more professional, better paid, and less dependent on patronage. Laurier ignored the recommendations save for one: creating a Public Service Commission in 1908 that would at least symbolize a willingness to reform the system. Small controversies involving petty issues of patronage and favouritism did not seem to throw the Liberals off track. The Conservatives had great difficulty in convincing voters that their issues around government efficiency were important: after all, no minister had been tarred by the controversies. Even the serious 1907 recession and Borden's idea of "A New National Policy" could not attract new voters. The country's unimpeded growth since 1896 had inoculated the Liberals. "These years will be remembered in the history of Canada," Laurier told a crowd in Cornwall, Ontario. "In them Canada has been lifted from the humble position of a humble colony to that of a nation.... In 1908 Canada has become a star to which is directed the gaze of the whole civilized world. That is what we have done."[24]

Laurier entered the contest of 1908 with a much thinner cabinet than ever (most of the strong arms of 1896 had resigned, from Mowat to Sifton), but the Conservatives, led by an "unstageable man" in the words of Augustus Bridle, showed themselves uninspired and uninspiring. The Liberal Party's strategy was simply to ask the voting public to "Let Laurier Finish the Job," and the voters agreed to give a twelve-year-old government four more years, but this time in fewer numbers. The Liberals collected 50.4 percent of the total vote (a loss of 1.6 percent), while the Conservatives earned the support of 46.9 percent of electors (a gain of 0.5 percent).

Still, it was an impressive showing for the Liberals, who still held 135 seats, three fewer than in 1904. They lost six seats in Nova Scotia (as the province finally warmed a little to its native son who had been Leader of the Opposition for seven years), but made spectacular gains in New Brunswick and Prince Edward Island. The showing in Ontario was also remarkably strong, with the Liberals holding thirty-seven seats, the same as in 1900. The contest in the new western provinces was more worrisome. Manitoba elected eight Conservatives to the house and two Liberals, including Sifton (who won his Brandon seat by only sixty-nine votes). Saskatchewan did the reverse, with one seat going Conservative blue and nine seats Liberal red. Alberta was more of a draw, with three Tories and four Grits elected. British Columbia, which had gone unanimously Liberal in 1904, was now divided with five Conservative and two Liberal seats. The West, now voting for the first time as four provinces, had given seventeen seats to both parties. The Liberal seat in the Yukon gave Laurier a small edge in the territory. There was a message here for the prime minister: the West could not be taken for granted. Borden, now twice defeated by Laurier, vowed to change tactics in the next campaign. The only way the Conservatives could beat the Liberals was to undermine Laurier at home in Quebec and to battle his policies, not necessarily to conceive of new platforms, he confided to Frederick Hamilton, an opinionated but Conservative-friendly journalist for the Toronto *Evening News* who enjoyed reporting rumours, impressions, and discrete conversations that could not make it to print to his editor, J.S. Willison, who had his own agenda in this saga.[25] Willison was originally a Liberal and the editor of the Toronto *Globe* (a Liberal organ), and undoubtedly one of the most influential journalists of his generation. In 1902, however, he left the *Globe* to assume new duties as editor of the Toronto *Evening News*, a Tory newspaper financed by Joseph Flavelle, and while writing a biography of Laurier, he began to move away from Liberalism. His allegiance to Laurier weakened with the 1905 Autonomy Bills, and would break after 1909, as he could no longer reconcile his views with those of the prime minister.

Laurier, who was always optimistic that he could rally people like Willison back to the Liberal fold, would not rest on his laurels, and instead set about to "finish the job" as his campaign slogan promised. If anything, the 1904 and 1908 elections had steeled the fist he concealed in his famous velvet glove. As ready as he had been to compromise in order to achieve higher objectives, he resolved to act more decisively. He created a Public Service Commission to improve the hiring and management of government employees, and a National Parks system to encourage the preservation of the environment. He established a Secretariat for External Affairs in 1909 to improve the management of the complicated relations between Canada and Great Britain as well as the United States. He would strike landmark agreements with both of them, but neither of was satisfactory to the Bourassa or the Sifton Liberals, let alone the Borden Conservatives.

On the issue of supporting the Empire, Laurier ordered that Canada equip itself with a navy. It would be a small one (two ships to start), but it would be Canadian. There was one proviso: if Britain needed Canada's ships in a time of war, Canada would make them available. What Laurier thought was a wise compromise was considered too clever by half. The opposition in English Canada condemned the Naval Service Bill as an empty gesture. In Montreal, Henri Bourassa saw it as an unconditional declaration of commitment to the Empire's wars. The issue quickly went beyond that of a simple navy.

On the issue of relations with the United States, Laurier also thought he had a breakthrough. At about the time Virginia Woolf said that human nature changed, the Canadian and American governments concluded their deal. What remained was to have the agreement ratified by both the House of Commons and the American Congress. Fielding presented this agreement to cabinet in January 1911 and then tabled it in the House of Commons. Borden and the Conservatives were incensed by the deal and absolutely refused to let pass the bill that would sanction the agreement. Laurier was itching for a fight, and even threatened to call an election on the issue. Instead, the debates were merely suspended until July so that Laurier could attend the coronation of George V. It was in this atmosphere of maddening frustration that Laurier found refuge in London, a place that was experiencing the most beautiful summer in memory, where again he delighted in finding friendly faces.[26]

The trip had something of tonic effect on Laurier. For a man of seventy, he appeared remarkably fit. He was slightly stooped, but in a manner that hardly diminished the fact that he had stood six feet tall. His eyes were more sunken and his face more deeply ingrained with the worry of the years, but his mane, while thin on top, was luxuriant and bushy behind his ears and gave a unique distinction to his appearance. Swayed by the enthusiastic crowd, Laurier declared upon his arrival in Montreal: "Henry of Navarre at the battle of Ivry said: 'Follow my white plume and you will find it always in the fore-front of honour.' Like Henry IV, I say to you young men, Follow my white plume — the white hairs of sixty-nine years — and you will, I believe I can say without boasting, find it always in the forefront of honour."[27]

Two days later he was back in Ottawa, acclaimed as a hero by a massive crowd on Parliament Hill. Surely the people were with him, he thought. But Conservatives did not see it that way, and for the next fortnight, as Parliament resumed, the Borden formation filibustered against the deal with the Americans. Laurier convinced himself that he had no choice but to turn to the voters. On Friday morning, July 28, Laurier grew concerned about a technicality: could the House of Commons be dissolved without a prorogation? He sent for Joseph Pope, the Undersecretary of State and the most experienced public servant, who informed the prime minister that the governor general had to issue two proclamations: the first to prorogue the House, and the second to dissolve it. Laurier then sent word to Lord Grey, the governor general, of what was required. In no time, Ottawa knew that the cabinet would gather on Saturday morning to come to a final decision. The town was on fire with rumour: "Nothing but election thought of at Ottawa" reported the Toronto *Globe*.[28]

TABLE 1.1

THE LAST LAURIER CABINET — 1911

Sir Wilfrid Laurier	prime minister
Allen B. Aylesworth	minister of justice
Henri Béland	postmaster general
Sir Frederick Borden	minister of militia and defence
Jacques Bureau	solicitor general
Richard Cartwright	minister of trade and commerce
William Fielding	minister of finance
Sydney Fisher	minister of agriculture
George Graham	minister of railways
W.L. Mackenzie King	minister of labour
Rodolphe Lemieux	minister of marine and fisheries
Charles Murphy	secretary of state
Frank Oliver	minister of the interior
William Paterson	minister of inland revenue
William Pugsley	minister of public works
William Templeman	minister of revenue

Laurier finished breakfast, and, unusually for a Saturday morning, took the regular streetcar to his office in the East Block (passing by the Hotel that already bore his name), to the room he had used since 1896 and that had first been occupied by George-Étienne Cartier, John A.'s legendary Quebec ally. He finalized some correspondence before the decisive lunch. The quorum being met, he met his cabinet colleagues in the corridor as he walked to the ornate Privy Council Chamber a few steps away. The ministers shuffled into the second-floor cabinet room, stopping in the small antechamber for refreshments and cigars before taking their seats around the rectangular table. Laurier sat in the throne-like chair at the far end and announced that the time had come to consider alternatives, to air fears and hopes, and to make a decision.

The meeting was short as he announced what was as obvious as inevitable. The Liberals were blocked in their project of free trade with the Americans, yet the people were with them. The timing was right to seek another mandate. As he wrote a sympathizer a few days later:

> Evidence are [sic] coming to me from every quarter that the action which we have taken was well timed. It was plain to me that the Opposition was simply bluffing and now that we have called their hand they commence to squeal. We will have a hard fight; I think it will be based on national prejudices, both in Quebec and in the other provinces. I am not a betting man, but I think the odds are very much on our side. I never was more full of confidence.[29]

Laurier was willing to dare Robert Borden and the Conservatives to a third fight. He had beaten them twice before and was confident that Borden's wooden delivery of a non-platform would not win many adherents. He was also willing to dare Henri Bourassa, who had campaigned bitterly against him on the Naval Service issue for over a year, and he was eager to challenge Clifford Sifton and the Toronto Liberals who had dared to criticize the Reciprocity Agreement.

Not least, he dared the people of Canada to turn their backs against a government that had delivered unprecedented growth and prosperity. *Belle époque* Canada was prosperous as never before in 1911. The new census showed that 1,800,000 people had settled into Canada in the previous decade (311,084 in 1910–11 alone — two-thirds of whom came from either Great Britain or the United States). Sydney Fisher, Laurier's minister of agriculture, confidently predicted in 1911 that by 1921 Canada's population would go from 7,204,527 to almost twenty million, and to forty million by 1940.

Foreign investment, mostly from Great Britain but also from the United States, was skyrocketing. Five hundred and forty-four new companies had been incorporated in the past year, with a capitalization of $458,415,800. As the editor of the *Canadian Annual Review* gushed in looking back on that year, "there could be no question as to the bounding development of Canada in 1911."[30] Canada's commerce per capita was the second highest in the world, with total exports reaching

$303,763,328 (over 12 percent increase since 1908) and imports at $524,850,792 (almost 80 percent higher than 1908). The earth was bountiful and half of working Canadians still laboured in agriculture. Investment in farm operations had gone from $1,761,000,000 in 1908 to over $2 billion in 1911. Land speculation had even become common in parts of the West — Hudson's Bay lands had increased from $8.78 per acre in 1908 to $14.00 in 1911. Canadian mining in copper, gold, pig iron, lead, nickel, and silver continued to expand, albeit more slowly given that Canada's increasingly important trading partner, the United States, was caught in a recession for much of that year. Fishery production in 1911 was the highest on record, almost $30 million. According to the Canadian Manufacturers' Association, investors had pumped $1.5 billion into the economy and production was over a billion dollars. Canada produced textiles, steel, cement, electrical machinery and motors, buttons, knitted gods, and shoes as it had never before. As the country was consolidating its expansion, the government was preoccupied with big issues, such as continuing railway expansion, the integration of new territory and new provinces, the changing of provincial boundaries, the schools questions, and a host of matters dealing with the settling of the West. Optimism, based on undeniable prosperity, was in the air — perfect economic weather in which to call an election.

CHAPTER 2

"GRASPING FOR NEPTUNE'S TRIDENT": THE NAVAL SERVICE BILL

One German cruiser in the mouth of the St. Lawrence
could put every Quebec farmer out of business.
— LORD GREY, 1909

The campaign of 1911 really started with the rumours of impending war that were circulating in London in late 1908. Laurier's cabinet had hardly met after its third re-election when the crisis that would shape its new mandate broke out. On December 8, 1908, the British government learned that the German Fleet had accelerated its procurement program for additional ships that would guarantee it sea supremacy by 1912, if not sooner. The First Lord of the Admiralty urged that six dreadnought ships were required immediately, and that another six be ordered in both 1910 and 1911. The revelation jarred the British government, at the time led by Liberal Herbert H. Asquith, who had slowed production to two dreadnoughts in 1908. After an acrimonious dispute, the cabinet agreed to the production of four ships in 1909 and four more in 1910 if Germany continued its production schedule. The proposal was tabled in the British House of Commons in mid-March 1909, causing general alarm in political and journalistic circles throughout the British Empire.[1]

Upon hearing the news, the government of New Zealand quickly offered to pay the cost of a battleship for the Royal Navy, sparking a similar fever of "dreadnoughtism" in neighbouring Australia. The world had changed. When Laurier had come to power, Kaiser Wilhelm II's fleet consisted of four small ships that could not survive modern warfare, while the British Navy boasted two dozen battleships. Within fifteen years, the Germans would threaten to overtake the British in naval superiority and Great Britain would fear a serious maritime adversary for the first time since 1805. Word of the crisis also reached the shores of Canada in no time, and the Conservative press reflexively responded that the revelations in London put the country in a situation where it had to react in terms of what it could do by way of help. The Montreal *Star*, for example, hoped to see Canada follow the New Zealand example and contribute to the Royal Navy.[2] "As a matter of fact, war is in progress," editorialized the Liberal-leaning *Globe*, as it equated shipbuilding to an act of aggression. "If the mother country were engaged in a deadly conflict Canadians could not get across the ocean fast enough to the aid of the motherland," it reasoned. "But we must remember that our aid is as much needed now as if a physical war instead of a shipbuilding war was on. It is Canada's duty, from every point of view, for our affection for the land of our fathers, and for our own self interest to take prompt and practical action."[3] The Liberal Winnipeg *Free Press*, by contrast, did not think that a gift to the Royal Navy was a solution for Canada, and instead supported the idea of creating a Canadian navy.[4]

The issue of contributing to the Royal Navy was pregnant with implications. It divided Liberals in government and stirred a crisis in the ranks of the Opposition. Frederick Hamilton, the *News* correspondent in Ottawa, gave his editor a sampling of the wide range of opinion among Liberals and Conservatives — from outright opposition to those who wished for a direct contribution — as the debates began in the House of Commons:

> Col H.H. Mclean (Lib, NB) Red hot for helping Britain. Wants two battleships. Not really in favour of a naval force of our own.

H.B. McGiverin (Lib, Ont) — in favour of a force of our own — not as of a direct contribution.

J.B. Carvell (Lib, NB) we can't go on as we are — favours imperial federation & one Navy.

Calvert (Lib, W. Ont) Doubts whether farmers & villagers (especially the "retired" element) wd favour it. These people averse to spending more money on preparation for war. Is inclined to the pact assuming a provocative attitude to German & doubted whether we cd spare the money. But inclined to debate the issue & apparently impressed a bit.

W.H. Sharpe (Con, Man) thinks the people in favour of action. Favours a force of our own.

Cowan (Con, BC) in favour of participation, by a force of our own.

The singular thing is that most of those favouring direct contributions are Liberals, while the Conservatives on the whole are sounder on the question of control.[5]

The pressure on Laurier's cabinet to act was intense, even though the prime minister himself, now hardened by having lived and survived numerous "crises," was slow to appreciate the nature of the arms race. He knew the country had already been split on this issue by the South African War and the intense feeling in English Canada that the country had to come to the aid of the Empire in defeating the Boer insurrection. Bourassa, who had left federal politics and now sat as a member of the opposition in the Quebec legislature, but who, more importantly, animated younger members of the *nationalistes* movement, such as Armand Lavergne and Olivar Asselin, was surely ready to pounce, but for the opposite reasons. The Liberals, Laurier surely knew, could never hope to strike a compromise that would convince both sides.

George Foster, the Member for Toronto North, and himself one of the most experienced parliamentarians in Ottawa, started the Canadian debate on the naval race in the House of Commons on

March 29, 1909. Foster, once a professor of classics at the University of New Brunswick, had entered politics in the 1882 federal election as a Conservative member of Parliament. John A. Macdonald immediately named him minister of marine and fisheries, and later minister of finance in 1888, a post he kept until the Tories were defeated in 1896. During the South African War, he was an ardent proponent of Canadian participation and was punished for it. He lost his New Brunswick seat in 1900 and moved to Toronto. Four years later, he returned to Parliament to represent the Conservative stronghold of North Toronto.

Foster spoke at length, rehearsing and responding to every argument raised in relation to Canadian military policy since the outbreak of the South African War, ten years earlier. He chided the government for doing nothing in terms of naval defence. He pointed out that many countries in the Empire, such as the Cape Colony, Natal (the Union of South Africa did not yet exist), New Zealand, and Australia, had made direct contributions to the Royal Navy in exchange for protection in the past: "Not only have we not put a dollar into the naval defence of Canada for her own coasts, but that not a ship in the procession bears the name of Canada and that not a stiver or a sixpence of the mighty expense of that great battle line has been contributed out of the money of Canada. Well, I say that this grips attention."[6]

He took on arguments that Canada stay away from global crises and dismissed the claims that the country had already assumed expenses in naval defence. Finally, he denounced the argument that expenditures in military preparedness were pointless in light of American capacity and its "Monroe Doctrine." In the speech that filled ten pages of Hansard, Foster showed himself well-acquainted with the contention that the presence of a navy would inevitably threaten Canada's autonomy. He called for a Canadian solution to an Imperial problem. "I want to see something grafted on the soil of Canada's nationhood," he said, "which takes root and grows and develops until it incites the spirit of defence in this country, leads to a participation in the defence, leads to that quick interest in it, its glories, its duties and its accomplished work, which is after all the one great thing that compensates a people for great expenditures either on land or on sea in the way of defence and of the maintenance of the right of the country."[7] Key to Foster's message was that prosperous commerce depended on the reassuring presence of a strong navy.

Foster leaned toward the creation of a recognizably Canadian navy — even one manned by British citizens — but that, in itself, would not be sufficient. He moved that Canada ought "no longer delay in assuming her proper share of the responsibility and financial burden incident to the suitable protection of her exposed coastline and great seaports," and concluded by challenging the government to follow the New Zealand example and "make a gift of dreadnaughts or the gift of money" to the British Empire. If the Liberals were still uncertain, the Tories seemed a little more united. They were comfortable with the Foster resolution because it seemed to take a high road to reconciliation rather "than to take some irregular course & appear to try to snatch a party advantage from a natural emergency."[8] Foster had thrown down the gauntlet.

Laurier responded with a speech that lasted more than half an hour, responding that the accusations that Canada had not done its share were false, and he trotted out statistics that had been used well before. For him, the idea of an outright gift to the Royal Navy was out of the question. He insisted that since 1885 Canada had absorbed all the costs associated with fisheries protection in the oceans and on the Great Lakes and that the cost should be considered to be an integral part of Canadian naval expenditures, considering it an "Imperial obligation." Laurier also reminded the Commons that Canada had a cruiser and was intent on building another at a cost of up to a million dollars. He reminded the House that Canada was assuming defence functions once carried out by the British in Halifax and Esquimalt. But in the end, Laurier argued, Canada shared the continent with a powerful international player whose navy now had global reach. Under the protection of the Monroe Doctrine, he insisted, Canada could sleep safely.[9]

Laurier then tabled a formal motion that acknowledged the historic role of Britain in Canada's defence — including a few lines that pointed out that, by assuming expenses at Halifax and Esquimalt, the Canadian government had relieved British taxpayers — and proposed that:

This House fully recognizes the duty of the people of Canada, as they increase in numbers and wealth, to assume in larger measure the responsibilities of national defence.

The House reaffirms the opinion, repeatedly expressed by representatives of Canada, that under the present constitutional relations between the mother country and the self-governing dominions the payment of any stated contribution to the imperial treasury for naval and military purposes would not, so far as Canada is concerned, be a satisfactory solution of the question of defence.

The House will cordially approve of any necessary expenditure designed to promote the organization of a Canadian naval service in co-operation with and in close relation to the imperial navy, along the lines suggested by the admiralty at the last Imperial Conference, and in full sympathy with the view that the naval supremacy of Great Britain is essential to the security of commerce, the safety of the empire and the peace of the world.

The House expresses its firm conviction that whenever the need arises the Canadian people will be found ready and willing to make any sacrifice that is required to give to the imperial authorities the most loyal and hearty co-operation in every movement of the maintenance of the integrity and the honour of the empire.[10]

It was Borden's turn to reply with a long speech that expressed support for the Empire and for a Canadian response to the naval race. He took exception to Laurier's statement that Canada effectively was protected by the Monroe Doctrine that guaranteed American protection against any foreign attack and indicated that while he was supportive of the thrust of the government, he was not happy with the motion. He suggested that the reference to the British taxpayer be removed, and that the second paragraph rejecting "the payment of any stated contribution" be deleted. There was considerable private discussion between Laurier and Borden, and they struck a compromise that came alive in the two middle paragraphs. The contentious phrase "payment of any stated contribution to the imperial treasury for naval and military purposes would not, so far as Canada is concerned, *be a satisfactory solution* of the question of defence" was changed to "payment of any *regular and periodical* contribution to the imperial treasury for naval and military purposes would not, so far as Canada is concerned, be *the most* satisfactory solution." In the third paragraph, the word *speedy* was inserted into the "promote the organization" phrase, thus lending more urgency to the resolution, and giving in both cases more flexibility to the government's response.[11]

Those who hoped for a more vigorous response were disappointed. Frederick Hamilton, for one, thought that Borden had scored points, and felt that Laurier had been caught off guard. "His speech was vague and windy as his amendment was picayune," he observed. "Borden, on the other hand, while starting heavily, wound up uncommonly well, and simply remodeled the whole resolution. He seems to me to have increased his stature by to-day's work."[12]

In reality, it was difficult to establish the winner with such assurance. Certainly, Borden has succeeded in imposing himself on the issue of urgency and in at least prying open some room so that a contribution be made if necessary. Laurier had agreed, hoping that the unanimity of the motion would give him political cover. All the same, it was his motion to create a Canadian navy that had won the day. Foster could claim that he had started the debate, but there was no uncertainty that Sir Wilfrid had had the last word. Canada was now committed to building its navy, and it would be associated with the Liberal government.

The governor general, Lord Grey, took a deep interest in the affair. A dedicated imperialist, "the most adept and most intelligent of English proconsuls" in the words of the young *nationaliste* Armand Lavergne, he did not shy from lobbying the government and the opposition to maximize the Canadian contribution to the Empire's naval strength.[13] Like his predecessors, Grey had an office on the second floor of the East Block with its own entrance on Parliament Hill. His office was only a few steps from the prime minister's own, making the man practically unavoidable to the members of cabinet who occupied the same floor. "The debate last night having ended with a unanimous expression of the recognition of the House that the maintenance of our Naval Supremacy is essential, and must be secured however great the sacrifice," Grey told Laurier. He continued:

> I am afraid your speech ... will not be regarded either in Canada or in England as a very effective contribution to the solution of the Defence Problem, unless it is followed up by a display of vigour in formulating a plan and in carrying that plan into effect such as past experience does not encourage us to hope from Mr. Brodeur [the current minister of marine and fisheries]. Do you not think the necessity of taking prompt business action in this matter does not make it desirable that the change of Minister at the head of Marine and Fisheries Department, which you have more than once informed me was impending, should be hurried up?[14]

Grey even suggested that Clifford Sifton, who had resigned four years earlier, be appointed minister of the marine. "There cannot be two opinions on the point that he is, of all your available men, the best man there is [in] Canada for that office," Grey reminded his prime minister. "I know you will have to face a little criticism from Quebec, but you are quite big enough and strong enough to disregard that criticism, if you share my view that the duty which Canada owes to the Empire is to put the best business man she has got at the head of the Marine Dept., and that Sifton is the best man."[15] Laurier must have winced.

A few days after the debate on the naval crisis, Grey travelled to Montreal to attend the "Dramatic Competitions" for his trophy to the Canadian professional football league (the idea of a game where two matched teams confronted each other in rank formation to either defend territory or to march forward obviously appealed to his martial senses and seemed entirely fitting for the times). "My going to Montreal to look on at a Competition will seem very frivolous to you who are engaged in a much sterner conflict — but what can I do? The stage on which you are principal actor is forbidden ground to me, even as an auditor!"[16]

Grey nevertheless persisted in pressing Laurier to action. "The only doubt is whether a nation of 40 odd millions [Britain] can compete against a Nation of 60,000,000 [Germany] which is resolved to wrench Neptune's Trident from our grasp.... 'The Genius of True Pacifism' would appear to require such action as will convince Germany that she has not only Great but Greater Britain to deal with. She may have realized that if she allows the Dominions to develop in strength before she makes her strike for the supremacy of the seas she may be too late.... The effect of the New Zealand offer has undoubtedly been very great, but apparently it has not yet slowed down the feverish preparations of Germany to increase her naval strength."[17] The Canadian prime minister was preparing his own response to the German threat.

A Conference on Imperial Defence (CID) was called that summer to discuss the crisis. Laurier himself would not participate, but instead sent Frederick Borden, Minister of the Militia, and Louis-Philippe Brodeur, Minister of the Fisheries, to attend the event, which was held in London in late July 1909. Even then, Grey persisted, arguing for a contribution of at least six million dollars. "I send this line to remind you that time is pressing, and that a cable if it has not already gone, ought to go at once if you wish Mr. Brodeur to make an announcement of the amount Canada is prepared to spend yearly on her Navy at the outset of the Conference."[18] Laurier responded that the government was willing to commit two million dollars, but not until 1912 at the earliest.[19]

The meeting of the CID did not change much in terms of Canadian policy. The British Admiralty urged Canada to provide a fleet on the Pacific coast. Frederick Borden gave a glimpse of the government's inclinations when he agreed that Canada would provide a presence on both coasts. The official report of the CID was released in late September 1909, and it reinvigorated the issue. It was clear from the report that the British Admiralty wished for the construction and maintenance of a single navy, and that "all parts of the Empire contributed" to its maintenance. The Admiralty also supported the creation of navies by dominion governments, as long as its component parts be available for use in time of war. It was clear that the Laurier government had not abided by the first wish, but certainly was inclined toward the second.

The Canadian government began to organize a ministry devoted to naval defence, and the thought was that the Ministry of the Marine and Fisheries was a logical first step until the "defence" navy could be brought into the ambit of the Militia Department. There were growing doubts regarding whether Brodeur was a good choice to lead it. A lawyer, he was elected in 1891 to the House of Commons, and within ten years was serving as Speaker. In 1903, Laurier appointed him minister of Inland Revenue. In 1906, he moved to the Ministry of Marine and Fisheries. He was popular in his riding of Rouville, and had been acclaimed in 1908.

But all was not well in his department. Frederick Hamilton, taking advantage of his easy access to the top echelons of the government, discovered that Brodeur was not popular among some senior public servants. He learned that Eugène Fiset, Deputy Minister of Militia, was asked to be deputy of "some sort of new navy dep't" but refused to serve under Brodeur because he did not have the confidence that the department would be allowed to run along strong administrative lines. Using "most striking language … about Brodeur — contempt & disgust for his weakness, want of will & lack of courage," Fiset told Hamilton that the Militia gave no contracts except by a rigid system of tenders and that the department was focused on creating efficiencies and economies. The fear, of course, was that Brodeur would change all that.[20] Nevertheless, Laurier gave Brodeur his confidence.

————•◦•————

The release of the CID report had a harsher effect on Conservative ranks. By the end of the summer of 1909, the Conservative premiers of British Columbia, Manitoba, and Ontario voiced their opinion that Canada had to make an immediate contribution to the British navy. The conservative circles were divided, with some favouring a "one empire, one flag, one navy" offer to the Royal Navy, while others hoped for the creation of a Canadian navy that could be deployed in aid of the Empire, should there be a need. A third group, the Quebeckers, wanted none of it.

Even Lord Grey thought he should give advice to the French-speaking Quebec Conservatives, and approached Frederick Monk, Borden's Quebec lieutenant. Monk was a difficult man to gauge. Born in 1856 of an Anglican father and French-Canadian mother, he studied in both languages and was called to the Quebec bar in 1878. He married into the family of a cousin of Louis-Joseph Papineau, thus making him a distant relative of Henri Bourassa. He taught law at the Université Laval in Montreal and managed a small practice. Active in local politics at first, he was elected MP for Jacques-Cartier in North West Montreal in 1896 and was re-elected in 1900, 1904, and 1908. Monk, despite his quiet, somewhat melancholy disposition, was popular in the party, but his allegiance was torn. He was deeply opposed to Laurier's policy of involvement in the South Africa War, but where most of his Conservative colleagues demanded a more vigorous contribution, Monk, like Bourassa, wished for Canada to stay neutral in this affair. The tension inside the party was so intense that he resigned as Borden's leader in the province. It was only the debate on Canada's navy that united Monk and Borden again, albeit for different reasons, and Borden asked Monk to take up duties in leading Quebec Conservatives in January 1910.

Grey wrote Monk a five-page letter that provided his survey of French-Canadian opinion on the issue of a naval force. Worth quoting at length, his missive aimed to show that an alliance with Bourassa would be contrary to popular opinion and to the Church. "There is no part of the British Empire which stands to lose more than the Province of Quebec, from any naval disaster that may befall the British Crown," Grey wrote. He continued:

> Agreeing as I do with you so fully on the question of Co-partnership and Proportional Representation, I shall indeed be much surprised if we do not find, on discussing the naval position, that we are of one mind here also. Monseigneur Mathieu of Laval, in

discussing the political position of the Province of Quebec with me last year, summed it up in these words: *"Nous sommes si contents que j'ai peur: un changement quelqonque serait un désastre."* [We are so happy that I am afraid that any change would be a disaster.] The talks that I have had with other Canadians of French descent, and with members of the Hierarchy, such as the Archbishop of Montreal, have convinced me that if there is an apparent slowness on the part of French Canadians to realize the gravity of the position, that slowness does not arise from want of patriotism, but only from want of education.

Monseigneur Bruchési, in describing his attitude toward the present crisis, said: *"Quand la cloche sonnera nous irons tous"* [When the bell rings, we will all respond], but, he added, the bell had not yet rung. It is difficult to *"sonner la cloche"* in such a question as this, but no patriotic and serious-minded man who studies the facts can fail to be anxious.... It looks as if the intention of Germany was to strengthen her Fleet with the view of defeating the British Fleet before the self-governing Dominions are strong enough to come to her assistance. If Germany waits until the self-governing Dominions have budded naturally into Dreadnoughts, she will be too late. At present the self-governing Dominions expose a vulnerable front to German cruisers all around the world. They are a present weakness, not a strength to the Empire in a naval battle. One German cruiser in the mouth of the St. Lawrence could put every Quebec farmer out of business.[21]

Monk could also read from another fellow Montreal Conservative on the issue of Canada's place in the Empire. Stephen Leacock, a forty-year-old professor of political economy at McGill University, published a long scholarly essay on "Canada and the Monroe Doctrine" in

University Magazine. Leacock directly addressed the points made by Laurier, among others, and rid the discussion on Canada's naval future of the idea that the United States would assure the North's safety and that therefore there was no reason in spending money in this pursuit. That notion, he wrote, "has acted as a soporific to the public mind," and the whole idea that the Monroe doctrine offered Canada protection "is the purest fiction, and has no warrant in history, in actual fact, or in common sense."[22]

Leacock favoured a muscular contribution from the Canadian government to the Empire. To accept the protection of the United States was simply "unworthy of a people as lofty in their own estimation as the people of this Dominion.... The nations of history have grown to greatness by sacrifice and self-reliance. There is no other path. We cannot accept unpaid the sheltering protection of another state. The future lies elsewhere. Upon the North American continent, there are not one but two great powers."[23]

"To put the matter on the lowest plane," wrote Frederick Hamilton in the same journal, "our material commercial interests require it." To Hamilton, who considered Canada's future to be tied to trade with Europe and parts of Asia, the naval defence of shipping was paramount. The threat of Germany on the waters of the Atlantic was evident, but Hamilton also pointed west: "On the Pacific coast we are confronted with grave problems which may develop into grave dangers ... it is imperative that we provide a coastal defence." Canada even needed to patrol its inland waters, if only to assert its independence.[24]

The Conservative cracks continued to widen in the fall of 1909. The Conservative premiers raised the tone of their attacks on the Laurier plan, with Premier Roblin of Manitoba denouncing it as having the makings of a "tin pot navy." Other Conservative leaders in the West, such as Frederick Haultain in Saskatchewan and R.B. Bennett in Alberta, denounced the deal. Clearly, opinion in Conservative ranks had moved in favour of a direct contribution to the Royal Navy, and that trend did not sit well among Quebec members of the party. Monk gave a speech at a Conservative rally on November 8, 1909, that called for any naval plan to be submitted to a plebiscite. Borden, who had hoped to organize a party convention in 1910, decided to withdraw his plans when he learned that Monk's position was widely shared to the point that the Quebec Conservatives would boycott the meeting in protest of the party's position on the naval issue.

As the House of Commons resumed its deliberations in mid-November, vague rumours continued to circulate as to what the Laurier government was finally going to propose in terms of a program to the House of Commons, revealing the hesitations in government circles. Laurier insisted that his cabinet was focused on the issue, and that the government was working diligently to craft a policy that would guide Canada's naval efforts. The comment elicited a cynical comment from Hamilton, whose understanding of the policy machinery put the prime minister at the core of the decision-making. "Laurier's remark about the subject having engaged the anxious consideration of the cabinet is laughable," he wrote privately, "apparently the anxious consideration was only when no application was before them, for when specific requests were made the cabinet did not even consult the militia department.... My criticism of Laurier ... was directed mostly against this attitude of 'we mustn't mention it'. I wonder if there is another English-speaking country in the world so full of reticence and cowardice in public writing and speaking ... by the wide gap between what we say in public and in private."[25]

Progress was indeed slow, even if Laurier insisted that a bill was forthcoming. "There seems no clarification of opinion yet on the naval defence issue," reported Hamilton, "there is talk, based on Laurier's remark, that the bill may contain a clause that the Canadian navy shall fight only if Canada orders it. I should advocate fighting any such proposal to the last ditch, on the ground that it means secession from the Empire."[26]

Monk, meanwhile, again raised the pressure on the government (and on his own party), warning them both not to make a mistake that would tie Canada to imperial war policy in a speech that greatly impressed Lavergne.[27] Borden greeted the prospect of Laurier's proposed naval law with grave reserve, but for completely different reasons. He wanted to commit the government to making a contribution to the Royal Navy, but was "anxious to keep his intention dark," noted Hamilton.[28] A few days later, Borden's thinking had moved some. "Borden's intention is to come out with a stiff proposal for a direct and effectual aid to the Royal Navy," reported Hamilton. "He is preparing his speech with great care and probably will read a good deal of it. It is drafted so as to convey the real meaning that if necessary several dreadnoughts could be voted, while it may bear the aspect of proposing only one Dreadnought — this for Quebec consumption — I don't like this phase of it at all. Borden is anxious not to let the gov't get any inkling of his attitude."[29]

Borden would have agreed. "The situation was full of embarrassment," Borden recalled in his memoirs. "On the one hand, Quebec Conservatives affirmed with vehemence that I had gone altogether too far; on the other hand, many Conservative leaders in the English-speaking provinces were firmly of opinion that I had not gone far enough."[30]

———•◦•———

On January 12, 1910, Laurier himself ended the speculations by tabling the government's response to the year-old arms crisis: the creation of a Canadian naval force. The Naval Service Bill allowed the government to create a fully integrated, permanent naval service that included acquiring ships and funding for all the activities necessary to sustain a navy, from a college to train officers to efforts to enlist volunteers. The government was committing funding for five light cruisers and six destroyers, but no battleships. The bill specified that at all times the navy would stay under Canadian control, although one clause explicitly allowed the government to use an Order-in-Council to allow the Canadian navy to participate in the wars of the British Empire: "In case of an emergency the Governor in Council may place at the disposal of His Majesty, for general service in the Royal Navy, the Naval Service or any part thereof, any ships or vessels of the Naval Service, and the officers and seamen serving in such ships or vessels, or any officer or seamen belonging to the Naval Service."[31]

The provision allowing the government to order the navy to battle without consulting Parliament was critical in motivating *nationaliste* opinion, but Laurier insisted that once the Parliament of Canada had voted the naval service into being, only it could mobilize it. He pressed his point so that there was no doubt:

If England is at war we are at war and liable to attack. I do not say that we shall always be attacked; neither do I say that we would take part in all the wars of England. That is a matter that must be determined by circumstances, upon which the Canadian Parliament will have to pronounce and will have to decide in its own best judgment.[32]

Borden decided to emphasize that speed was of the essence and that if war was imminent, Canada had to keep open the idea of making a direct contribution to the Royal Navy: "Has that peril passed? No, Sir, we are nearer to it by nearly a year. Has Germany's policy been modified in the meantime? No, on the contrary Germany has since put forward the greatest naval budget in her history ... without war, without the firing of a shot or the striking of a blow, without invasion, German naval supremacy would bring the Empire to an end. It is idle to assure that there will be no war. The war has already begun, the war of construction, and victory will be as decisive here as in actual battle." Borden insisted that Canada had "the resources and ... the patriotism to provide a fleet unit or at least a dreadnought without one moment's unnecessary delay."[33]

"Things are very unsettled here politically," privately reported Hamilton about the dissidence inside the Conservative Party. "There also are murmurings against R.L. Borden; how serious I cannot determine. On the whole my judgment is that they are confined to a younger & more irresponsible element. The Frenchmen are behaving very badly & the party seems inclined to let them go to the devil."[34] Hamilton also reported that Laurier was having "a very bad time with his English Liberals who are very anxious for him to add a dreadnought to his policy." There were rumours that a petition had been circulated among some of them appealing to the cabinet to include a direct contribution to the Royal Navy. Hamilton's cynicism could not be held in check as he related one explanation: "It is surmised that the round robin [the petition] was really inspired by [Laurier] to give him an excuse to drop the whole bill. From an Imperial standpoint it would be a calamity & the prospect disturbs me."[35]

Finally, Borden made his decision known: he would oppose the government on the Naval Service Bill because it had no mandate to act on this matter. "Lay your proposals before the people and give them if necessary the opportunity to be heard," he said, while also reminding the government that it had to act: "Do not forget that we are confronted with an emergency which may rend this empire asunder before the proposed service is worthy of the name." Borden demanded that the government give the British government the necessary cash or "provide a fleet unit or at least a Dreadnought without one moment's unnecessary delay." When the bill was presented for second reading in early February, Borden this time moved an amendment to the bill, requiring that no permanent navy be created until the measure was submitted to the people of Canada and had received approval. Monk moved his own amendment, calling for the bill to be submitted to the Canadian people in a specific plebiscite.

Both amendments were voted down (Monk's motion only won the support of eighteen MPs); a line had been drawn in the sand. Borden's final words on the third reading of the bill contained two commitments: first, that the naval emergency of the Empire required "immediate and effective aid," and that "before a basis of permanent co-operation in the naval defence of the Empire is entered upon, the people of this country have a right to be consulted and to give their mandate."[36] Borden's policy was clear: he supported a direct contribution, and wanted Laurier's navy to be stalled until an election was called to debate it. By early March, even the fervent naval enthusiast Hamilton had grown despondent about the debate: "If we had to force a hand as of yore I think I would feel disposed to drop heavily on the naval debate, which is becoming very bad. While it has interesting aspects it has brought out a wonderful quality of rot & some very poisonous rot at that."[37] Some of the Conservatives were thinking (again!) that perhaps Sifton should join their ranks. Hamilton reported, "I am advising any Conservatives I talk to to leave Sifton alone for two years — and then see what will happen. If we have a real blow-up, such as the German war, he should come to the front."[38]

In early April 1910, Borden wrote a letter to George Taylor, the party's chief Whip, announcing his retirement. (He recalled in his memoirs that no less than four groups within the Conservative Party were clamouring for his withdrawal from the leadership at the time.) Borden did not hide his disgust at his own party. "He is very sick of it … his wife is sick of it — so he told me," reported Hamilton. "That being said, there was no agreement on who would or could replace Borden." The rumour again ran that Clifford Sifton was itching to fight the government. "His whole attitude suggests that he is getting ready to do something — and that something not a mere retirement into private life," Hamilton noted. The only good news was that Borden, by working with Monk, was gaining popularity in Quebec because the Quebec Tories were "wild with Monk."

"They have an ingrained habit of following a Frenchman," Hamilton continued, "but apparently wd [*sic*] welcome a French leader who wd work with Borden. This is the most cheering news (speaking as a Borden man) I have heard."[39]

As William Burrell recalled, these were "beastly days." The party was racked by doubt in its cause and in its leader. Caucus met on the evening of April 12, and Borden spoke in no uncertain terms. He was "anxious to retire" in light of the lack of support and "the talking behind [his] back." Borden eventually left the meeting to let the caucus decide his fate, but it continued to weigh the merits of keeping Borden as leader until the small hours of the morning. Finally, a motion of support was proposed and carried with some unanimity. Some members of the caucus got up "with evident reluctance."[40] Taylor and others insisted Borden withdraw the letter of resignation, and he did.[41]

The political situation was untenable. For the *nationalistes*, the naval bill that was finally passed on April 20, 1910, was the last straw. "It was a formal renunciation by a clear statement of law, of the policies of Sir John A. Macdonald, of Mackenzie, or Blake and of all Laurier's predecessors from the days of the United-Canadas and Confederation," remembered Armand Lavergne.[42] He would join Henri Bourassa to take the fight to the street. "Do you hear any whispers of an election in the autumn?" Hamilton wrote to Willison. "There is some such suspicion in Conservative circles. Lady Laurier's health is very bad, Sir W. is very anxious to pull out, and he may be rushed into seeing them through one more election before retiring."[43]

———•◦•———

Bourassa, who had been working on the idea of creating a daily news-paper for years, had a choice opportunity in the context of the Naval Service Bill to justify his new venture — a daily newspaper entitled *Le Devoir*. It would appeal to Montrealers who were concerned about the growing presence of Empire affairs in Canadian politics. For him and for others, Laurier's policies amounted to yet another capitulation — the "most complete retreat Canada has made in a half-century — the worse compromise of our autonomy since the beginning of responsible government."[44]

Bourassa liked to point out that at the 1902 London conference, Laurier had refused to enter what he called "the vortex of militarism." Following the defence conference of 1904, when the need for a stronger militia was put to the dominions, the Canadian government responded by proposing a militia act that limited Canadian defence to the ter-ritory. For Bourassa and the emerging *nationalistes*, the creation of a navy seemed to reverse the course of Canadian autonomy, and pro-vided further proof that the government had to be defeated. *Le Devoir* greeted the introduction of the *Naval Service Act* as a justification for its existence in its first edition of January 10, 1910, and promised to fight it.

Le Devoir's crusade started immediately, and Bourassa and the *nationalistes* took their battle to the people a few weeks after the bill was signed into law. The first demonstration against the law creat-ing the Navy was held in Beauport, outside Quebec City, on July 10, where Monk, Armand Lavergne, and Pierre-Edouard Blondin (the Conservative MP for Champlain) spoke. A week later, a rally of over seven thousand people was organized on the square in front of the historic church of Saint-Eustache — the site of the famed *Patriote* resistance in 1837 — where Blondin and Monk joined Bourassa in denouncing the law.

Bourassa drafted a set of seven resolutions that would be debated and adopted. The first resolution was a commitment to defend Canadian soil as loyal subjects of the King. The second resolution opposed any policy that would lead Canada into foreign wars unless Great Britain shared, on an equal footing, the formulation and execution of foreign and defence policy with the autonomous dominions of the Empire. The third resolution claimed a right of freedom of expression, but also recognized that "the majority of the Canadian people have the right to determine a new orientation in our relations with the other parts of the Empire, as long as the choice is made in all consciousness." The final resolution censured "the attitude of Mr. Borden and the members of the

Courtesy LAC, C-5110.

Henri Bourassa, 1910.

opposition who have pursued the adoption of a policy that would be no less nefarious" than the government's own law, and finally declared its unequivocal support for "Mr. Monk's loyal and courageous attitude."[45]

Monk and Bourassa were in full crusade mode, claiming that Laurier and the Liberals were turning back on their own positions of 1902 and 1907. Their argument was that Canada was now headed to a full engagement in Britain's wars, and the only one to blame was the prime minister, although Borden was not entirely spared: they were both "cowards and traitors." Bourassa was particularly acerbic in his critique of Laurier:

> Laurier nowadays likes to drive around in his official car, like the Caesars of yesteryear who would visit their provinces ... Laurier made a deal with Lord Grey.... He uses his authoritative voice, his honeyed eloquence to confuse and lie to the men who believe in him.... He presses French Canadians towards imperialism, hoping that they won't notice.... He has, with the stroke of a pen, decreed that in half of this country, Catholics have no right to have their children taught in the faith and language of their forefathers. I say that when a man, no matter his personal qualities, when a man so disdains the confidence and the love a people have had for him, to betray his own with such ease, I say that a man like that is more dangerous for the faith, for the country, and even for the British crown, than the worse of the Orangemen.[46]

The speech was a resounding hit. Two weeks later, Bourassa repeated it in front of the college in Saint-Henri where Armand Lavergne and a few others joined him. On August 6, the *nationalistes* gathered in Saint-Hyacinthe, the town Bourassa represented in the Quebec legislature. The campaign hit its apogee a few weeks later. On Sunday August 21, rallies were organized in eight different parts of the province, and on the following Sunday yet more rallies were held in eight other areas. Through the summer, the Liberals and the Conservatives had been quiet. Laurier, for one, was travelling in Western Canada and could not answer the *nationaliste* campaign.

Laurier was also preoccupied with the lingering effects of botched attempts to reconcile people of different views within his own party. Over the fall of 1909, Laurier had been pressed to act on another Quebec matter that would complicate the nature of the support of Liberalism in Quebec. Liberals in Quebec had long relied on Godfroy Langlois, as editor of the daily *Le Canada*, to tow the party line and to win for it more adherents. Langlois was no ordinary journalist. Since his earliest days in the daily press in the mid-1890s he had distinguished himself as an uncompromising reformer whose tirades in favour of school reform, state involvement in the economy, and against corruption and the *nationalistes* of Bourassa's ilk had secured him a place as the head of the party's radical wing in Quebec. Laurier had acquiesced in allowing Langlois to spearhead the creation of the party's new daily, *Le Canada*, in 1903 in recognition not only of his talents, but also of the strength of Liberal progressivism in Montreal (Langlois also sat as a member of the legislative assembly in Quebec).

With the years, however, the acidity of Langlois's critique had worn through the friendliest of Liberal shields. "The newspaper has ceased to be the organ of the party in Ottawa and in Quebec; it has become and becomes even more with every day that passes, the organ of Langlois," Senator Frederic-Liguori Béique, a key organizer in Montreal and part owner of *Le Canada*, told Laurier in early 1909, "He has alienated numerous friends we had among the clergy for a long time now, and the newspaper is now despised by a large number of Liberals. This situation has favoured the *Action Nationale* newspaper and will help Bourassa's paper."[47] Laurier concurred. "I have indeed spoken about *Le Canada*'s position with many friends and I informed them of my hesitations to break with the radical group of our party," he wrote to the Senator,

> That notwithstanding, I note that it is time to take sides and that the time has come to act. Our friend Langlois has given to *Le Canada* a slant that, as you know, does not suit me. I had always hoped that he

would eventually understand that it is not loyal on his part to substitute his personal ideas to those of the party, but since he now considers it to be his business, there is only one thing for us to do and that is make him understand that it is not his business, but ours. I am ready to do my part. I trust your judgment as to what should be done; just let me know what you expect me to do.[48]

Still, Laurier hesitated. "I understand that you are perplexed by the possible effect Langlois's departure from *Le Canada* would have on his friends," Senator Béique allowed.[49] Through the spring and summer of 1909, the Archbishop of Montreal intensified his pressure on Laurier and others, to the point in late August of threatening to ban the Liberal daily if something was not done about Langlois. When the revelation was made in the fall of 1909 that Langlois was, to top it off, the leader of the Loge L'Emancipation in Montreal, the anti-Catholic masonry lodge that took its cues from headquarters in Paris, even friends like Senators Raoul Dandurand and Béique had to rethink their support. Dandurand had to deliver the *coup de grâce*:

Your presence at *Le Canada* hamstrings our newspaper during the battles where moderate liberalism should fight. We are hamstrung and the critics mock our impotence.... You are viewed as an adversary of the doctrine and we are handicapped and unable to broach the many other questions that should be within our reach. A debate could arise at any moment when it would be critically important that our sincerity and our collective orthodoxy could not be called into question. I ask you in all sincerity: Do you think that in these conditions we are not justified in asking of you a sacrifice in the interest of the party for which this newspaper was created to defend?[50]

Langlois was finally convinced to leave when yet more evidence of his Freemasonry emerged during the Christmas holidays of 1909, and *Le Canada* quietly announced that its founding editor and director had accepted a post as Canadian Secretary to the newly created International Joint Commission on Boundary Waters. Langlois never assumed that post. Instead, in the same cold January week of 1910 that Henri Bourassa launched *Le Devoir*, Langlois published the first edition of *Le Pays*,with a mission to "open the minds of the population to the new ideas of social progress, of intellectual independence and of egalitarian democracy."[51] It would take almost a year before the Liberals realized what they had lost, especially as the *nationalistes* ramped up their campaign to actually repeal the *Naval Service Act* and build support for the "Saint-Eustache resolutions." The government response came with a rally on October 10, 1910, when Laurier spoke for two hours refuting Bourassa at a Montreal rally:

> I am the same man. In 1910, like in 1902, I am resolved to organize territorial defence, and now the principle of local autonomy. The *Naval Service Act* does not contain any gift to Britain that was refused to it in 1902. It contains not one word that takes away control of the navy from the government, from parliament or from the people of Canada. In 1902, Mr. Bourassa congratulated me; in 1910 he insults me. Who changed?[52]

Laurier decried Bourassa's raising of the spectre of conscription, but did acknowledge that Canada's youth could be called to service "by the people of Canada and the parliament of Canada." The Liberals were so confident that the *Naval Service Act* would be popular in Quebec that they were willing to test the waters with a by-election. Daring the Conservatives to mount a campaign against him, Laurier offered a Senate position to Louis Lavergne, the uncle of Armand, the Member for Drummond-Arthabaska (surely one of the most "red" ridings in the province) and called the by-election for November 3.

The Liberal choice to replace Louis Lavergne was Joseph Edouard Perreault, the scion of a wealthy Montreal family with no ties to the riding. Laurier himself travelled to Drummondville to preside over the nomination of the young man who was in part selected for his age. This time Laurier took on the arguments Bourassa had addressed to women: "Let them be reassured. They can continue their duties, because their children will not be called to serve despite them.... The Nationalists and the Conservatives should stay home with their wives and their children if they are afraid. We are not counting on them."[53]

The *nationalistes* were concerned that Perreault was strong in Drummond-Arthabaska and that only Armand Lavergne himself could win the by-election. "If you fight in Drummond-Arthabaska not only the eyes of the province of Quebec and of the entire dominion but also those of England's will be turned to those counties because the result of this fight will shape the fate of militarism and imperialism in this country," he was told. [54] Lavergne chose not to run (supporting instead a local candidate, Arthur Gilbert) but invested himself heavily in the campaign, giving speech after speech.

"The whole Quebec business is dirty politics," wrote Frederick Hamilton. "I really think that if Laurier had gone the whole hog and omitted the order-in-council clause he would have found no fiercer opposition than he has actually encountered and would have saved a very awkward episode for the Canadian gov't (perhaps his own) when the next big war breaks out."[55] A few days later, he reported a phone call he received from Brodeur indicating Liberal optimism in the result. "The Liberals seem to be putting some reliance on the English vote," he wrote.[56]

The beginnings of the campaign were promising for the Liberals, but they gave contradictory accounts to Laurier and Grey. Brodeur spoke in Drummondville and encountered some of the opponents of the Canadian navy. "I am glad to say that the audience, which was composed almost exclusively of French Canadian farmers," he reported to Grey, "seemed to be favourable to the idea and Messrs Bourassa and Monk had a very cold reception." He was sanguine that the by-election would end the issue: "I was happy to see that the

French Canadians who composed almost entirely the audience generally appeared to appreciate the importance not only of maintaining our connection with Great Britain but also of assuring by all means possible her naval supremacy. It was very consoling to me to hear such an expression of opinion on the part of my compatriots."[57]

Laurier received different reports from Henri Béland. "The navy is not popular among the farmers," Béland wrote to the prime minister on October 26.[58] Three days later, with a note of exasperation, he wrote, "I'll repeat it for the twelfth time: there is nothing to neglect ... the 'silent vote' is to be feared."[59]

Laurier, for his part, dreaded the result. "This is getting on my nerves," he wrote.[60] Liberals lost the by-election one early historian called the most important in Canadian history by just over two hundred votes. The verdict was a punch to the government that left it speechless. On the night he heard the verdict of Drummond-Arthabaska, Laurier said it hurt too much to laugh, but that he was too old to cry.[61]

One of the first to single out the reasons of the defeat for the Liberals was Godfroy Langlois in Le Pays. The Drummond-Arthabaska fight showed how intellectually impoverished the party had become. "One would believe that our friends were afraid to confront their adversaries. They gave the impression of muted dogs," he wrote. He perceived the by-election's result as the product of a faltering Liberal Party, the product of massive demoralization. "For fifteen years, the Liberal Party has been the manipulation of a few men. It is when that little group of men is seen, men who sell jobs and promotions, who traffic in influence and believe that the supreme ambition of a man is to indulge in profitable politics, that one understanding why so many people in our party are demoralized and disgusted."[62] For Langlois, who was now free to highlight the corruption of leading Liberals, had openly asked how it was that individuals who were known to be dirt poor (he was mostly referring to Senator Dandurand) could emerge wealthy from their years in the Senate.

While some blamed young Perreault himself for running a poor campaign,[63] Brodeur was livid at the way the nationalistes had behaved and what they had gotten away with. "In Drummond & Arthabaska they [the nationalistes] could never say things strong enough against the English and against England, but in the House their courage is weakened and they can't even keep their positions," he wrote with some resolve. "So be it! Their deceits are revealed and it shows once again how our population is wrong in allowing itself to be attracted by the disloyal denunciations of these demagogues."[64]

Le Devoir, not surprisingly, was jubilant. "It was the roughest setback, the most complete and especially most personal setback Laurier has suffered since his own defeat in the riding of Arthabaska in 1877," it editorialized. "*It is the beginning of the end*: that is what people were saying."[65]

Emboldened by the win, Monk presented an amendment to the naval law a few weeks later by again calling for it to be the subject of a referendum that tested positions on both sides of the aisle. Some thought that even Brodeur might vote for it so that the issue could be resolved for good. The Conservatives were unsure. "I don't think that Borden has made up his mind," Hamilton reported. "The Conservatives probably will divide on the Monk amendment, some for and some against. The Monk ... crowd ... like Borden; but that he doesn't go down in Quebec & so they are playing for the nationalists; & after the election all will be well. Sweet party game is it not?"[66]

A few days later, it was decided that Borden would vote against Monk. "It is as nicely balanced a bit of political judgment as I ever saw. The thing that influences me for it is the certainty that the future Nationalist campaign is certain to be as rabid as that in Drummond & Arthabaska. Ontario's likely will be as angry next year, and 2 years from now, as she is now. On the other hand, Ontario is very keen for an appeal to the people and to vote for and against such as demand in the same way would have a curious look and would embarrass countless Conservative speakers." Many of the Conservatives wanted to vote for Monk's amendment because they were convinced that an appeal to the people on the naval issue would win in English Canada. It was, as Hamilton wrote, "deadly orange."[67]

The government, meanwhile, had gone shopping and had appropriated two ships from the Royal Navy to seed its new navy: the *Niobe*, a cruiser, and the *Rainbow*. As the *Niobe* sailed into Halifax Harbour in mid-October 1910, the Canadian Navy was born.

The cost of purchasing and adapting the *Niobe* was estimated in November 1910 at $1,125,000, while the much smaller *Rainbow*'s cost would amount to less — $290,000. The cost of a Bristol-class ship was estimated at $7,540,000 and six "river-class" destroyers at $3,600,000. The total for ships amounted to $12,555,000, but would cost more if built in Canada. The cost of upkeep in 1910 for the Canadian Navy was estimated at $3,816,000, including the maintenance of four Bristols, the cost of a naval college, staffing, and whatever accoutrements would be required.[68]

"This event tells the story of a dawning epoch of self reliance," Brodeur declared in Halifax as the *Niobe* sailed into port. "It proclaims to the whole British Empire that Canada is willing and proud to provide as rapidly as circumstances will permit for her local naval defence and to safeguard her share in the Commerce and trade of the Empire…. This event appeals to all classes, conditions, political hues and racial origins."[69]

Brodeur took "a great deal of pride" in the *Niobe*, because he felt "sure that this nucleus of our Canadian Navy will prove of great benefit in advancing the ideas that we all cherish."[70]

Archives of Ontario, C 301, Newton McConnell collection, circa 1910, #10007739.

"The Dog of War." A commentary on Laurier's defence policies and the Naval Service Act.

"I was much pleased with Brodeur's speech in welcoming the *Niobe*," wrote Hamilton, again offering inside gossip. "It was far more courageous than Laurier's…. Privately I hear that he was jacked up to do it. His speech was written by a committee, prominent on which (I infer) is my great friend Commander Roper. It was written, and Brodeur removed all oratorical effect by laboriously reading it out, with the copy about 6 inches from his nose. It reads better than it sounded."[71] All the same, even the crusty imperialist reporter had to admit that the government's acquisition made sense. "The *Niobe* seems to me an excellent acquisition," Hamilton observed. "She is a very powerful vessel & the things that make her rather a white elephant of the Admiralty (her size & the number of men she requires) are rather a recommendation for us. She amounts to this — she can lick almost anything in the German navy short of their armoured cruisers; they could not spare their armoured cruisers to come over here, and so the *Niobe* should make our coast a very unwholesome place for their small fry and old cruisers. At the same time, she is not important enough to make her absence from British waters a deduction from British strength. The admiralty had destined her & other obsolescent large protected cruisers for the patrolling of trade routes…. If we had an *Indomitable* & kept her on our side of the Atlantic … It would not do to keep her habitually with us & send her on the approach of danger to England."[72]

The twenty-month debate on the naval question left both Laurier and Borden politically bloodied and physically exhausted. It had not started well for Borden. As the debate started in the early weeks of the spring of 1909, his good friend Frederick Hamilton would report: "His face has an oddly haggard look."[73] A year later, he was not feeling much better as he battled some sort of respiratory ailment. The stress of this period did not help, and he suffered the second-guessing from various factions in his party. Not surprisingly, he again came very close to resigning his position as leader in the spring of 1910.[74]

Laurier did not fare much better. He had grown tired with many parts of his cabinet and let it be known to Charles Fitzpatrick, the

Chief Justice of the Supreme Court, that "things have become corrupt and he has lost control of them; and that he is sick of it all." Fitzpatrick left the impression that Laurier was planning to retire before the end of 1911 and that there would be an early dissolution of the House. Fitzpatrick also revealed that if one had to do business with Laurier, "it is necessary to see him in the morning; in the latter part of the day he cannot concentrate his attention." Frederick Hamilton noted that this account tallied with "some curious instances of forgetfulness etc. which the opposition have [sic] noticed this session on his conduct of the house."[75]

Laurier, who had tried to apply the Solomonic touch that had seemed to work in resolving the Manitoba schools question in 1896, the question of Canada's participation in the South African War and the creation of Alberta and Saskatchewan, recognized that his approach was creating enemies. His party was now ripping at the seams he had so carefully sewn over issues of Empire in both English and French Canada. This was costing him party support. Parts of Ontario and the Maritimes, where imperialist sentiment ran strong, were increasingly unsure that Laurier spoke for them on the issue of defence. In French Canada, Bourassa used the issue to undermine the prime minister, who had failed him on the South Africa War and the use of French in the West.

Imperialist discontent with the Navy hinged on two arguments. First, that it was insufficient, and second that it was ineffective. Many also took exception that the Navy would only be deployed when it suited the whim of the government. As the editorialist of the *Halifax Herald* put it, "It is doubtful if the bulk of the people of Canada who are putting up the money for this 'order-in-council' navy realize that their hands have been completely tied by the voluble opportunist who sits at the head of the cabinet table."[76]

There was discontent about the role the Canadian government would play in that the Navy could not be of assistance to Britain unless the government authorized it: "It cannot even fire a gun without permission and England might be swept from the sea before the machinery of government gave the word which would pull the trigger."[77]

The conclusion by the summer of 1910 was that "we have failed to range ourselves proudly and gladly by the side of the old land.

She asked for bread and Sir Wilfrid Laurier politely handed her a stone… Sir Wilfrid Laurier looks calmly on while millions are frittered away on the National Transcontinental, on Quebec bridges which collapse, on saw dust wharves which help to elect supporters of the government, on Hudson Bay railways, on public works which do the most political good and the least public benefit, and on the hundred and one expenditures which have taxed the credit of Canada to the limit."[78]

French Canada had handed a stone of its own to Laurier. The Liberal Party had lost the support of its progressive wing, for one thing, but that ailment could be repaired. It was also losing the support of its more nationalist supporters, as the result of the Drummond-Arthabaska by-election showed. Brodeur could report at the end of 1910 that his end-of-year meetings with voters in his riding showed strong support for the party, and that the Drummond-Arthabaska result was nothing more than an accident. But this could only be cold comfort to Laurier; the events of the preceding months had made one thing clear: he could be beaten.[79]

The *Naval Service Act* episode had practically taken a full two years of the government's time, and, according to Henri Bourassa, threatened to become for Laurier the poisoned shirt of Nessus that had killed Hercules. He had to find a way to shake it off in order to be able to fight the next election.

CHAPTER 3

NEGOTIATING RECIPROCITY

The old man [Laurier] is getting many jolts nowadays
and doesn't like it.
— Martin Burrell, Conservative MP

In his dealings with the world outside the Empire, Laurier had every reason to be positive about his government's policies. Over the course of his four administrations, Canada had broadened its international activities, and its relations with the United States in particular had undergone what can only be called a quiet revolution. Canada's domestic growth and economic prosperity were mirrored internationally, and Laurier's conduct of foreign policy — limited as it was — was generally considered to have protected and furthered the country's national interests.

In the late nineteenth century, Canadians looking around the world for potential threats could usually find only one — the United States. The century was filled with American military incursions (both organized and spontaneous), border disputes, and economic rivalries, and was permeated by Canadian fears and injudicious American musings over the potential annexation of Canada by the United States. By the turn of the century the issue of annexation languished in the United States and was confined to the dark recesses of Canadian minds, but still ready to be stirred at the first hint of aggressive American rhetoric.

Under the leadership of President McKinley, the United States sought improved — what we would today call "normalized" — relations with both Canada and Great Britain. Accelerated by their respective wars against Spain and in South Africa, in which the Americans and British found themselves with few international friends other than each other, the turn-of-the-century Anglo-American rapprochement became a reality. To complete the new Anglo-American relationship, however, the slate of problems between the two North American states needed to be cleaned.

In the decades following the end of the Civil War, the governments of the United States, Great Britain, and, increasingly, Canada, met in a series of joint high commissions to solve mutual problems facing the "North Atlantic Triangle," including border disagreements, fishing disputes on the Atlantic coast, and sealing disagreements in the north Pacific. The Canadians came out of these negotiations rather well. There were a few occasions — the 1903 decision on the Alaskan Boundary, for example — when the Canadians felt poorly served by the British as they pursued friendly relations with the United States. In any relationship between a very large country and a small one, however, breaking even can rightly be interpreted as victory.

As Laurier started his fourth mandate, most of the pressing North American problems had been settled amicably, usually in ways acceptable to Canadians. The few remaining border disputes had been settled: a treaty had been signed to regulate salvage and wreckage operations in joint waters, and in 1907 Laurier had agreed to send the nagging east coast fisheries dispute to arbitration before an international tribunal at The Hague. This effectively removed the issue from public contention and, ultimately, it was agreed to establish a Canadian-American commission with authority to set the regulations for the use of the inshore fisheries. Similarly, agreement in the Bering Sea pelagic sealing dispute — and compensation for Canadian sealers — was reached in a 1911 treaty.

The new relationship was now less about Fenian invasions and border squabbles and more about continental industrialization, economic development, and trade, and it was best symbolized by the Boundary Waters Treaty, signed by the United States and Great Britain in 1909 to regulate the use of the lakes and rivers that spanned the Canadian-American border. Part of the treaty — which was largely negotiated by Canadians — called for the establishment of an International Joint Commission, which would work quietly behind the scenes in settling cross-border water issues, from irrigation and water diversion to electric power generation.

Credit for these much-improved relations rested with James Bryce, the British Ambassador in Washington; but that did not mean that Laurier could not try to claim some of the glory for himself on the campaign trail. Equally, his creation of a Department of External Affairs in 1909 seemed to reflect well on his government and the growing international stature of Canada, even though at first the department had a tiny permanent staff and even less to do, nestled in its offices above a barber shop on Ottawa's Sparks Street.[1]

If there was a weak spot in Laurier's record it was in trade relations with the United States. Laurier was a liberal in an era of American conservatism, and a free trader in a continent of protectionists. His party was dedicated to lower tariffs, and doomed, it seemed, forever to co-exist with a neighbour who had repeatedly raised some of the highest tariffs in the world. In 1910, seizing on an opportunity to grasp a prize that had eluded all previous Canadian governments — both Liberal and Conservative — he entered into negotiations for a reciprocal trade agreement with the United States.

———

Canada's quest for reciprocity or freer trade with the United States predated the living memory of most of those people involved in the 1911 election. Great Britain's repeal of its "corn laws" and adoption of free trade in the 1840s panicked Canadian farmers, dairy producers, and some manufacturers who feared for their livelihood with the loss of British North America's preferential status in the British market. Feelings were so strong that a group of Anglo-Montreal businessmen came out in support of annexation by the United States as a way of dealing with their economic distress. The annexation movement was short-lived but survived long enough to publish a manifesto and burn down the parliament buildings in Montreal in 1849.

To placate the Canadians, the British government initiated trade negotiations with the Americans to find new outlets for Canadian products to offset what might be lost in the British market. Years of negotiation led to the signing, in 1854, of the Reciprocity Treaty, which allowed free entry of Canadian natural and some processed goods into the American market and the reduction of duties on a number of other products. In addition to reduced tariffs, the Americans were granted access to the inshore fisheries in the Maritime colonies.[2] Ironically, in 1911 much would be made of the connection between reciprocity and annexation, with the argument that the one (reciprocity) would inevitably lead to the other (annexation), even though, in 1854, reciprocity was seen by the British government as a way of *preventing* annexation.

A mixture of rising protectionist feelings in the United States and the souring of Anglo-American relations during the Civil War led the United States to abrogate the treaty in 1866, triggering more than four decades of Canadian efforts to resurrect some kind of reciprocal trade agreement. Canadians always wanted reciprocity more than Americans did (it was getting access to the Maritime fisheries that was key for the Americans in the early negotiations), and all subsequent efforts ended in failure. In the 1871 Treaty of Washington, for example, the Americans agreed to pay for access to the Maritime fisheries but offered no trade concessions in return. Indeed, Republican-inspired protectionism dominated U.S. fiscal policy for most of the rest of the century and American tariff levels were raised repeatedly.[3]

It was partly because of his inability to revive reciprocity that Sir John A. Macdonald introduced the National Policy in 1879. The National Policy was far more than a simple tariff implemented to foster the growth of industry in Canada. It was part of a broad scheme of continental expansion to orient the economic development of Canada on an east–west basis even though geography suggested that the natural way would be north–south. The National Policy tariff was set at a rate high enough to protect and promote manufacturing at home in an effort to supply Canadians all across the country with the homegrown products and jobs that they desired. The National Policy would open the West to new waves of immigration (in a pattern similar to that successfully applied in the United States) and its backbone would be the construction of the Canadian Pacific Railway to physically tie the country together. The steel spine of a transportation network would bring immigrants and eastern manufactured goods to the West and return the produce of Western farmers for Eastern consumers and foreign markets overseas. The National Policy was, in the words of a later historian, "a Declaration of Economic Independence."[4]

The National Policy was wound around fidelity to the imperial connection with Great Britain, and Macdonald was able to ride these twin forces to a series of electoral victories from 1878 to 1891. In 1891 he savagely attacked the Liberal policy of unrestricted reciprocity, or free trade, under the Conservative banner of "the old man, the old flag, and the old policy." Accusations of treason were hurled at the Liberals with abandon and Macdonald, wrapping himself in the Union Jack, declared "a British subject I was born — a British subject I will die." The Liberals joked that they, too, would die as British subjects, but perhaps not as soon as Sir John, to no effect. Combatting charges of disloyalty is one of the most difficult of political tasks, as the Liberals discovered in both 1891 and 1911. For the Conservatives, however, "remember 1891!" became something of a rallying cry in the 1911 election.

Even though a standing offer of reciprocity in natural products was a part of the National Policy (and repeatedly rebuffed by the Americans), Macdonald's careful mixture of economic policy and patriotism emerged as a formidable political force. So much so that the Liberals, under their new leader, Wilfrid Laurier, muted most of their free trade rhetoric after the humiliating defeat in 1891. Why trumpet an idea or cause like free trade when it meant a seemingly permanent seat on the opposition benches in Parliament — especially when the Americans showed no inclination to adopt it in any event?

The Liberal Party largely accepted the tenets of the National Policy and, after their 1896 election victory, showed little inclination to change its basic structure, instead advocating tariff reductions and "freer" rather than "free" trade. In 1899 Laurier announced that the "general feeling in Canada is not in favour of reciprocity." A few years later he went farther, stating that "there was a time when we wanted reciprocity with the United States, but our efforts and offers were put aside. We have said good-bye to that trade, and we have now put all our hopes in British trade."[5] He may have succumbed to the enthusiasm of the moment and given his audience what he believed they wanted to hear, but he said enough then and at other times to convince many Canadians that he had shifted his views away from reciprocity.

Later, during the 1911 election campaign, a heated debate flared over whether or not the Liberals had ever officially abandoned their commitment to reciprocity. For some, the Liberals had turned away from free trade to embrace the National Policy and, as a result, attracted considerable support from the business community and others who benefitted from the higher tariffs. Adopting reciprocity in 1911, therefore, was a serious breach of trust for those who had supported Laurier for fifteen years, and his opponents were quick to remind him of his earlier statements. Others argued that the Liberals always remained true to the spirit of reciprocity but because the Americans were so unforthcoming it made little sense to continually try — and fail — to negotiate freer trade. But, they argued, the commitment was maintained, and when the opportunity for reciprocity arose in 1910, the Liberals stood by the fundamental principles of liberalism by negotiating a trade agreement with United States. Either way, it was believed that matters of great principle were at stake.

What could be agreed upon was that under the Liberal government Canada's trade policy became more diverse and sophisticated, reflecting a growing and prosperous economy. In 1897, Finance Minister William Fielding introduced a budget containing a new imperial preference tariff that was essentially a lower tier tariff, about 25 percent below the National Policy level (which now became the general/maximum rate). It was a brilliant move for the Liberals, who in a single stroke could claim to be both taking a step toward freer trade and being patriotic to the Empire (even though the new tariff was technically applicable to all states that reciprocated). The move was widely popular in both Canada and the mother country and fed into the popular talk of "tariff reform" in Great Britain, which had already led to calls for the creation of a vast imperial preferential trading bloc. Then, in 1907, Fielding added a new intermediate rate between the imperial preference rate and the general National Policy level. The new intermediate rate was to be negotiated in return for concessions from other countries on exports of Canadian goods. Trade agreements exchanging these intermediate rates were negotiated (and several existing agreements were updated) with Germany, France, and Italy over the following years.

Even more important was the trade relationship with the United States. Although imperial preference helped increase Canadian imports from Great Britain, imports from the United States were growing even faster. With or without reciprocity, Canadian–American trade rose steadily virtually every year from the Civil War to the outbreak of the First World War.[6] The United States now exported far more to Canada than it had in the past. These facts were not lost on those who cared about Canadian–American relations in Washington. In addition, talk in Canada and Britain of an imperial preferential trading scheme troubled many in Washington who had never before given much thought to trade with Canada — what if Canada developed as an industrial nation at the heart of a global empire?

Thoughts of a military annexation may have diminished with time, but few Americans wanted to see Canada develop as an economic competitor with the United States. American government and business leaders far preferred a Canada that would buy American manufactured goods and sell its natural products to Americans. The "open door" was general American economic policy and, although it may have been fine-tuned for local consumption, it was applied to Canada as well. By 1910 one of the goals of American policy was to detach Canada economically from the Empire and to tie it to the American economy.[7] One way to achieve this goal was through a trade agreement.

"No such opportunity will ever again come to the United States," American president William Howard Taft warned an audience of the Associated Press and the American Newspaper Publishers Association in New York, on April 27, 1911. Without a trade agreement with the Canadians, he added, the only ones to benefit would be the "forces which are at work in England and in Canada to separate her by a Chinese wall from the United States and to make her part of an imperial commercial band, reaching from England around the world to England again, by a system of preferential tariffs."[8]

A call for lower tariffs had also emerged from important segments of the American population. Low tariff Democrats were growing in number and demanding tariff revisions. Some manufacturers, especially in New England, called for tariff reductions to make it easier for them to gain access to raw materials and to increase markets for their goods. All those who depended on the import of Canadian raw materials and food could see some benefit in reduced tariffs, and few American manufacturers saw any harm in the reduction of Canadian tariffs on their goods. Most important, the rapidly growing American newspaper industry, which relied on massive imports of Canadian pulp and newsprint, came out in support of tariff reductions. Their case was no more logical or important than anyone else's, but they were able to pursue a vigorous campaign through the pages of their newspapers and maintain intense pressure on American politicians.[9]

All the calls for tariff reductions had their effect on the American government, but not exactly in the way that was at first anticipated by its supporters. President Taft pledged his administration to the lowering of tariffs with all countries and looked to Congress for new legislation, but by the time a bill passed both Houses it was significantly compromised. The 1909 Payne-Aldrich tariff lowered the duties on some goods (including on newsprint, lumber, and a few other products) but it also included a punitive higher tariff (about 25 percent above the general level) and compelled the administration to apply it against those states that were seen to be discriminating against American exports. Several governments caved in to the threat of punitive retaliation and lowered their rates on American imports, but the Laurier government refused.

Washington looked at the 1907 trade agreement Canada had signed with France (and other European states) and announced that it was discriminatory against American exporters. They demanded equivalent treatment to the French (i.e. rates at the intermediate level). To the Canadians it was an outrageous demand for trade concessions when nothing was offered in return — while the French had earned the reductions in the Canadian tariff by reducing their own tariffs, the Americans were demanding equal reductions and in return offering only the threat of an even *higher* tariff. There also was a time deadline, and the Canadians had until March 31, 1910, to comply or the higher rates would be imposed. A trade war threatened.

"The temper of the average Canadian is very satisfactory," wrote Lord Grey, the governor general, about the American threats. "He won't be bullied; he would prefer to suffer. The United States pretension that we have no right to negotiate a commercial treaty with another Power is monstrous!"[10] Ironically, despite the outrage, Canada's tariff legislation contained a not dissimilar "surtax" that was to be applied against states that treated Canadian exports less favourably than those of other states. It was very rarely applied, and never against American imports, but if a trade war erupted this surtax would have been Ottawa's key weapon of retaliation.[11]

Neither government wanted a trade war, but they needed a way out. The Americans made the first move. President Taft wrote to his wife that he "was very anxious not to have a war with Canada." But something had to give, he continued, "If they will only give me some-thing upon which I can hang a decision, I will be glad to seize an excuse and make the announcement required."[12] An opportunity soon arose: two American government officials were dispatched to Ottawa in February to discuss the situation, and in March Taft travelled to Albany, New York, for a speech before the Albany University Club. On the prompting of J.A. Macdonald, the editor of the Toronto *Globe*, who had encouraged Taft to pursue trade negotiations, the president invited Lord Grey and Laurier to attend the speech.

Finance Minister Fielding attended in Laurier's place, as the prime minister could not leave Ottawa, and Fielding and the Americans worked out a compromise of sorts on the spot. The Canadians agreed to reduce to the intermediate level tariffs on thirteen American imported products, including soap powders, nuts, dates and figs, arti-ficial feathers, and various kinds of perfume — none of which were of anything more than minor significance. Taft accepted the offer and declared the Canadians in compliance with the Payne-Aldrich tariff (the tariff penalized "undue discrimination" but it was up to the president to decide what was "undue"). With a nod and a wink a trade war was averted; or, as Laurier's biographer O.D. Skelton wrote, a "phantom concession had been made to remove an invented grievance."[13]

This small success led Taft to believe that the moment was right to initiate broader trade negotiations with Canada. He realized that a trade war might have hurt the already ailing American economy and its growing reliance on imports of natural resources. American industry wanted Canadian raw materials and it was the American consumer who ultimately paid for the tariff duties on Canadian imports. An agreement of some kind would help silence his pro-reciprocity critics at home and further American economic interests in Canada. Taft invited Fielding to Washington for more trade discussions. Later in the spring, Fielding visited the White House for preliminary talks, and an official invitation was issued for full trade negotiations — not specifically for reciprocity, but, in the words of Secretary of State Philander Knox, for the "consideration of a re-adjustment of our trade relations upon the broader and liberal line which should obtain between countries so closely related geographically and racially."[14]

It was a strategic moment for Laurier, Fielding, and the rest of the government. Reciprocity, lower tariffs, and trade negotiations had been Liberal objectives for years — however muted — but the Americans had shut the door every time. Now, not only was the door opening wide, a welcome mat was thrown before them. It was an offer that Laurier just could not refuse. His party had been in power for fourteen years and was under attack on a daily basis for its naval policy; a trade agreement with the United States might be just the thing to re-energize the Liberal Party and the government, and return the party to the true faith.

Laurier had time to think it over, however. Fielding was soon off on a European trip that would keep him out of the country until September, and he himself was about to embark on a long-planned trip across the country. A voyage to the West would provide him the opportunity to feel the pulse of the country on any possible "truck or trade" with the Yankees.

Laurier left on his western trip on July 7. The journey took him in a private railway car from Port Arthur and Fort William to Winnipeg and, following the tracks across the Prairies, to most of the major towns and cities of the West (including Brandon, Regina, Saskatoon, Moose Jaw, Calgary, Edmonton, and dozens of places in between), all the way to Vancouver and Victoria and then back again, bringing him home to Ottawa in early September. He had crossed the country sixteen years before, but this was the first time as prime minister and he must have wondered how the country had changed in the intervening years. "I undertook the same journey in 1894," he wrote his old friend and minister of justice Allen Aylesworth as he left Ottawa, "and what makes me diffident now is that I am just sixteen years older than I was then. At that time I was full of enthusiasm and fully enjoyed the *'gaudium certaminus.'* It is not so now; I have not the same enthusiasm and my only hope is that it may come as the trip progresses."[15]

All reports of the Western tour, including from Laurier himself, suggest that it was a great success, with large, enthusiastic crowds at almost every stop willing to listen to speeches at virtually any hour of the day. "Everyone is in agreement that this voyage has produced very positive results," he wrote his colleague Rodolphe Lemieux as his train approached Prince Rupert, British Columbia. "I am beginning to believe it myself."[16] The Manitoba premier wrote that Laurier was looked upon "as a political humbug" in the West,[17] and one Conservative MP wrote of the "noticeable lack of enthusiasm" in British Columbia for "the old Frenchman," but these comments were in the minority.[18] The whole affair went off without a hitch, save for a collision of Laurier's railway car with a freight train outside of Moose Jaw in which the prime minister was shaken but not seriously hurt.[19]

Wherever he went, Laurier made an impression. In contrast to modern politicians who don casual clothing, baseball caps, aprons, or hard hats, as each situation warrants, most photographs of Laurier on his western tour — speaking from the back of the train, at receptions, standing in a farmer's field — show him fully dressed in an elegant suit and the ubiquitous top hat, often in what must have been scorching summer heat. He had the common touch that transcended his fashionable clothes and which allowed him to connect with people, but he never pretended to be *of* the people; with his demeanor, his elegant looks, and flowing white hair he always maintained an air of grace and even nobility.

Ten-year-old Arthur Irwin, a future diplomat, newspaper publisher, and editor of *Maclean's* magazine, remembered for the rest of his life the larger-than-life Laurier at one of his Winnipeg speeches in 1910. Eighty years later, three of Laurier's words stuck out in Irwin's memory, each punctuated by a grand sweep of his arm: "Canadian! Pacific! Railway!"[20] In Saskatoon, where Laurier arrived to lay the cornerstone for the new University of Saskatchewan, he bought a newspaper from a young John Diefenbaker. The future prime minister later wrote that he had "the awed feeling that I was in the presence of greatness." The elder statesman and newsboy talked for a few minutes before Diefenbaker reportedly ended the conversation with: "Sorry, Prime Minister, I can't waste any more time on you, I've got work to do."[21]

There was no shortage of issues of concern to westerners. On the Prairies, freight rates, control of the grain elevators, and the scourge of (especially eastern) graft and corruption were constants on the political agenda. The construction of a railway to Hudson Bay had long been debated and had become something of a political football, tossed around between the political parties before each election. Moreover, provincial control over natural resources, which was maintained in the hands of the federal government at the time of the creation of Alberta and Saskatchewan, was a constant source of friction between Ottawa and the new provincial capitals and would remain a bone of contention throughout the election campaign.

In addition, the control of Asian immigration — an issue in which neither central nor western Canadians particularly distinguished themselves — was of special interest to the residents of British Columbia and had been an election issue in both 1904 and 1908. From 1896, the Liberal government built on the restrictions introduced by the previous Conservative administration, and throughout the Laurier years stiffened the limits on immigration from India, Japan, and China (although in different ways from, respectively, restrictive legislation, to "gentlemen's" agreements, to the raising of the infamous head tax). But it never seemed enough; when Laurier reached Vancouver Island he was met with a deputation from the Victoria Trades and Labour Council on Asian immigration, "a subject of first importance to the working people of this City and Province." While the Liberals were applauded for their efforts to keep the foreigners out, it was argued that a $500 head tax was no longer sufficient and needed to be raised to $1,000 and applied to all Asian immigrants.[22]

The central issue on the Prairies, however, especially for the majority rural population, was trade and, in particular, the demand for tariff reductions on natural products and farm machinery. At almost every stop on the tour Laurier was met by farmers' delegations and political groups armed with local petitions and resolutions demanding action on trade policy. Laurier was told how the tariff discriminated against farmers for the benefit of eastern industry, by making imports of American farm machinery and tools more expensive and diminishing Canadian farm exports to the United States. The tariff affected farmers both ways — by reducing their income while raising their overhead costs.

Early in the tour a delegation from the Manitoba Grain Growers' Association advised Laurier that there were "no trade relations our Government could enter into with any nation that would meet with greater favour or stronger support from the farmers of Western Canada than a wide measure of Reciprocal trade with the United States including manufactured articles and the natural products of both countries." It would not be easy to accomplish, they added: "We know the protected interests will oppose with all their united strength any attempt to lower our present Canadian tariff, or to enter into reciprocal trade with the United States, but these protected interests have had control of our fiscal policy too long."[23] Farther west, the Liberal Association of Edmonton made comparable entreaties for tariff reductions as the government tried to "eradicate the selfish interests of protection." Laurier was urged to make the "decisive move" and to remove all duties on agricultural machinery.[24]

Similar requests awaited Laurier at virtually every train station, luncheon, ceremony, parade, reception, and garden party. He made no promises in return, beyond general platitudes, and gave no account of the ongoing discussions with the Americans. But a couple of things were clear as he returned home to Ottawa in September: if he needed any confirmation of the desire for reciprocity or encouragement and support for his movement into trade negotiations with the United States, he had found them on his western trip.

Formal trade talks began in Ottawa on November 5, with Fielding and William Paterson, the minister of customs, on one side and Henry Hoyt and Charles Pepper of the State Department on the other. No final agreement was reached but the Canadians were startled at how far the Americans were willing to go to secure an agreement. Fielding argued that eliminating the Canadian tariff on imports of American manufactured goods was impossible (he was well aware of the opposition to such a move among Canadian business leaders) and the Americans apparently accepted the argument. In general, the Canadians seemed to put their faith in the American desire for a reduction in the cost of living that would be derived from cheaper Canadian imports, and hoped that this would be enough for them to agree to lower American tariffs on Canadian goods.[25]

There was, however, accord on two issues. First, the two sides agreed to meet again, this time in Washington, to sign a formal agreement. Second, on the suggestion of the Canadians, it was agreed that the final result of the negotiations would not be a formal treaty but, rather, an exchange of letters between governments outlining the agreement and a commitment to put that agreement into legislation in both countries. The argument was that a treaty would be more formal, harder to amend, and would need the involvement of the British government on the Canadian side and a two-thirds majority in the American Senate. Legislation was easier and could be passed in both countries with a straight majority, and the agreement could be amended relatively easily over subsequent years.

News of the preliminary discussions spread quickly and the scrutiny and pressure on Laurier increased throughout the late summer and fall of 1910. Not everyone agreed on the best course of action, and the first cracks in what would become major fault lines during the election campaign began to appear. For some supporters the possibility of a reciprocity agreement was cause for celebration, if only that it might deflect some attention away from the naval issue and back to more traditional Liberal strengths. To others, however, reciprocity with the United States was nothing but a dangerous gamble.

The greatest pressure on Laurier continued to come from rural Canada. Western farmers were well-organized, with Grain Growers' Associations in each of the Prairie provinces and the newly launched Canadian Council of Agriculture, an umbrella organization representing a variety of farmers' groups from across the country. Although unrest was widespread and there already was some talk in the West of forming a regional or farmers' political party and other kinds of non-partisan organizations to express western grievances, most farmers were willing to maintain their support for the Liberal Party, providing it spoke for their interests. To ensure that Laurier would not forget, a large Farmers' Convention was held in Ottawa in the middle of December. Organized by the Canadian Council of Agriculture, the Convention — variously known as the "Siege of Ottawa" or the "Siege of 1910" — included more than eight hundred representatives of farmers' groups from Ontario and the West.

At a mammoth rally on December 15, a series of resolutions were adopted unanimously, and presented to Laurier the following day. The resolutions became known as "The Farmer's Platform," and included, among others, a call for the construction of a publicly owned railway to Hudson Bay, the demand that Ottawa acquire and operate the terminal elevators at Fort William and Port Arthur and establish similar facilities on the Pacific Coast, and a plea for legislation to reform and curtail the powers of the banks. Most important was tariff reduction: "in view of the fact that the further progress and development of the agricultural industry is of such vital importance to the general welfare of the state, that all other Canadian industries are so dependent upon its success, that its constant condition forms the great barometer of trade, we consider its operation should no longer be hampered by tariff restrictions."[86] Laurier met with a delegation from the Convention and accepted the resolutions. Beyond that he made few comments other than promising to take their demands under consideration.

Critics of a trade agreement with the Americans also publicly aired their concerns. A number of critical articles appeared in major newspapers and, in the House of Commons, a few MPs rose from their seats to let off ominous warnings of the dangers of tinkering with the National Policy. The boards of trade in several Ontario towns, including Oshawa, Brockville, and Berlin (Kitchener), passed resolutions protesting the negotiation of reciprocity with the Americans. The Canadian Manufacturers' Association also protested, and organized a more formal presentation of their concerns in a lengthy document presented to Laurier by a delegation of businessmen in mid-January 1911. Even without knowing the details of the agreement the Association anticipated several problems; in particular there was concern over the impact of reciprocity on Canadian manufacturers, as it would be "obviously impossible for them to withstand the competition that would inevitably follow reductions in the present Canadian tariff."[27]

"So far," one businessman wrote in a letter to Laurier, "Liberal manufacturers as a whole have supported the Liberal Government, but, I am free to say that if in dealing in reciprocity with the U.S. Mr. Fielding would lower the tariff on manufactures, he would lose the support and influence of the said Liberal manufacturers."[28]

Even within the Liberal Party there were rumblings of discontent. In November 1910, Sir George Ross, senator and the former Liberal premier of Ontario, proclaimed that the American goal in negotiating a reciprocity agreement was simply annexation by other means.[29] Liberal Senator James McMullen warned Laurier that he was "treading on dangerous ground." Writing from his home in Mount Forest in southwestern Ontario, McMullen raised two points that the Conservatives would later use effectively to attack the government. First, after a decade of prosperity the economy was doing well — why risk that prosperity on an agreement that might make things worse and potentially "raise a storm that may be hard to control?" Second, he expressed his concern over the effect of reciprocity on the American branch plants that had established themselves in Canada as a way to circumvent the National Policy tariff. "By lowering the tariff," he noted, "you are moving in the direction of putting a stop to the establishment in Canada of such institutions."[30]

The centre of the discontent was in the larger manufacturing centres, especially in Toronto. From Vancouver, the American consul-general informed Washington, "I do not find any active interest at present taken relative to the subject,"[31] but Robert Chilton, the consul-general in Toronto, reported that the "sentiment of this community is opposed to any reciprocity arrangement." The American State Department closely followed the unfolding Canadian events. Only "among some farmers" was there support for reciprocity, Chilton added. Toronto was, after all, "a great manufacturing centre and a strong Conservative stronghold and therefore both for business and political reasons is in favor of maintaining a protective tariff, especially against the United States."[32]

For Laurier there was no turning back at this stage, however, and the final negotiations began in Washington on January 7, 1911. As in November, the discussions were easygoing and productive, although there were a few snags. First, the Americans asked for fishing rights in Canadian waters in return for the free entry of Canadian fish into the American market, but Fielding rejected the proposal. A compromise was reached with an agreement on a flat one-dollar fee for American fishing vessels to enter Canadian waters (in return for the free entry of Canadian fish). The division of powers in the Canadian constitution led to a second problem. Several provinces, in particular Quebec and Ontario, applied export taxes on pulp and paper in an effort to stimulate the processing of paper in their home provinces. The Americans offered to include imports of pulp and paper on the free list, providing the Canadians agreed to remove their restrictions. Fielding responded that this was an issue upon which he could not take action as it was a matter for the provincial governments. The two sides agreed to leave it at that and the agreement stated that pulp and paper would be allowed into the United States free of duty providing the province in question removed its export restrictions.[33]

The Reciprocity Agreement was signed on January 21, 1911. As agreed, the final text was an exchange of letters between Fielding and Secretary of State Knox, with four attached schedules setting out in detail the various items and rates that would now apply between the two countries. The Free Trade Agreement signed in 1987 ran to over a thousand pages; in 1911 they needed fewer than a dozen.

Schedule A listed those items that were to be allowed into each country free of duty and contained a broad range of natural products, including live animals, poultry, corn and maize, wheat, rye, oats, barley, and other grains, fresh vegetables and fruits (potatoes, turnips, onions, cabbage, apples, pears, peaches, grapes, berries, etc.), dried fruit, dairy products (including cheese, butter, fresh milk and cream, eggs), honey, various seeds, fish "of all kinds," fish oils, wood products from timber and sawed boards to railroad ties and telegraph poles, and a host of other items. A few manufactured goods were on the list, as well, including cream separators, typesetting machines, and iron and steel wire.

Schedule B comprised a list of items to be allowed in at a common lower rate of duty by both countries, including more processed foods, such as fish packed in oil, bacon and hams, wheat flour, barley malt, prepared cereal, macaroni, biscuits, maple sugar and maple syrup, roofing slates, bells and gongs, and printing ink. This schedule contained more manufactured goods, including musical instruments, motor vehicles (including automobiles), canoes, clocks and watches, plumbing features, cutlery and knives, and, most important, agricultural machinery (and parts), including ploughs, harvesters, and threshing machines.

Schedules C and D listed a variety of different items and their new lower rates to be applied on Canadian exports to the United States (C) and American exports to Canada (D).

It was not complete free trade but it was the closest thing to it in Canadian–American trade relations in over forty years. Most Canadian natural products would enter the United States without duty and a few others had the duty cut considerably. In addition, the reduced Canadian tariff on agricultural machinery (to 15 percent on all machinery) would be a particular benefit for western farmers, who for years had clamoured for lower rates on agricultural machinery (before the agreement the rate fluctuated between 17.5 and 25 percent).[34] And, given that the American tariffs had generally been higher at the start, the reduction in American tariffs was on average greater than the

Canadian. In return, the Canadians had had to give up relatively little: a few manufactured goods were given reduced rates (and the producers of agricultural machinery would not be happy) but, overall, Canadian industry had seemingly little to fear from this agreement.

Courtesy LAC, PA-025973.

William S. Fielding, August 1911.

———•◦•———

"The arrangement still rests in reality on the growing realization of the fact that a high tariff wall between contiguous countries whose products are economically interchangeable is an injury to both, and opposed to sound fiscal principles," reported Ambassador Bryce to London. He had watched the negotiations carefully, to help if necessary but also to watch over British economic interests in the agreement. He was convinced that the Reciprocity Agreement would benefit Canada without harming imperial trade, and he dismissed any notion that the agreement would impinge on Canadian sovereignty. "No more in Canada than in the republics of Latin-America," he concluded, "to which the United States Government has sought to extend its Pan-American propaganda, does there seem a likelihood that a freer interchange of commodities is likely to lead to closer relations of a political kind."[35]

Others were not so sure. The countries of Latin America did not share a language, culture, and a three-thousand-mile border with the United States. Many Canadians began to ask: Could you have closer trade relations without sacrificing some part of your independence in the bargain? Would the flag always follow trade? Others even wondered how Fielding got such a good deal — what were the Americans really after? Did they see this as the first step toward a second agreement on manufactured goods? For more than forty years these questions were only theoretical in nature; now they would have to be confronted directly.

In Washington, President Taft largely agreed with Bryce that the agreement would not produce closer political connections between Canada and the United States. But he might have added that the United States was not seeking political connections with Canada — Washington's goal was to integrate Canada *economically*. And here he felt he had achieved some success. He soon was referring to the Reciprocity Agreement as one of the most important acts of his administration, and he explained his views in a private letter to former president Theodore Roosevelt just days before the announcement of the agreement. Under the proposed agreement, he wrote, the "amount of Canadian products we would take would produce a current of business between Western Canada and the United States that would make Canada only an adjunct of the United States. It would transfer all their important business to Chicago and New York, with their bank credits and everything else, and it would increase greatly the demand of Canada for our manufactures." Making Canada an "adjunct" of the United States had not been on the negotiating table and obviously not what Laurier and Fielding had in mind. "I see this as an argument against reciprocity made in Canada," Taft added, "and I think it is a good one."[36]

The night before the signing of the agreement, Fielding reported to Laurier that an understanding had been reached. He began making plans for his return home and the best way to introduce the pact to the country. He would return to Ottawa for, first, a cabinet meeting and then the announcement of the Reciprocity Agreement in Parliament. "I feel persuaded," he wrote Laurier from his hotel room in Washington, "that when we are able to spread the details before you, you will come to the conclusion that we have not made a bad bargain."[37] It was meant to be the beginning of a new era in Canadian–American trade relations and to enhance Canadian economic prosperity; it turned out to be the beginning of the end for Laurier and his government.

When Laurier announced to cabinet on January 18 that an agreement was at hand, Mackenzie King, the young minister of labour, only saw dark clouds on the horizon. That night, he confided to his diary that he "spoke out strongly about the danger to Ont. of interfering much with mffrs. [manufacturers]" and that he "wd. not be returned if we did, & that there was danger in many cities." King asked if furniture (a prime industry in Berlin) was included in the deal, and was told that it was. He pointed to the industry in Grand Rapids, Michigan, that would likely swamp Canadian markets and he asked Laurier if this objection could be cabled to Fielding. After many other objections, Laurier asked King to write out what "he wanted" and that he would convey it to the minister of finance.

As the midnight hour approached that evening, King wrote in his diary:

I must frankly confess I see great danger in whole tariff negotiations at this time. Americans will be lowering tariffs anyway & we could manage our own tariffs. Agreements are poor affairs. I question if we will satisfy the farmers and we may prejudice other interests to the extent of suffering defeat at their hands. The West just now is affording a good market to Eastern mffrs. [manufacturers]. We are building an internal development, trade east & west, mffr. development, getting capital from U.S. & other lands & well enough had better be left alone. That is my feeling. We could meet the farmers by tariff reductions in agric. Implements. This has been the view I have taken, it is the Ont. view I believe, & is in national interest, as well as in the interest of Govt.[38]

King, demonstrating remarkable prescience and a fine flair for the affairs of his province, could not dissuade cabinet from this pursuit.

CHAPTER 4

THE TORONTO EIGHTEEN
AND THE DECISION TO FIGHT

Although I am a Liberal, I am a Canadian first of all.
— SIR BYRON EDMUND WALKER

Reciprocity had always been a dream of economic salvation. It was a prize that many Canadians liked to talk about and even anticipate, but it was not something many people thought would actually happen. But it did happen, and the announcement of the agreement in Parliament in January marked the unofficial launch of the 1911 election campaign. Within days the lines of debate were drawn clearly and they remained virtually unchanged until election day the following September. Regional and ideological tensions — east vs. west, rural vs. urban, imperial vs. continental — were brought more sharply into focus and partisan political divisions were unleashed. In the winter of 1911, longtime friends chose different sides and new alliances formed within and between the major parties. By the spring, both parties and their leaders were willing to fight an election on the issue of reciprocity. And both were convinced that they could win.

William Fielding and William Paterson gave their account of the negotiations in Washington to cabinet, followed by an hour-long presentation by Fielding on the structure of the agreement on January 26. Mackenzie King noted in his diary that "there was a general consensus of opinion that the agreement reached was a most exceptional one for the Dominion, while it was likely to prove equally advantageous of the U.S." William Templeman, Minister of Mines as well as Inland Revenue, observed that fruit growers might suffer, and King thought to himself that the tariff reduction on clocks might affect his "good friend" Arthur Pequegnat, whose factory was located in Berlin (Kitchener). "All had to suffer a little," he wrote in his diary — hardly a ringing endorsement.[1]

Fielding rose to his feet in the House of Commons later that afternoon to unveil the Reciprocity Agreement and to outline its terms to a hushed audience of MPs and a packed visitors' gallery. Everyone had read in the newspapers about the negotiation of the agreement, and so everyone in the House that day knew that this would be a historic juncture in Canadian political history. But the details of the agreement were kept secret, so no one — other than Laurier, Fielding, the cabinet, and a few others — knew the scope and scale of the agreement. As the eminent journalist John Dafoe later wrote, Laurier "was somewhat addicted to the habit of confronting his followers with the accomplished fact."[2] Later, many would remember this day as a moment when Canadian politics changed.

"We have conducted negotiations first at Ottawa and afterwards at Washington, covering the whole question of trade relations," Fielding began. "We have now been able to come to an understanding, and if we are able to bring about some of the good results which this country has been seeking for many years, I earnestly hope that the action will be one in which all parties in this House and in this country will be able to join and say that this was for the good of Canada and for the good of the United States as well." But Fielding was not there to inspire Canadians, he was there to inform them, and the speech continued at some length reviewing the agreement. The four schedules outlining the lists of reciprocal actions were tabled and the correspondence with the American secretary of state was read into the parliamentary record. "We present the arrangement to you today," he concluded, "not as a triumph of one country over the other, but as the result of an effort to do justice to both; we commend this arrangement, Sir, to the judgment of this parliament as the President of the United States will commend it to the judgment of the Congress. The one fear I have is that there may be people who will say that we have made so good a bargain that the Congress should not approve of it."

The reporter for the Liberal-leaning Montreal *Herald*, looking down from the visitors' gallery, described the historic moment:

> [T]he limited list had swelled and swelled and swelled and as it grew to the proportions of a nation's commerce, and members leaned forward to catch every word, triumph was written on the faces of the Liberals and dismay painted on the visages of the Opposition. There was not much cheering. Interest was too keen to tolerate interruption. But there were occasions when enthusiasm mastered curiosity. Free fish, free wheat, oats, barley, and buckwheat, free potatoes, free dairy products and free hay conceded by the United States brought forth a tumult of appreciation which for a moment halted the Finance Minister in his triumphant recital. And when he closed the Liberals cheered and cheered again.[3]

Mackenzie King noted that the Liberals "most heartily" received the announcement, but that the opposition was "visibly non-plussed." Borden, as Opposition leader, rose to respond when Fielding finished speaking, but he had remarkably little to say. He asked about the duration of the agreement and, interestingly, questioned its potential impact on Anglo-Canadian trade relations and the British connection. It was as if he had been caught off guard and as unprepared as everyone else over the breadth of the agreement. The following day the Conservatives met in caucus to consider their strategy. Borden recalled the atmosphere among his colleagues as one of "deepest dejection." Sir George Foster, the veteran Conservative, announced that his heart fell into his boots during Fielding's speech, and several western Conservatives warned that they could not be re-elected in the West if they opposed reciprocity. "Many of our members," Borden wrote, "were confident that the Government's proposals would appeal to the country and would give it another term of office."[4]

Borden did not like the Reciprocity Agreement even though it appeared to include everything that both political parties had called for in decades past. Rural Canadians would clearly benefit because their products would reach American markets at an even more competitive price. A few manufacturers, on the other hand, would see their tariff protection reduced, allowing American goods to enter Canada more cheaply: they would have to be more competitive. He was well aware of the fact that for large segments of the population reciprocity would be welcomed. Still, for Borden, there was an opportunity here and any doubts he may have had quickly vanished. But at first he had to draw back and regroup his party. He found allies among friends, naturally, but a few of them were found in unexpected places.

One of the first colleagues Borden approached was Sir James Whitney, Ontario's Conservative premier. Borden asked for advice on how the Opposition should respond to the reciprocity issue. Whitney was an able but cautious man and he rarely gave Borden direct advice, and on this occasion he offered nothing more than his views on the Liberal messenger: "Fielding has never been loyal to Confederation," he wrote, "and from childhood up his political vision was apparently bounded by the New England States and the City of Boston." Then he added that many Maritimers were "limited in the same way."[5]

Borden's relationship with the Ontario premier was to some degree a testament to his less than firm hold on his own party. As noted earlier, Borden had barely survived a direct assault on his leadership over the Naval Service Bill. It was almost impossible to imagine how to bridge that gap in the party. Some openly accused Borden of allowing the party to drift and criticized his ineffectual leadership. Borden again threatened to resign but his supporters rallied and convinced him to stay.[6] Still, the voices of discontent in his own party lingered and, as a result, the one source of support upon which Borden could rely came from the provincial Conservative premiers: Richard McBride in British Columbia, Rodmond Roblin in Manitoba, J.D. Hazen in New Brunswick, and, of course, Whitney in Ontario.

Borden's own character didn't always help; he was diffident and occasionally withdrawn and lacked the easy and casual manner that made personal relations so much easier to manage. He could offer a warm smile and there was a more relaxed side to his character, but they were not often on public display. His colleague and supporter Sam Hughes described him as a "most lovely fellow; very capable, but not a very good judge of men or of tactics."[7] Privately the governor general was less kind, labelling Borden "a man who is wanting in courage and conviction — a high-minded gentleman who commands the goodwill of everyone because of his amiable qualities and his Parliamentary ability — but a bad leader because of the readiness he shows to be frightened out of his course by any group who point a pistol at his head."[8]

Like a boxer waiting for the first bell, Borden scrutinized his opponents and the agreement, searching for weaknesses. He found little from a technical perspective, but retained a sentimental one — the potential impact of reciprocity on Canadian nationhood. "We are face to face with the fight of 1891 but under circumstances of greater difficulty," he wrote A.E. Kemp, the wealthy businessman and one of Borden's most able lieutenants in the House of Commons and a leading Conservative organizer in Ontario. Reciprocity might produce benefits in the short term, but "from the national standpoint the Government's proposals destroy the whole meaning of Confederation and will ultimately disintegrate its fabric."[9]

In the House of Commons the Conservatives began to hammer away on this point, turning attention from the specifics in the agreement toward an analysis of the "larger" issues. Foster took the lead and attacked the agreement by introducing an element of anti-Americanism. The United States "covets the rich natural resources of the Dominion of Canada," he announced, and the agreement "will not have been in operation for five years before the big trusts and moneyed interests of the United States will own everything that is loose in this Dominion in the way of great natural resources."[10] The Conservatives felt they were on to something here: combining Canadian patriotism with its evil twin of anti-Americanism. It was a potent brew.

For most of February and March the Reciprocity Agreement was debated in the House of Commons, while a groundswell of opposition to the deal rose away from Parliament Hill and in the boardrooms of the nation. In Montreal, where Bourassa and the *nationalistes* were at first fairly neutral on reciprocity (there was even some sympathy because the agreement was perceived as a further weakening of the imperial tie), the business community was up in arms. On the motion of Huntley Redpath Drummond, president of the Canadian Sugar Refinery Company, the Board of Trade denounced the agreement within days and insisted that it be put to the country in an election before allowing it to pass. As it was, the agreement "might easily prove to be the entering of a wedge that would eventually result in a separation of our interests from those of the Motherland."[11]

Boards of trade in Quebec City, Winnipeg, Vancouver, and several Ontario cities, including Brampton, Sault Ste. Marie, Deseronto, Brockville, and Port Hope, all passed resolutions protesting reciprocity. So did the Associated Boards of Trade of Ontario. Similar actions were taken by the Montreal Produce Merchants Association, the Toronto Live Stock Exchange, the Dominion Millers' Association, the Fruit-Growers of Eastern Canada, and the Canadian Manufacturers' Association. The Grand Black Chapter of Ontario West, a group connected to the Orange Association, condemned reciprocity while at the same time calling for the abolition of French in Ontario primary schools.[12] In Hamilton, the city council denounced the agreement; soon provincial Tory governments in British Columbia, Manitoba, New Brunswick, and Ontario did the same.[13]

As might be expected, newspapers across the country were divided along party lines. Liberal papers such as the Halifax *Morning Chronicle*, *La Presse* in Montreal, and the *Manitoba Free Press* in Winnipeg immediately endorsed the agreement. But soon, Conservative and some independent papers launched a much more concerted and spirited attack. The Montreal *Daily Star*, for example, quickly published a sarcastic appeal to Laurier as "the one man who can save Canada." Reciprocity was an American Trojan Horse, the newspaper claimed; it was a "gift" so vast and far-reaching that "it engulfs our commercial independence and endangers our national existence." Sir Wilfrid could save the country not by pursuing the bargain that he himself had made but by walking away from it.[14] Sir Hugh Graham, the *Daily Star*'s publisher, sent the article to Laurier for his comments.

Prominent individuals also voiced their opposition through letters and public debate. One of the most vigorous attacks came from Joseph

Flavelle, one of Toronto's leading citizens and president of the William Davies Company, the large meat-packing company. Although a lifelong Conservative, Flavelle remained aloof from politics and had prospered under the Liberal government, but the announcement of reciprocity prompted him into public action. In a lengthy letter to the Toronto *Daily Star*, published the day after Fielding's speech, Flavelle outlined how reciprocity would adversely affect the meat-packing industry by sucking Western Canadian cattle into the United States market and flooding eastern cities with cheaper American meat products. Within two weeks Flavelle led a delegation to Ottawa from the Ontario and Quebec meat-packing industries to protest and to impress upon the government their deep concerns over the impact of the agreement on their businesses.

Similarly, in Montreal, Sir William Van Horne — railway builder, former president of the Canadian Pacific Railway, and another business-man who had happily co-existed with the Laurier Liberals since 1896 — came out of retirement to take aim at the Reciprocity Agreement. Even though he was born in the United States (and would soon be buried there), he argued that reciprocity would destroy everything the country had tried to build for thirty years behind the protective wall of the National Policy. "To my amazement and distress and shame I now see the magnificent work of a generation traded away for a vague idea or a childish sentiment — the splendid commercial and industrial position we have reached, and our proud inheritance, bartered for a few wormy plums," he wrote. "Was there ever such an exhibition of crawling and cringing as Canada's representatives have just now given us at Washington?"[15] Almost immediately, and despite his major fear of public speaking, Van Horne was campaigning, as he told one reporter, to "bust the damn thing."[16]

Opposition to reciprocity gradually coalesced around two main themes: there was what the agreement *said* and what the agreement *meant*. The former made bad economic sense; the latter made even worse sense in terms of national autonomy and survival. The agreement would harm specific industries and, whatever immediate gains it might contain, the long-term consequences for the country were far more serious. Ultimately what was at stake was the country's future — Canada's autonomy and its membership in the British Empire.

On the economic front, the fruit growers of Ontario and British Columbia argued that free trade in fruits and vegetables would lead to the flooding of the Canadian market with American fruit, which, thanks to a generally longer growing season, ripened before Canadian fruit did. Similar fears over the influx of American products were expressed by the dairy and milling industries and, as noted above, the meat-packing industry. More generally, it was argued that reciprocity would kill any hope for the future establishment of American branch plants in Canada, with the resultant loss of thousands of jobs. The branch plants were set up only as a way to circumvent the protective tariff; if you remove the tariff, the logic ran, you remove the raison d'être behind the branch plants. Moreover, the agreement focused on natural products and over time would emphasize the export of Canadian raw materials to the United States. There would be less processing done in Canada and, ultimately, less manufacturing, turning Canada into nothing more than a supplier of raw materials for the American economy.

There were also concerns about the way the agreement was made. Legislation was less binding than a treaty in that it could be amended or overturned at the whim of one of the parties (supporters saw this as a good thing). The Canadian economy would be forced to go through a difficult process of realignment under the terms of the agreement and then the Americans could simply throw the legislation out and create havoc in Canada. Others argued that without a treaty binding the Americans they could change their tariff legislation at will, and who would protect Canadian interests then? And knowing the economic dislocation that might follow the agreement's termination, the Americans could use the threat of cancellation as a way to secure even greater concessions from the Canadians.

In a more general way there was some question whether or not the agreement was even necessary at all. Canada had experienced more than a decade of prosperity and significant economic growth over the thirty years since the implementation of the National Policy. If the National Policy had proven itself successful, why tear it down? Reciprocity may have made sense in the 1870s, but now it was unnecessary and potentially dangerous if it disturbed the prosperity that Canadians had worked so hard to achieve.

The progression from what was said in the agreement to what it meant was therefore an easy one for critics to make — that beyond the specifics in the agreement there was a larger issue at stake: the survival of the country. The agreement announced by Fielding was merely the first step. If free trade worked, then the pressure to expand the agreement to other sectors of the economy would be too great. Indeed, the deal might work so well that the temptation to expand it would be irresistible, and before too long it would be broadened to include manufactured goods, which would destroy Canadian manufacturing, which was unable to compete against much larger and more powerful American enterprises. "Thus the logical conclusion of such a policy is complete free trade and a Washington made tariff," Borden wrote to Premier Whitney. "From an economic standpoint this may be of advantage; from a national standpoint it is suicide."[17]

If this deal was accepted, critics charged, Canada would be at the starting point of a process that inevitably would lead one after another to an expanded agreement, economic dislocation, the realignment of trade along geographical lines, the commercial union of North America, and, ultimately, the severance of the imperial tie and absorption of the country into the United States. The "thin edge of the wedge" became the cliché of choice for opponents of reciprocity in 1911. As the governor general, Lord Grey, reported to the colonial secretary, "those who are swayed by these considerations do not dread the reciprocity agreement so much for the changes which it proposes to effect at the moment as for those which they expect to follow from it in the course of time."[18] The old bogey of annexation was back with a vengeance, this time in the form of an economic policy.

Such arguments were lost on Laurier and most Liberals. Reciprocity, they argued, had been in one form or another the goal of every government since Confederation, and the agreement reached in 1911 left the great majority of manufactured goods under the protection of the National Policy. The only important exception was in agricultural machinery, and there the tariff was only reduced, not removed (even though the Western farmers had demanded its elimination). Plus, nothing in the agreement would undermine or threaten the existing imperial preference tariff or trade with Great Britain (a point consistently repeated in private correspondence between the governor general and the British government). And more trade would inevitably lead to *more* railway traffic, not *less*, and more activity between the provinces and along the east–west axis.

On the specifics of the agreement, supporters asked what could be bad — let alone threatening — about expanded trade with a friendly neighbour and the addition of a huge market for Canadian products. Canadians, moreover, were not likely to import very much more in the way of natural goods from the United States under the Reciprocity Agreement. Even if they did, any losses would be more than offset by the addition of new exports to the United States. American fruits may ripen earlier, but later-ripening Canadian fruits could then flood the American market *later* in the season. The same applied to the other industries — any loss of sales of wheat in the Canadian market, for example, could be more than made up through expanded sales in the United States.

Supporters of the agreement were also repulsed by the resort to patriotism and fidelity to the Empire to denigrate what was simply an

Archives of Ontario, C 301, Newton McConnell Collection, circa 1910, #1008925.

"The Workman: We'll have to stand together, for if he gets you, he'll get me next." A commentary on Reciprocity.

economic agreement. The deal with Washington could be amended at any time if Canadians believed their interests were in jeopardy or if it was in any way perceived to be threatening Canadian industries or the country's autonomy and relationship to the Empire. And as for threatening the National Policy, Westerners, in particular, were quick to point out that they had long borne the burden of the National Policy by paying the higher costs for the protected products of Eastern Canada. To them the National Policy tariff was a *cause* of regionalism and its removal would not only enhance prosperity but also promote national unity. Surely, it followed, that a prosperous country was better able to withstand any annexationist threats and to play a stronger role in the Empire.

Furthermore, most of the agreement dealt with the lowering of American tariffs on Canadian goods — something Washington could do unilaterally at any time if it chose to. If that happened, Canadian business leaders would be far more likely to rejoice at the expanded market south of the border than to complain that it would lead to annexation. The opposition of the business community, at least in the eyes of reciprocity's supporters, was not only unwarranted by any-thing written in the agreement but a nakedly self-serving campaign to preserve its own privileged position in Canadian society. It had more to do with pocketbooks than patriotism. As one Liberal supporter wrote Laurier from Toronto, the "absurd attempts to stir up hostility by assertions of a pseudo-patriotism would be ridiculous if they were not so mischievous."[19]

The two sides were far apart. One thing that was clear, however, was that in a matter of weeks the parameters of the debate had shifted dramatically. The issues were elevated beyond the simple pros and cons of the proposed trade legislation onto a new level. The contest over reciprocity was now a struggle for the heart and soul of a nation. And with stakes this high, all bets were off.

———————

Following his resignation from Laurier's cabinet over the 1905 Autonomy Bills creating Alberta and Saskatchewan, Clifford Sifton remained a Liberal MP but had relatively little influence over Laurier, the party, or the government. What should have been clear to Laurier, however, was that Sifton had long shed his "Western" viewpoint on tariffs and reciprocity in favour of general support for a protective tariff and the National Policy. He was, Toronto's *Saturday Night* magazine observed, "by nature a business man, first, last and all the time." Several times in the preceding decade he had made public declarations against reciprocity, including in a speech to the Montreal Canadian Club just days before the announcement of the Reciprocity Agreement.[20]

Sifton found common cause in fellow businessman and Liberal MP Lloyd Harris from Brantford, Ontario. Both men had business concerns that led them to oppose reciprocity; Harris, for example, had close family and business connections to Toronto's Massey-Harris Company, a major manufacturer of agricultural machinery. Sifton and Harris, along with four other Liberal MPs, approached Laurier within days of the reciprocity announcement, asking him to withhold all discussion of the issue in Parliament until after the Americans had approved the agreement. The Americans might never ratify it — there were precedents here, they noted — so why stir up emotions at home (and divisions within the Liberal Party at the same time) until everyone knew how the American Congress would react?[21] Laurier rejected any thought of stalling the bill, however, and for Sifton this was the last straw, even though he was not yet ready to sever completely his ties to the Liberal Party.[22]

The disillusionment and discontent of a small group of Liberal MPs echoed in the financial and business communities of virtually every metropolitan centre of central Canada. In this group were many businessmen who had prospered during the Laurier era and had come to call themselves Liberals. Their support was already slipping; many Ontario Liberals were politically closer to Sifton than Laurier when it came to Catholic education and French-language rights, and provincially they found a more congenial home in the Ontario Conservative Party. Others were staunchly imperialist and at odds with Laurier's naval policy and the creation of an independent Canadian navy, which seemed to be unnecessarily antagonistic to the Empire and the British connection. On this issue there had already been speculation that several Toronto businessmen would shift their support from the Liberal to the Conservative Party.[23]

In Toronto, Liberal and Conservative businessmen frequented the same clubs — the Toronto Club, the York Club, and the Royal Canadian Yacht Club — and sat side by side as trustees of public institutions from the Toronto General Hospital to the University of Toronto. The Liberal and Conservative Toronto business elites were so intertwined as to be indistinguishable: they knew each other, lived next to each other, and sent their children to the same schools. However looked at, the interests of the Ontario Liberal business class coincided far more with Ontario Conservatives than with the large Quebec wing of the Liberal Party.

By 1911, therefore, the commitment of many Ontario Liberal businessmen to the Liberal Party was only as strong as the strength of Laurier's attachment to the National Policy. When Laurier challenged the National Policy by introducing reciprocity, that support began to weaken rapidly. Liberal businessmen who had supported Laurier with their votes, influence, and money for fifteen years began to walk away from him within hours of the announcement of the Reciprocity Agreement.

"I have had opportunities of hearing the views of some of our leading Canadians," wrote Toronto lawyer Zebulon Lash to Laurier early in February. The Newfoundland-born Lash was brought to Ottawa in 1876 as deputy minister to Justice Minister (and future Liberal leader) Edward Blake. Lash returned to Toronto in 1882 as a member of Blake's law firm to become one of the foremost corporate lawyers in Canada. He was connected with the upper crust of Toronto society for decades as a lawyer for the Canadian Northern Railway, a director of the Canadian Bank of Commerce, and a member of the board of directors of a handful of Canadian companies. His political ties, although not robust, were Liberal, and he wrote Laurier as a concerned colleague. "I have been trying to eliminate all considerations except those for the welfare of Canada as a whole," he continued. "We believe that the subject has not been long enough before the country in its present form to elicit sober second thoughts and conclusions."[24]

Laurier replied that he was surprised at Lash's reaction and quoted directly from Macdonald's National Policy legislation, which contained a standing offer for a very similar agreement — "almost word for word."[25] But Laurier focused on what the agreement *said* and did not address Lash's concerns about what it *meant*. Lash quickly wrote back, mentioning his concern over the hundreds of thousands of "newcomers" in the country, many from the United States, who would soon be able to influence public policy decisions. Reciprocity might throw everything into question: "There is a principle involved in it which seems to me to go to the very root of Canadian nationality and unity and autonomy, and to affect very materially the future of Canada as part of the British Empire."[26]

Others felt the same way. Self-interest, nationalism, and fidelity to the Empire and all things British came together — with a touch of anti-Americanism tossed in for flavour — into a powerful mixture and potent political force. Liberals, former Liberals, semi-Liberals, and fair-weather Liberals chose principle (and business) over party and came out in opposition to reciprocity.

In Toronto they began to organize. The scene was the meeting of the Toronto Board of Trade on February 16, called to protest the Reciprocity Agreement. "We are here not to discuss men, but an agreement," announced board president R.S. Gourlay, "so I would ask everyone here to eliminate all political bias from the discussion."[27] That sage advice was promptly ignored. After some debate, a resolution was passed (the vote was 302–13 in favour) outlining the dangers of reciprocity, especially regarding its negative impact on Canadian autonomy and the imperial connection, and calling for its termination. The agreement "is opposed to the true interests of Canada," the Toronto business community resolved, "and should not be consummated."[28]

During the meeting, several now quasi-Liberals stood up one after the other to denounce the agreement. Among the most prominent was Sir Byron Edmund Walker, one of the country's leading bankers. Walker was the epitome of the self-made man. Born near Caledonia, Ontario, he grew up in Hamilton and began working at the age of twelve. In 1868, barely twenty years old, he joined the Canadian Bank of Commerce as a clerk, and from there he worked his way up (including several years working for the bank in the United States) to the presidency in 1907. A founding member of the Canadian Bankers' Association and prominent member of the Toronto Board of Trade, Walker lived and worked within the elite of Toronto society. An amateur collector, arts patron, and philanthropist (including pivotal support to institutions as varied as the Royal Ontario Museum and the Champlain Society), he was knighted in 1910. Walker was not actively involved in politics, but he was a great "Empire-man" and was already moving away from Laurier politically. He knew Sifton, had been unofficially offered a cabinet seat in a future Conservative government, and was in the process of organizing a Canadian branch of the Round Table group to help promote greater co-operation within the Empire.[29]

"Although I am a Liberal," Sir Edmund announced, "I am a Canadian first of all." The Reciprocity Agreement might put an end to that because it had "aroused once more the dormant hope in the minds of millions of people in the United States that Canada would someday become a part of the Union." He surveyed the problems as he saw them — the deal was unnecessary, it would harm transportation interests, Winnipeg would be ruined as all Western trade would flow via Duluth and Minneapolis, et cetera — but it was the emotional patriotic argument that had the greatest force. "Our alliance with the Mother Country must not be threatened. We must assimilate our immigrants and make them good Canadians. And this Reciprocity Agreement is the most deadly danger as tending to make this problem more difficult and fill it with doubt and difficulty. The question is between British connection and what has been well called Continentalism."[30]

Details of the meeting flowed to the prime minister, and most were critical. "Walker was, when an obscure clerk in New York, a strong continentalist," wrote one observer, "but Toronto social circles of ... Imperialists have spoiled him and you know it's the very few who can wear an Imperial title without making D--d fools of themselves."[31] Another explained how the manufacturers of Toronto were uneasy with all the talk of free trade and that they were determined to stop Laurier now to ensure that they wouldn't have to fight an expanded trade agreement later.[32] Laurier's reaction, however, was sanguine, bordering on nonchalant. "I am at a loss to understand why our friends in Toronto should be driven from their moorings on a question which has been the policy of the party for forty years," he wrote.[33] He felt fairly confident that the "people," especially in rural Canada, were behind him, and he was nonplussed by the bellows emanating from Toronto. To another colleague, he added, "I am not at all surprised at the opposition which is offered to our policy. We have been very familiar with it all through our life. It seems to me perfectly evident that those shrieks are falling very flat and that the country is decidedly with us."[34]

But something significant was happening. The Conservatives immediately saw businessmen like Walker and politicians like Sifton as potential allies. After all, Conservatives were among the organizers of the board of trade meeting to denounce the agreement. Walker's home on St. George Street, near the University of Toronto, was a few doors south of Premier Whitney's house and not far west of "Holwood," Joseph Flavelle's mansion on Queen's Park. Flavelle clearly must have sensed that Walker was a neighbour, not only geographically but philosophically as well, and he quickly encouraged his banker friend to speak out against reciprocity. It was a "fitting time for you to exercise the commanding influence which you possess," he wrote.[35]

A.E. Kemp, one of Borden's lieutenants and chief organizer in Ontario, closely monitored the malcontent Toronto businessmen and planned to turn Liberal discontent into Conservative advantage. "Some of the strongest Liberals in this City would be willing to take almost any legitimate steps if they could prevent this Treaty coming into force," Kemp reported to Borden.[36] Conservative organizers encouraged sixty boards of trade to pass anti-reciprocity resolutions; they wrote more than one hundred businessmen asking them to raise petitions among their workers; and they began to organize mass meetings and to circulate thousands of copies of anti-reciprocity speeches.[37]

Borden wanted even more. Action was needed, now, to save the country (and, he might have added, his political life). "If the preservation of Canada to the Empire is worth fighting for," he wrote Premier Whitney, "men who can exercise powerful influence over public opinion ought to make their voices heard." Borden clearly had Whitney in mind and wanted the Ontario premier to come out fighting for the cause. But he also looked to others for help: "If the business interests of the country believe that this crisis can be met by a few casual meetings and an occasional vigerous [sic] protest, they are living in a fool's paradise," he added. "We have got to fight and fight hard."[38]

Liberal opponents of reciprocity were organizing, and they began talking with Conservatives about working together. Both groups connected with Clifford Sifton, who was increasingly seen as the linchpin between the disgruntled Liberals and the Conservative Party. Walker, for one, travelled to Ottawa from Toronto on February 17, the day after the Board of Trade gathering, with a plan to meet Sifton. Ironically, he spent most of his afternoon in Ottawa with Laurier and Fielding — the very two men he was plotting to denounce and within whose company he had to remain silent over his true intentions. Later that night, however, after leaving the prime minister, Walker went to meet Sifton. Despite his efforts, no meeting with Sifton took place that night, but "arrangements" were made nevertheless, and Walker informed Sifton soon to expect a "significant" statement to be released by "at least twenty prominent Liberals."[39]

On February 20, the Toronto *Mail and Empire* published a "manifesto" signed by a group of Toronto's leading Liberal businessmen. It listed ten points outlining the opposition to reciprocity, repeating much that had been said at the Board of Trade and in other meetings. The government had no mandate to negotiate such a deal, the businessmen proclaimed: the agreement would destroy the east–west trade that had "involved the expenditure of hundreds of millions of dollars upon railways, canals, steamships, and other means of transportation"; it would inevitably lead to a wider agreement including manufactured goods, which would weaken the imperial tie and "make it more difficult to avert political union with the United States"; and with all the "newcomers" arriving, resisting annexation in the future would be more difficult. "Believing as we do that Canadian nationality is now threatened with a more serious blow than any it has heretofore met with and that all Canadians who place the interests of Canada before those of any party or section or individuals therein should at this crisis state their views openly and fearlessly, we, who have hitherto supported the Liberal Party in Canada, subscribe to this statement."

There were eighteen Liberal signatures attached to the manifesto, and the group was instantly dubbed the "Toronto Eighteen." The group comprised a who's who of Toronto's financial and business elite, with Walker at the top and others, including Thomas White, vice president and general manager of the National Trust Company, and John Blaikie, the president of the Canadian Landed and National Investment Company. The exclusive Eighteen also included a mixture of presidents and general managers from banks and insurance companies, officials from the Board of Trade and Canadian Manufacturers' Association, several lawyers (including Zebulon Lash), and businessmen such as John Eaton, president of the T. Eaton Company. Also on the list was Sir Mortimer Clark, a one-time member of the anti-Catholic "Equal Rights" Society and a former lieutenant-governor of Ontario, who had once been described by the Montreal *Witness* as a "ripe scholar" and "a Liberal, but free from party entanglements."[40]

Critics were quick to point to the interwoven connections between the members of the Toronto Eighteen (the Board of Trade, director-ships, banks, insurance companies, et cetera) and between members of the group and the Canadian Northern Railway (Walker was the railway's banker, Lash its lawyer, Blaikie a director). Questions were also raised about the strength of the commitment of several members to the Liberal Party. Laurier kept a list of the group members in his personal papers, with comments beside each name. One member was ambitious to be president of the Board of Trade, according to the list, and therefore went along with the majority. Other comments simply stated "Never knew he was a liberal" or "They have certainly kept their liberalism to themselves." Another member was with the Canadian Pacific Railway, and it was assumed that he thought the same as Van Horne in Montreal. Thomas White worked under Joseph Flavelle at National Trust, and therefore no more needed to be said about White's views. R.J. Christie, the president of Christie, Brown & Co., was listed as "disgruntled," not having "given us a liberal vote for years on account of English biscuits being allowed to come into Canada." Hugh Blain, a businessman and a director of the Toronto *Globe*, was dismissed as "one of the hysterical class who was carried away from us before when Sir John waved the flag"[41] (a reference to the 1891 election). Mackenzie

King, Laurier's minister of labour, dismissed the Toronto Eighteen as a group who "read the success or prosperity of the nation in terms of their own success or prosperity. This is Toryism — that is all, and though they cling to the name of Liberal, these men are in reality Tories."[42] But what could not be dismissed or underestimated was the devastating blow that had been inflicted by the Toronto Eighteen on reciprocity, Sir Wilfrid Laurier, and the future of the Liberal Party.

The same day that the Toronto Eighteen's manifesto was published in the Toronto press, Clifford Sifton made his move — privately, behind the scenes at first, but then more publicly. He wrote Walker in Toronto saying that he had been discussing things with Montreal friends and that he might have to meet with Walker soon. "I think the arrangements we have talked of are going forward satisfactorily," he wrote.[43] Next, he informed the prime minister of his decision formally to break his ties with the Liberal Party and to oppose reciprocity.[44]

Sifton rose in the House of Commons a few days later to deliver one of the most important speeches of his career. One reporter noted how silent the House was at the start, but as Sifton spoke, the opposition Tories began to cheer loudly, giving Sifton a thunderous round of applause when he finished.[45] Sifton laid out the arguments against reciprocity that were followed for the rest of the campaign, and thousands of reprinted copies of the speech were distributed across the country.[46] "His out and out condemnation of the reciprocity agreement," observed the governor general, "has greatly impressed the public mind and cannot fail to be a severe blow to the Government."[47]

"I cannot follow the leader of the party with which I have been identified practically all my lifetime," Sifton told the House. His points against the Reciprocity Agreement by now were familiar, but he laid them out in a clear and concise manner. The way it was done was wrong; the deal itself would lead to a revolution in Canadian fiscal policy and destroy some industries in the process; it would bring dislocation and suffering in its wake; and it would realign trade on a north–south axis and would bind the regions of Canada to the United States. "The United States beckons from Washington and we are asked, the first time anybody beckons, to turn from the path that leads to the capital of the empire, and to turn towards the path that leads to Washington. I say, so far as I am concerned: Not for me."[48]

The opponents of reciprocity now had perhaps their most effective tactician and leader, and steps toward a more formal alliance with Borden and the Conservative opposition soon followed. Sifton encouraged Walker and a few others to come to Ottawa to discuss

Courtesy LAC, PA-025966.

Clifford Sifton, June 1910.

strategy.[49] Walker was about to leave on a trip, so in his place he sent Lash, the Toronto lawyer and leading member of the Toronto Eighteen. "I am prepared to stand by anything and to have my name made use of in connection with anything to which he agrees," Walker informed Sifton.[50] Also included was journalist John S. Willison, editor of the Toronto *Evening News*. Prompted into action by Flavelle, Willison came out swinging against reciprocity in his newspaper and, tapping his deep connections among Toronto Liberals, he worked behind the scenes with Walker and Sifton to organize the Toronto Eighteen.[51] The day after Sifton's speech, these men launched their campaign to undermine Laurier and his policy.

The key meeting took place in Ottawa on Wednesday, March 1. Sifton and Lloyd Harris, the other Liberal renegade, were there, along with Lash, Willison, and Robert Borden, the Conservative leader of the Opposition. The four one-time Liberals had met earlier in the day and agreed on how best to achieve their goals, which now consisted of far more than merely the defeat of reciprocity[52] — they wanted that, of course, plus the defeat of the government, and the establishment of a "basis of co-operation" with Borden and the Conservatives. It was the latter goal that was the focus of the meeting with Borden, and the four presented the Conservative leader with their terms of alliance with the Conservative Party. Borden was ready to listen to what the former Liberals had to offer.

There were seven conditions to be met by Borden in exchange for their co-operation in bringing down the government, and, according to Willison's memorandum of the conversation (and the only contemporary source documenting the meeting), they all dealt with the formation of the next government and the appointment of suitable candidates to key government positions.[53] The first struck at the heart of the ageless ethnic divisions that had bedeviled Canadian society: the appointment of Roman Catholics and francophones. While the government would need a fair representation of Quebecers and Catholics, the future government "should not be subservient to Roman Catholic influences in public policy or in the administration of patronage." In addition, the four conspirators demanded the rather more vague commitment of the government to "strengthen Canadian nationality and the connection with the Mother Country." Presumably this included maintaining the National Policy and eschewing all talk of reciprocity. They also asked Borden to pledge that his future government would reorganize the Department of Trade and Commerce, establish a Tariff Commission, and put control of the "outside" civil service under the Civil Service Commission. Borden was also asked to bring "men of outstanding national reputation and influence" into his government, implying that the talent of the individual rather than party affiliation should be paramount in some cases. Finally, Borden would be expected to consult with Walker, Lash, and Willison before forming his first cabinet, "in order to ensure that his Ministry should be so constituted as to guarantee the effective adoption and application of this policy, and that there should be reasonable representation therein of the views of those Liberals who may unite with Conservatives against the policy of Reciprocity."

According to Willison, Borden expressed his "sympathy" for the points raised and pledged to do his best to implement all of them when he became prime minister. He even went so far as to offer to resign as Conservative leader if the Liberal conspirators wanted another person better able to implement their demands. In his memoirs, Borden was somewhat less forthcoming; he acknowledged the meeting (indeed, he calls them conferences and suggests that they met more than once) and the offer of co-operation but not the specific terms. Sifton wanted to discuss "certain aspects" of Conservative policy but Borden made no reference to agreeing with the Liberal demands other than in a general way.[54] Borden's biographer suggests that Borden already agreed with most of the demands of the Liberal conspirators and that he would have been inept and naïve not to. But, by agreeing to these demands he had not formed an "insidious alliance."[55] Later, in a letter to the journalist John Dafoe, Borden mentioned his offer to step down as leader, but remembered Sifton rejecting the proposal as "unwise."[56]

Regardless of the small gaps in detail of how the meeting actually unfolded, it was one of the most remarkable political bargains in Canadian history. Without consulting his party, the Leader of the Opposition had sealed a deal with a small group of discontented Liberals in his effort to bring down the government. In return for their co-operation, he not only offered to ally himself with Liberal

MPs — who presumably could at some later date cross the floor in Parliament and sit as colleagues — he also agreed to consult with Toronto business leaders, altogether outside government, in the formation of his first cabinet. As with Borden's relationship with Bourassa and the *nationalistes* in Quebec, there were would be much speculation over whether or not he had made an official "alliance" with the Liberals and the Toronto Eighteen. Either way, it was a risky gamble that could backfire at any given moment.

At first Borden may have doubted his own judgment in forging this deal with the Liberals. The initiative had been his alone; he had not consulted with his party before meeting with Sifton and the others. Word of the bargain soon leaked, however, and he faced another challenge to his leadership from within his own party. The "disaffected party seems very formidable in point of numbers," wrote journalist Frederick Hamilton. "Sir Edmund Walker mentioned it to me on Saturday & I looked about a bit today, with the result that I am told that the majority of the party is hostile to him [Borden]. The talk is McBride. It will be out soon."[57] Borden was accused of potentially destroying the party by allowing the "ascendancy of Liberal elements." But no serious rival rose to stake a claim on the leadership and his political opponents were too divided among themselves to mount an effective challenge. The provincial Conservative premiers also maintained their support for Borden (and refused all offers to come to Ottawa as his successor). As before, Borden threatened to resign the leadership, more as a tactic than a specific intent, and, as before, his supporters rallied behind him. He went home, told his wife that he was finished in politics, and then a knock on the door brought a few supporters "almost in tears" begging him to reconsider. Soon there was a petition with the same request signed by most caucus members, and Borden was leader again.[58]

It must have been an incredibly frustrating moment for Borden. The Liberals had presented his party with an ideal election issue and several leading Liberals had been delivered up to him like room service — now, if only his party did not let the opportunity slip away. "To me it seemed madness that we should refuse the effective aid of powerful elements within the Liberal Party," he wrote in his memoirs.[59] The party would not have to *become* liberal in order to *defeat* the Liberals.

And taking on Laurier and reciprocity ought to have been a unifying force for the Conservatives, but the divisions in his party ran very deep. With his leadership reaffirmed, however, Borden put the internal divisions behind him and turned his attention to defeating the Liberals at the election which now appeared closer than ever.

CHAPTER 5

THE UNOFFICIAL CAMPAIGN BEGINS

*But believe me there is a disease of soul, highly contagious that afflicts
the peoples of that land of luxury. Do we need no barriers of Protection
here? Or is soul so little important compared with body?*
— WILSON MACDONALD[1]

March arrived in 1911 with the warming winds that hinted at
the approach of spring, but the air was saturated with talk of
reciprocity. Newspapers were crammed with stories of the progress of
the reciprocity legislation in the United States and the growing debate
at home. Editorialists talked past one another in their enthusiasm for
one side or the other. Business groups, workers' organizations, wom-
en's groups (which celebrated the first International Women's Day
that month), and entire communities discussed the ramifications of
the deal and weighed its potential benefits and risks. Governments
— federal, provincial, and municipal — debated it and passed resolutions in favour or against.

Even the writers became involved. Wilson MacDonald, a young
Toronto poet who reportedly gave up a lucrative job in the United
States in exchange for poverty in Canada, and whose claim to fame
was that he had lived in all the provinces except Prince Edward Island,[2]
saw reciprocity as the harbinger of much darker forces: "the vision of

a flame clothed negro feeding the carrion lusts of a mob stands to disturb our dreams of peace," he wrote in his diary. "A divorce court's restless grinding sounds across our virgin fields with damning music. We look from our windows upon a nation riding furiously upon a hopeless quest, and there are men and demons in our midst who would entangle us in the chase. They call for Reciprocity and their echoes carry back from the far Rockies with tones suggestive of a more intimate embrace."[3] Reciprocity, reported the governor general, "continues to provide the one absorbing topic of public interest."[4]

In Montreal, business leaders formed the Anti-Reciprocity League with members from the Montreal Board of Trade and a cross-section of the Montreal business community. The elderly Charles Chaput, a former merchant and member of the Chamber of Commerce, chaired the new organization, and another key figure was Thomas Chase-Casgrain, a member of a distinguished Montreal law firm who had been junior Crown counsel at the trial of Louis Riel and a leading Conservative who would later be a member of Robert Borden's government. J.S. Willison travelled to Montreal to attend the inaugural meeting and brought several Toronto supporters with him. Within weeks, the leading women of English Montreal formed a Woman's Branch of the Anti-Reciprocity League. Ethel Ewing, the wife of a prominent Montreal businessman and granddaughter of writer Susanna Moodie, was selected secretary. The Woman's Branch raised a petition with a gendered spin against reciprocity, stating that "Reciprocity means Annexation, injury to home life and the marriage tie, [and] a lessening of national religion, morals and patriotism."[5]

In Toronto, two organizations were created although there was considerable overlap in membership and activity between the two groups and with the Toronto Eighteen. In March–April, the Canadian Manufacturers' Association (CMA) established the Canadian Home Market Association to educate the public about tariffs and the pros and cons of reciprocity. It was ostensibly a non-partisan group but it was little more than an anti-reciprocity propaganda organization supported by conservative businessmen.[6] It wrote dozens of articles and distributed these stories and pamphlets to hundreds of newspapers across the country and gave direct financial support to a number of other publications. A.E. Kemp was on the executive committee of this group, and, although it tried to keep its activities out of the public eye and distinct from the CMA, by August, the Home Market Association had distributed over nine million copies of material at a rate of twenty thousand pieces per day.[7]

Similarly, the Canadian National League was established as a propaganda organization to oppose reciprocity, protect the National Policy, and to develop inter-provincial trade. Zebulon Lash was selected president and Thomas White, also of the Toronto Eighteen, as nominal treasurer. Filling the role as secretary of the Canadian National League was Arthur Hawkes, a British immigrant and former reporter for the Manchester *Guardian*, who freelanced for different newspapers in Canada and was a director of publicity for the Canadian Northern Railway. An expert in public relations and propaganda, Hawkes devoted his time to public speaking, writing newspaper articles, and producing campaign material, most notably his imperialist pamphlet *An Appeal to the British-born*, which was produced for distribution among the large number of British-born Canadians. Hawkes later wrote that the League was really the product of an afternoon meeting at Toronto's York Club, and he recalled that the Toronto Eighteen's Zebulon Lash paid for everything out of his own pocket. Clifford Sifton, although not an official member, was "the rock on which the secretary most surely relied. He was there at every call. When others were in perplexity he was in his element."[8]

Lash dipped into his own pocket to support the Canadian National League, but he was not its only benefactor. Other members of the Toronto Eighteen contributed to the League, while the Canadian Home Market Association received money directly from the CMA and from subscriptions by individual members, raising a total well over $50,000 for the anti-reciprocity campaign.[9] In Montreal, similar funds were delivered to the Anti-Reciprocity League, and Henri Bourassa himself later acknowledged receiving money for the *nationaliste* campaign from Sir Hugh Graham of the Montreal *Star*.[10] By the end of March, the journalist Frederick Hamilton was reporting to J.S. Willison on the rumours that the Canadian National League campaign chest had reached $500,000, although even Hamilton believed this figure to be exaggerated. "Many of the Conservatives," he added, "are frantic at the prospect of these funds being managed by Sifton & not by themselves."[11] The Liberal journalist, author, and civil servant W.T.R. Preston felt no such restraint, writing of the connections of Lash, Walker, and railway promoter and businessman Sir William Mackenzie, who were united via the Canadian Northern Railway, the Bank of Commerce, and their mutual dislike for Laurier. "Mackenzie gave a blank cheque guaranteed by the Bank of Commerce," Preston wrote, "which it is said was filled in afterwards for $2,000,000." With that kind of money floating around, Preston concluded, "an orgy of corruption was inaugurated."[12]

There is rarely sufficient evidence left behind to document accurately all the money that changes hands in situations like these, but two things are fairly certain: first, the Conservative campaign against reciprocity was well-funded from private business interests, and second, the Liberals had nothing by way of comparison with which to fight back. There were no private groups or leagues established to support reciprocity and the Liberals were slow off the mark in responding to the propaganda campaign that these groups launched. Plans for a series of meetings in Ontario to promote reciprocity were delayed and efforts to match the anti-reciprocity forces in print all failed. "Not a blow has been struck," complained Liberal cabinet minister George Graham, "It is discouraging here — not a single envelope." Another Liberal organizer added, "unless a very vigorous educative campaign is undertaken, taking township by township and polling subdivision by polling subdivision, I would not like to do any prophesying as to the result."[13] Late in May, William Fielding was still raising the need for "an abundant supply of literature dealing with the reciprocity question."[14]

These anti-reciprocity organizations were uncomplicated in their methods and approaches. Rallies were organized at which "invited" speakers railed against reciprocity (supporters of reciprocity were usually specifically not invited); their views were widely disseminated through letters to the editor and newspaper articles, petitions were circulated, signed, and delivered to the government, and a host of anti-reciprocity, pro-Empire pamphlets were produced, reprinted, and distributed across the country. One, produced by the Canadian

National League — *Reciprocity with the United States: Canadian Nationality, British Connection, and Fiscal Independence* — although some twenty-four pages long, told readers all they needed to know in its title.[15] Another was the equally popular reprinting of Sifton's House of Commons speech denouncing reciprocity. Equally important, these organizations provided information to politicians, newspaper editors, and just about anyone who was eager to fight the Reciprocity Agreement. They also proved very effective vehicles for raising and distributing funds for the election campaign.

On March 9 the Canadian National League staged a mammoth rally at Toronto's Massey Hall. The theatre was filled to capacity with an audience of some four thousand men and women, and untold hundreds more were turned away at the door. Sir Mortimer Clark emceed the event and shared the stage with Toronto's mayor George Geary and R.B. Gourlay of the Board of Trade. The Toronto Eighteen were well-represented, with Lash, Thomas White, and others making speeches (virtually all the speakers were ex-Liberals). There was a band to launch the affair and Union Jacks were draped everywhere in

Archives of Ontario, C 301, Newton McConnell Collection, circa 1910, #10008929.

The Anti-Reciprocity Quartette: "Every little movement has a meaning all its own."

the Hall. Behind the speakers was hung a huge map of Canada with the track lines of the transcontinental railways prominently displayed. According to news reports, the crowd enthusiastically waved their flags and applauded vigorously with each reference to the Empire and the imperial connection and hissed at any mention of the stars and stripes. "The disturbance of our trade and trade channels would be widespread and revolutionary," Lash declared, turning frequently and pointing to the imposing map with the railway lines. Others lumped together Laurier and Fielding as "co-conspirators" who had fashioned this "great betrayal" of a trade agreement, reported *The Globe*.[16] A few Liberals and supporters of the agreement were in attendance and heckled several of the speakers, especially Lash. Although the disturbers were quickly drowned out by the audience and speakers, they did introduce a note of discord into the evening.

White's speech was warmly received by the crowd and was declared by the Liberal Toronto *Star* to be the "speech of the evening," although this was not an accolade that White might have welcomed. White spoke of the Reciprocity Agreement as an American "gift horse" that he would have to "not only examine as to his teeth but would keep away from his heels." As the *Star* reported, with some sarcasm, "he early discovered that it was not flag waving, met by cries of 'British preference,' not the talk of injury to the railway companies, or to the Manufacturers' Association, not the prosperity leave-well-enough alone talk, met by cries of 'Laurier did that,' that was most effective, but that it was an appeal to a spirit of resentment against Uncle Sam that roused his attitude quickest and easiest."[17]

Lash introduced an anti-reciprocity motion (similar to the Toronto Eighteen manifesto) calling on the government to hold an immediate election before proceeding with the reciprocity legislation. White seconded it, and it was easily adopted by the co-operative crowd. With that, the audience rose to leave what was, for most opponents of reciprocity, a very satisfying evening. "The gathering," concluded Montreal's *Gazette*, "was on the whole a most convincing expression of Toronto's opinion on the reciprocity proposals."[18]

Montreal's Anti-Reciprocity League sent a message of support which was read out at the Massey Hall rally. Not to be outdone by their Toronto allies, the League also staged its own rally at Montreal's Windsor Hotel on March 20. A large enthusiastic crowd arrived for speeches by Anti-Reciprocity League notables, including Chaput and Chase-Casgrain, Lash from the Toronto Eighteen and Canadian National League, and Clifford Sifton, the *eminence grise* of the anti-reciprocity movement.

Earlier in the night Sifton gave a speech at McGill University where he was frequently interrupted by a crowd of pro-reciprocity students. The plan was for Sifton then to be escorted to the nearby Windsor Hotel in a carriage pulled by some friendly students, followed by a band and torchlight demonstration.[19] Accompanying Sifton was a fellow speaker for the night, Stephen Leacock, the McGill economist and a founding member of the Anti-Reciprocity League. Showing no respect for one of their university's most respected faculty members (or for Clifford Sifton, for that matter), another group of McGill students attacked and overturned the carriage, forcing Sifton and Leacock out into the muddy street. The carriage was filled with wood, torched, and then dragged as it burned through the streets of Montreal, while the students smashed store windows and broke into automobiles. The police arrived and, as the Toronto *Globe* reported, "a rush was made, and there was some clubbing."[20] The students escaped to the local YMCA, where they relied, in true Canadian fashion, on snowballs to keep the police away. The student riot was quelled and a few arrests were made. It was all something, reflected *The Gazette*, that "almost reminded older citizens of the days when Montreal had a Parliament building"[21] (which was burnt to the ground by an annexationist mob in 1849). Sifton and Leacock, meanwhile, walked the rest of the way to the Windsor Hotel.[22]

Sifton and Leacock's late arrival did not dampen the enthusiasm of the crowd, which also filled the hall and overflowed into nearby Dominion Square, where they were entertained by bands and a torchlight procession. As in Toronto, the stage was dominated by local notables, and Lash and Leacock both spoke, as did Casgrain, who spoke in English to inform the audience that French Canadians could also be counted on to vote against reciprocity. Fielding, the author of the agreement, was denounced as a separatist and closet annexationist by more than one speaker.[23] Also, as in Toronto, the crowd almost unanimously endorsed a resolution condemning reciprocity.

But the star of the show was Sifton, who, perhaps energized by his earlier misadventures, gave a rousing two-hour speech. Laurier was his main target and he attacked the prime minister for resurrecting a policy that had been abandoned years before. If Laurier really had maintained reciprocity as a Liberal policy, Sifton argued to great applause, he would have quit the party long ago. Sifton also repeated the argument that because of Canadian economic prosperity an agreement with the Americans now was unnecessary and potentially dangerous. "The great beneficiaries of the agreement," he said, "would be the American Newspaper Association, and Chicago Beef Trust, the U.S. Steel Company, the Minneapolis Milling Company, and the Hill railway interests. It will mean that these vast aggregations of American capital will be invited to come in and dictate to our country and to take from us the business we have built up by the past 25 years of hard work."[24]

The meetings in Toronto and Montreal were repeated in smaller venues across the country for the rest of what was now the unofficial election campaign. In most cases the opponents of the agreement had it easiest. They could attack the government and its supporters on the issues of patriotism and the imperial connection, discerning, as the Toronto *Star* editorialized, "some subtle connection between selling hay and selling loyalty."[25] The supporters of reciprocity could only dream of reaching that level, but there was absolutely nothing patriotic about being in favour of a trade agreement with the Americans. So, while the Liberals held their own public meetings and processions, preaching the virtues of trade and consumer prices,[26] the Conservatives aimed for the heart and soul of the nation, making it seem that if you simply desired the economic benefits that reciprocity would produce you were somehow unpatriotic.

John Foster, the American consul-general in Ottawa, watched these developments with growing amazement and reported to Washington about the "violent and irrational character of much of the opposition" to reciprocity. "It is difficult to indicate to you," he informed the State Department, "how bitter and excited the public opposition is becoming in Canada. Many of the people one meets in society are almost beside themselves. I have rarely known such manifestations of extreme feeling. They claim that reciprocity would destroy the home because divorces would immediately become prevalent, that the present judicial system would be replaced by an elective judiciary, and that every conceivable kind of ill would be let loose."[27] Momentum was building for the Conservatives.

———•·•———

The legislative debate in Parliament over the Reciprocity Agreement dragged on for weeks, with speaker after speaker venting over the agreement's strengths or weaknesses, over what was said and what it all really meant. The rhetoric was highly charged and it appeared that the fate of the nation hung in the balance. Laurier was attacked for coming back to reciprocity, as one MP stated in a colourful metaphor, "like a dog returns to its vomit." Frederick Monk, the leading Quebec Conservative MP, tried to embarrass the government by introducing an amendment to a House motion, dramatically reinforcing Canada's attachment to the Empire and stating without reservation Canada's ability to control its own fiscal policy and autonomy. Laurier had no choice but to accept the amendment and it passed unanimously. "With his back to the wall," *The Gazette* reported, Laurier "was forced to drop the mask of cynical amusement at the utterances of [annexationist American politician] Champ Clark and had to swallow the motion, lock, stock and barrel."[28]

The Conservative strategy was becoming clear: stall the legislation as long as possible to force the government to dissolve Parliament and go to the people in a general election. In his memoirs, Borden quite candidly affirms his party's intention to obstruct the agreement in Parliament.[29] Borden weighed the pros and cons of forcing an election; he wrote Whitney in Toronto asking whether he would "consider it good tactics to hold up supply and force the Government to a dissolution."[30] Whitney offered no clear direction, but he was encouraging about Borden's electoral prospects and minimized all of Borden's "cons."[31] More important, the caucus was behind him and by the end of April the Conservatives were committed to fighting reciprocity to the end.[32]

Borden also had two advantages. First, the use of closure to limit debate was unheard of in the Canadian Parliament, so his party could extend the debate as long as it wanted. "It cannot be said that the Opposition has been resorting to unfair methods of obstruction," the governor general observed, "but there is nothing to prevent them, even without the use of such methods, from prolonging the debate almost indefinitely."[33] Second, Laurier was scheduled to travel to Great Britain for the Imperial Conference in May, where he anticipated that he would have to fight for both Canadian autonomy and his navy. In addition, the coronation of King George V was scheduled at the same time and Laurier's presence at this ceremony was expected. Time was on Borden's side.

The Liberals wanted a vote on reciprocity before Laurier left and threatened to cancel the prime minister's trip if they failed to get one. The Conservatives wanted to continue the debate; they were willing to adjourn Parliament temporarily to permit the prime minister to travel to Britain, but fully intended to resume the debate on his return. The Conservatives had the upper hand, and as each day passed — and as May 12, Laurier's sailing date, approached — their advantage increased. Despite their rhetoric of fighting to the finish the Liberals blinked first, agreeing to a two-month adjournment from the middle of May to the middle of July. The reciprocity legislation remained in limbo.

For Borden it was clear that an election on the reciprocity issue was more certain than ever, and he stepped up his preparations. With Laurier out of the country and Parliament in recess he could focus his attention on organizing for the campaign. One of his biggest plans was to tour the West — as the prime minister had the previous year — to test the Conservative message on the Prairies. Meetings and political rallies were scheduled, speakers readied for all occasions, and the different anti-reciprocity leagues and associations stepped up their propaganda campaign on his party's behalf. Equally important, he scouted for potential candidates to stand by him in the election campaign. He believed that he had a particularly strong one waiting — overseas.

"I have definite and reliable information that the Laurier government contemplate an early dissolution," he wrote Max Aitken, a fellow Maritimer. "Reports from all parts of the country excepting Alberta and Saskatchewan are exceedingly encouraging and there is every reason to believe that the Government will meet defeat on this issue."[34] Max Aitken (soon to be Sir William Maxwell Aitken and, ultimately, Lord Beaverbrook and minister in the British government and confidant of Winston Churchill) was a young, brash, dynamic, and hugely successful businessman and the entrepreneurial kingpin in the wave of business mergers that had swept Canada in the previous decade. A millionaire many times over, Beaverbrook had migrated to Great Britain where he found a seat in the House of Commons. He never lost his devotion to Canada, however, and Borden approached him to return home to stand as a Conservative in the upcoming election. There would have been no doubt of a cabinet seat for Aitken if the Conservatives won the election, and his presence (and financial support) would give an enormous boost to the Conservatives, not only in his native New Brunswick, where a seat was ready for him, but across the whole country.

"The result of [the] election will have a very important influence upon the destiny of the Empire, it may even determine that destiny," wrote Borden, appealing to Aitken's imperial sensibilities. "I realize that you owe a duty to your constituents in Great Britain; but you owe a closer duty to Canada at this juncture. We want you here in the forefront of the firing line where you will be fighting not only for Canada but for the whole Empire." Aitken was a great supporter of closer imperial unity and imperial trading preference and he was quick to perceive the potential threat of reciprocity to that goal. As for many other imperial-minded Canadians, the choice to be made was for more than a simple trade agreement, it was for the future direction of the country. "A man of your driving force," Borden concluded, playing to Aitken's vanity, "is especially needed in your native Province; and victory or defeat in New Brunswick may mean victory or defeat in the whole Dominion."[35]

Aitken appeared eager to accept Borden's offer. He opposed both reciprocity and Laurier's naval policy, and he had been criticized by Liberals and others for his role in the series of business mergers leading up to the creation of the Canada Cement Company. Aitken was attacked by farmers for price-fixing and for gouging consumers, and the government responded with the *Combines Investigation Act*, which, even though it turned out to be rather toothless in its application, did not enamour Aitken to the Liberal government. With the announcement of reciprocity, Aitken launched a full-scale attack on the government through his newspaper, the *Canadian Century*, which began to publish a steady stream of articles on the navy, imperial relations, and reciprocity.[36] Ambitious, politically motivated on the issues, and wealthy, Aitken was a natural for the job.

The fly in the ointment was the legacy of Aitken's Canadian business dealings. As the man who had engineered the creation of several large business enterprises via a series of mergers and acquisitions, Aitken made, along with millions of dollars, a number of enemies and rivals who for business and personal reasons would be happy to see him fail. In particular there was Sir Sandford Fleming, the Scottish-born Canadian engineer and surveyor who had helped build the Canadian Pacific Railway, had invented standard time, and, in 1849, was reported to have run into Montreal's burning parliament buildings to save the portrait of Queen Victoria. In 1911, the aging Fleming was the president and shareholder in two companies that were part of the merger creating the Canada Cement Company. When, thanks to Aitken's manoeuvrings, he found himself on the wrong side of a large debt, Fleming made public allegations against Aitken of fraud and various other wrongdoings. It became a very public spat and a national issue, with newspaper editorials attacking the upstart businessman and his reputation.[37]

Fleming also approached Sir Wilfrid Laurier with a list of allegations against Aitken and a demand for government action. "I have under advice omitted the name of the person who has pocketed so many millions wrongfully (Sir William Maxwell Aitken)," wrote Fleming.[38]

The two men met on April 10, but the prime minister was not optimistic that Aitken's misdeeds could be investigated under the *Combines Act*; although he apparently encouraged Fleming to try.[39] There also was a political advantage to be had. A parliamentary committee was established and the allegations against Aitken were given a good public airing but proved to be little more than an exercise in tarnishing Aitken's reputation; nevertheless, more publicity only added to the growing calls for a full inquiry into the whole affair. Suddenly, Aitken became a political liability for Borden and the Conservatives. None of the directors of the Canada Cement Company wanted an investigation and Aitken gradually came to believe that he could not win in New Brunswick. Ultimately, a deal was made. One of the directors of the company went to Ottawa and arranged a bargain with Laurier — Aitken would stay in the United Kingdom and not run as a Conservative; in return there would be no public investigation into the Canada Cement merger.[40]

Aitken never returned to Canada. His struggle with Fleming continued, but after the election he had his friend and new Conservative MP, R.B. Bennett, in Ottawa to fight on his behalf, and eventually an out-of-court settlement was reached with Fleming.[41] (Fleming died in Nova Scotia in 1915.) In the short term, Aitken maintained his attack on reciprocity through the pages of the *Canadian Century* and he made contributions of a different sort to the Conservative campaign, donating an estimated $10,000 for the Northumberland riding and the candidate who stood in his place and an additional $16,000 for

"*The naval debate progresses at Ottawa.*"

Archives of Ontario, C 301, Newton McConnell Collection, circa 1910, #10007757.

other candidates.[42] The money was helpful, and the moral support from across the ocean was welcome, but this was one small setback for Borden and the Conservatives in what had otherwise been a very successful spring.

———•◦•———

The Conservatives could celebrate as the end of spring approached. Their tactics had enabled them to corner the government and to keep the Reciprocity Agreement before the Canadian public. And the longer the people got a chance to look at it, the more they began to distrust it. Equally important, reciprocity had helped unify the disparate elements within the party, and the potential of electoral victory seemed greater than at any time in the previous fifteen years. As Laurier sailed to Britain for a conference that would keep him away from home for two months, Borden set to work organizing, raising money, and travelling the country. Election talk was in the air: by the end of May, *Saturday Night* magazine was predicting — based on "conclusive information" — a general election to be called for late September.[43]

Laurier read the signs somewhat differently, and he may not have seen the trap that was opening up in front of him. He continued to receive support from across the country and encouragement to call an election, but the reports he received likely were more optimistic than they should have been.[44] A number of workers' organizations endorsed the Reciprocity Agreement, but that did not mean that the working class as a whole would vote for it: rural Canadians tended to back freer trade, but many had other reasons not to vote Liberal in the next election; he was also the favourite son of Quebec and could likely count on a majority of the francophone vote, but the nationalist winds of change were blowing, even across his own province. Laurier even took Sifton's defection in stride. Colleagues labelled the defector variously as *"cet homme dangereux,"*[45] and "a complete moral degenerate without a redeeming trait in his character,"[46] but Laurier seemed more resigned, calling Sifton's resignation "a loss," but concluding that "he will do himself more harm than to his former friends."[47]

Laurier continued to believe that the country was behind him and that he could win on the issue of reciprocity. "Sir Wilfrid has given me privately to understand," the governor general reported to London, "that he would have no objection to a General Election if the Opposition, by obstructive tactics, were to force him to advise a dissolution of Parliament, and that he would have no fear of the result."[48] He left for England in a confident mood; it was a mood not shared by all of his colleagues.

It was widely believed then — and later — that, had Laurier dissolved Parliament immediately in February and called a snap election, the Liberals would have won easily.[49] The agreement looked spectacular at first glance and the Conservative opposition was disorganized and caught flat-footed. But Laurier let the moment pass. He gradually came to believe that the best course of action was to pass the agreement first and then appeal to the country. The census underway that year meant redistribution and more seats for the West and potentially more Liberal seats, so waiting made some sense at first. But as the debate dragged on and the opposition mounted, Laurier was forced to fight on the Conservative's terms, not his own.

The question remained: why go to the country on an issue that had sparked so much anger and opposition? Laurier is reported to have explained to a friend, "My dear fellow, it is the breath of life to the dying."[50] However apocryphal such a statement was, it spoke to the central issue that, given the other weaknesses of his government — the loss of talented colleagues, the by-election defeat in Quebec, the fallout from the Autonomy Bills and other religious and linguistic divisions, the Naval Service Bill, and immigration policy — fighting an election on reciprocity was, all things considered, probably the best shot he had.

CHAPTER 6

THE SUMMER OF DISCONTENTS

Mr. Speaker, this is not reciprocity. It is revolution.
— WILLIAM MACLEAN, MP (CONSERVATIVE, YORK SOUTH, ONTARIO)[1]

Laurier left Canada and the reciprocity debate on May 12, and arrived in London like an aging lover greeting an old flame. The smile was reassuring and there was real pleasure in renewing acquaintances in the most exciting, dynamic city in the world. But Laurier was weary of the imperialist fever that again gripped the capital, and London reminded him of why he was only a visitor. He had long hesitated in going because the debate on reciprocity was unresolved, and he had lost the taste for the rigours of intercontinental travel. The Conservatives, on the other hand, were horrified by the prospect that Canada would not be represented by its leader at the coronation of George V, so Borden and Laurier made a deal: the debate on reciprocity would be suspended for two months, and resumed in July upon the prime minister's return. Eight members of the Laurier government would attend the Imperial Conference, as well as five Conservatives. Borden would not travel to London; instead, he headed to the Canadian West.

Canada had been a participant in these global summits for over twenty years by 1911. The first such conference was the Colonial Conference of 1887, held in London — the year, coincidentally, when

Bismarck publicly called for a much larger German army. It did not accomplish much that was notable, but that the event happened at all was significant. Seven years later, a Conference of the self-governing colonies met in Ottawa. The more mundane but still critically important Empire-building questions of cable- and mail-service infrastructures, as well as trade relations, were discussed at this conference. The next event, the 1897 Conference in London, was called to coincide with the sixtieth anniversary of Victoria's accession to the throne, and proved a notable success for its talks on preferential tariffs among members of the British Empire. It was Laurier's first conference — the one where he was knighted — where his charming repartee made an impression on the British press that was nothing short of spectacular. He was Canada's first international superstar, rivalled only by the celebrated opera singer Emma Albani (*née* Cécile Lajeunesse), a Chambly, Quebec, native who had been a star in Covent Garden for a generation.[2]

The Colonial Conference that followed in 1902 was very different. It had been called to coincide with the coronation of King Edward VII, but all the talk focused on the Treaty of Vereeniging (that ended the South African War), that had been signed a few weeks before the leaders gathered in London. It provided a critical opportunity to take stock of the Empire's defence ambitions and capabilities. Australia and New Zealand had participated actively in the South Africa campaign, as did Canada, albeit to a much lesser extent, and from this experience many had come to believe that a more integrated approach to defence was required. The Conference started with great anticipation as the British, led by Colonial Secretary Joseph Chamberlain, hoped to convince the dominions to contribute to the Royal Navy. The brand new country of New Zealand revealed itself eager to pledge help, and strongly argued against any policy of "localization" of the navy, but that appetite was not widely shared. Laurier's position was that the heavy costs of building Canada's infrastructure precluded any contribution to the British navy; Australia claimed a similar predicament.

Laurier was accompanied by Frederick Borden and William Fielding, and, together with Australia, managed to derail any notion of "empiremanship." Chamberlain's ideas for a "Council of Empire" were ignored, and British appeals for direct colonial contributions to imperial defence were ultimately rejected. Trade negotiations remained inconclusive. All the same, a Colonial Defence Committee was created to consider various ideas and proposals around subsidies and contributions, and to make recommendations on how collaborative actions could be taken.

For the British Admiralty, the idea of creating a fleet that operated under one command as a bulwark against Germany would remain a driving ambition. Laurier's position was that Canada should not integrate its defences — slight as they were — with the British government's, but he was willing to ensure that there was some compatibility should the need arise for joint action. He considered the construction of transcontinental railways as militarily strategic, and was open to the suggestion as early as 1902 that Canada assume the cost of the bases at Halifax and Esquimalt. Still, he was firmly opposed to an entrenchment of imperial decision-making that would systematically involve the autonomous dominions of the Empire. As Governor General Lord Minto put it, Laurier thought "that much more [would] be got out of the future in imperial sense by sentimental connection between Canada and the Old country than by any stipulated conditions having Imperial Federation as their aim…. An Imperial Council composed of Colonial representatives he thoroughly disapproves of."[3]

Laurier shared his thoughts and tested the popularity of his views with personal friends. "With regard to the question of Imperial Defence, I am prepared for a storm, but this is a thinking as to which I have my mind firmly made up," he wrote to the journalist J.S. Willison before leaving for London in April 1902. "I am not disposed to go into military expenditure any more than we have done in the past. There is a movement on foot to bring the Colonies into the vortex of expenditure which Great Britain [sic] situation and warfare make incumbent upon her. The principal item of expenditure in Great Britain's budget is land and marine armaments; the principal item of Canada's Budget is public works and we have as yet so much to do in that line that to divert any portion of that expenditure to throw it into armaments should seem to me like suicide."[4]

The British proposed that the members of the Empire work together to form a trained reserve that could be deployed for overseas service. Canada again refused the idea. The argument was that such a special force would require special training and equipment, something Canada could ill afford, but that instead Canada would work to improve and strengthen the existing forces. Again supported by Australia, the Canadians managed to end the discussion. On the general topic of imperial defence, Laurier was mysterious. "Sir Wilfrid is never very clear as to this, but I think on the whole is inclined to recognize the principle that Canada should guarantee the efficiency of its own forces as the garrison of the Dominion and thereby perform its duty as a factor in the defence of the Canadian portion of the Empire," reported Minto. Laurier made it known that he considered Canada safely removed from harm, particularly from south of the border, something the governor general did not share entirely.[5] In London that year, he openly opposed any commitments and refused to drag Canada into a "vortex of militarism," and said that if Canada was to be engaged in foreign wars, it would be on its own terms. In his last speech in London before leaving, Laurier offered "eloquent platitudes," according to Lord Minto, that were "negative in the Imperial sense."[6]

The next meeting of the Imperial Conference took place in London in 1907, and there again Laurier held fast to the idea that Canada's contribution to imperial defence would be limited to the safe maintenance of its borders. Although it appeared that the Australians grew warmer to the idea of helping the Empire militarily, Laurier continued to insist on preserving autonomy, and the 1907 Imperial Conference further cemented the idea that a fully integrated scheme of Empire defence was not going to be forthcoming.[7]

When the 1911 conference began on May 26, Canada had not submitted any resolutions in advance to be discussed. "I have the happy privilege of representing here a country which has no grievance to set forth and very few suggestions to make," Laurier declared upon arriving. "We are quite satisfied with our lot. We are happy and prosperous, but we recognize that there is always room for improvement, and we approach with an open mind the suggestion which shall be made by our colleagues for what they conceive to be the better interests of the Empire."[8]

Laurier was on the defence from the beginning, as he would be throughout the conference when demands were repeated for a more integrated, imperial foreign and naval policy. The first idea presented was that the conference be held openly before the press. Laurier noted that the same issue had been raised and rejected in 1907 and promised to vote against the motion once again. His views carried the day. The second motion was that an "Imperial Parliament of Defence" be created, where High Commissioners would meet and discuss policy. The British had no appetite for it. Laurier declared it "absolutely impracticable," and again spoke for the majority. The idea was dropped.

Clearly, Laurier, the elder statesman at the conference, commanded attention. "The most picturesque figure at the table was probably Sir Wilfrid Laurier," noted John George Findlay, a reporter at the conference. "He is still the same verbal epicure. His is choice English, picked phrase, and he seems to savour his words as he utters them. French is his language, and he pronounces the longer words of our tongue with a slight French accent and with a deliberate precision which are very agreeable. He has the grand manner — always courtly. He spoke with a greater air of assured authority than any other man at the Conference, save, of course, Mr. Asquith."[9] Findlay was most complimentary. "His cast of mind is French — quick, delicate, dialectic, elusive. His prestige is already great, and prestige usually affects our judgments favorably; but if he were placed alike unknowing and unknown amid a multitude of strangers, his appearance, bearing and abilities would soon attract attention and win respect."[10]

The conference then considered proposals aimed at restructuring the way imperial policy was discussed and decided. The first was that the British government's department of colonial affairs would be divided: one for the free-standing dominions, the other for the Empire's colonies. Laurier boiled the issue down to one of communication between the imperial government and the autonomous governments of the Empire. "Such a means of communication already exists, and, for my part, I must say that we are quite satisfied with the present system."[11] Again, his views won the majority over.

The second idea was that High Commissioners (ambassadors to London from the former colonies) should be given greater roles in defining imperial policy. Under this scheme, they would be admitted to the Committee of Imperial Defence for any discussion of the defence of Colonies. More importantly, the high commissions would be the sole channel of communication between the British government and the dominions. Laurier again led the charge in rejecting the motion, pointing out that issues between autonomous governments and the imperial government would be more quickly settled on a one-on-one basis (i.e., between him as prime minister and the governor general) than if referred elsewhere.[12]

Joseph Ward, the intensely imperialist New Zealand prime minister, who constantly prodded Laurier, responded that the very same objections could apply to meetings such as the Imperial Conference itself. "No," Laurier insisted. "We are representatives here, and we are not dealing with actual questions which we have to decide, but simply offering suggestions."[13] The British government proposed a "Standing Committee of the Imperial Conference" to act as permanent secretariat that would ensure the coordination of proposals between summits. Laurier, supported by the South African Louis Botha, waved the idea away as unnecessary and again made it be known that he would not support the idea of a Standing Committee that might "in the slightest way lead to interference in the work of Responsible Government in any one of the Dominions."[14]

Laurier, concerned by the potential for imperial meddling in Canadian affairs, challenged his colleagues to discussing a concrete example of how a Standing Committee would work, and proposed immigration as an issue that affected all parts of the Empire. The committee, it was said, could make recommendations. Laurier responded with disbelief: "I would be very chary for my part of having a recommendation which would be suitable to one section and not suitable to another." It was pointed out that recommendations could be ignored. "But if you have a recommendation sent to you and you do not act upon it, you give a weapon at once to somebody to attack you upon it," Laurier argued in defending Canada's autonomy.

> There is such a position in Canada.... I would not like a Committee to pass and send to us a resolution which we could not act on. Take a concrete case. Take the Asiatic question: there is no more difficult question

than that to deal with. The Home Government has views upon this question which perhaps we do not entertain. They have difficulties in India which they must take cognisance [*sic*] of, but we have difficulties in our countries also. You have questions of this kind debated by this Committee and they pass a resolution and send it to you and me and Mr. Fisher, calling for either administrative or legislative action which for my part I would not like to take, perhaps, or it might be suitable to you and not suitable to another. I do not see clearly what good point could be served. I see very clearly what adverse point might be made.[15]

It was suggested that immigration policy had to be made at the imperial level in order to ensure, for instance, that South Asian migrants did not imperil New Zealand's "white colony." Laurier grew irritated, again resisting the idea of imperial involvement in domestic affairs, showing a generous humanitarian streak: "I understand you think that the character of the population should be an Imperial question?" he asked. "If I understand you aright, you say that the country would be flooded by those outside people, as so become less British than it is to-day, and possessed of a different spirit." The New Zealand prime minister replied in the affirmative: "If a majority got into our countries, it would be so." Laurier refused the proposition: "I do not admit that conclusion at all."[16] The idea was shelved.

On the eighth day, June 13, the issue of immigration turned to naturalization, and here Laurier did wish for a more cohesive imperial approach. Laurier held that the power of granting citizenship was "one of the most important attributes of sovereignty," but argued that, should "a man" be made a British subject in one country, then that attribute should be extended to all countries of the Empire.[17] It was Britain, led by Winston Churchill, that resisted the idea, and both Churchill and the Canadian prime minister debated the issue at length. Laurier noted that a man who obtained letters of naturalization in Great Britain could move to Canada or Australia, or anywhere else in the Empire and be recognized as a British subject. He wanted a reciprocal agreement, again affirming equal rights for the former colonies, so that a man naturalized in the dominions would also be recognized anywhere as a British subject.

Laurier also anticipated objections, particularly in regards to race. He supposed that Great Britain was "perhaps more easy on the colour question" than were Canada, South Africa, or New Zealand, but dismissed the potential difficulties: "I, for my part, do not see any serious difficulty in that because the colour question will never be a problem in this country," he declared. "The men of the coloured races who would be naturalized in Great Britain would be of higher education and of the higher class. You would not have in this country a rush of such immigration as we would have in Canada, Australia, and New Zealand unless it is limited. That is really the true difficultly at the bottom of every mind here, that you may naturalise a class of subject generally undesirable."[18] Inspired by Laurier's eloquence, the Conference unanimously agreed that a scheme of imperial citizenship should be adopted, but the initiative was not pursued.[19]

Most of the discussion on defence took place in the secret meetings of the Committee of Imperial Defence (CID). The first one took place on May 26, when the CID was briefed on the international situation. A good deal of the attention was devoted to Europe, but the issue of renewing the Anglo-Japanese alliance was presented. It was due to expire in 1915, and Britain was considering an extension to 1921. Laurier hailed the alliance with the Japanese as "one of the happy events of the last century" and supported the idea of extending it. The second meeting took place three days later, and this time focused on naval defence. The British portrayed the relationship between the British navy and the dominion fleets as "sister members of the King's Navy" and suggested that "in time of war the Admiralty of the United Kingdom [would] control the whole of the King's Navy" but that a dominion government would be "at liberty to withdraw its fleet from membership with the King's Navy before joining in hostilities."[20]

Laurier saw the contrast between what was proposed at the CID and the Canadian *Naval Service Act* that had been voted in Parliament exactly the year before. He took "very strong exception to this language."

"The spirit of our Act," he told his counterparts, "is that in time of peace our navy is under our own control, but in time of war we may place it at the disposal of His Majesty the King." He clarified his position in a speech worth quoting at length, as the discussion that ensued clearly stemmed from his vague opening:

> It is the policy which would bring Canada in to take part in all wars that I object to.... The point I make, and the point of policy of our Act is that we are going to war only when the Canadian Parliament has so determined. The point you have taken is that we cannot help being at war and taking part in a war the moment war is declared between Great Britain and some other Power. If war were declared with Germany probably our duty would be to go to war at once, but I can conceive there are many smaller nations who might be at war with Great Britain in which war we should take no part whatever, and that is the reason we have framed our policy as we have framed it. This point is, however, clear that we do not hold ourselves bound to take part in all the wars in which Great Britain may be engaged.... The way you put it is that you have the right to depend upon our assistance, and to make your calculations accordingly, at the last moment we may withdraw and thus make your calculations all wrong, which would make it in a position infinitely weaker than the position in which we want to regard it ... what I want to impress upon the Conference here is, that so far as we are concerned in Canada we must stand by the principle that we have the control of our own fleet until we place it in the hands of His Majesty.[21]

Laurier scored some points, and the principle was recast and presented at the third meeting of the CID on May 30, but not in a manner that was entirely acceptable. The new resolution stipulated:

In time of war when the Dominion Fleets, in whole
or in part, have been placed under the control of the
Imperial Government, the ships to form an integral part
of the Imperial Fleet, and remain under the control of
the Admiralty of the United Kingdom, and be liable to
be sent anywhere during the continuance of the war.[22]

Herbert Asquith presented the principle that if the Empire was at
war, so was Canada. Laurier considered the proposal, and tried his best
to find a way to work with it. Certainly, he had supported this principle
when he had tabled the *Naval Service Act* in the winter of 1910. But
with the protests of that summer and the hard lesson learned in the
Drummond-Arthabaska by-election, he had to reconsider its political
implications. When it came time for him to speak, Laurier indicated
that he took some comfort in that this clause could only be applied
"when" the dominion fleets were put at the disposal of the British government, implying that dominions still held the right not to grant them.
He personally did not like it, but Laurier accepted the new formula. All
the same, he grew exasperated:

You people in Britain, if I may say so, do not appreciate the different conditions in which we stand in
the Dominions beyond the seas compared with the
centre of the Empire here. All the nations of Europe
today, in my humble estimation, have gone, if I may
say so, mad. I think Great Britain would willingly
limit her armaments but every nation in Europe
today is spending I suppose one-half of its revenue
in military precautions against its neighbours. We are
not in a position to do that in Canada.[23]

On the third day of CID talks, June 1, Andrew Fisher of Australia
moved that all the dominions should be consulted upon *all* treaties to
be negotiated by Great Britain. Laurier abhorred the idea and tried to
dissect it. In terms of its commercial treaties, he observed that Great

Britain did not involve the dominions, and that this principle should be applied for the dominions also. "Liberty is left to us to be included or not included in such a treaty as that, and I think that is very satisfactory." Laurier — who, after all, had left Canada in the middle of a debate on a trade agreement with the most important economy in the world — did not wish to see further entanglements with Britain, especially if they (as they inevitably would) had implications on defence treaties. "This is a thing which, in my humble judgment, ought to be left altogether to the responsibility of the Government of the United Kingdom for this reason: this is a treaty which lays down certain rules of war as to in what manner war is to be carried on by the Great Powers of Europe. In my humble judgment if you undertake to be consulted and to lay down a wish that your advice should be pursued as to the manner in which the war is to be carried on, it implies, of necessity, that you should take part in that war. How are you to give advice and insist upon the manner in which war is to be carried on, unless you are prepared to take the responsibility of going into the war?"

Ward again interjected: "Do not we do that in a manner by coming here?"

Laurier was categorical. "No, we come here to discuss certain questions; but there are questions which seem to me to be eminently in the domain of the United Kingdom," he said, explaining his thinking:

> We have taken the position in Canada that we do not think we are bound to take part in every war, and that our fleet may not be called upon in all cases, and, therefore, for my part, I think it is better under such circumstances to leave the negotiations of these regulations as to the way in which the war is to be carried on to the chief partner of the family, the one which has to bear the burden in part on some occasions, and the whole burden on perhaps other occasions.[24]

Opinion in English Canada was not entirely supportive of Laurier's nationalist positions. *Saturday Night*'s correspondent lost patience: "This is mere bunkum. What foreign war in which Great Britain could be conceivably engaged would not involve Canada?" The prime minister's motives and calculations were scrutinized. "He [Laurier] is talking for the benefit of those French-Canadian electors who have been misled by the calculated misrepresentations of Bourassa and the wild fulminations of the tail twister Lavergne. He is apparently trying to prove to them that he is just as un-British as his assailants of the Nationalist Party. He boggled the whole matter of naval assistance by a somewhat similar attempt, and now he is trying to remedy matters by a still worse mistake, which is likely in the not distant future to alienate from him English-speaking Liberals who take second place to none in their loyalty to the British Imperial ideal."[25]

Though he had not revealed any intentions either before leaving Canada or upon arrival in London, Laurier presented a resolution on the fourth day of talks, June 2, that further emphasized for disentanglement from imperial affairs, allowing "for any of these Dominions which may so desire to withdraw from the operation of the treaty without impairing the treaty as respects the rest of the Empire." Laurier argued that should this resolution be accepted, it would have the effect of asking the government of the United Kingdom to enter into negotiations with those respective nations with a view to securing to the dominions the liberty of withdrawing from the operation of such treaties. For many, this motion represented an attempt to undermine the conference. A friend from Canada wrote to Laurier that Willison's Toronto *Evening News* had called him the wet blanket of the Imperial Conference. "I notice from the reports that Botha has the good sense to back you up. The idea of little New Zealand laying down a policy for Canada is absurd," the correspondent wrote.[26] Laurier, for his part, was satisfied with the progress at the conference: "The conference is going on famously here, and so far we have everything our own way," he wrote to Sydney Fisher.[27]

There was ample time for socializing in London. The highlight was a luncheon on June 16 hosted by the Canadian High Commissioner, Lord Strathcona, at the Westminster Palace Hotel — the same hotel where the *BNA Act* forming Canada had been negotiated in 1866. The event was organized to unveil a plaque in the dining hall to commemorate that event, and featured as an honoured guest Sir Charles Tupper, who was present at those negotiations. It was a celebration of Canada that brought together its governing class. George Foster was present, as was Clifford Sifton, the premiers of Alberta and Saskatchewan, and Sir Edmund Walker and other notable bankers. The toast was given by Sir Henry Kimber, the eminent British parliamentarian who had acted as legal counsel for the British government in 1866, and Laurier replied, paying tribute to the founders of Canada, including Tupper, his adversary in the 1896 election. Sir Charles was cheered when his turn came to speak. He showed little signs of aging, and as the correspondent for *Saturday Night* described it, "his voice and his sentiments were alike clear and strong."[28]

Fresh from lunch, Laurier returned to the talks and formally introduced a resolution that called on Great Britain to allow dominions like Canada to withdraw from commercial treaties it negotiated. This resolution emphasized points he had made before about ensuring dominion autonomy. He explained that the policy of Canada was to develop trade as much as possible, first with Great Britain, and secondly with other countries, and that whenever trade arrangements were agreed to with nations outside the Empire, efforts should be made to extend them to Britain also. But his key message was that the dominions be allowed to conduct their own trade arrangements, and not be bound by whatever the British government managed to negotiate for itself or the Empire. The prime ministers of Australia, New Zealand, South Africa, and Newfoundland all quickly announced themselves in favour of the motion. Noting that Britain functioned under similar rules for some fifteen years, the British Minister for the Colonies, Sir Edward Grey, voiced no objection.

Laurier followed up with other thoughts on resolutions that might have the effect of entangling Canada. Australia had proposed a resolution "that every effort should be made to bring about co-operation in commercial relations and matters of mutual interest" and that "it is advisable in the interests both of the United Kingdom and of the British dominions beyond the seas that effort in favour of British manufactured goods and British shipping should be supported as far as it is practicable." Laurier had also gone to London to ask for an end to the obligation that the former colonies honour whatever treaties the British government signed with other countries. It was simply a declaration that countries could decide for themselves which nations they should consider "most favoured." The principle was accepted by the Conference. Laurier stated clearly his position on the autonomy of countries like Canada in the British Empire and again returned to the possible implications such treaties might have on defence issues: "It might seriously embarrass the Government if they had to consult the dominions, as they might have advice from Australia in one direction, advice from New Zealand in another, and advice from Canada in a third. Although the Empire was a family of nations, by far the greater burden had to [be] borne of the shoulders of the Government of the United Kingdom, and it would be going too far to say that in all circumstances the dominions beyond the seas were to be consulted." He then added an important principle: "If a dominion insisted on being consulted in regard to matters that might result in war, that would imply the necessity that they should take part in the war."[29] Again, Laurier had underscored that, while his imperialist sentiment could not be questioned, he had no interest in taking part in initiatives that might lead to international entanglements.

The last of the Conference's activities was to consider Laurier's motion that a Royal Commission be created to examine the trade irritants between the members of the Empire before further commitments were made on trade.[30] The proposal served two purposes. First, it set aside tedious issues of tariff reform that no longer were burning, and instead focused on other trade obstacles that effectively hamstrung freer trade. Laurier had cleverly channelled the call for general collaboration with an urgent plea for more intelligence on a key issue of trade. The resolution was hailed as "another step in advance in the path of what has been the governing note of this Conference — the path not of Imperial concentration, but of Imperial co-operation," and Laurier's resolution was unanimously adopted.

The conference ended after twelve days of discussion on June 20. The coronation ceremony itself took place three days later at St. Paul's Cathedral. Laurier took his place in one of the front pews along with other prime ministers, monarchs, generals, and high clergy. It was a beautiful day; the service itself was short and simple, and the music beautiful. Laurier joined the Canadian delegation in various gatherings that week, including the king's garden party, the Festival of Empire, a Dominion Day Dinner, and a reception at the Imperial Institute.

The Conference had accomplished a few things that bore the marks of Laurier's statesmanship. He had defused the idea of an "Imperial Parliament of Defence"; he had stood against the separation of the Dominions Department from the Crown Colonies Department, the creation of a Secretary of State of Imperial Affairs, the establishment of an independent secretariat, and the broadening of the powers of the High Commissioner. He had also been influential in getting support to appoint a Royal Trade Commission, and in securing the understanding that any dominions wishing to withdraw from the operations of British treaties would be allowed to do so.

To some, Laurier was actively working against the idea of imperial integration. "The 'jingo' papers of London," he wrote to a friend, "have been fierce on me for my attitude at the Conference … every day

Archives of Ontario, Newton McConnell Collection, circa 1910, #10008903.

"*Obstructing the Imperial Conference.*" *The figure of Laurier and the voice of Bourassa and Monk.*

makes me more certain of the fact that the policy which I defended here is sound in every point, and everything else would simply lead to trouble and disruption of the Empire."[31]

In English Canada, Laurier's positions in London were presented as further evidence that he did not care for the affairs of the Empire. "Sir Wilfrid Laurier seems to have practically capitulated to Mr. Bourassa and his fantastic following. His whole attitude since the opening of the Imperial Conference in London has been one that, however satisfactory it may be to the latter group, absolutely misrepresents the rest of the people of Canada's," wrote *Saturday Night*:

> [His] whole course became obstructionist. No proposal has come from himself as to how the difference[s] [within the Empire] "might be harmonized towards union," and any suggestion that has come from the lips of other Premiers has met with criticism and opposition from his lips. His whole attitude has been "I object"…. He has strived to convince his French-Canadian compatriots that closer relations between the various parts of the British Empire have no friend in him. In his old age he returns to the separatist ideas of his youth, or if he still believes as he once professed to do, that the British Empire is the chief civilizing force in the world to-day, he successfully conceals the fact. In truth, it looks as though Sir Wilfrid has been badly scarred by the Nationalist bogey, and was willing to sacrifice its professed convictions and those of the rest of Canada in order to get back a solid French-Canadian support. Will the day ever come when our leading politicians shall be willing to give up the idea of considering only a "solid Quebec" and adopt the ideal of a solid Canada?[32]

Laurier's actions were equally greeted with disdain by the *nationalistes*, who accused him of being the opposite: an ardent imperialist with secret agendas and a diplomat *manqué*. In a series of articles published through July 1911, Bourassa hammered the Canadian prime minister's performance in London and "his duplicity, his delays and excuses, his sinuous and unprincipled politics."[33] For Bourassa, Laurier was an absolute failure as a statesman, "chained to the pettiness and the demands of our miserable party discipline, diminished by the tricks and expediencies of the opportunist politics that he has pursued over the past fifteen years."[34]

Bourassa simply had no patience for the man of "honourable compromises," the "just middle," and "conciliation." Even if the Canadian prime minister was greeted on his return with banners hailing him as the "Nestor" of the London conference (Nestor was the wise and heroic character in Homer's *Iliad*), the *nationalistes* painted him as a self-dedicated imperialist who had abandoned his policy of neutrality on military matters and who now did London's bidding. Laurier could defend his position by arguing that he had protected Canada's autonomy in an Empire that he fully supported — he was an imperialist if necessary, but not necessarily an imperialist — but not all his audiences were convinced. In English Canada, his London trip confirmed impressions: Laurier was *against* the Empire and *for* the United States. In French Canada, the London trip showed that he was against Canadian autonomy and *for* the Empire.

Bourassa objected to the thought that Laurier might have been a "Nestor," portraying Laurier instead as having played Ulysses with his mix of self-serving prudence, smarts, and skill to simply ensure survival. He would have agreed with George Cowan, the MP for Vancouver, who likened Laurier's performance to yet another mythical figure: Narcissus, the hunter who fell in love with his own image.[35]

For Bourassa, Laurier had abdicated Canada's autonomy. He argued that Laurier had gratuitously extended to Britain the right to decide "in all circumstances" what might be the foreign policy of the colonies and even ceded the right to be consulted on its participation in war. While conceding that some of Laurier's actions were useful in protecting some aspects of autonomy, they had contributed much more to "the formal recognition of the absolute supremacy of England."[36] Bourassa also noted that the London Conference had taken a wrong turn — that instead of furthering issues around commerce, it had focused too much attention on imperial defence. He observed that the 1902 and 1907 conferences had focused preponderantly on commercial issues. Laurier's purpose in London had amounted to serving the political interests of the Asquith government and of its "liberal imperialism" that called on the colonies to support the military needs of the Empire.

Laurier, he wrote, had taken extraordinary precautions to "veil his attitudes" and "hide from the public the nature and range of his actions."[37] Bourassa argued that the Canadian prime minister had been more subdued and less active than in the previous three conferences. More confusing was Bourassa's perverse championing of Joseph Ward, the hyper-imperialist prime minister of New Zealand, as an autonomist — "not to say nationalist."[38] The only really "autonomist" position Laurier had taken was in supporting Joseph Ward's resolution that the colonies be allowed more latitude in navigation and maritime commerce matters. Laurier had risen against the Imperial Council, but only because most delegates opposed it anyway. "The conduct of Mr. Laurier in London will certainly not please either the imperialists or the nationalists," wrote Bourassa.[39] On that score, he was most prophetic:

> Indeed, the sincere Imperialists and Nationalists consider that the time has come when vital questions must be asked in Canada as in the rest of the Empire. Is it surprising that the man of the "just middle," of the "honorable compromises," of the false conciliation and to put it in one word: the pontiff of opportunism — the only doctrine he has ever followed — has seen the end of his reign? He has no reason to complain or to claim persecution. We would be wrong to blame him too severely. He has pursued his path and it has come to an end. He has been, more than any other, the creator of his system, of its success and of its glory. He is today the instrument of his own downfall, far more than the "jingo imperialists" and the "jingo nationalists."[40]

Bourassa even found fault with the Laurier initiative of a Royal Commission on trade irritants. "Either this commission is a farce or it is serious. If it is a joke, it is only a vulgar electoral maneuver," he wrote, insisting on seeing only the darkest consequence: "If it is serious ... it will serve to delay for some time imperial discussion of the two most controversial questions: imperial tariffs and American reciprocity."[41] Laurier had insisted throughout the conference that uniform measures applied across the Empire were not likely to work and that problems had to be dealt with locally. He had resisted all attempts to consolidate the management of the Empire or of institutionalizing further imperial co-operation. Even Grey seemed to agree with him: "I do not see how you could have taken a line different from that which you did ... without laying the foundation of an agitation all over Canada."[42]

The Conservatives were quick to call the conference a failure. While Sir Wilfrid toasted royalty, Robert Borden sniffed the political winds of the Canadian West, content to point out that Laurier's views in London were hardly unanimous. In Winnipeg, he was greeted by a band that played a medley "which sounded like a cross between 'The Maple Leaf' and 'Where is My Wandering Boy To-night?'" This was, by some accounts, a very different Borden than the one who had toured the West in 1902. His speaking ability seemed to improve markedly, and he connected with his western audience as he had never done before. There was vigour in his approach that caught many by surprise. "And the fact was demonstrated that the manly West loves a manly man," noted *Saturday Night*'s reporter: "That Robert Laird Borden is the man of the hour in the West nobody can deny. He has met the grain growers and reasoned with them as a father would with a naughty son."[43]

This tour was dramatically different than his earlier one. He showed humour and seemed more relaxed. "He dominated every meeting, and his driving, tireless energy was remarkable," noted *Saturday Night*. "He caught the ear and eye of the West. They liked the bluntness of his speech, the pains he took to make his position clear beyond the shadow of a doubt. His honesty of purpose and desire to discuss with them in a straightforward way the issues of the day made a deep impression on the prairie farmer." What also caught the attention of the reporter was the organization of the tour, which seemed to go off without a hitch. The Conservatives were evidently ready for battle once Sir Wilfrid returned to Canadian shores.[44]

Liberals in English Canada were more supportive. The Toronto *Star* promoted Laurier's ideas on the naturalization laws of the Empire and again noted that the prime minister of Canada had secured a unanimous vote. It saw the endorsement of the declaration of London to support Britain in war as a distinct step toward the peace of the world.[45] Some of the more imperialist Liberals argued that Laurier's position was sometimes misconstrued and that he was, at heart, an ardent supporter of the Empire. "Some have attempted to argue that his statement involved a declaration that Canada might take a neutral position in case Great Britain was at war," Newton Rowell said in Toronto. "Sir Wilfrid Laurier's whole record in the administration of the affairs of Canada shows that such a construction is entirely unwarranted. He has repeatedly and truly stated that when Great Britain is at war, Canada, as part of the Empire, is at war."[46]

Canada, for now, would continue to avoid entanglements. While Laurier sailed home, the Germans deployed a gunboat to the Moroccan port of Agadir to take advantage of a political crisis and stake a claim to the area. The bold move was a challenge to the French government and, inevitably, to its British ally. As part of the negotiations to resolve tensions, Germany asked France to cede Tahiti in return for a free hand. Laurier received a telegram from John Caroll, the acting prime minister of New Zealand (Joseph Ward had not yet arrived in Wellington), indicating that "New Zealand prepared [to] join Australia in remonstrance like joint action with Canada."[47] Laurier's telegraphed response was curt: "Question new to us in this part of the world. Will be happy to give it most sympathetic consideration."[48] Nothing more was done on this imperial question as the Agadir crisis was slowly resolved.

———•·•———

The Canadian prime minister left London on July 1 and landed at Quebec ten days later. The crowd waiting for him on the docks was impressive, as if welcoming a long-gone prince. Election talk was in the air because the stalemate that Laurier had left behind in May showed no sign of possible resolution. "If Borden wants an election, he can have it" was the attitude of many Liberals, according to the Toronto *Star*.[49]

Laurier took the government's steamer, *The Druid*, to Montreal, stopping along the way in Trois-Rivières and Sorel. He arrived in Montreal on Tuesday evening, June 11, and was greeted by an estimated 150,000 people and a display of fireworks. The prime minister was driven to the elegant Place Viger Hotel. "It is impossible to describe the wonderful

Wilfrid Laurier at Sorel, Quebec, August 1911.

Courtesy LAC, C-106748.

scene of welcome which was accorded Sir Wilfrid by the citizens of Montreal," reported the Toronto *Globe*, "no public man in Canada was ever accorded such a hearty and tumultuous welcome as that given Sir Wilfrid Laurier tonight." Laurier was understandably buoyed. His Reciprocity Agreement with the United States would pass, he said. The opposition of the manufacturers would likely dissipate. "They are sensible men, and would not be so foolish as to arouse opposition to that measure," he declared. The real source of the opposition to reciprocity came from those who wanted Canada to commit to the Empire fully. "These Imperialists and Nationalists both attack me from the opposite sides. After the present fight is over, you will find them devouring one another and the Imperialists will swallow the Nationalists."[50]

Laurier returned to Ottawa the next day and was feted by four thousand people on Parliament Hill before being driven in a parade of automobiles to his home where Zoë waited with yet another reception. He had been gone for almost two months and was eager to return to work. He went to the office in the East Block on the following day and had a meeting with cabinet to plot strategy.

Robert Borden arrived in Ottawa on July 11 and also declared himself ready for a fight. "I am satisfied," he said, "that the more thoroughly the Western farmer understands the true import of the reciprocity compact the less he will approve of it. We made our position exceedingly plain not only at our public meetings, but at the interviews with delegates of the farmer organizations at many points. It is needless to add that we shall maintain that position to the end."[51]

When the House of Commons convened a week later, on July 18, it was clear that the deadlock of the spring had only hardened. The Liberals wanted passage of the reciprocity bill; they also wanted to pass a "redistribution bill" that would accord more seats in the House of Commons to the Western provinces in a manner that would reflect their population growth. The problem here was that the final figures would not be ready until September. The Liberals, sensing that growth in the West would work in their favour, were willing to wait it out, even if passage of the bill took six months, as it had in 1905. For their part, the Conservatives were ready to filibuster and present amendments to the bill that would provoke endless and meaningless debate and to paralyze the legislature's consideration of reciprocity. For Borden, the government had received no mandate to "surrender to the United States our fiscal autonomy."[52]

On the opening day of Parliament, Fielding moved that the House immediately transform itself into a committee on Ways and Means to consider the bill regarding the Reciprocity Agreement. Borden responded with a resolution that showed that the Opposition was not going to allow the government to proceed. Instead, the Conservatives proposed that the House recognize "in some substantial manner" the services of the Fenian Raid veterans of 1866 and 1867. It was surely not lost on the members of the House of Commons that the Conservatives suddenly took up the issue of the Fenian Raid veterans as a way of illustrating their solidarity with those who defended Canada from an American-based peril. Regardless, Laurier mocked the motion, noting that his own negligible military services had been rewarded with a medal. "But I did not deserve it. I had no claim," he said; his garrison had arrived too late and all he did was sentry duty. The Opposition persisted for two hours until Borden himself rose to accuse the government of having "humbugged" the matter.

Electric fans were brought into the House of Commons to accommodate the parliamentarians, but the afternoon was wasted. Only at 9:00 p.m. did the House consider Fielding's motion and by 11:00 p.m. some members complained that they had travelled for six days to be in Ottawa and wanted to retire for the evening. Laurier, a marathon parliamentarian, would have none of it. If the Conservatives wanted to filibuster, he was willing to wait them out. The Liberals said practically nothing while the Conservatives attacked the government. When tempers flared, the Liberals responded with taunts of "go on, go on."

"It is grossly unfair," one Conservative backbencher complained, "to require a private member to speak at this hour, when the member of the Government representing this Province is not physically able to occupy his place. There should not be one rule for a Minister and another for a private member." Laurier turned to him: "Go on," he smiled. The House adjourned after midnight on its first day of debate.[53]

The House of Commons resumed its affairs at 3:00 p.m. the following day. Fielding again moved that the debate on reciprocity continue, but the Opposition proposed instead to discuss the Imperial Conference and to debate the nature of coal strikes in Western Canada, and the Conservative "obstruction brigade" continued to needle the government. The Tory MPs from Ontario made their mark and would lead the charge from the Opposition. John Reid, the MP from Grenville, harangued Mackenzie King, Laurier's young minister of labour, noting that the Department of Labour was "evidently useless."[54] Borden continued with an attack on Sydney Fisher, the minister of agriculture, complaining that he had not been personally canvassed as part of the census. "I would like to have one point cleared up," the Leader of the Opposition said, "and that is to ascertain whether I am enumerated in this census. I do not know whether I have the honour to be included in this census as a citizen of Canada.... I would like very much to find that out." Fisher replied dryly, "I will find out," but was subjected to another twenty minutes of Borden's indignation and accusations that he had been deliberately excluded from the census.[55]

Half the day was gone before the matter of reciprocity finally made its way to the floor. The Conservative attack was led by Uriah Wilson, the Member for Lennox and Addington in Ontario. Wilson spoke until the dinner break and was on his feet again at 8:00 p.m., pointing out the inconsistencies of the Reciprocity Agreement in light of what commitments the government had made in the past. Wilson spoke for an hour and then was relieved by two other Ontario MPs, Guss Porter from West Hastings and William Thoburn of North Lanark. Thoburn had the merit of being blunt: reciprocity was "causing more unrest in the minds of the business men of Canada than any other question since the national policy came in to force. What is the cause of this great agitation? They are affected by this reciprocity agreement."[56] It was past 10:30 when Thoburn pointed out that manufacturing was well-represented by eight men in the Commons and asked why they did not speak out. The irony was lost on Thoburn, who continued his filibuster until past midnight.

Tempers flared again when the House resumed the following day. The Conservatives focused their filibuster on a recent report on Asian immigration, a topic of great concern in British Columbia, but the subject was turned into a pretext for more personal attacks. Mackenzie

King was accused by George Taylor of using "willful and malicious" language: "If the prime minister finds that a minister would make statements which are not true, he should expel him from the government immediately."

"Order" responded Laurier numerous times. "I did not rise to reply to my friend," he continued, "because I had concluded that his speech was not made for the purpose of securing information but for the purpose of killing time in obstruction."[57] Borden demanded an apology, to which the prime minister again only smiled. By this time, the House had been in session for twenty-one hours, twenty of which had been dominated by the Opposition. Laurier had made a point of being in the House most of the time and with his colleagues teased the Conservatives with calls to speak "louder." Laurier even mused that the House might start its deliberations earlier in the morning, thus ensuring that the Conservatives would have to stand all day to maintain their filibuster.

After midnight, William Thoburn again was on his feet, calling for a break: "I appeal to the prime minister. I cannot go on at this hour. I ask [for] an adjournment," he said, but Laurier shook his head. Instead, Fielding asked that his motion on reciprocity be carried. The Opposition roared in protest while the Liberals laughed, and Thoburn had no choice but to stand and continue speaking. When he finished, another backbencher, John Best from Dufferin, Ontario, also asked for an adjournment. Fielding again objected: "I think I may say frankly now that the desire of the government is that this reciprocity debate shall be continued in a reasonable manner from day to day so that we may make progress. In intervening proceedings, I will not say objective proceedings — that might be objected to — but if intervening proceedings occur to prevent the consideration of reciprocity in what we think a reasonable manner, then we think we should sit later and advance what we regard as the paramount business of the House at this moment."[58] Borden responded to Fielding by claiming the right to discuss what the Opposition considered to be in the public's interest — such as "the loss to the people of this country of a million dollars by a system of boodling."[59] Best was allowed to finish his speech on reciprocity at 1:30 a.m.

The session of Friday the 21st was hardly more productive. The Conservatives focused on three topics: voter enumeration (demanding that seats be redistributed according to the census that had been carried out in the spring), parcel post delivery, and Asian immigration. The issue of reciprocity was finally tackled when the House resumed following dinner. This time, it was Angus MacDonell, the MP for South Toronto, who led the charge for the Conservatives. He spoke against reciprocity most of the night until he was relieved by William Smyth of East Algoma, who did the same. The House adjourned at 11:30 p.m. for the weekend.

In the meantime, the American Senate ratified the Reciprocity Agreement. The new tariff rates would go into force when Canada reduced its own. When the House of Commons resumed on Monday the 24th, Laurier rose to state the case that the Americans had spoken and that it was now up to Canada to respond, either through its parliamentarians or directly from the people, and taunted the Opposition. "Surely these honourable Gentlemen do not object to an election. They say they want an election and when I tell them that they do not object, they cheer; but when we take steps to have an election, they find fault. But we understand all this. The last thing they want is to go before the country."[60]

"This is the reciprocity that we begged the United States for thirty years to give us," added William Fielding. "This is the reciprocity that was in view when the leading gentlemen on the opposite side of the House went down to Washington — shall I say wore much shoe leather in the elegant phrase of the Leader of the Opposition — they went there to ask for the very reciprocity that is now before this House."[61]

Laurier was the first to speak when the House of Commons resumed the next day. He moved that until the end of the session the House would meet starting at 11:00 a.m. Both parties had met earlier in caucus and the Liberals emerged confident (to the point where their caucus was called a "war council"); there were rumours that some western Conservative MPs were hesitant about an election on reciprocity.[62] But if Laurier expected the Conservatives to expedite matters on reciprocity, he was quickly disabused as Borden led a charge demanding that the government release reports from the recent Imperial Conference, that the grievances of old settlers in the West be addressed, and that voters' lists be revised. Reciprocity was not discussed until the evening. Again it was Smyth of East Algoma who occupied the floor, with helpful assistance from Samuel Sharpe (Ontario North). The next day, the papers were openly speculating on when the election would be called. The Liberal-leaning *Globe* reported that "the Liberals confidently believe they will sweep the country." The Ottawa *Citizen*, which favoured the Conservatives, was less enthusiastic. "The government," it said in an editorial, "seems to have the inside track on every phase of the situation."[63]

Debate on reciprocity started early the next day, Wednesday the 26th, but did not last long. The mood in the House soured as accusations were traded across the floor. This time, the Liberals were on the attack. William Pugsley, the minister of public works, quoted a letter written by the president of the Riordon Paper Company that supported reciprocity despite the fact that George Perley, the Conservative MP for Argenteuil, but who was also vice-president of the Riordon Paper Company, was in the front ranks of the campaign against it. Perley protested that he had little to do for the company, implying that he could not speak on its behalf and that he opposed the deal on principle. The Liberals, led by Laurier, roared with laughter in the face of the Conservative accusations. Borden then raised the ante. "Are we going to have a debate on this sub—" Pugsley interrupted him: "The [Honourable] Gentleman has heard enough?"

"On the contrary," replied Borden, "we have heard too little from the [honourable] gentleman; we are likely to hear more from him particularly with regard to some of the insinuations he gives out, which … do not come very well from a gentleman with the record in dealings with the treasury of New Brunswick that the [honourable] gentleman has."

Pugsley, who had been battling rumours of petty corruption for months, was as angry as he was embarrassed. "I have dared the gentlemen who I have accused to come into the courts against me and bring an action for libel for the charges I made against them," he thundered. Borden was in a fury. "The House witnessed the unusual spectacle of Mr. Borden utterly losing control of himself. The Opposition leader was white with passion," noted the *Globe*'s reporter, as Borden demanded an apology for quoting a confidential letter and then demanded that all correspondence on the reciprocity deal be released to the House.[64] The affairs of the House were consumed by attacks led by Arthur Meighen on various dredging contracts in New Brunswick that also involved Pugsley, as minister of public works. Again, it was almost 1:00 a.m. when the house adjourned, reciprocity hardly being addressed.

The next day's debate took a different turn. "There is, Mr. Speaker, a growing feeling of uneasiness in Canada at the anti-British attitude of this government," said Thomas Beattie, the MP for London, Ontario, "and that feeling has not been allayed by the Premier's boast in Quebec of having preserved Canada's autonomy at the Imperial Conference, and his coolness towards pro-British proposals generally. It is a lamentable fact that at the coronation ceremony in the capital of the country not a single cabinet minister thought it worthwhile to attend His Excellency, or to step onto the lawn in front of their offices where the celebration was being held. Indeed, it was said that some of them were looking out the windows at the ceremony in their shirt-sleeves."[65] It was subsequently revealed that there were only three ministers in town on the day of the celebration and they had not been invited to what was understood to be a municipal affair.

Laurier grew impatient. "The House is engaged at the present time in passing the reciprocity agreement. We have had it before us for some months, and it seems to me that for all the information drawn from the debate, we could pass upon it today. At any rate, we could have a vote upon it and know whether we are in favour of it or not."[66] The prime minister's wish was not granted as discussion moved again to consider the post office, the alien labour law, and the Commission on Chinese Immigration. It was only as the hour approached 10:00 p.m. that the issue of reciprocity was broached, this time by James Donnelly, the MP for South Bruce.

It was evident that a clear confrontation in the legislature on reciprocity was not going to happen. The Opposition had managed to give it only sidelong glances, focusing instead on the issues of Asian immigration, government administration, and imperial designs. Clearly, the intention was to embarrass the government and to portray it as insensitive to local needs.

With Parliament at an impasse, various ministers tabled documents, clearly aware that the legislature would not be in session much longer. On Friday July 28, Mackenzie King tabled a special report on comparative prices in Canada and the United States from 1906 and 1911 and Laurier announced that training of the Canadian navy would now begin under the supervision of British naval officers, reminding the House that "in time of war, when the naval services of a dominion or any part thereof has been put at the disposal of the Imperial government by the dominion authorities, the ships will form an integral part of the British fleet, and will remain under the control of the Admiralty during the continuance of the war."

Later that afternoon, Thomas Beattie resumed his speech on the Reciprocity Agreement and, after dinner, yielded the floor to James W. Maddin, the MP for South Cape Breton and, importantly, the only non-Ontarian to voice opposition to reciprocity. As he neared the end of his three-hour speech, a few Liberals gave signs to the speaker. Mackenzie King moved a motion that the documents he had tabled earlier in the day be printed; Sydney Fisher tabled more figures regarding agricultural products affected by the pact with the United States as well as the report of the Defence Committee of the Imperial Conference that had finally arrived from London. "Might I ask what business will be proceeded with on Monday?" asked George Taylor. Fisher responded dryly: "Reciprocity will be interesting, I think."[67]

The long death rattle of Parliament had finally ended. The House of Commons had talked itself to death and there was nothing left but to appeal to the people. Laurier had made plans earlier in the week to call the election, and arrangements had been made to have the governor general, at that time enjoying a holiday in Murray Bay (today La Malbaie, Quebec), to sign off on the dissolution of Parliament.

There was tension in the air on Saturday morning, July 29, as cabinet members gathered. After Laurier introduced the agenda, it was pointed out that the Liberals had been seriously delayed in distributing their campaign literature. The intention was to send as much material out while members could avail themselves of their free postage costs as sitting members of the House. With the House dissolved, so would franking privileges, leaving piles of Liberal pamphlets on loading docks.

There would be no recourse but to do so under a minister's frank now that Parliament was dissolved. The issue pointed to the Liberal Party's lack of preparation.

Frank Oliver asked to speak. He was against calling the election, in part because organizational issues such as the mailings were unresolved, but also because the government was not popular in many parts of the West. He also said that Liberals had to increase the number of seats in cabinet from the West before calling an election. Noting that Nova Scotia had two portfolios while the entire West had only two, he argued that the Militia portfolio be transferred to a western province, since Frederick Borden was going to be named High Commissioner to the Court of St. James. Fielding took exception to the idea, noting that Borden had not been named and that the Liberal weakness in the West might be attributable to the fact that Oliver was still under the investigation of a parliamentary committee on the charge of having accepted a "slush fund" of $69,000, paid to his bank account by the Canadian Northern Railway as a reward for allowing the railway to change subsidy lands from Manitoba to Saskatchewan. The *Halifax Herald* reported that the argument in cabinet "waxed so warm at one point that blows were exchanged and that the other ministers had to interfere to maintain peace."[68] One reporter was told that Laurier even threatened to resign if peace was not at hand. Frustrated beyond words, and with his plea to wait defeated, Oliver articulated his discontent by leaving as Laurier informed his men that the election would be held on September 21. The cabinet broke up at 1:30, and he led them down the small corridor toward the main hallway of the East Block. There, more Liberal MPs joined the prime minister.

Smiling and confident, he met the reporters who had been impatiently waiting in the heat at the door of the council chamber. "Gentlemen," he smiled, "Mr. Fielding has some news for you." Fielding, who had been by Laurier's side for fifteen years and who had captained the debate on reciprocity, chimed in without wasting words: "Gentlemen, Parliament has been dissolved." The news spread like wildfire across Parliament Hill. "Some of the French-Canadian Liberals cheered and sang in the corridor," the *Globe*'s reporter wrote. "The English speaking Liberals were a little less demonstrative, but all were evidently in fine mettle and not a doubt was expressed as to what the people's verdict would be. 'A greater majority than has been' is the confident verdict of every Liberal member of Parliament."[69]

Parliament had broken up over reciprocity, and it looked as though the election would be fought on that issue, but Borden made up his mind that it was the issue of Canada's place in the Empire that had bedeviled Laurier in London that would make the difference. "I feel even more convinced than ever that it involves the British connection and the future destiny of this country," he wrote Premier Whitney of Ontario.[70] Laurier was cautiously optimistic. The imperial issues he had wrestled with in London the month before and the frustrating stalemate on reciprocity weighed on Laurier's mind, but he was hopeful: "We will have a vicious fight. The appeals to the prejudices of Ontario and the prejudices of Quebec will be more villainous than before, but the current running on our side is very strong and I think we will resist such efforts."[71]

CHAPTER 7

"THE PARTING OF THE WAYS": THE FIRST STEPS OF THE CAMPAIGN

Canada is at the parting of the ways. Shall she be an isolated country, or shall her people and our people profit by the proximity that our geography furnishes?
— PRESIDENT WILLIAM HOWARD TAFT

Any way he looked at the campaign, Laurier faced an uphill fight. He would focus on Quebec and Ontario, with perhaps a visit to the Maritimes, and the West would be under the supervision of William Templeman in British Columbia and Alberta's Frank Oliver. Liberal standing in British Columbia (two of seven seats) and Manitoba (two of ten seats) was already on life support and, although the Liberals had held their seats in Ontario in 1908 (thirty-seven of eighty-six seats), the party was clearly in a minority position in that province. Laurier could be fairly confident that his support on the Prairies would be maintained, thanks to the great support for reciprocity, but he already held thirteen of seventeen seats in Alberta and Saskatchewan and there was relatively little room for growth. Reciprocity would be a much harder battle in the more urbanized Manitoba and British Columbia, given the larger manufacturing base in the former (including agricultural implements), and in the latter, the large fruit and dairy industries, two groups of rural Canadians who would not necessarily prosper under reciprocity.

In Quebec there was a little uncertainty; the Liberals could expect to hold most of their seats, but who could tell how big a challenge Bourassa and his *nationalistes* would pose? Laurier knew he could rely on Rodolphe Lemieux to manage the race. In the Maritimes, Laurier could afford to be more positive; the Liberals held a slight advantage going in and reciprocity might give his party a boost; he also had Nova Scotia's Fielding and Frederick Borden and New Brunswick's William Pugsley as strong regional voices. Ontario would be the key battleground: it was the manufacturing centre of the country; its large meat-packing industry was solidly opposed to reciprocity; its rural industries were less dominated by wheat farmers (the ones likely to benefit the most from reciprocity); and it was the cultural centre of Anglo-Tory-Protestant-imperialist Canada.

In addition, the Liberals were less prepared for an election campaign than the Conservatives, and Laurier was slow in getting his candidates confirmed. Complaints came in from British Columbia about the level of dissatisfaction and lack of organization — and hope — within Liberal ranks in that province.[1] Laurier was not so much dismissive of these concerns as he was out of touch with the seriousness of the situation. He had just visited British Columbia, he wrote, and he had "never heard of any complaints."[2] In another letter he added, "at the last election, in making our calculation before the dissolution, I had put British Columbia in the black list. I am afraid that whenever the next elections take place, I will have to do the same thing again."[3] In Quebec, J.A.C. Ethier announced his retirement as MP for Deux-Montagnes, and Laurier was urged by Arthur Cantin, a Sorel postmaster, to intervene to remove J.E. Perreault, the Liberal candidate in the riding of Drummond-Arthabaska, because the latter had proven to be a poor campaigner.[4] When Laurier refused, Cantin announced that he would run against the Liberal incumbent Adélard Lanctot in the riding of Richelieu.[5]

From Prince Edward Island he had reports of additional disorganization from J.J. Hughes, Liberal candidate in the riding of King's. Hughes wanted to organize the upcoming campaign but claimed that he could not finance his campaign from his own resources: "My friends are all farmers and fishermen who will contribute nothing, but look for something." Indeed, for Hughes there was the added confusion as to who was the minister responsible for Prince Edward Island — was it Pugsley or Fielding? With all the confusion, Hughes was "obliged to apply to you and if I am to get no assistance I must drop out of the fight."[6]

It was even worse in Ontario. Members of Parliament with a large urban population in their ridings faced a difficult campaign selling reciprocity. As early as March, Laurier learned that reciprocity was not catching on "even among the farmers" in Ontario, and that more time and a more vigorous campaign might be necessary.[7] From the southwestern part of the province he received complaints about the lack of a morning daily Liberal newspaper to counteract the Conservative anti-reciprocity campaign at this "most critical time in the history of the party."

"It is too bad we don't have a paper in southwestern Ontario," Laurier noted with a degree of resignation.[8]

Finding suitable candidates in Ontario was also more of a struggle than it should have been. There were the expected personality clashes; in Peterborough, for example, J.R. Stratton, one of the Liberal candidates in the two Peterborough ridings, disparaged his colleague as an "absolute impossibility" and a "dam [sic] conceited little runt without any brains whatsoever."[9] Stratton got his way, but his preferred choice for candidate was passed over in favour of F.D. Kerr. In nearby Russell County, an ugly dispute erupted over the Liberal nomination between Irish and French-speaking Catholics. Charles Murphy, Laurier's secretary of state, was a young and rising Liberal, but in 1911 he faced a challenge from the francophone Catholics in the riding. Warnings flooded in to Laurier about the "deepest resentment" that would surface among Anglo-Catholics if he lost the nomination.[10] Laurier blamed "certain firebrands" who had long been "working to throw the seeds of discord between English speaking and French speaking Catholics," and he stood strongly behind Murphy.[11] Murphy won the nomination, but the affair was a reminder of the simmering linguistic and religious tensions in 1911 Ontario.

More seriously, several candidates and sitting MPs declared their intention not to run and Laurier was forced to scramble to keep his troops onside. Charles Hyman, a former cabinet minister, rejected any thought of running again: "I could not hope to carry the city of London at the present time, the party organization is gone, the party itself only a skeleton of its former self, and enthusiasm over reciprocity in a city constituency could hardly be expected."[12]

Laurier had a little more success recruiting Leighton McCarthy, the eminent partner of the McCarthy, Osler, Hoskin and Harcourt law firm in Toronto, to run in Simcoe North.[13] "My own opinion is that I will not be able to win," wrote McCarthy. "Had I … six or eight months I would be quite of the contrary opinion … the fight is coming far too quickly to enable me in the heat of battle to awaken the kindly feeling the people of that riding once had for me."[14] His prediction proved correct.

Laurier had to plead with others to stay. Alfred Clarke, the MP for Windsor, begged to resign his seat even though he thought reciprocity was "popular in the riding and the Conservative candidate … not strong."[15] Laurier responded a few days later: "The important thing at this moment is to put up the boldest run everywhere. Your failure to run would dishearten some of our friends; your presence in the field will give courage even outside of South Essex."[16]

Manley Chew, the MP for Simcoe East, also announced that he would not run. "I am distressed to hear that you did not feel inclined to run again in the coming election," Laurier wrote him. "We depend on you to keep this constituency for us. Let me ask you as a personal favour to again accept the candidature."[17] Laurier also appealed to J.J. Ward to run in the riding of South Toronto: "You know that you have always been my candidate…. Can I hope this time that you will come forward and redeem my constituency for us?"[18] All three agreed to stand in September; only Clarke kept his seat.

Laurier's personal papers contain many such examples documenting his efforts — with mixed success — to attract and maintain quality candidates, especially in Ontario.[19] It is a telling point, however, that he had to do it at all. The fact that Laurier was forced to carry so much of this burden was an indication of the lack of organization and preparedness within his own party. Here the loss of his colleagues over the years was really felt, as few suitable replacements had been found to take care of the provincial organization and at the local level. It is another indication of his growing isolation within the party and perhaps of a willful blindness to his party's disarray. Without a solid grassroots organization he would be left to rely on his charm, his prestige, and the force of his personality alone to pull off another victory.

In Ontario the party was falling apart. Laurier and his predecessor Edward Blake had worked hard to bring Anglo-Protestant Ontario around to support a Franco-Catholic as prime minister. Much of the credit went to Laurier's stand on provincial rights, his apparent support for non-denominational schools in the West in 1905, and his preferential tariff policy. Liberalism in Ontario also benefited, however, from the strong organizational hand of Sir Oliver Mowat, the former Ontario premier who joined Laurier's cabinet in 1896. A strong and effective provincial leader was an essential ingredient for Liberal electoral success in Ontario,[20] but Laurier never found a suitable provincial leader to replace Mowat following his retirement in 1897. From there, things started to unravel.

Laurier put his faith and trust in Allen Aylesworth, a brilliant lawyer who had been one of Canada's nominees on the tribunal established to settle the Alaska boundary dispute in 1903. Aylesworth was enticed into politics in 1905 and was quickly appointed minister of justice and the leading Ontario Liberal in Laurier's government. He enjoyed Laurier's trust and confidence, and the two became close colleagues, but he never demonstrated the necessary political instincts to control, maintain, and build the party in Ontario. He alienated much of his party through several controversial decisions — not supporting a bill that would outlaw gambling at race tracks and ridiculing the bills' supporters, and by releasing early, on two occasions, prisoners serving time for obscenity convictions — and by his apparent lack of interest in party organization.[21]

By 1911, Aylesworth was under attack from within the Ontario party,[22] and his increasing deafness only made it that much harder for him to be effective. Two younger cabinet ministers — Mackenzie King and George Graham — were taking on more of the responsibility for the party in Ontario, but their time had not yet come. Laurier stood by

Aylesworth, probably longer than he should have, even after the latter informed him that he would not stand for re-election. During the 1911 campaign, Laurier discussed possible replacements for Aylesworth and asked his minister of justice to stay on "until after 21st September,"[23] but the Liberals in Ontario were effectively leaderless.

Mackenzie King at Simcoe, Ontario, August 15, 1911.

Just as the Conservatives were faster off the mark in mobilizing against reciprocity in the spring, they were better organized for the campaign when it began in August. Borden left Quebec to Monk and Bourassa and their allies, and in English Canada he could count on several provincial premiers, their organizations, and their party faithful for help. Ontario, British Columbia, Manitoba, and New Brunswick each had Conservative governments with provincial premiers who were determined to defeat Laurier, his party, and his policy — even before the announcement of the Reciprocity Agreement. If there was a symbol of how much things had changed, it was here: in 1896 Laurier had three provincial premiers as colleagues in his government; in 1911 he had four provincial premiers opposed to him and ready to fight to the end.

Premier McBride in British Columbia had stood by Borden during the challenges to his leadership and his commitment to the Empire, and opposition to reciprocity guaranteed his vigorous support during the campaign. A similar situation appeared in Manitoba and New Brunswick, where the Roblin and Hazen governments passed resolutions condemning reciprocity and committed their active support for the Conservative campaign. Hazen's support for Borden was limited and his own political position less secure, but McBride and Roblin were dedicated to a Conservative victory. Both premiers had clashed with Laurier over increased provincial subsidies and both had their own provincial grudges over Laurier's hesitation to extend Manitoba's provincial boundaries and his disallowance of several bills passed in British Columbia to restrict Asian immigration.[24]

It was not just chance that brought this support to the Conservatives in 1911. For years Borden actively courted these Conservative provincial premiers by promising to end patronage and to clean up government and reorganize the civil service. The Conservative 1907 Halifax platform also included a strong statement on provincial rights and its opposition to the centralizing tendencies of the federal government. These issues were attractive to the provincial premiers.[25] When their concern over the French-Canadian Laurier and his focus on Quebec clashed with their strong attachment to the Empire and all that it stood for, working to defeat the Laurier government made perfect sense.

In Ontario, the co-operation of the Whitney government was even more vital to Conservative success. Whitney did not like Laurier's navy and he questioned his whole imperial policy; he also clashed with the federal government on several other issues and generally felt that Ontario's interests had been ignored by Ottawa.[26] Even before reciprocity was announced he was allied with Borden; reciprocity served to galvanize Whitney and his whole political organization. Not only did he personally back Borden and help preserve his leadership, he allowed the federal Conservatives to raid his provincial party for candidates for several Ontario ridings. When the federal party approached several potential candidates without Whitney's permission, however, it became a bit of a problem, but once Borden agreed to consult Whitney on all those involved, the relations between the two wings operated very smoothly.[27] It was extremely important for Borden, because in a majority of the Ontario ridings there was only one riding association for both wings of the party, and in the remaining ridings the relationship between the federal and provincial riding associations was very close.[28]

As early as December 1909, Borden and close to a dozen Ontario Conservatives had dined together at Toronto's King Edward Hotel and formulated an organizational game plan, with J.S. Carstairs, a leading Conservative organizer, and A.E. Kemp in place to oversee its implementation. Overall direction of the Ontario campaign was put in the hands of Frank Cochrane, another one of Whitney's provincial Conservatives.[29] As we saw in chapter four, within days of the announcement of reciprocity in Parliament, the Conservatives moved to mobilize opposition to reciprocity through the boards of trade, the Toronto Eighteen, and various business groups. Throughout the spring and summer, the organization secured candidates, disseminated literature, held meetings, raised money, encouraged friendly newspapers to increase their support for the party, and focused attention on key ridings in the province. The Conservatives were remarkably perceptive of Conservative chances and carefully selected suitable candidates and targeted important ridings for extra effort, and, even without reciprocity as an issue, the Conservatives were likely heading for victory in Ontario.[30] As Carstairs wrote a few months after the election, "I think it can be safely asserted without fear of contradiction, that it was largely owing to the successful working out of our plans that Ontario elected so large a number of Conservative Members on September 21st, 1911."[31]

The Conservatives also benefited from the contribution of supporters outside the party, in particular Clifford Sifton. From the moment of his defection from the Liberals the previous winter, Sifton pursued his own anti-reciprocity campaign, a campaign he maintained (with a brief respite to attend the coronation in June) until election day in September. He collected the telephone lists for Manitoba, Saskatchewan, and Alberta and turned them into mailing lists, with the plan to send every Prairie home a copy of his House of Commons speech and an anti-reciprocity pamphlet. He remained involved in the activities of the Anti-Reciprocity League and kept in contact with the leading Conservative organizers about specific details of the campaign.[32] He spoke regularly against reciprocity, and during the election campaign undertook an exhausting speaking tour of Ontario, Quebec, and the Maritimes.

In the West he was lampooned as "Clifford Snifter."[33] In Ontario he was attacked by former colleagues who questioned whether he had ever really been a Liberal and then painted him as a self-serving capitalist who was out only for himself.[34] But in Saint John, New Brunswick, he appeared at a rally with Premier Hazen, rising to "deafening applause." He condemned reciprocity and warned of the dangers of annexation from Halifax to Windsor, claiming that he spoke not as a Tory but "as one who has put above that his duty to the British flag."[35] He inadvertently made more trouble for the Liberals by not running as a candidate in his old Brandon riding, freeing up for a Conservative challenge what once had been a fairly safe Liberal seat. He agreed to disagree with John Dafoe, the editor of his newspaper, the *Manitoba Free Press*, and did nothing to challenge its support for reciprocity, and he maintained a personal reluctance to speak in the ridings of former colleagues,[36] but otherwise he proved to be an effective ally for Borden and the Conservatives. As the prime minister–elect wrote at the end of the campaign, "the victory seems to be very decisive. Your own splendid efforts contributed in no small measure to the result."[37]

No other individual matched Sifton for his vigour, determination, and stamina, but a few of the Toronto Eighteen added their voices to the Conservative campaign. In particular, Thomas White, of the National Trust Company and a leading member of the group of former Toronto Liberals, made a significant contribution to the Tory campaign, speaking at rallies in Berlin, Brussels, and Paris, without ever leaving southern Ontario. He was quoted as saying that he believed there was "no healthier sign of the times than that an honest man should change his party in the interests of his country,"[38] and he put those views to the test, formally running as a Conservative in one of the first by-elections held after the September election (following his selection as Borden's first finance minister).

Other members of the Toronto Eighteen spoke on various occasions during the campaign and gave interviews to the press,[39] and the Canadian National League, the Anti-Reciprocity League, and other groups took out political advertisements and organized events at which speeches were made and reciprocity denounced. Arthur Hawkes, the ubiquitous secretary of the Canadian National League, wrote steadily throughout the campaign, and his work on the "British-born" received considerable attention; in August he had a hand in the formation of the Canadian-British Association in Toronto. In the Ontario capital, J.S. Willison observed the election campaign and made his contribution from the Toronto *Evening News*'s editorial office. In Montreal, Huntley Drummond, the prominent business leader, along with a handful of other businessmen, spoke out against the agreement. Another asset for the Conservatives was Sir William Van Horne, who spoke for Canadian nationalism — and the railways — in ridings in Ontario, Quebec, and the Maritimes. On several occasions in New Brunswick he appeared alongside Robert Borden. At the Queen's Rink in Saint John, Van Horne denounced the hideous reciprocity because it "would destroy our fiscal independence; because the underlying idea on the part of our American neighbours is our estrangement from the Empire."[40] The message was familiar, but it was a message that the Conservatives liked to hear repeated everywhere across the country.

It should also be pointed out, however, that most business-men and members of the leagues and the local boards of trade and manufacturers' associations did not participate directly in the election campaign, beyond voting, and did not involve themselves too closely at the local riding level. Joseph Flavelle, for example, watched from Toronto, but made few public appearances. Sir Edmund Walker received several requests to speak, but does not appear to have made many appearances,[41] while Zebulon Lash, one of the guiding forces behind the Toronto Eighteen, the Canadian National League, and the alliance with Borden, rejected the idea of actual campaigning. It "was never intended that the 'League' should take any responsibility in connection with the Election Campaign in the Constituencies," he wrote to Sifton.[42] Personally, he could not "be away from home for more than a day or two at a time," and, in August, "home" for Lash was in the Muskokas, just north of Toronto.

Finally, the luxury of opposition was to be able to attack the government on its record without having to explain in detail how they would have acted differently. The year 1911 was no exception; the government was attacked for its extravagant spending since 1896, especially for the rising costs associated with the transcontinental railways, and Laurier was condemned for the sins of his government and for the eruption of a variety of corruption scandals. For example, Edmonton's Frank Oliver, the minister of the interior, was accused of accepting money in return for helping the Canadian Northern Railway select land in Saskatchewan, but Parliament was dissolved before any investigation was complete. Enough other allegations of bribery, influence-peddling, and graft appeared, however, to create an aura of corruption around the Liberal government.

Reciprocity was, without doubt, the issue of the 1911 campaign in English Canada and it was a major secondary issue even in Quebec. It was the most frequently debated question, it dominated newspaper coverage and editorial commentary from July to September, and it was the most regular topic of political speeches. Reciprocity was the focus of debate not only among bankers, manufacturers, railway promoters, and newspaper editors, but also among farmers' groups, workers' organizations, and fishers on both coasts. It was the only issue to prompt the creation of outside political groups dedicated to its success or failure. There were no leagues to promote the Hudson Bay railway, or pressure groups to support harbour development in Victoria or to dig a tunnel to Prince Edward Island. Reciprocity was the one inescapable issue of the campaign. A quarter of a century later, when he came to write his memoirs, Borden's chapter on the 1911 election was simply entitled "Reciprocity."

Everyone had a stake in reciprocity, and everyone, it seemed, had a theory or a view on how it might affect them, their city or region, and the country as a whole. There were several angles to the debate: How would reciprocity affect the economy — would it create or destroy jobs? What impact would it have on prices? Would it promote or shun American branch plants from establishing themselves in Canada? Was it possible, as some argued, for the farmers to earn more for their produce, for the manufacturers to earn more profit on their goods, for the businessmen

to prosper, and for the consumers to see lower prices in the stores —
all at the same time? Another dimension focused on the greater — or
national — meaning of reciprocity, debating the impact of the agreement
on Canada's survival as a British nation, with charges and countercharges
on the questions of loyalty, patriotism, imperialism, and annexation.

Both parties launched their campaigns with more than enough
statistics to bombard the opposition — not to mention their own supporters — into submission. Prices would fall to historic lows or rise
to unbearable levels, depending on your views of reciprocity; business
would expand with new markets and bring prosperity for all or be overwhelmed and destroyed by American competition; the average working
family would see a real improvement in its standard of living or fall
under the dominant boot heel of the evil American trusts. Either way,
Canadians would demonstrate their loyalty, their independence, their
common sense, and their intelligence and integrity by the way that they
voted on the issue.

The two sides condemned each other and paraded out former
opposition politicians and supporters who had seen the political light
and crossed the floor to make new political friends. The Conservatives,
in particular, produced a steady stream of businessmen who once had
voted Liberal and now had embraced their love of country and come
forward in opposition to reciprocity. Hundreds of meetings were
held with resolutions passed in favour of or opposed to reciprocity;
hundreds of petitions condemned or heralded the agreement. Both
parties organized parades and street-light processions for their candidates, hired bands, church choirs, and orchestras for the occasions,
and copied the words of their candidates for future distribution. Each
side spoke boldly of the promise of Canada and the golden future that
their policies would ensure, while victory for their opponents would
lead to financial ruin, destitution, and despair.

Both parties had newspapers that trumpeted the cause — for and
against reciprocity and their parties — emphasizing how this campaign
was the election of the century, with the fate of the country hanging
in the balance. Most cities had at least two dailies supporting one or
the other side, and the reciprocity debate was fought out in print over
and over again. Occasionally they attacked one another, describing

their competitor's coverage as fatuous, misguided, silly, and just plain wrong. In Halifax, for example, the *Herald* and the *Morning Chronicle* were both confident of victory until the very end of the campaign. The *Herald*, which began most days with a thin banner on the front page containing a quotation denouncing reciprocity, accompanied Borden and Sifton as they crossed the eastern half of the country on their way to ultimate triumph. The Liberals, meanwhile, were in disarray and floundering thanks to internal dissension that had, on at least one occasion, dissolved into a cabinet fist fight.[43] Across town, the *Morning Chronicle* predicted a Liberal sweep and called all the talk about annexation a "red herring"[44] as it followed Laurier and local hero William Fielding on their way across the Maritimes. Whereas Robert Borden, the other Nova Scotian, faced sullen and dispirited crowds, Laurier and Fielding were met by enthusiastic demonstrations and wild applause, usually of a historic nature.

Regional variations of similar campaign stories can be found in newspapers in Saint John, Montreal, Toronto, Winnipeg, Calgary, Victoria, and a dozen other cities in between. Liberal papers in one part of the country picked up and repeated Liberal stories from other parts; the Conservative papers did the same. They filled their pages with stories from the campaign trail, editorials supporting their party and reviling the opposition, and editorial cartoons poking fun at everyone. All of them predicted victory on election day. The day after, Conservative papers would claim that victory had been obvious and inevitable from the start; Liberal papers would place the blame for their misfortune on a variety of sources, none of which was the responsibility of their party, its leader, or reciprocity.

The other major national issue was the debate over Laurier's *Naval Service Act*, the plan to build an independent Canadian navy, and, more generally, Canada's relations with the British Empire. The Empire and the naval issue dominated in Quebec but the debate was somewhat more subdued in English Canada and a bit of an appetizer before the main course of reciprocity. Moreover, in English Canada the focus was less about the specifics of Laurier's naval policy, and the navy was usually raised in a different context than in Quebec. For example, there was much less rhetoric about Canadians being dragged into imperial wars, or over the possible implementation of conscription. For the most part, however, the Conservatives and their sympathetic newspapers raised the matter in the context of reciprocity and used Laurier's naval policy as another platform from which to attack the allegiance and loyalty of the Laurier government and Liberals in general. The flipside of Laurier selling out the country to the Americans with reciprocity was Laurier turning his back on the Empire and effectively declaring independence by establishing an independent navy that theoretically could remain neutral when the Empire was at war. It is hardly surprising. Borden rarely mentioned the specifics of the naval issue in English Canada for it was not something that would attract many votes for his party and likely would draw unfavorable attention to his party's close co-operation with the *nationalistes* in Quebec. But emphasizing the contest as a struggle between, on the one hand, patriotism and allegiance to the Empire and, on the other, annexation and independence from the Empire played very well to audiences in English Canada.

When the Liberals raised the naval issue in English Canada, it was to focus public attention on Quebec and the *nationalistes* and to highlight — and condemn — the "unholy alliance" of Borden and Bourassa. What Borden was saying in English Canada was compared to what Bourassa and Monk were saying in Quebec. "While the right wing of the Conservative army, under the leadership of Commander-in-Chief Borden, is giving battle to reciprocity, with loyalty to the Empire as the slogan," wrote John Dafoe in the Liberal-leaning *Manitoba Free Press*, "the left wing, led by General Bourassa, under the Nationalist colors, is assaulting the Dominion Government in Quebec with the slogan that Laurier is an Imperialist who has betrayed his country to the British jingoes." The Leader of the Opposition is "careful in every utterance to say nothing that would sound in Quebec ears as indicating the faintest lack of harmony and co-operation between himself and Mr. Bourassa." This alliance, Dafoe concluded, "cannot be regarded otherwise than as involving possibilities of the gravest national peril."[45]

Sometimes the Liberals expanded the unholy alliance into the "Borden-Bourassa-Sifton" triumvirate, and the connections between the three leaders were closely scrutinized, with allegations that the Anti-Reciprocity League in Montreal was secretly financing the *nationaliste* campaign in Quebec.[46] Comparing the three to Caesar, Pompey, and Crassus, the famed First Triumvirate of ancient Rome, the Toronto *Star* rose up in rhetorical anger: "Mr. Borden and Mr. Sifton have both been appealed to, to denounce Mr. Bourassa and his campaign. They have declined to do so. Why?" The answer was clear: Borden had sold out to Bourassa and amended his naval policy in a cheap grab for votes in Quebec.[47]

The Conservatives tried unsuccessfully to turn the tables. In a way that would be repeated in the 1980s by the Liberals over the "Mulroney" free trade deal, in 1911 the Conservatives often referred to the Reciprocity Agreement as the "Taft-Fielding Agreement," in an effort to associate potentially unpopular names to a policy, and in this case labelling it as the "real" unholy alliance. "There IS an 'unholy alliance,'" proclaimed the *Halifax Herald*, "between the forces of annexation in the United States and the Laurier reciprocity forces in Canada."[48] Laurier easily brushed aside such allegations with his stump speech, repeated many times during the campaign: "I am represented in Quebec as an ultra-imperialist in Ontario, while in Ontario I am represented as an anti-imperialist in Quebec. In Quebec I am represented as subservient to the English, in Ontario as subservient to the ultramontanists of Quebec."[49] These may have been the most memorable words to come out of the campaign.

Even more serious for the Liberals, Laurier's navy not only failed to resonate well in English Canada, it cost him support in rural Ontario, the very part of the province that he needed to hold in order to win in 1911. Opposition to the building of an independent Canadian navy arose in many rural communities and in the Farmers' Association of Ontario, and it was officially rejected at a 1909 farmers' convention in Toronto. The opposition of rural Ontarians was not based in an imperialist call for solidarity within the Empire; it was more an attack on the extravagant spending that a navy would entail, a reflection of the prevailing concern that a navy would drag Canada into needless foreign wars, and an expression of the belief that there was no need for a navy at all. It was more isolationism than imperialism.[50] It was one of the many small ironies of the 1911 election campaign that Laurier was assailed for his lack of imperial enthusiasm in urban Ontario while being accused of militarism in rural Ontario. The Liberals were already weak in Ontario cities where Anglo-imperial enthusiasm was its greatest, but they depended on the rural vote.[51] Without the rural ridings behind them, Laurier and the Liberals were in deep trouble in Ontario.

One other "national" issue that was notable — if only in its absence from the campaign — was women's suffrage. This election was the last federal election in which all Canadian women were excluded; by the end of the First World War, most Canadian women could vote either federally or in one of several provinces. But 1918 seemed a long way away in 1911, when there was little apparent effort to make extending the franchise into a national issue. Few candidates spoke on the subject; none made it a basis of his campaign. Robert Borden was cool to the idea and did not become a convert until the First World War — when he needed the votes of soldiers' female relatives to save his government; others, like Henri Bourassa, were openly hostile to the whole idea of granting women the vote.[52]

There was a considerable women's movement in late-nineteenth-century Canada affecting all aspects of social life (Women's College Hospital, founded in the summer of 1911 in Toronto, was but one reminder of its emerging strength). Several suffrage organizations comprising both men and women were active throughout the country, and various suffrage bills had appeared in Parliament over the previous thirty years. But thanks to Laurier's *Franchise Act* of 1898, the franchise and voters' lists were relegated to provincial control.[53] This gave Laurier an easy excuse to do nothing. During the campaign, a representative of the Canadian Suffrage Association complained to the prime minister that it was an "insult" to Canadian women to deny them the vote any longer. "Surely Canadian women have the well-being of their country more at heart than the average foreign immigrant," she wrote. "We have no Dominion franchise," Laurier replied, dodging the issue, "the electoral vote is exercised under franchise granted to each provincial legislature."[54]

There literally were no votes in extending the vote to women and, as a result, women's suffrage was a non-issue in the election campaign.

Nevertheless, that did not stop women from participating in political affairs during the campaign. Women's groups and individual women helped with campaign work, organized petitions, and attended political rallies all across the country. Campaign rallies were social occasions that attracted all kinds of people, including many who could not vote. And it did not stop candidates from both parties from appealing to women or using gender-based stereotypes to make their case. "Every housewife should welcome reciprocity," proclaimed the Toronto *Star*. "It will mean cheaper food for her family."[55] Appeals were also frequently made to women as mothers to sway their husbands to the cause. At one stop in Quebec, for example, Laurier called on "the women to use their influence on the right side."[56] But the election of 1911 did little to question — let alone challenge — the prevailing views of the place of women in Canadian society.

It should also be noted that in English Canada the 1911 election was very much a two-party race. There was no group or party comparable to the *nationalistes* outside Quebec, and no significant third party on the left or right. There were more than a dozen independent candidates in ridings across the country, including a few Labour candidates and socialists. In Winnipeg, the Social Democratic Party nominated

Wilfrid Laurier in Moose Jaw, September 1910.

Courtesy LAC, PA-073657.

labour leader R.A. Rigg; in Edmonton, Arthur Masters ran under the Socialist banner. In most cases the labour candidates supported reciprocity, and shortly before the election the Trades and Labour Congress executive endorsed the agreement. Reciprocity was in the interest of the Canadian people, they announced, "If other proof of this were wanting, the fact that the Canadian Manufacturers' Association is against it, would be sufficient to prove it must be of some value to the workers."[57] None of these candidates, however, were elected; Rigg, for example, even lost his deposit.[58] However it is measured, 1911 was a fight between Liberals and Conservatives.

Every time an opponent of reciprocity stood up during the election campaign to speak about the agreement, he or she had a wealth of supportive material from the United States to back up his or her position. Consequently, in 1911, Canadians were inundated with a flood of rhetoric that was a mixture of patriotic bombast, nationalistic fear-mongering, jingoistic support for the Empire, and pure anti-Americanism. For Conservatives it was the icing on the cake.

President Taft's administration introduced the Reciprocity Agreement to the American Congress on the same day in January that Fielding addressed the House of Commons, and from that moment the pros and cons of reciprocity were debated in the American government, in the press, and, to a far lesser degree, on main streets across the United States. Congress adjourned early in March, but the legislation was reintroduced into the new Congress in April and, following more debate, it passed through both houses of Congress by the early summer. As noted earlier, Taft formally signed the bill into law on July 26, just as the election campaign was set to begin in Canada.[59]

Throughout the whole period leading up to the September election no formal or official statement was ever issued suggesting that reciprocity with Canada would lead to the annexation of Canada by the United States. In fact, virtually every official statement coming out of Washington stated the exact opposite: that the two countries were just that — *two* countries looking for the mutual benefits of an improved trading relationship. The legislation, accordingly, had no political overtones at all. By the first decade of the twentieth century, overt annexationist thinking in the United States had largely disappeared, to be replaced, at least among those who cared, by a more gentle pro-union feeling. The former was a remnant of the old "manifest destiny" and involved the threat of war and the use of force to bring Canada into the Union; the latter was a more benign understanding based on the thinking that union of the two countries was still a good — even an inevitable — idea, but that the United States would have to wait for the Canadians to come to their senses and openly and freely ask for union with the United States.[60]

There was a distinction between these two streams of American thinking that was lost on many Canadians. For Canadians living in 1911, annexation was not just an ancient historical or theoretical issue. Laurier and Borden were both old enough to remember the war fears along the Canadian-American border during the American Civil War, the Fenian invasions that occurred in the years that followed, and the purchase of Alaska in 1867. Many other Canadians had heard stories at their grandparent's knee of American invasions dating back to the War of 1812, the border crossings of the rebellions era, and the American war with Mexico and the annexation of Texas. Everyone remembered more recent events such as the annexation of Hawaii, the Spanish American War, when the Americans grabbed the Philippines, Guam, Cuba, and Puerto Rico, and the heavy-handed way the Americans acted during the negotiation of the Alaska boundary a few years earlier. Fears of annexation may have been unwarranted, but they were at least understandable. Thus, while Canadians could be thankful that most Americans no longer believed a war to annex Canada was justified (and cross-border talk of celebrating the centenary of the "undefended border" was just then ramping into full gear), it seemed to many Canadians that the American *goal* of annexation remained. Canadians, as a result, took great interest in deciphering comments made about reciprocity in the United States. And usually they didn't need a dictionary or thesaurus to understand what the Americans were saying.

The fact that the Taft administration officially ruled out any movement toward annexation did not prevent Canadians — especially those whose inclinations were to oppose reciprocity — from surveying American newspapers for editorial content and digging into the Congressional Record for nuggets of American annexationist wisdom. Reporters found hours of work in 1911 sifting through stacks of American statements, speeches, newspaper reports and editorials, magazine commentaries, and published letters in search of the damning phrase. If they did not quite stumble across the smoking gun of annexation, they did find plenty of ammunition to be used back home. And, of course, once a quotation was found it took on a life of its own, to be reported, then repeated, distorted, taken out of context, and, in the worst cases, rephrased for emphasis, often conveying a meaning completely unintended by the original source. Clarifications were issued, and occasionally retractions demanded; but by then it was usually too late — the damage was already done.

The American consul-general in Toronto surveyed the press reports and the various resolutions condemning reciprocity in Canada and reported to Washington that "they practically ignore the utterances of the president and Secretary of State on the subject and continue to harp on utterances by others which they think or pretend to think point to annexation as the ultimate purpose and result of the agreement. The Liberal press continues to show the folly of this idea but those who have adopted it refuse to be convinced as they no doubt find it a most useful means of fighting a measure to which they are opposed either on business or party grounds or both."[61]

President Taft set the tone himself in a speech to the Illinois state legislature on February 11. "Canada is at the parting of the ways," he told an American audience. "Shall she be an isolated country, as much separated from us as if she were across the ocean, or shall her people and our people profit by the proximity that our geography furnishes and stimulate the trade across the border that nothing but a useless, illogical and unnecessary tariff wall created?"[62]

No matter how many times the president subsequently tried to explain, modify, or backtrack on his remarks, the phrase "parting of the ways" echoed across Canada until election day and defined the tone of the campaign. Taft had lobbed an easy one for the Conservatives to hit right out of the ball park. The choice was clear:

maintain with faith and honour the connection with mother Britain and the Empire or sell the Canadian soul for thirty pieces of American silver. "It cannot be denied," Borden wrote Premier Whitney with not a little understatement, "that his speeches have been of the greatest possible assistance to us."[63]

Similar kinds of assistance arrived from other sources. Congressman James "Champ" Clark, leader of the Democratic Party in the House of Representatives, repeatedly made a point of saying how much he wanted Canada to be a part of the United States and then feigning surprise when Canadians and others got upset. Clark issued the definitive statement connecting reciprocity to annexation in a speech to the American House of Representatives: "I am for it because I hope to see the day when the American flag will float over every square foot of the British North American possessions, clear to the North Pole," he informed the House. "They speak our language, their institutions are much like ours, they are trained in the difficult art of self-government. My judgment is that if the Treaty of 1854 had never been abrogated the chances of a consolidation of the two countries would have been much greater than they are now. I have no doubt whatever that the day is not far distant when Great Britain will joyfully see all her North American possessions become part of this Republic. That is the way things are tending now."[64]

But it was not just Taft, Clark, and a few other politicians. By the time one clarification was made explaining what such American speakers really meant, two or three more indiscretions were uncovered and printed in Canadian newspapers. One senator from Minnesota explained that he could "see only one prospective benefit in this Reciprocity Agreement. It may lead to Canadian Annexation. We cannot hope to annex the rest of the world, but if we can annex Canada we will accomplish a great deal." New York Republican congressman W.S. Bennet went so far as to introduce a congressional resolution calling on the president "to enter upon and prosecute from time to time such negotiations with the British Government as he may deem expedient for the annexation of the Dominion of Canada."[65] The resolution was defeated, of course, but how do you issue "clarifications" for statements like these?

Others pointed to the migration of thousands of Americans to the Canadian West and followed the fact to their own logical conclusions. One Illinois congressman explained it this way:

> What is the history of the American people? We might as well be frank and honest. Americans went to Texas and Americanized it, and it was annexed as a part of this great Union. Americans went into Hawaii, Americanized it, and annexed it. And if these bright young men that the President speaks of in his speech, these clever, active, virile, vigorous young men from the farms of Illinois and the other northern States, thousands and hundreds of thousands of them, go up into that north land, what do you think will be the effect of it? We have 92 millions of people in the United States as compared with seven millions in Canada. Have I not a right to say that it is the first step toward annexation? Have I not a right to believe it? Why have not the Americans that go to Canada a right to believe it?

Some newspapers agreed; the Newark *Star* reported that "every American farmer who settles in Canada takes his nationality with him and helps to loosen the tie which unites Canada to Great Britain. The thousands of American farmers who settle in the northwestern Provinces look to Washington rather than to Ottawa. The time is not far distant when the question of the Annexation of Canada to the United States will have become a burning issue on both sides of the border. And when that time comes the American element in Canada will make itself felt and heard."[66] When the business leaders in Toronto, Montreal, and other cities read words like these in their morning newspapers they must have gasped. All their anxiety about reciprocity seemed confirmed: it would lead to treasonous actions in the West, to the demise of Canada, and to the demise of their transportation and business interests.

The campaign itself only generated modest interest in the United States and elsewhere outside the country. Canadians living abroad wrote many letters home that were published in local newspapers supporting both sides in the debate, and a few major American and British newspapers covered the campaign. Most American papers favoured reciprocity, with the chain of newspapers controlled by William Randolph Hearst being especially keen.[67] There were also a few sensational international stories that did little to help improve relations between the two countries. On September 10, for example, the Seattle *Sunday Times* warned of potential attacks on American consulates in Canada and falsely reported that thousands of Americans were returning to the United States as the election approached. "So unpleasant are things in Canada at this time for Americans, that our people… are coming home early."[68]

The American consul-general in Vancouver downplayed such hysterics, but was aware of the tensions unleashed by the debate over reciprocity. Earlier in the summer the American flag above the American Consulate in Vancouver had been stolen by a local teenager and the consul-general declined to press charges. If the story leaked, he wrote, there would be "no telling of what the sensational newspaper reporters, of whom there are plenty here as well as at home, would have made of it." He thought it best, owing "to the pending reciprocity proceedings to handle the matter in a quiet way, to keep it out of the Press and to await instructions from the Department."[69]

American ruminations became so embarrassing during the campaign that Laurier asked the American government to tone it down, as such comments were doing more harm than good. The message to the White House was clear: "Silence is golden," and "the least said the soonest mended."[70] "This talk of annexation is bosh," said Taft over and over again in different ways, but to no effect. Right up to the end, Taft remained confident that Canadian opinion would come around to the agreement. He expressed "great surprise" to the British ambassador just days before the election that "it should have been supposed in Canada that there was any design in the United States to bring about a political union of the two countries, or that this Agreement looked in the smallest degree thereto."[71] However considered, the constant flow of indiscreet comments from American politicians and newspaper editors handed a huge advantage to the Conservative opposition and Canadian opponents of reciprocity.

For the Conservatives, the persistent comments and indiscretions from south of the border were a godsend, and as the Tory candidates left for their ridings to launch their individual campaigns, each carried a strong message for the country that could be hauled out at every street corner, church picnic, and town hall: reciprocity meant annexation and the end of the British Empire in Canada and, perhaps, even the end of Canada as a separate entity. This was a powerful message and it was a message for which the Liberals had little to offer in return other than statistics that promised more trade and lower prices.

As the formal campaigning began in August the lines of the campaign were sharply drawn. The Liberals had the advantages of power and, despite the glaring organizational problems, in reciprocity they had an issue to fight for and a policy that likely would appeal to a broad cross-section of the country, but especially to rural Canadians and westerners. And they had a leader whose charisma and charm remained strong, not only in Quebec but across the whole country. Laurier's personal appeal to Canadians was a factor that the Conservatives would never underestimate.

Conversely, the Conservatives, hungry for power after fifteen years in opposition, had more reason for optimism than at any time in years, and the prospect of victory only whetted their appetite for a fight. They also had considerable advantages in that they were better prepared and organized at the local level, and Borden had brought together a broad informal coalition of groups and individuals in support of his party — including provincial premiers, the Toronto and Montreal business communities, Bourassa and the *nationalistes* in Quebec, and individuals from Clifford Sifton to Sir William Van Horne. Intentionally or not, he had also sharply polarized the country — urban Canada versus rural Canada, central Canada versus the Prairies — and he was playing one part off the other. That all these groups and individuals were united more by their desire to defeat Laurier and the Liberals than by anything else might not have been the best recipe for constructing a future government or for governing a country like Canada, but in the weeks leading up to the 1911 election it began to look more and more like a winning combination.

CHAPTER 8

THE CAMPAIGN IN ENGLISH CANADA

It is her own soul that Canada risks today.
— RUDYARD KIPLING

"They're off!" proclaimed *Saturday Night* magazine. "From now until the eve of polling, the land will be deluged with showers of oratory." It would be a tough campaign, and not always a fair or high-minded one. "The campaign now proceeding bids fair to be a record-breaker for personalities, and the exchange of lurid compliments. Both parties are likely to be mutual sinners in this respect, and the candidate who can convince the electorate that his opponent is a knave, paltroon [*sic*], and totally unfit to sit in Parliament, is the one who will win out. Politics in Canada are yet in the elementary stage of development, and the slogan will be: 'When you see a head hit it!'"[1]

The first two weeks following the dissolution of Parliament were filled with planning, the preparation of campaign literature, and the nomination of candidates for each constituency. Following the last cabinet meeting, the government ministers travelled to their ridings and began preparing for their own campaigns. Laurier worked in Ottawa and conferred with various strategists and allies as they passed through the capital, including Liberal premiers A.L. Sifton of Alberta and Walter Scott of Saskatchewan, who were returning home from the coronation.

He also met with A.K. Maclean, the Nova Scotia Attorney General, while William Fielding and Sir Frederick Borden met with Premier Murray of Nova Scotia in Montreal. All the provincial Liberals, including Premier Lomer Gouin of Quebec, promised active support for the party in the election.[2] Robert Borden was equally busy and his party's organization was primed and ready to go. "Undoubtedly we shall be confronted by desperate tactics on the part of the Government," he wrote Premier Whitney.[3] But Borden had recently returned from an exhaustive and what he believed to be a very productive western trip, and his spirits were high.

Although he spent far more time in his native province, Laurier opened his campaign in Ontario, at Simcoe, in Norfolk County, on August 15. The town was decorated with flags and banners, and Laurier was escorted from the train station to the local park by a procession of automobiles. The *Canadian Annual Review* recorded that it was "an immense out-door gathering" of mainly rural folk, where Laurier rallied the crowd with words that would soon be repeated many times: that Sir John A. Macdonald had been "the Moses of Reciprocity who failed to reach the Promised Land; he would be the Joshua who would lead the people of Canada to the goal." He dismissed all thoughts of disloyalty and annexation, telling the crowd, "If I were privileged to address an American audience I would tell them: 'We want to trade with you but if the price we are to pay for it is the sacrifice of our manhood, keep your trade, we will have none of it.'"[4] His focus was reciprocity and the benefits the agreement would bring to the country — "reciprocity was his theme from start to finish, and he showed clearly that reciprocity was the big issue of the battle."[5]

Laurier left for Quebec shortly after his speech, but the style established the first day in Simcoe remained for the duration of the campaign in English Canada: at every stop the people would be provided with a healthy portion of the benefits of reciprocity served up with plenty of warmth and charm. "He was in good form," reported the Ottawa *Citizen*, "and the sunny smile being oft in evidence, and time after time the great audience cheered him to the echo."[6] Laurier was also accompanied on the stage in Simcoe by several younger regional ministers — George Graham, Mackenzie King, and Rodolphe

Lemieux — and this, too, became common during the campaign. Most candidates stayed in their own ridings and looked after their own campaigns, occasionally making an appearance in a nearby constituency. For these candidates, it was an added bonus if the prime minister or party leader came through town. Cabinet ministers, however, had regional responsibilities and usually were called away from their ridings to appear with the leader or to help other candidates in their ridings. For example, at a large Liberal meeting in Stratford, Ontario, on September 8, Laurier shared the stage with several Liberal candidates, including Graham, King, and Hugh Guthrie. Trains were hired to bring people to the meeting from Woodstock, Sarnia, Mount Forest, and elsewhere in the region.[7]

The Opposition leader launched his campaign in London, Ontario, on August 15. He lunched with the Conservative Association and gave a speech that night at the opera house. An automobile procession, a band, and some two thousand people made it a memorable occasion. A day earlier, Borden had issued an election manifesto which reflected fairly standard Conservative policies that had been adopted over previous years. The Conservatives promised to build the Hudson Bay Railway, extend state control over terminal grain elevators, promised help for the "chilled meat industry" and various other rural improvements from free mail delivery to the extension of public highways. They also promised to grant the Prairie provinces control over their natural resources. Much closer to Borden's heart, the Conservatives also promised broad civil service reform and a new method to oversee and supervise public expenditures. Conservative naval policy was noticeably muted, although Borden did indicate that his government's policy would be submitted to a plebiscite, a commitment that did not escape the *nationaliste* press in Quebec.

The focus of the Conservative platform, however, was reciprocity, and it reasserted everything that the Conservatives had been saying since February. The Liberals had no mandate to introduce reciprocity and it would overthrow everything that had been accomplished under the National Policy. It was a bad economic idea that would hurt business as well as the farmers, fishers, and workers of Canada, and it would tie Canada too closely to the United States. Accepting reciprocity would open up the Canadian market to foreign competition and domination by American trusts and threaten all the prosperity and economic growth that Canada had experienced for more than a decade. Most important, it would mean turning against the British connection. It was about the survival of the country: "The true issue is this. Shall we continue in the course which has led us to our present enviable position of prosperity and national development, or shall we, at the moment of greatest success and achievement, lose heart and abandon the fight for national existence?"[8]

Borden made reciprocity his issue in English Canada and closely linked it to patriotism and loyalty to the Empire. Like Laurier, he also appeared with party candidates, although instead of ministers he was usually accompanied by provincial politicians and other luminaries, such as Clifford Sifton. Other leading Conservatives — especially those who might desire a cabinet seat should Borden win — undertook regional campaigns that often overlapped with Borden. Sir George Foster, one of the leading, if not the most popular, Conservatives, juggled his own riding campaign duties with a gruelling provincial campaign that crisscrossed Ontario. "So begins what will prove one of the most important elections ever held in Canada," he wrote in his diary on August 6. Foster was the Conservative candidate in Toronto North, but he spoke in North Bay, Paris, Brampton, Cobalt, Wingham, Hanover, and several other towns. At Woodstock, Ontario, he filled in for Borden when the latter's voice gave out. Late in August he travelled to the Maritimes (and had an unexpected meeting with Laurier en route) and spoke at Moncton, Picton, Antigonish, and Halifax before returning to Ottawa on September 6.[9]

Borden spent the first two weeks of the campaign in Ontario, arriving in Simcoe two days after Laurier, on August 17. From there he travelled through much of rural southwestern Ontario, with stops in Woodstock, Harriston, Owen Sound, Berlin, and Guelph.[10] In Harriston, when challenged by a heckler who cried out "Let us have what Sir John A. Macdonald wanted when he went to Washington in 1873," Borden replied that in 1891 Sir John had called reciprocity "veiled treason," and how times had changed. Reciprocity might have been attractive then, but in the new, prosperous Canada it was no longer necessary and even dangerous.[11] His statements were regularly punctuated with references to President Taft and other Americans with apparent annexationist designs on Canada. In Berlin, he faced a somewhat hostile crowd of Liberals who reportedly broke out in cheers at the very mention of Mackenzie King, the Liberal candidate and minister of labour.[12] But it was not the only time that Borden made speeches in the ridings of Liberal cabinet ministers.

On August 23 he arrived in Toronto for a massive rally at Massey Hall where he was accompanied by Foster, Thomas White, and several others of the Toronto Eighteen. From Toronto he travelled east to Peterborough, Napanee, and Brockville before crossing into Quebec on August 29. He travelled by car, over the rolling hills of eastern Ontario, visiting Campbellford, Belleville, and Napanee. "Two dead chickens and a frightened old lady, who fell in the road as the car slowed up," wrote the Toronto *Star*, "made up the score of casualties." In Napanee he was joined by the eminent senator Sir Mackenzie Bowell, one of the last Conservative prime ministers, who was old enough to tell the audience of his active opposition to the Reciprocity Treaty of 1854.[13]

Everywhere he went, Borden essentially repeated the same speech with a few local variations, but it did not matter whether he was addressing a crowd of thousands in Massey Hall or the eight hundred who came to hear him in the rain in Warkworth, he attacked reciprocity and wrapped himself in the Union Jack in an effort to save Canada from certain ruin.[14] "The people seem very greatly impressed," he explained to one reporter, "with the very grave significance of President Taft's utterances, and especially with his declaration that Canada stands 'at the parting of the ways,' and that the bond which unites this Dominion to the Mother Country is 'light and almost imperceptible.'" To the same reporter he refused to comment on "the situation in Quebec."[15]

As noted above, there was no reason for Borden to discuss "the situation in Quebec" while in Ontario. Nevertheless, Quebec and what it represented — the French language and Roman Catholicism — was an undercurrent in the Ontario campaign, more a presence than a specific issue. The uproar over French language education in eastern Ontario that would soon explode into a national debate, the various blasts of

Ontario Orangemen over the spread and apparently sinister nature of Catholicism, the tensions between Irish and French Catholics within Ontario, the angry outbursts over the *Ne Temere* decree, which suggested that mixed marriages between Catholics and Protestants were invalid, all combined with the general pro-British, imperialist enthusiasm that pervaded the time. Anti-French and anti-Catholic feelings rarely emerged in speeches, or at rallies and demonstrations, or in the mainstream newspapers, and it is hard to estimate how many Ontarians voted on this basis, but these feelings were real and they lingered under the surface throughout the campaign. As one Liberal organizer wrote, "the whole tory campaign in Ontario to-day is an anti-French crusade because of our Leader's French-Canadian origin."[16]

Once Borden left the province for the east, the local candidates and the provincial party carried on, led by Premier Whitney, who had agreed to make at least ten appearances during the campaign.[17] The message of loyalty and anti-reciprocity was heard from one end of the province to the other thanks to the thorough canvassing of Whitney, Foster, Frank Cochrane, a variety of federal and provincial Conservative politicians, Sifton, White, other members of the Toronto Eighteen, former Liberal businessmen, and their sympathetic newspapers. The campaign was well-organized and financed. "The enemy seems to have so much money that they are spending it in a lavish and reckless matter," complained George Graham in Brockville. Graham remained optimistic about Liberal chances but he was aware of Conservative strength, even in his own riding.[18]

Laurier visited Ontario again on September 4, but only spent five days touring before returning to Quebec. He campaigned to his strengths — in eastern Ontario with stops in Glengarry County and Cornwall, to the north with speeches in Sudbury and North Bay, and then to the south — to Barrie, Stratford, London, and all the way to Windsor, where he was met by a crowd estimated (by Liberals) at ten thousand.[19] In Sudbury he was met with a loud chant of "down with Bourassa" from the mixed anglophone and francophone audience.[20] In Cobourg, he again evoked the name of Sir John A. and then made a personal attack on Borden, describing the Conservative Party "like a ship without a rudder, mast, or captain."[21] Laurier bypassed the Tory stronghold of Toronto altogether, and by September 10 he was gone, off to finish the campaign in Quebec.

Without Laurier the campaign in Ontario fell to a mixture of old and new Liberals. As noted above, cabinet ministers Graham, King, Charles Murphy, and William Paterson made multiple appearances across the province, in some cases ignoring the problems in their own ridings. Other Liberals who were not seeking re-election, including Allen Aylesworth and Sir Richard Cartwright, canvassed on behalf of other candidates. Senator Cartwright, the son of a Loyalist, a former Liberal minister of finance, and still a member of Laurier's government, took special umbrage at the accusations of disloyalty. "So far as I have been able to trace it," he told a Toronto audience with a sexist flourish, "this cry of loyalty appears to have taken its origin from certain hysterical women of the male sex, chiefly resident in Toronto."[22]

The provincial wing of the party also contributed, in particular Newton W. Rowell, the well-respected Toronto lawyer and soon-to-be provincial Liberal leader. Rowell, like many Ontario Liberals, displayed strong Protestant views tinged with anti-Catholicism and was attracted to many things about Borden, including his call for civil service reform and the removal of patronage from politics. But he also supported Laurier's naval policy and reciprocity, which put him at odds with many of his friends, including several of the Toronto Eighteen.[23] Rowell did not contest a seat in the election but he made dozens of pro-reciprocity speeches and was particularly scathing in his denunciation of the "unholy alliance," turning the patriotism argument on its head. "Liberals are true Loyalists, not merely lip Loyalists," he wrote in the Toronto *Globe*. "Who gave us British preference? The Liberals. Who gave us the Imperial penny postage? The Liberals. Who sent the first Canadian contingent to cover itself with glory by aiding Britain? Sir Wilfrid Laurier. Who refused to send a contingent to aid Britain in the Egyptian campaign [in 1885]? Sir John A. Macdonald."[24]

Two influential Toronto papers, the *Globe* and the *Star*, and their editors (J.A. Macdonald and J.E. Atkinson respectively) also gave steady support for the party and reciprocity, and the *Star* was partly responsible for one of the oddest events of the campaign. In an effort to show how the lower prices for meat purchased in Buffalo would be transferred to Toronto as a result of reciprocity, the *Star* set up a display in its office window of refrigerated meat products and the differing prices from the two cities. When Joseph Flavelle and Willison's *Evening News* found out they responded with angry letters to the *Star* and with their own competing displays of cooked hams and choice meat cuts in their office windows in downtown Toronto.[25]

The Liberals were at a general disadvantage in Ontario; still, the contest was very close in many ridings and in each there were local issues and circumstances that played on the outcome. The urban ridings, especially in Toronto, were Conservative, but outside Toronto many ridings included both urban and rural districts and a different balance between Protestant and Catholic. Also, in several eastern and northern ridings there was a significant francophone population, and in many others it was suspected that the ethnic makeup of the riding shaped the way people voted.

Mackenzie King's riding of Waterloo North, for example, was a bellwether constituency and a good indicator of Ontario attitudes. Waterloo North contained a mixture of urban and rural areas, including parts of the towns of Berlin and Waterloo. In 1911 the riding population was a little over 33,000, with a 60/40 urban–rural split. What made it a little different was that over two-thirds of the population was of German descent. Mackenzie King realized that reciprocity would be a very difficult sell in his riding, especially if it included manufactured goods. Berlin was a regional manufacturing centre and hundreds of workers depended on manufacturing jobs.[26]

King was a strong candidate — a sitting MP and cabinet minister, an emerging leader of the Liberal Party, an effective orator, and a thorough campaigner. He knew his riding and decided to focus on canvassing the factories over the rural areas, probably believing that he could count on rural support. As a cabinet minister and rising Liberal star, he was expected to help in other ridings and to appear at larger rallies with the prime minister and others. By the time the election was over he had campaigned in every part of his own riding and made appearances in seventeen other ridings.[27]

King's opponent was William George "Billy" Weichel, a local merchant and mayor of Waterloo. He did not have King's national profile but he could count on considerable support from the urban population, he was popular candidate, and he spoke German fluently. King had studied German in school and made speeches in German in the 1908 election in an effort to appeal to his German constituents, but in 1911 he did not, perhaps because he did not share Weichel's fluency and could not compete in that language. Like Conservatives everywhere, Weichel spoke of the dangers of reciprocity and of the threat it posed to Berlin's manufacturing interests and he warned of the prospects of annexation should the Liberals win.[28]

King was also hampered by his record as a cabinet minister. In 1910 he had acted as a mediator in the strike of the Grand Trunk Railway's conductor and trainmen unions. He helped end the strike and earned considerable initial praise for his actions, but the company's truculent refusal to implement all elements of the settlement's terms, especially dealing with the reinstatement of the employees and the workers' pensions, sparked criticism of the government and King for their inaction and inability to resolve the problem. King maintained the support of several of the union's leaders, but the criticism of his action was a factor in the loss of Liberal support, especially in ridings with a large population of railway workers.[29] He also shared in the criticism of the government following the collapse of the Toronto-based Farmers' Bank. Neither King nor the government was responsible for the bank's failure, but the government was attacked for its lack of action and apparent indifference to the plight of those affected.[30]

King also caused a minor stir on the naval issue when he attacked Borden for his willingness to send money to Great Britain, as he told the people of Berlin, "to build warships to fight Germany." King was accused of playing for the "racial vote" in appealing to the German-Canadians of Waterloo North to oppose Borden because of his naval plans. The *Halifax Herald* exploded in sanctimonious rage, labelling King "worse than Bourassa or Monk" for besmirching Borden's character. "Better, a thousand times better," the *Herald* announced, "a Bourassa or a Monk preaching a crusade of indifference to Canada's honor and Britain's safety through the parishes of Quebec than a W.L.M. King seeking to rouse Canadians of German origin against R.L. Borden."[31] The Liberal

naval policy was not popular among the German-Canadian population in the riding, which was largely opposed to both a direct contribution to the Royal Navy and an independent Canadian navy because
both were seen to be directed against a perceived German threat.[32]

Ontario was the key for both campaigns, and it was here that
the election would ultimately be decided. Both parties claimed the
advantage and appeared confident of victory, but the Conservatives
had more reason for confidence. "The main issue is strong," Laurier
reported to the governor general, "but there are in several constituencies local troubles which are likely to jeopardize a few seats."[33] This
turned out to be a bit of an understatement.

Both party leaders toured the Maritimes. The Liberals held the edge from
1908 with twenty-six of the region's thirty-five seats, and two provinces
(Nova Scotia and Prince Edward Island) passed pro-reciprocity resolutions, but in 1911 both parties saw potential growth in the Maritimes.
The Conservative leader was a Nova Scotian, and his home province had
increasingly come to embrace him, while the Liberals offered several
powerful Maritime cabinet ministers, including Fielding, Pugsley, and
Frederick Borden. The Liberals believed that Maritime fishers, farmers, and miners would benefit from an open American market and that
reciprocity would help stop the flow of young Maritimers to the New
England fishing industry. With better access to the American market,
there would be more trade — and more jobs at home. The Conservatives
countered that reciprocity would destroy the growing east–west trade
within Canada for the products of the Maritimes. Under the expanding
concept of Confederation, central Canada was the "home" market for
Maritime products. With reciprocity, would Ontario not buy more of its
coal from Pennsylvania rather than from Cape Breton? In the general era
of prosperity, they argued, why take a chance on a new policy that might
damage or threaten what they already had?[34] Plus, there was the loyalty
argument that reciprocity meant severing the bond between Maritimers
and the motherland. Given that no one could be absolutely sure what the
consequences of reciprocity would be, the campaign in the Maritimes
was guaranteed to be wide open.

Laurier's entourage travelled in a private rail car and passed into New Brunswick on August 28. His first stop was Saint John. Over the next six days he travelled to Digby, Halifax, Truro, New Glasgow, across to Charlottetown, with stops in Summerside and Montague, and then to Moncton on September 2.[35] At every stop, and at many more along the way (Shubenacadie, Nova Scotia, for example, got him for fifteen minutes), he was accompanied by local candidates and a variety of cabinet ministers, and many times also by lights, flags, bunting, choirs, children, a procession of some kind, and throngs of adoring supporters. In Stellarton, Nova Scotia, Liberal supporters were treated to the spectacle of a baseball game with Laurier pitching to William Fielding — "it must be said that political doctrines are safer than his baseball curves," reported the Toronto *Star*.[36] In Saint John he lunched at the Union Club, then was brought to the Victoria skating rink by sixty illuminated automobiles and half a dozen bands and was honoured to review the parade before entering the rink to make his speech.[37] It was a reception "never before witnessed in the Loyalist City of St. John."[38]

Crossing the Bay of Fundy was a challenge for Laurier, who was prone to seasickness; he spent most of the voyage on deck "hanging on to the stanchion and gazing gloomily into the fog. In the flying spray, with his white plumes drooping and limp, he made a mournful and solitary figure."[39] At Digby, even though the sea trip had "worked havoc with his inward organizations,"[40] there were close to three thousand people to hear him speak in the pouring rain under a giant "welcome" arch on a platform with the words "Our leader: the man we trust."

That night an equally large gathering received him at Kentville. The biggest event was scheduled for Halifax, where almost eight thousand attended the Halifax Arena. Banners surrounded the hall: "Reciprocity and Prosperity," "You can trust Laurier and Fielding," "Now is Nova Scotia's greatest opportunity," and other similarly uplifting platitudes.[41] Laurier shared the stage with many Liberal luminaries, including Fielding, Frederick Borden, Premier Murray, a variety of senators, and several local Liberal candidates. In Prince Edward Island, where it was still raining, there were a reported "10,000 welcomes" for the prime minister.[42]

At most stops Laurier repeated the same message about the benefits of reciprocity, sometimes dressed up in local colours for local consumption. In Nova Scotia he raised the memory of Joseph Howe and pointed to Fielding as the "father" of reciprocity and the British preferential tariff.[43] Over and over again he reviewed the details of the agreement and denounced Borden, the "unholy alliance," and all anti-reciprocity forces for trying to lead the people astray. More often than not he raised the memory of Sir John A., not always with the "He was the Moses, I am the Joshua" line, but always with the intent of linking himself, Sir John A., and reciprocity together.[44]

Borden focused on Ontario for the first part of the campaign and, following a very brief stop in Quebec, carried on to the Maritimes at the start of September to finish out the last three weeks of the campaign. He visited many of the same towns as Laurier had, including Saint John, Charlottetown, Summerside, Moncton, New Glasgow, and Halifax. He spoke alongside various Conservative notables, including Premier Hazen of New Brunswick (who also accompanied Borden to Prince Edward Island), local Conservative candidates and provincial politicians, and, on different occasions, Clifford Sifton and Sir William Van Horne. In Halifax he was joined on stage by his old law partner Sir Charles Hibbert Tupper, former cabinet minister and son of the venerable Nova Scotian and Father of Confederation Sir Charles Tupper, who travelled all the way from Vancouver to save Nova Scotia from reciprocity.

Throughout Borden's tour, the crowds and demonstrations matched those given to Laurier and his meetings were widely reported as festive and historic moments in Maritime political history. In Charlottetown there were two bands and a torchlight procession; later that day, among the farmers of Souris, Borden's attack on reciprocity was so moving it reportedly provoked a spontaneous outbreak of "Rule Britannia."[45] In New Glasgow the meeting was "joyous, glad, enthusiastic and attentive," reported the *Herald*, and Borden was met with "an enthusiasm far more intense and spontaneous" than the one experienced by Laurier ten days earlier.[46] In Liverpool, Nova Scotia, with less than a week left in the campaign, Borden's meeting coincided with a rally for Fielding. Borden had the Court House while the Liberals hired a tent for Fielding. Both sides had a band, flags, and cheering crowds.[47] Mutual challenges for a debate were issued, but none was accepted.

Everywhere he went Borden ridiculed the Liberals for promising harbour development and shipbuilding contracts for every port from Halifax to Victoria, but he was quick to promise railway extension in eastern Nova Scotia and to alleviate freight rates, highway development, and other public works expenditures across the Maritimes, and, if feasible, a tunnel connecting Prince Edward Island to the mainland.[48] But the thrust of his speeches again focused on reciprocity and the British connection. Rather than referencing Moses and Sir John A., Borden repeated the names Taft and Champ Clark, and with them the spectre of annexation, and he appealed to the sons of Loyalists to think of their children and to do what was right for them.[49]

The campaign in the Maritimes also consisted of regional issues and multiple individual contests. Not unexpectedly, the impact of reciprocity on the region's industries was extensively debated; railway expansion, highways, and harbour development all were regional issues. The debate over reciprocity also revealed regional overtones and was denounced or heralded as the solution to Maritime economic problems. For some it would destroy the growing integration of the Maritimes in the Canadian economy and set the region adrift; to others, reciprocity was the key to future prosperity for the region — the chance at last to retrieve fragments of that "golden age" that once had been. Even for some of those who supported reciprocity, it was expressed with a degree of regionalism; no one needed to teach Nova Scotians anything about loyalty, announced the *Morning Chronicle* early in the campaign. The Upper Canadians had stolen Maritime trade and markets, and now the "big interests" in Upper Canada "are hiring newspapers and cheap politicians to tell us that we are disloyal to think of recovering what we lost to them."[50]

In Saint John, William Pugsley faced a significant Conservative challenge, and the stalled railway expansion in the province was regarded as a major hindrance by some,[51] but by the end of the campaign he was ready to predict a Liberal sweep in the province.[52] He proved to be over-optimistic. Premier Hazen campaigned for the

Conservatives; his enthusiasm for Borden increasing once he received a promise for a subsidy for a Saint John Valley railway line.[53]

In Nova Scotia, Fielding was hampered by bad health and a voice that gave way fairly early in the campaign. Newspapers from both sides reported on his inability to speak; in New Glasgow the prime minister refused to let him speak even though he was on the platform

Frederick Borden, July 1905.

Courtesy LAC, PA-025997.

and appeared willing.[54] Sir Frederick Borden was less of a factor in the campaign, as he remained in Ottawa anticipating an appointment as high commissioner to Great Britain. When the appointment evaporated (Lord Strathcona had long indicated that he wanted to retire, but stubbornly did not step down) he rushed to Nova Scotia, but he missed much of the campaign.

The weak showing of these two cabinet ministers only put more of the responsibility on the prime minister and it also led to difficulties in their own ridings. In Shelburne-Queen's there was reluctance to take a chance on reciprocity, especially in the important fishing and lumber sectors, and Fielding, perhaps suffering from a little over-confidence, did not campaign extensively or effectively. In Frederick Borden's riding of Kings in the Annapolis Valley, the fruit growers saw little benefit in a larger American market, and his absence for much of the campaign put his seat in jeopardy. He did not help matters when he defended reciprocity by saying "let Winnipeg gets its apples from the Middle States."[55] On September 21, local conditions worked to undermine the re-election of both these cabinet ministers.[56]

———◦—

Neither of the party leaders ventured farther west than Ontario during the campaign, but the comings and goings of the national leaders and other major players were followed closely by rival newspapers all across the West. Consequently, no westerner needed to have been unaware of the major issues, personalities, and events of the campaign. The specific western campaign was left on its own, however, with its own regional and local leaders. In reality, there were several election campaigns in the West unfolding simultaneously, with dozens of unique local contests evolving independently of the national campaign.

There were a few shared regional issues. For one, the census redistribution would have meant more seats and a stronger western voice in Ottawa, but the calling of the election put that off to a later date. In addition, all the Western provinces shared a growing sense of isolation from Ottawa and the government, which having been Liberal for the previous fifteen years could only favour the Conservatives. Moreover, by 1911, the provincial demand for "better terms" reverberated all through the West. Alberta and Saskatchewan were equally united in their demand for the transfer of control over their natural resources from the central to the provincial governments. It was an issue that had rankled relations with Ottawa for years. There was also a kind of unity in rural areas for tariff reductions. The Prairie farmers' organizations all participated in the "Siege of Ottawa" in December 1910, and they expressed their continuing support for lower tariffs when meeting both party leaders during their western trips. This support was maintained during the election campaign, although the active engagement of the farmers' organizations varied from province to province.[57]

In British Columbia the economy was booming under the leadership of Premier McBride, known variously as "Glad-hand Dick" and "the people's Dick." Described by *Saturday Night* magazine as a "manly man" who made "no bones of the fact that he hates reciprocity and will join with Mr. Borden in fighting it 'to the bitter end,'" McBride crossed the province making dozens of speeches, including stops in Victoria, Vancouver, Cranbrook, Kamloops, and Revelstoke, and warned of the dangers of reciprocity and annexation and the threat to Canada's nationhood and the British connection should the Liberals win.[58] Early in the campaign, McBride promised that he would oversee a "clean sweep" for the Conservatives in British Columbia.[59] It was one promise he was able to deliver.

One of the very few bumps for McBride was in Vancouver, where his hand-picked candidate for the Conservative nomination was challenged by a young Conservative businessman, H.H. "Harry" Stevens. McBride was unable to insert his Attorney General, William Bowser, over the objections of the riding association, and Stevens went on to win both the nomination and the seat with a huge majority in September. Like most other Conservatives, the British-born Stevens avoided the naval debate and ran on his opposition to reciprocity and on local issues.[60]

The Liberals, both federal and provincial, were less prepared and ultimately no match for McBride and his provincial organization. One Liberal, even when trying to be optimistic about Liberal chances in the province, warned Laurier that "we have a powerful organization arrayed against us in the local Government machinery, and are fighting against heavy odds."[61] William Templeman, Laurier's minister of mines, in particular, was attacked and forced to defend the Liberals' immigration policy. Despite raising the Chinese head-tax, tightening immigration restrictions, and passing various other kinds of restrictive legislation, the Liberals were seen as not vigilant enough in restricting the influx of Asian immigrants to British Columbia and were rumoured to be willing to relax some of the rules.[62] Reciprocity was also a harder sell in the urban areas of Vancouver and Victoria and among the fruit growers of the Okanagan Valley.

Reciprocity was a popular policy in Alberta and Saskatchewan and other than in a few urban ridings the Liberals were confident of victory. Earlier in the year the Liberal provincial government in Saskatchewan, led by Premier Walter Scott, passed a resolution endorsing reciprocity, and even the provincial Conservative leader, F.W.G. Haultain, spoke in favour of it and voted for it. Haultain tried to backtrack on his support during the election campaign, but to little effect.[63] Liberal newspapers insisted that the only issue was reciprocity and condemned the Conservatives for trying to "drag in extra issues and run the fight along the usual lines of insinuation and scandal."[64] So long as reciprocity remained *the* issue, the Liberals had reason to be confident, and the predictions were that the Conservatives would fail to win a single seat.[65]

Similarly, in Alberta the Liberal government endorsed reciprocity and the United Farmers of Alberta broke with their normal policy and urged their members to vote in favour of it.[66] There were a few Conservative newspapers in Calgary and Edmonton that supported the Conservatives and fought along the lines of Empire and loyalty, but it was an uphill fight. The Liberal provincial government led by Premier Arthur Sifton (Clifford Sifton's brother) supported the Liberal candidates and Sifton and other provincial politicians spoke many times during the campaign. Sifton publicly raised the issue of provincial control of natural resources during the campaign but this act neither damaged the Liberal vote in Alberta nor prompted any response from Ottawa.[67]

Liberal confidence was so high that it might have inadvertently aided one Conservative candidate. In Calgary, R.B. Bennett, the wealthy lawyer and businessman, had refused offers to run for the

Conservatives in 1908, choosing, instead, to run provincially in 1909. In 1911, Bennett returned to federal politics and heartily endorsed the Conservative platform. Bennett saw it as a great opportunity to get out of provincial politics, and he ran in Calgary against reciprocity, against continentalism, and against Liberals in general.[68] Bennett was a great "Empire-man" and he sincerely believed that reciprocity was a move in the wrong direction. Bennett was also one of the brightest and most talented persons anywhere in Alberta politics and his personal popularity alone attracted votes. As the publisher of the *Calgary News Telegram* wrote to Laurier, "we fear a considerable number will take it for granted that reciprocity will win and will vote for Mr. Bennett for the sake of the quality of representation he is capable of giving."[69]

In what became the most interesting race in the Alberta campaign, Bennett confronted a difficult challenge in Calgary, where even with the backing of most of the business community, he faced formidable opposition from the provincial and federal Liberals. But Bennett spoke well, was rich enough to finance his own campaign, and he faced down all Liberals, farmers, and hecklers with his patriotism and commitment to the Empire. As the Toronto *Globe* described it, Bennett, "ex-C.P.R. solicitor, has been getting after the newcomers, especially the British newcomers, and working on their feelings with fearful tales of what will happen when Canada has become an annex

Courtesy LAC, PA-181093.

Richard B. Bennett, Delaware, Alberta, September 4, 1911.

of the American Republic."[70] The Calgary *Eye Opener*, which had "ever and anon experienced hard feelings towards R.B.," came around to endorse him because of his personal qualities.[71]

In Manitoba, things were a little different. The population consisted of a greater percentage of people with roots in Ontario and Britain; there was a sharper contest between rural and urban than in Saskatchewan and Alberta; and reciprocity faced a major opponent in Premier Rodmond Roblin. Robert Rogers, Roblin's minister of public works and a man who, according to Regina's *The Morning Leader*, "has developed the art of machine politics to a science," organized the Conservative campaign in Manitoba, and the opposition to reciprocity was much more focused.[72] Roblin toured the province, speaking in multiple ridings right up to election day, all the while denouncing reciprocity and linking it with continentalism and annexation while defending the National Policy and linking it with honour, imperialism, and the Empire.

This was the message embraced by the relatively new backbencher Arthur Meighen in Portage la Prairie. Meighen had not participated in the debate on reciprocity earlier in the year but he was a staunch protectionist and supporter of the National Policy. His loyalty to the British connection was fundamental (even though he had, five years earlier, named his son Theodore Roosevelt Meighen) and he saw the tariff as an arm of economic policy, to be used in nation-building. In Portage la Prairie, where reciprocity was popular, he argued that the benefits of the deal weren't as good as might be expected and that the agreement would re-orient the east–west nature of Canadian trade. Never one to avoid a good debate, Meighen went so far as to attend the meetings of his Liberal opponent, the Reverend Robert Patterson, and interrupted and challenged him on his statements.[73]

Even more important than reciprocity, however, the Conservatives focused on other provincial issues that had appeal to the average Manitoban — both rural and urban. There were enough issues on the table: the demand for boundary extension, the desire for a Hudson Bay railway — all reasonable Manitoban demands that were apparently stymied by the Laurier Liberals. As Roblin told a crowd in Beausejour on August 26, "every vote polled for a Laurier candidate is a vote polled to shackle Manitoba; to cripple her enterprise and to handicap her future; to prevent the widening of her horizon and keep her from that place in the Confederation of Canada that she should occupy by virtue of the industry, enterprise, and patriotism of her people."[74] It was an effective strategy.

Liberal strength was in rural Manitoba and support for reciprocity was strongest among farmers and the Grain Growers' Association, and much of the work of the campaign fell on the shoulders of T.C. Norris, the provincial Liberal leader. With no eastern national leader visiting the province, Liberals brought in support from the other Prairie provinces, including Premier Scott from Saskatchewan, who spoke several times in Winnipeg. Not surprisingly, Liberal candidates repeatedly had to demonstrate their loyalty to the Empire and British-connection. J.H. Ashdown, the Liberal candidate in Winnipeg, for example, reminded his constituents that he was "an English-born and an Englishman to the end," but still supported reciprocity, and that support for reciprocity was very high in the United Kingdom itself.[75] Adding to their problems was the fact that Manitoba Liberals could be held accountable for the sins of Ottawa and forced to defend the actions of the Laurier government, and this was not always an easy thing to do, given the existing tensions between Ottawa and Winnipeg.

In Winnipeg, John Dafoe carried the torch for reciprocity through the pages of the *Manitoba Free Press*. Dafoe supported reciprocity for economic reasons and saw no annexation threat behind it; conversely, he loathed imperialist Tories both in Ottawa and Winnipeg and, as noted above, he was scathing in his denunciation of the "unholy" Borden-Bourassa alliance.[76] Editorials regularly explained the benefits of reciprocity and demonstrated the wrong-headedness of its critics. He attacked the "determined and persistent efforts of the Opposition to distort and misrepresent the provisions of the agreement," even though the government had distributed thousands of copies.[77] "The Conservatives show a desire to switch the discussion to other questions," he wrote on another occasion. "This is particularly noticeable in the West. These devices are, however, vain. Reciprocity must remain the sole issue of the campaign."[78] Vain it might have been, but it was also effective.

With less than a week to go in the campaign, *Saturday Night* magazine published its last pre-election issue. By the next week it would all be over, the magazine editorialized, and the "people of Canada will have settled the issue of reciprocity and the present exceedingly rancorous campaign will have ended. Then it is to be hoped that everybody will settle down to business and enjoy the pleasant autumn weather with contented minds. Then many of the arguments that have been raucously shouted and glaringly printed by campaigners on both sides may well be banished to the limbo of oblivion.[79] Two things stood out according to the magazine: the way that the "national side of the agreement has elbowed the more material economic from the canvas and hustings," and the "development of Mr. R.L. Borden as a platform speaker." Earlier, Borden's performances were "as heavy as the average 'home-made' pie," but no more.[80]

The Conservatives also gained a little momentum as the campaign wound down, again from sources outside the party. On September 7, the Montreal *Star* published a front-page story with an appeal to all Canadians from the imperial poet and novelist Rudyard Kipling. "It is her own soul that Canada risks today," he wrote. "Once that soul is pawned for any consideration, Canada must inevitably conform to the commercial, legal, financial, social and ethical standards which will be imposed upon her by the sheer admitted weight of the United States." Continuing with a leap in logic that was not unusual in this campaign, he warned that Canada might be compelled "to admit reciprocity in the murder rate of the United States, which at present, I believe, is something over one hundred and fifty per million per annum." Anyway you looked at it, he concluded, reciprocity would offer Canada little more than "a little ready money which she does not need, and a very long repentance."

Kipling had been prompted into action by his new expatriate-Canadian friend Max Aitken, who was still nursing his wounds after being prevented earlier in the year from returning to Canada to stand for the Conservatives.[81] His words were splashed across Conservative newspapers over the next week; as journalist and author Beckles Willson wrote, Kipling's message was "read and digested by virtually the whole English-speaking voting population of the Dominion."[82] The Liberals had no clear response and Aitken was apparently particularly delighted with the angry reaction of the Liberals to the reference to "the high murder rate on the American side."[83] Queen's professor O.D. Skelton later asked if Kipling "could sell his poetry for hundreds of thousands of American dollars without injuring the perfect bloom of his patented patriotism, could not a Saskatchewan homesteader sell a beef or a loaf of wheat without selling his soul with it?"[84] It was a "bitter and disgraceful appeal to Canada," concluded the *Saint John Globe*. "Surely such trash as this can not affect the mind of any reasonable person."[85] The Conservatives were hoping for just that, however.

With five days to go, other papers were filled with more stories from the United States and calls for annexation. The *Southern Lumber Journal* was quoted with a blunt call for the American government to "straightway demand that negotiations be instituted without delay … for the peaceable annexation of Canada, but for annexation if it should have to come about through conquest." Everywhere across the United States it seemed, at least in Conservative newspapers, that reciprocity was seen as the first step to the inevitable union of the North American continent. The Montreal *Gazette*, for example, published similar comments from several newspapers, including the Detroit *Free Press*, the Washington *Star*, the Cincinnati *Enquirer*, the Philadelphia *Ledger*, the Chicago *Record-Herald*, the Milwaukee *Free Press*, and the New York *American*.[86] Again the Liberals had little rebuttal for this kind of attack.

In a way Kipling was right. By the time English Canadians went to the polls on September 21, the issues had risen far above the material and economic, and Canadians were deciding, if not about their souls, then at least about the future direction of their country and its place in the world. This is not to suggest that self-interest had been removed from the equation or that character and circumstance were absent as factors in the hundreds of ridings across the country, but something greater was at stake. It is hard to imagine many voters disagreeing with the editors of the Ottawa *Citizen*, who wrote on the eve of the vote that "the election to be held tomorrow will be the most important so far in the history of Canada."[87]

CHAPTER 9

"SHAKING OFF THE SHIRT OF NESSUS": THE QUEBEC CAMPAIGN

There is no doubt that the high-fallutin Conservatives of Toronto are hand in hand with the Nationalists of Quebec.
— WILFRID LAURIER, AUGUST 2, 1911[1]

"I need to see you here immediately," Laurier cabled Henri Béland, the MP for Beauce (Quebec) moments after he called the election, "Please answer."[2] Laurier had good reason to summon Béland back to Ottawa. The Quebec campaign was going to be critical because the Liberals faced an unprecedented challenge in being pitted against the Conservative-*nationaliste* alliance. Some ridings still did not have candidates, and the party leadership had to ensure that moneys and strategies were aligned. Laurier was central to the campaign. His first move was to remove Louis-Philippe Brodeur as minister responsible for the navy. Brodeur, whose performance in defending the government's naval policy had been lacklustre at best, was given a seat on the Supreme Court. In his place, Laurier's trusted knight Rodolphe Lemieux would take up the battle, and Béland, a forty-one-year-old doctor, hurried to Ottawa to be sworn in as Lemieux's replacement for Postmaster General. Béland was a friendly man; Laurier liked him very much, but more importantly wanted to give a new face to Quebec Liberalism.

The race in Quebec was different. For one thing, the leader of the opposition was Henri Bourassa, a man who was neither a candidate nor a member of the opposition. The Conservatives, for their part, were not sufficiently strong in the province. Frederick Monk, of course, was still a force to contend with, but his wife was in the last stages of a terminal cancer and he would only make a few appearances in the next seven weeks of the campaign. The other prominent Conservative in Quebec was Herbert Ames, an inveterate imperialist who only spoke a little French. Robert Borden, who did not speak French, avoided Quebec almost completely, except in one game-changing way. On August 14 he adopted the Monk position and announced that any naval policy would be put to a plebiscite and that subtle change to his platform — unanswered by Laurier — galvanized the *nationalistes*. As Bourassa saw it, "Mr. Borden's acceptance of the principle of popular consultation, thereby acknowledging the right of Canada to decide for or against contribution to Imperial defence, made it possible for the Nationalists to fight the Laurier government alongside of him and his party."[3] Laurier was categorical on the use of the navy during his Quebec campaign: it would not be an "imperial navy." He denied that it would participate in Britain's wars unless Parliament agreed and the population agreed, but he never offered a plebiscite. This proved to be a fatal mistake.

Borden visited Montreal only once, on August 30, to give a speech at His Majesty's Theatre. It had a decidedly imperialist flavour, with repeated song cycles that included "O Canada," "The Maple Leaf Forever," "Rule Britannia," and "God Save the King." *Le Devoir*, now unequivocally friendly to Borden, reported that the songs were rendered with gravity and coldness, "perfectly corresponding to the [anglo] saxon audience."[4] Interestingly, the naval issue was not raised by either Borden or the others who spoke that night, but for one oblique reference: G.F. Johnston, one of the Conservative candidates in Montreal, pointed out that the Americans were still willing to field warships on the Great Lakes (they had done so in 1907 and then declared that they would no longer do it). The purpose, simply, was to depict the United States as hostile to Canadian interests.

Borden was introduced by former Montreal mayor Hormidas Laporte as "the only man who merits respect and consideration ... a man of honesty and loyalty whose unassailable reputation commands respect."[5] Borden insisted on the reciprocity issue, pointing out that the best markets for farmers were local ones, followed by British shops. More than that, he was a democrat, a man who wanted to give to the people the right to decide the issue. "I consider, in the name of the Conservative Party, that I have done my duty in giving you the right to express yourself on this question," he said. He took aim at President Taft, and particularly took exception to the message of thanks the American president had sent to the notoriously anti-British William Randolph Hearst for supporting reciprocity with Canada in his many newspapers. He then delivered a message from Ontario: "I have arrived from Ontario," he said, "and I am delighted to know that the people of that province are fully aware of the gravity of the issue that will be decided on September 21st. And that question will be decided in the same manner that the people of Canada in 1891 decided — with a strong expression in favour of Canadian nationality and the British link." Borden travelled the next day to Sherbrooke and Richmond before ending his visit to Quebec. Those events went well, with the attendance of over five thousand people.

The anti-American undertones of the campaign across Canada resonated in Quebec also. Among French-language newspapers, *La Patrie* was most obvious. Beyond stories about how reciprocity would close the port of Montreal and most industries, it likened reciprocity to the wedge of assimilation. "The Americans hate our faith and detest our language," it explained. "A Roman Catholic has never been elected president of the United States. No Catholic school receives its just shares of public taxes in the whole of the United States. Louisiana used to be a French province. The Americans bought it; and now they have extinguished our race, degraded our language into a dialect, and have put our religion aside.... This is not a question of political parties. What must be done is to protect our language, our laws and our faith."[6]

An odd touch of anti-Americanism was the active pursuit of William Randolph Hearst, whose papers were loudest in supporting reciprocity. Early in the campaign, rumours were that his New York *Herald* was likely to open a foreign bureau in Ottawa — a sure sign that annexation was near, according to *La Patrie*.[7] In early September, copies of the so-called "Canadian edition" of the Hearst *Boston American* were seen being handed out for free in Ottawa. Louis-Philippe Pelletier, the Conservative candidate in Quebec County, and Rufus Pope, a former Conservative MP, challenged Hearst to come north and attend a debate in Montreal. "If the trusts function in Canada [against reciprocity]," said Pelletier and Pope, oblivious to the fact that a good portion of the business community in eastern Canada was against reciprocity, "we can see it ourselves. His impudent intrusion cannot be tolerated.... The assertion that the trusts are fighting reciprocity is most absurd. It's a cover-up behind which Hearst is hiding. The annexation of Canada — that is what Hearst wants."[8]

Travelling in Europe, the newspaper magnate surely never received the invitation. "No one here has the slightest authority to speak in his name," came the reply from New York. "He might see fit to answer a courteous telegram sent to him in London; but I certainly would not undertake to forward him a telegram composed of ridiculous misstatements and couched in boorish language and conveying nothing but a convincing impression of the ill-breeding, inaccuracy, and unimportance of the two individuals signing it," wrote back his secretary.[9] The protest against Hearst took place as scheduled, with almost eight thousand people present and most of the local Conservative and *nationaliste* candidates spoke at the event.

Borden could also rely on anti-reciprocity forces in Quebec. *La Patrie* carried regular editorials examining the impact of the agreements on a host of economic activities. It published the "Messages" produced by the Anti-Reciprocity League that highlighted the uncertainties and the risks involved in adopting the trade deal. "Of all the cities in Canada," it wrote, "Montreal has the most benefited from the protective tariff Mr. Fielding wants to tear up."[10] The message in Quebec was essentially the same as in the rest of Canada: "Let's keep Canada for Canadians!"[11] The anti-reciprocity forces targeted the fruit and vegetable growers as well as Montreal manufacturing workers. *La Patrie* was so effective in defending financiers and manufacturers that it actually ran an article on the day after the election reporting how its coverage had won the plaudits of the presidents of the Lake of the Woods Milling, Ogilvie Flour Mills, Montreal Street Works, the Banque Hochelaga, Tooke Brothers, and Alaska Feather & Down.[12]

A number of captains of industry were actively involved in the campaign. Huntley Drummond, the president of the Canada Sugar Refining Company, for instance, convened employees in the plant and explained that reciprocity was contrary to their interests and to the company. He also asked C.J. Doherty, the Conservative candidate in Sainte-Anne, and Louis Coderre, the *nationaliste* candidate in Hochelaga, to speak to the workers.[13] A few days before the election, another dozen companies united forces and held a meeting in the yards of the Belding Paul Company on Saint-Patrice Street in Montreal. An unusual appeal went to the female employees: "If they cannot vote, they still have a father, a brother, a husband who votes. May they make them vote against the reciprocity that will be the ruin of our manufacturers, and consequently yours also because if there is no work, there is no salary."[14]

If Borden could afford to spend so little time in Quebec, it was to make sure the *nationalistes* had the opportunity to occupy all the stage. Bourassa thundered out of the starting gate on August 3 with an all-out attack on Laurier's imperialism and his unreserved support of "participation of the Canadian people in men and money in Imperial wars where the fate of Canada is not at stake." He accused Laurier of entering into secret agreements during the London conference, where "millions of dollars expended and thousands of lives [would be] sacrificed in foreign war, just and unjust." The election of 1911 was nothing but a diversion designed "to impose silence or throw a veil of deceit over his actions in London. [Laurier] wishes at all costs to have his Navy Act forgotten and to shake off the shirt of Nessus which the electors of Drummond-Arthabaska fastened on his back."[15]

Nationaliste candidates ran in thirty-four ridings across the province, although only one actually listed himself as such (Arthur Gilbert in Drummond-Arthabaska), while another identified himself as nationalist-conservative (Olivar Asselin in Saint-Jacques in Montreal). One labelled himself as an "independent" and one as an "independent conservative." The rest all ran under the Conservative banner. The Bourassa candidates, identified as such because he campaigned in their favour, spoke in their favour, or were identified as such in newspaper accounts, were: David L'Espérance (C-Montmagny), Georges Cloutier (C-Beauce), Louis-Philippe Normand (C-Trois-Rivières), Arthur Gilbert (N-Drummond-Arthabaska),Wilfrid Potvin (C-Kamouraska), Louis Morin (C-L'Assomption), Joseph Bégin (C-Lévis), Eugène Paquet (C-L'Islet), Wilfrid Laliberté (C-Lotbinière), Joseph Guilbault (C-Joliette), Emile Léonard (C-Laval), Edmond Marion (C-Montcalm), Elzéar Lévesque (Ind.-Chicoutimi-Saguenay), Herménégilde Boulay (C-Rimouski), Joseph-Avila Masse (C-Sainte-Marie), Paul-Emile Lamarche (C-Nicolet), Joseph-Arthur Lortie (C-Soulanges), Luc Lebel (C-Témiscouata), Wilfrid-Bruno Nantel (C-Terrebonne), Louis Cousineau (C-Wright), René Leduc (C-Québec Est), Louis-Philippe Pelletier (C-Quebec County), Joseph Lavallée (C-Bellechasse), André Fauteux (C-Deux-Montagnes), Joseph Rainville (C-Chambly-Verchères), Albert Sevigny (C-Dorchester), Ernest Guimont (C-Saint-Hyacinthe), Louis Coderre (C-Hochelaga), Honoré Achim (C-Labelle), Tancrède Marsil (C-Bagot), Olivar Asselin (NA-C-Saint-Jacques), Frederick Monk (C-Jacques Cartier), Adélard Bellemare (Ind-C-Maskinongé), Louis-Philippe Gauthier (C-Gaspé).

Among the *nationalistes*, the anticipation of success ran high. In Bagot, Tancrède Marsil was considered to have a good chance. In the Beauce, Georges Cloutier also was a contender because the incumbent, Dr. Béland (now a cabinet minister), chose to run also in the riding of Montmagny as a precaution.[16] Philippe Normand was a threat in Trois-Rivières, in part because the *nationaliste* appeal was well-received, but also because Liberal ranks were in dispute about their nomination.[17] Arthur Gilbert, who had won in Drummond-Arthabaska just ten months before, was confident he could be re-elected. Other promising candidacies were Potvin in Kamouraska, Morin in L'Assomption, Bégin in Lévis, Paquet in L'Islet, Laliberté in Lotbinière, Asselin in Saint-Jacques. In Chicoutimi-Lac Saint-Jean, Elzéar Lévesque showed a great deal of promise, to the point where the Liberal incumbent Joseph Girard ran a very strange campaign. After the start of the campaign, he started insisting that he was a *nationaliste* who would oppose Laurier on the *Naval Service Act*. Despite protests from local Liberals, Laurier insisted that Girard was his man.[18]

In Montcalm, Marion had a great chance, as the Liberal incumbent David Lafortune was mocked mercilessly by *nationalistes* as a "grotesque buffoon."[19] In Montmagny, L'Espérance was a popular candidate, although Bourassa detested him.[20] In Chambly-Verchères, Joseph Rainville presented himself against Victor Geoffrion, the Liberal Whip, and *nationalistes* thought he would be a vulnerable target, yet Chambly had not voted Conservative since 1882 and Verchères had never leaned that way. In Champlain, the incumbent Conservative Blondin had good chances, but there was some danger in that the hay-growers were favourable to reciprocity. The less promising candidacies were J.A. Masse in Sainte-Marie, young Paul-Emile Lamarche in Nicolet, Lortie in Soulanges, Lebel in Témiscouata, Nantel in Terrebonne, and Louis Cousineau in Wright — few gave them much chance of winning.

In Quebec-Est, René Leduc, the owner of *La Libre Parole*, a small *nationaliste* weekly, waited until mid-September to announce that he would run against Laurier. André Fauteux ran as a Conservative in Deux-Montagnes — with strong support from Bourassa — against the incumbent Liberal Joseph Éthier.

Éthier himself did not feel up to it. In a letter to Laurier shortly after Parliament was dissolved, he announced that he would resign his seat.[21] Laurier was saddened: "I think you are wrong," he wrote back, and ultimately prevailed.[22] Éthier threw himself into the race and did not shrink from challenging Bourassa directly and publicly on August 30. That candidacy did not last long as Fauteux's nomination papers were disqualified on technicalities and Éthier was acclaimed.

In Montreal, chances were divided. Monk ran in Jacques Cartier and would likely be re-elected. Louis Coderre, the *nationaliste* candidate in Hochelaga, had a good chance. In Saint-Jacques, Olivar Asselin's candidacy was a real question mark as observers wondered if the journalist could convert his invective pen into a vote-getter. In a letter to Henri Bourassa dated September 1, 1911, Asselin complained of Monk's unsupportive attitude toward his candidacy.[23] Others complained that Asselin's abrasive personality would damage the *nationaliste* chances of taking a riding that was leaning in that direction.[24] All in all, the *nationaliste* movement fielded candidates in over half of Quebec's sixty-five ridings. As one writer put it, "There are large parts of the Province which have no more than heard of Mr. Bourassa and his teachings … the nationalist program is as unknown as Mohammedanism."[25]

The first big event of the campaign in Quebec occurred on Sunday August 13, two weeks and a day after Parliament was dissolved. The Liberals decided to take the fight directly to the *nationalistes* and challenged them to a public debate in Saint-Hyacinthe, Bourassa's constituency in the Quebec legislature situated some fifty kilometres east of Montreal. The Liberals fielded a team composed of Lemieux, the new minister of the marine, Béland, and a few local candidates. Bourassa, who normally detested debates, changed his plans and urged Lavergne to get involved in order to take part in this "battle of the bulls."

"It's a dirty business," he said, "but a necessary one: so let's do it … with exquisite care" ("*aux petits oignons*").[26] It was plucky on the part of Lemieux to face the *nationaliste* leader in his own stronghold, but the Liberals knew how symbolically important this riding was. Lemieux relished the opportunity of a faceoff with the former Liberal in a provocative debate in the *nationaliste* chief's own backyard. The Liberals thought they could hold on to this seat. As much as Saint-Hyacinthe had supported Bourassa provincially, it was also a hotbed of radicalism under the guidance of the local journalist and rabble-rouser Télésphore-Damien "TD" Bouchard.[27] For their part, the *nationalistes* looked forward to bringing down the sometimes condescending Lemieux, who was characterized in their newspapers as "haughty," "ridiculous," "autocratic," and "pretentious."[28] Bourassa, who had had a running feud with Lemieux for years now, was also personally scrapping for a fight. In an editorial published at the end of June entitled "Lemieux: The Underside of a Vile Soul," Bourassa had vented his spleen.[29] (Even inside the Liberal Party caucus, Lemieux was not popular. "A singular feature here is the intense dislike felt for Lemieux by most of the French Canadians," noted Frederick Hamilton in a private note that betrayed his hostility to French Canadians. "You seldom hear a good word for him from them. My explanation is that he has good manners. Another is that he has held aloof from the machine end of the work and that the practical politicians resent his rise."[30])

Courtesy LAC, PA-027994.

Rodolphe Lemieux, July 1911.

The weather on that Sunday afternoon was glorious, and estimates vary widely as to the number of people who attended. By some newspaper accounts, upwards of fifteen thousand people were present in a town that counted less than nine thousand inhabitants. The Grand Trunk Railway alone furnished five trains, carrying five thousand people from Montreal. It was a warm day and ginger beer was sold at a premium price of fifteen cents a bottle. "The scene was a lively one and the hotels and tradesmen reaped quite a harvest," according to the Quebec *Chronicle*, with "eatables running short and after the meeting it was impossible to even get bread in some of the hotels."[31] T.D. Bouchard remembered precisely that one merchant made $184 in selling glasses of water at five cents each.[32]

Lemieux was the first to speak, claiming this opportunity to set the record straight and welcoming the opportunity to confront the *nationalistes* who had insulted him so mercilessly. A good portion of his remarks were devoted to recalling Bourassa's incessant demands for government postings. The real source of the latter's opposition, he argued, was disappointment after disappointment for not securing patronage. He painted *Le Devoir*'s editor as consumed with hatred for Laurier, for the government, and for all French-speaking MPs. "Between the work of prosperity, the work of peace, the work of conciliation of Laurier and the work of envy and hatred of Bourassa, the people will not hesitate," he assured the audience.

Armand Lavergne mocked him with hand gestures. Lemieux, Canada's cool diplomat, representative of his country to Japan and ambassador for his government, lost his cool, interrupted his speech, and literally threatened to punch out Lavergne. After regaining some of his composure, the new minister of the marine claimed that the election was not about the navy, but rather reciprocity, and offered a survey of the history of the issue as well as the key contents of the draft agreement with the Americans. This time it was Bourassa who interrupted Lemieux, again provoking the minister to a fury. Confrontation was only avoided at that moment when the portion of the hastily mounted stage, where a number of journalists and dignitaries were sitting, collapsed.

It was then Bourassa's turn to speak. He argued that he had not taken a position on reciprocity, but that the measure was simply designed to distract electors from the real issue of the election, namely the navy. Most of Bourassa's remarks focused on the naval policy, pointing out that it could only lead to conscription. Henri Béland was the third speaker. In essence, his remarks aimed at weakening Bourassa's credibility by pointing out that the latter had no plan for prosperity and no compelling vision for the country, "almost like a child or a parrot that can't say anything but 'navy.'"

Lavergne then spoke, implying that the Liberal Party had offered a seat on the Supreme Court of Canada to his father (Sir Wilfrid's old friend) if he chose to sit out the election. He tore into Lemieux, calling him a traitor. "Gentlemen, here is the man who has asked the English majority to sacrifice the French language in the west, by saying that there were more Doukhobors there than French Canadians." Lemieux again lost it, leaped from his seat and grabbed Lavergne's arm, declaring him as having lost his mind. By the time the last speaker, the Liberal MP for Yamaska Oscar Gladu, had spoken, the debates had lasted almost four hours.[33]

The Saint-Hyacinthe match set the tone for the campaign. For the *nationalistes*, who liked to mock Laurier's "white plume," the election was as much a referendum on his leadership as it was on the naval issue or reciprocity. In one of its final editorials before the election, *Le Devoir* argued that to vote for Laurier was to "vote for the ratification of the treason of minorities," it was a vote "for the decline of French as an official language in Western Canada" and "a glorification of the thefts of the administration" the "prostitution of justice" and a number of minor "scandals." It argued for Borden, based on his promise that he would consult the electorate before deploying the Canadian navy. Finally, "Mr. Laurier is an old man: he repeats it so often that one need not emphasize it."[34]

Laurier started his home-province campaign on August 16. The first order of business that morning was a private meeting at the Windsor Hotel with Lemieux as well as Mackenzie King and George Graham, who had accompanied him back from the launch in Simcoe the day before. A few hours later, Fisher and Béland joined them, and in a third round of consultations, Brodeur, Raoul Dandurand, and Séverin Létourneau, the key organizer in Montreal, shared the strategizing. Clearly, some ridings where candidates still needed to be selected were a priority. It was also confirmed that Laurier would travel around the province with the Quebec members of his cabinet: Jacques Bureau, the Solicitor General; Sydney Fisher, the minister of agriculture; Henri Béland, the new Postmaster; and also Rodolphe Lemieux. Montreal and Quebec City would have to wait. "My supporters certainly have a right to complain that I don't often visit," Laurier wrote to his old friend François Langelier, "but it's impossible for me to do more for them and I know they understand."[35]

The key concern was the performance of the Liberal team in the face of Bourassa's stormy presentation at Saint-Hyacinthe and what adjustments needed to be made to the upcoming tour. The Liberals had to confront him at every opportunity, something they knew he absolutely hated.[36] Laurier knew the Liberal coalition he had built in the province since the early 1890s was increasingly divided. He had lost the support of many of the more nationalistic Liberals over imperial and school issues. There was another weakness: the absence of the progressive wing of the party. Godfroy Langlois announced that he would not participate in the Liberal campaign because the Party simply did not deserve it. He continued to take aim in *Le Pays* in denouncing the conflicts of interest of many Quebec Liberals, and there is little doubt that his readers followed his example.

Laurier's campaign started at Trois-Rivières that same day, a place that Bourassa considered critical to the success of the *nationaliste* campaign.[37] "I met many people of Ontario yesterday at Simcoe, but my welcome here [over 12,000 people] is far more important than

Courtesy LAC, C-023167.

Wilfrid Laurier at Trois-Rivières, Quebec, August 1911.

even that meeting." He immediately sought to squelch the *nationaliste* momentum gathered at the Bourassa-Lemieux debate and emphasized the contradictions of the Bourassa-Borden alliance. The massive turnout, he said, was "the answer to the meeting at Saint-Hyacinthe last Sunday, and I am satisfied with the reply."[38]

Laurier lost no time before he tore into Monk and Bourassa:

> I had read Monk's mealy-mouthed speech — Bourassa's speech is not so mealy-mouthed. They speak about everything except reciprocity. Monk is for it; Bourassa is against it. The only policy of the *nationaliste* party is to overthrow Laurier. They want it, but that does not mean that it is going to happen. If those people only knew how little I care for power, they would not be so happy with my downfall. I've faced many challenges and I have had my share of success.... If I had to bet, I'd bet on the Old Liberal Cock."[39]

As the rain started, Laurier then spoke about the naval policy and his personal stake in it with eloquence worth quoting at length:

> We are not the small tribe of fifteen years ago. It is an unfortunate necessity to have to protect oneself. When I was here 44 years ago for the first time, the city, which was very small, did not have a police force. Since then, it has grown, and it was necessary to organize the defence of citizens. It is the same for nations. They must have a police force and that police is the navy. Look at the riots in Liverpool where authorities required troops. We must protect ourselves. The navy will only cost four million dollars. No taxes needed to pay it. This expense is less than two percent of our revenue. Some say that we will come to take your children. You ask yourself how it is that Laurier is capable of such a thing. Remember me, I have not

changed. When there are men who say that the naval bill exposes you to war, I am embarrassed for them. Such assertions are outright lies. I can take hits, but I do my best to hit back. The nationalists don't dare repeat that the navy will snatch your children. I will prove to you that this is not true. An Ontario MP asked if we expected to impose conscription for the navy. I told him that we were not disposed for such a thing. Mr. Bourassa says that he wants to defeat Laurier. I tell you this: he cannot defeat Laurier. He has to create an alliance with the Conservatives. Borden and Monk formed a plot to overthrow me. They have based their campaign by saying in Ontario that Laurier is anti-British, disloyal to England and in Quebec by saying that he is an imperialist and a traitor to his race.

The storm erupted, and the assembly began to move to the nearby drill hall, as Laurier continued to harangue his adversaries. Soon high winds and hail lashed the outdoor crowd and instantly it disappeared into nearby shelter. Unfazed, Laurier stood on the dais, venting his rage as Béland, Lemieux, and others begged him to come inside.[40] The message was clear: the Liberals were not taking Quebec for granted, and Laurier, who would not even be daunted by the elements, was up for the fight.

The prime minister resumed his trip down the St. Lawrence to touch base in his own riding of Quebec East. He settled into the Château Frontenac, then addressed a friendly audience in Saint-Roch. He spoke alongside Dr. Béland and the Liberal Quebec premier, Lomer Gouin, who made one of his very rare appearances. The campaign then started a second phase with a focus on the agricultural belt around Montreal — an area that had always been friendly to the Liberals but that needed some reassurance on the issue of freer trade with the Americans. Laurier started in Sainte-Julienne, a town about fifty kilometres northwest of Montreal, and spoke before an audience of about two thousand people, including many women and children.

"The French-Canadian women are just as keen politicians — perhaps more so than the men. I have heard them heckle the speakers with all the energy of a suffragette, and woe be it to the orator who cannot reply right off the reel to some of these feminine interruptions," wrote "The Mace" in his weekly column of *Saturday Night*.[41]

Laurier's objective was to shore up David Lafortune's candidacy in Montcalm. Accompanied by Rodolphe Lemieux and Senator Casgrain, Laurier spoke of infrastructure and transportation, but raised his invective a few degrees for Bourassa and the claims that the navy would inevitably lead to a "blood tax" and the kidnapping of young men for military service. He responded this time to accusations of treason. "The *nationalistes* want to overthrow me because I allegedly betrayed my province in favour of the English provinces. If that were so, the English provinces would support me. Well, it's the opposite. In the English provinces I am accused of having betrayed the English provinces in favour of the province of Quebec. I could not have betrayed everyone. The truth is that I betrayed no one but I did disappoint the *Nationalistes* and the jingoes and it is the disappointments of both groups that are considered to be my betrayals."[42]

Laurier returned to his lair at the Windsor Hotel in Montreal that night, visibly tired. The next day he, along with a number of ministers, travelled to Saint-Hyacinthe to attend the funeral of Aimé Beauparlant, the Liberal candidate whose untimely death added yet another headache in a riding that was vitally important in the fight against Bourassa. He returned to Montreal early in the afternoon and then set out for a rally of about two thousand people in front of the historic church of Saint-Eustache, where Monk and Bourassa had held one of their first rallies against the *Naval Service Act*, and pointed out the contradictions in the *nationaliste* plan. "Mr. Bourassa was a lion in Saint-Eustache a year ago," Laurier charged, "but if you read the speech he gave in Lachine last week in English, you would say, 'why, he's become such a lamb.'" Laurier also denounced Clifford Sifton and condemned Monk as Bourassa's puppet. He again assured his audience that nothing in the naval act authorized the *nationaliste* claim that the children of French Canadian mothers would be torn from their families and marched to the war ships. This time, Lemieux

spoke almost exclusively about reciprocity and its promise of prosperity for local farmers.[43]

The Liberal travelling show returned to Montreal, but not without
a stop in the village of Ahuntsic, in the riding of Laval. The spectacular
evening rally, attended by at least four thousand people, most coming from Montreal (a thirty-minute tramway ride did the trick), was
festooned with torchlights, Chinese lanterns, and flags bordering the
assembly area. Laurier commented that this was probably the most
beautiful demonstration he had ever seen in his long political career.
He then gave his "salad speech," railing against the alliance between
Bourassa and Sifton, and denouncing it as the product of "English
jingoes who want Canada to trade only with the British Empire and
close its doors to all other nations."[44] He took to task the opposition's
posture on freer trade with the United States:

> Reciprocity has been the policy of every public man
> in Canada for fifty years.... It is time the farmers of
> Canada had their turn ... I could scarcely believe my
> ears when I heard Mr. Borden oppose this agreement,
> nor my eyes when I read Mr. Bourassa's declaration
> that he was neither for it nor against it. I don't know
> where Mr. Monk stands. The more I see of him the
> less I understand him. But when I see Mr. Borden, Mr.
> Sifton and Mr. Bourassa united against me, I say to
> myself, "What a salad."
>
> I suppose Mr. Sifton furnishes the oil for it, and
> I am sure Mr. Bourassa supplies the vinegar, while
> poor Mr. Borden has to eat it. The Conservative Party
> has fallen just as it reached the gates of paradise.
> What was the tempter that caused it to fail? Was it
> the Canadian manufacturer? I have been told so, but
> I do not believe it. It was the English jingoes and the
> Canadian jingoes, the *castors* in Quebec and Ontario
> jingoes, the men who say that the different parts of
> the Empire should trade only within the Empire. Our
> policy is grander. We believe that we should trade

with the Empire, but also with all the world. We have given a special preference to Great Britain, we have negotiated an agreement with France, and now we come to you with one with the United States.

What about the Navy? Men of Laval, we will not leave our defence to anybody but ourselves, that is our policy, a virile policy, a proud policy, a policy worthy of Canada. We have the rights of a nation; shall we not have its responsibilities? We have those rights and we demand the privilege of defending ourselves. Appeals have been made to passion, and to the basest passion of all, that of fear. Only one word in conclusion that I may close the mouth of some calumniator who may come to you saying that the naval service has been obligatory. That is not a fantasy. It is not even a calumny, it is purely and simply a lie.

I have been attacked as an imperialist and as an anti-imperialist. I am neither. I am just a Canadian, a Canadian first, last, and all the time.

If there is one man Mr. Bourassa, one man he has insulted, it is Mr. Sifton. Now they are exchanging the kiss of peace and singing the chorus "we must overthrow Laurier."[45]

Laurier left Montreal on the morning of the 24th in the direction of Sorel, where he had launched his Quebec campaigns in 1904 and 1908 before crowds of over ten thousand people. This time, only half the audience presented itself to see the prime minister. Wearing his favourite light morning coat, he was there to support Arthur Cardin, a candidate who had been selected at the last minute to replace Adélard Lanctôt, a "gaffe-prone drunkard," long associated with petty corruption.[46] Lanctôt, who protested to Laurier that the nomination convention was "fixed," even threatened to run as an independent Liberal.[47] Laurier acknowledged the displeasure in the audience, but noted that Cardin had won the nomination contest fairly. "I ask you to be gracious and to put aside your personal interests and forget personality conflicts. Remember the Liberal ideals because there is only one way of looking at this election: either you are with us or you are against us."[48]

On August 25, Laurier headed northwest again, to Saint-Jerôme, where he introduced his remarks by saying that he really wanted to speak to the Conservatives in the audience, in that the Liberal platform was essentially Conservative. "It's a policy program that aims at finding new markets for the products of our soil," he argued. "Those products are so abundant that local consumption is not sufficient.... New outlets are needed and that is why all the parties have consistently asked for reciprocity with the United States. Sir John Macdonald asked for it as did [George-Étienne] Cartier and [Adolphe] Chapleau. Even I did. When I arrived in power my first act was to send representatives to Washington to open negotiations. Our advances were rebuffed, and that is when I declared that 'we will no longer ask Washington.' I was affirming Canada's dignity. But today it is not us who went to Washington. It is the United States that found us. Could I have turned them away? No, because it would have been a crime against civilization."[49] He then dropped a bombshell: he announced that he would resign if his government was not re-elected. The emotion in his voice was unmistakable to the three thousand people who heard him. Laurier had raised the stakes again.

Laurier left the province for a seven-day swing in the Maritimes, returning to Montreal on the evening of Sunday, September 3. He convened his electoral team in his suite in the Windsor Hotel the following morning and reported himself in good shape as the campaign entered its second half — and a second tour through Ontario. A few decisions were finalized. Laurier announced he would run in Soulanges against the incumbent Conservative, a Dr. Lortie, who had strong *nationaliste* support, in addition to Québec-Est. (Individuals were allowed to present their candidacies in more than one riding.) Lemieux would, after much debate, present himself in Gaspé and in Rouville. The group emerged from their meeting to encounter journalists in the hotel lobby when Clifford Sifton, who had been tailing Laurier through the Eastern provinces, arrived. The adversaries did not exchange glances, let alone greetings as the former Liberal minister was hurriedly whisked to his room. The tension could be cut with a knife.

That night, Laurier hosted a reception at the Mount Royal Club before leaving for the rural areas of Farnham and Sherbrooke the following morning. These meetings were intended to support Sydney Fisher and the other Liberal candidates of the area, Frederic Kay and F. McCray. "Our adversaries repeat in each province that reciprocity will lead to annexation. Let us reason a bit," Laurier pleaded. "Annexation will only happen in two ways: by violence or persuasion. It would be ridiculous to contend that, once the treaty is adopted on both sides, our neighbours, those with whom we have lived in peace for over 100 years now, will invade Canada with their army and conquer us. As for persuasion, it would be a grave insult to the patriotism of Canadians to hold that they will consent to give up the nationality that they have won through hard labour for a few pennies."

Four thousand people gathered in Farnham and more than five thousand people heard him speak in the Sherbrooke Stadium at 8:00 p.m. when the rally started, but many lost interest, especially when Laurier and other speakers spoke in English. "The French Canadians that were the majority of the audience at first proved cruelly indifferent to the appeals of the prime minister," observed the *Le Devoir* reporter.[50] At Valleyfield the next day, eight thousand came to hear Laurier and Fisher ("a miniature whirlwind on the stump" who had "the habit of breathing out fire and slaughter against his political enemies"[51]). Laurier and his team introduced a new argument at this meeting as they denounced the "exorbitant and extravagant" profits of packers and middlemen, citing the case of the Wm Davies Company of Toronto, "which had made profits as high as one hundred and twenty percent per annum out of the packing business."[52]

In the final ten days of the campaign, the Liberal train stretched northwards to Victoriaville, Laurier's old home, because the prime minister desperately wanted Drummond-Arthabaska back and knew that victory was at hand in this riding.[53] In front of seven thousand people, Laurier was emotional, adding poignancy to his voice as he delivered what many considered to be his best speech in the whole campaign.[54] "You know me," he said, "and you know that I have never misled you. I am ashamed of Bourassa, the demagogue and his demagogue friends. By means of their lies and false stories, they make your wives and mothers cry. They frighten children with their stories and cause dissensions in happy families. Bourassa and his anti-navy policy are causing strife and sorrow where none is required."[55]

In Beauce-Junction the next day, Laurier spoke in favour of Dr. Béland and commented on the campaign tactics used against the Liberals. "I have never fought a battle in which the opposition uses such insidious and dishonest tactics," he said. "But thank God, I still have enough vigour, even though I'm on the threshold of my seventieth birthday, to face it and to fight it to the end. Never will the imperialists of Toronto nor the *Nationalistes* of Quebec manage to beat Laurier." He repeated the same themes at Thetford Mines that night before five thousand people. Laurier finally spoke in Quebec West, making it a priority because the race had been lost by the narrowest of margins in 1908. More worrisome was the declaration by nineteen shoe manufacturers (mostly located in that riding) that reciprocity would undermine their business. Laurier had courted William Power, a local lawyer, to run in the bilingual riding, but the feeling was that the race was too close to call. The speech went off splendidly, as journalists noted the well-organized rally. Power was ably aided by his son Charles (nicknamed "Chubby"), whose job it was "to see to it that the banners and placards were taken down as soon as Laurier's meeting was over. [He] carried them to the next town or village which was to be favoured by a visit from the Chief." Charles Power later became a minister in Mackenzie King's government.[56]

Laurier devoted the major portion of his last week to Quebec, and it started with a very curious episode. He learned on September 14 that he was challenged in Quebec East by the *nationaliste* René Leduc. A day later, Leduc announced that he had to withdraw. On the morning of Saturday, September 16, Leduc's wife found him so ill that she called the doctor. The story seemed to have come to an end when, just before lunch on that day, Laurier was declared elected by acclamation in Quebec East. Within hours, however, Leduc had recovered his energy and declared to the press that Liberal organizer Louis Létourneau had gotten him drunk on the night of the 15th and made him withdraw his candidacy. Leduc's wife went further, claiming that Létourneau had offered her husband a five-thousand-dollar bribe to withdraw his opposition to Sir Wilfrid. George Perley, the Conservative Whip, immediately created a sensation by alleging that Leduc had been drugged in order to ensure Laurier's acclamation. On the following day (a Sunday) Leduc sent a telegram to Laurier that was quickly made public. "One of your most important chiefs in Quebec East, extorted from me, while I was under the influence of liquor, my resignation as candidate against you. I have asked the returning officer to whom the document has been delivered to give it back to me. He has referred me to the Clerk of the Crown in Chancery. I have telegraphed the latter and I hereby ask you to give instructions that my extorted resignation be given back to me and that the election be not stolen. The people of Quebec East desire to vote and they trust you will not take advantage of the mistake made."[57]

Laurier mocked the allegations and said that if they were proven he would resign his seat. On Monday, Létourneau revealed in court that he had indeed received a request from Leduc to see him that Friday evening. Létourneau said that when they met, Leduc expressed his willingness to resign if he was given a position, ideally something at the Canadian Commission in Paris (Leduc was a relatively recent French immigrant). Létourneau did not deny that he offered to help him. Apparently another phone call at 10:30 that night yielded more discussion, but no offers, and according to Létourneau, a perfectly sober Leduc, who had hoped to leverage his candidacy into some sort of blackmailing vehicle, indicated that he would not pursue the race and recover his deposit before it was too late. "Everybody here laughs at this stupid story," wrote the *Globe*'s reporter. "Everybody knew Leduc's candidature was a joke and the Liberals did not care a cent about it. The truth seems evident that Leduc found he was injuring himself and decided to drop out and save his deposit."[58] (The affair triggered a series of lawsuits that were not resolved until mid-November, when Leduc was found at fault for making false allegations, and both the *Quebec Chronicle* and *L'Évenement* were ordered to pay one thousand dollars each to Létourneau for libel.)[59]

While this crazy affair unravelled, Laurier travelled to Joliette and Grand'Mère before taking a swing in Eastern Ontario (to give a speech in Rockland) and then in Hull, where he spoke exactly where Bourassa had addressed a crowd a few days earlier. Over five thousand people gathered to hear the prime minister, who appeared tired and who only spoke for a few minutes before returning to Montreal for a series of grand events that would cap the campaign.

The last evening of the campaign was frenzied. Wilfrid Laurier had dinner at the Windsor Hotel and left after 8:00 p.m. for the first meeting on Atwater Street, in the Hochelaga riding. A stand had been erected opposite the Church of Saint-Irénée and over twenty-five thousand people stood in the street.[60] Few people could actually hear the prime minister as he gave his hour-long speech, but according to a reporter, "all cheered when Laurier, his hair shining in the brilliant light, lifted his arm to drive home a point."[61]

"The venerable city under the mountain went raving crazy in sorts," wrote the reporter. Laurier was then hurried to a car, barrelled down to Bonaventure station, up Windsor Street, along Dorchester, and, according to the Toronto *Star*'s colourful account, "Presto! There was the white head above the swaying crowd of the St. Lawrence Boulevard at the corner of Ontario." Laurier re-boarded his car for another stop at the corner of Ontario Street and City Hall Avenue before finishing his parade at the Marché Saint-Jacques, "the Kingpin of them all," where a crowd of over twenty thousand invaded the small square, spilled in the adjoining streets "crawling up telegraph poles, climbing trees about as thick as walking sticks, threatening to invade the speaker's stand, doing a good deal of good natured … swaying and singing *'Tiens, c'est le vieux coq.'*

'Hourra pour Laurier' was the signal cry, swelling into an ear-splitting roar, as the Old Cock came spinning into sight with the speed of a comet. For nearly ten minutes the roar continued, breaking into a thunderous song, and dropping back again to cheers."

Laurier made his final arguments. "How can the consumer pay less for what the farmer gets more for?" he asked. "The solution lies in the two buyers for the farmer, and the saving on duty for the consumer," he answered. The first mention of Bourassa and *Le Devoir* created an uproar of hisses that silenced Laurier, but only for a few moments:

At Marieville Mr. Bourassa had said that Laurier should be defeated to save him from his friends. "Doctor, cure thyself" is a good motto for Mr. Bourassa. Who is the real chief? Is it Mr. Borden, and do you know the naval policy of Mr. Borden? Who will finally triumph, the Nationalist lamb or the imperialistic lion? The latter will devour Bourassa, and why? Because before English audiences Mr. Bourassa is a lamb; instead of roaring, he bleats. As to Mr. Bourassa saying that whether or not reciprocity would be passed, the farmers would still work twelve hours a day, I agree with him, but there is a difference. Today, the worker gets a $1 per day for his work, but under reciprocity he would receive $1.50 per day....When I first knew Mr. Bourassa he had a good attitude, but it has changed since he kept different company. But I say to Mr. Bourassa to go back to school and learn before trying to teach others, and I will say a prayer for him as it is the Good Book: "Pardon him Lord, for he knows not what he says, or does." Mr. Bourassa knows quite well he is in favour of reciprocity, as he always has been, but he does not wish to say so. He is against it on account of his alliance, but he is presenting the humiliating spectacle of a splendid human mind not knowing whether he is for or against reciprocity.[62]

Laurier would have spoken to close to fifty thousand people that day, and, according to *La Presse*, another fifty thousand would have seen him drive through the city. Laurier then proceeded to the Place Viger Station to catch the train, and ran into a *nationaliste* student crowd that had gathered to hear Bourassa speak from a balcony of the Hotel Viger after their own final rally at the Patinoire Ontario, a sizeable arena. Young men blocked Laurier's car and physically threatened the prime minister.[63] Again, an altercation between young partisans took place, and while a few black eyes were exchanged, Laurier boarded his private car without difficulties and arrived in Quebec City a few hours later. The Liberals in Saint-Hyacinthe vowed their revenge on Bourassa the next day.

For his part, Laurier gave his final speech as a campaigning prime minister in Sainte-Anne-de-Beaupré on the morning of September 20, and then retired to the Château Frontenac to wait for the results.

———•·•———

The *nationaliste* campaign in Quebec was energized. It focused on two aspects: the first was Laurier himself and the second was the naval bill. On the subject of the man, the *nationalistes* could be cruel. "The elderly, and the old cocks themselves cannot escape the general rule — the elderly often have the habit of focusing their remembrance of this past on a particular subject," wrote *La Patrie*. "For Mr. Laurier that subject is reciprocity. This is a mistake. Even if reciprocity could produce the miracle of having us pay less money for the products the farmer will sell for more money, what will be the purpose of the economy if we are consistently condemned to the same administration of frauds and theft that has almost quadrupled the expenses of the country over the past fifteen years?"[64]

Bourassa, the effective head of the campaign, retraced the steps taken by the prime minister. Bourassa's speech at Farnham highlighted Laurier's personal stake in the *Naval Service Act* as he addressed himself to families with children:

> It is all very well for him [Wilfrid Laurier] — he has no children. Ten years hence, or perhaps sooner, he will have disappeared from the scene of politics. For fifteen years he has trodden on everything sacred to his compatriots in order to make a pedestal for the English who distribute titles, medals and decorations. Perhaps we men of today will not suffer very much from such a policy. You heads of families, old men who have one foot in the grave, you perhaps will sleep in death before the disastrous effect of this ignominious policy are felt; but you have children. I see some in this meeting who smile over the future of their country.

They are eight or ten years old. They were brought up on the knees of their mothers and they count on you to protect them from all the danger which may reach them, but when, fifteen years hence — you heads of families will be no longer here — when fifteen years hence your wives will see the agent of the government, having in his hands this accursed act and addressing each one of them, he will say, "Good mother, thou must give thy sons, but to fight on all the lands and the seas of the world on behalf of the English."

Then when your wives will learn some months later that an Austrian shell, a Japanese cannon ball or a German bullet will have disemboweled their children and that they have fallen over the precipices or collapsed on the deck of a ship, do you think they will then say, "very well, my husband was rouge and it is Mr. Laurier who passed that act. He did well." No, they will curse you and it will be only right.[65]

At Lachine, Monk and Bourassa spoke together at length in English to explain their position on the navy. The explanation began with a history of Canada's position in imperial affairs since Confederation. When the provinces united, according to Monk, the Dominion undertook the defence of the country, but some few years ago a new school of thought was inaugurated and this school felt that Canada should not only maintain her own defence, but should share in the defence of the Empire. In the 1880s a definite scheme of imperial defence was drawn up by Great Britain to which the colonies agreed. By this scheme England was to maintain her supremacy of the sea and the overseas dominions were to provide ports and coaling stations for the fleet. Canada's duty lay in Halifax and Esquimalt, and it was promised that these two points could be properly equipped. Canada, according to Mr. Monk, has fulfilled her duty.

Monk, in one of his few appearances during the campaign, underlined the change in Laurier's policy, comparing his positions in the Imperial Conferences of 1902 and 1907 with the most recent one.

At the first two, he stated, Sir Wilfrid and the other Canadian representatives absolutely refused to consider the proposal that Canada should share in the maintenance of the navy. He then argued that Canada had agreed to create a navy in order to serve the Empire and that the decision was made undemocratically. "We have spent $70 million on our militia since the Laurier Government went in power … and people say it is useless," Monk said. "Would it not be better to rectify these mistakes than to spend as much at least for a navy?"

Bourassa took the stage and raised the accusations of corruption that still swirled around Frank Oliver. He then tackled the issue of reciprocity: "Upon the question of reciprocity, I have been charged with having no set ideas. It is true, I confess it. The more I study the question, the more I am puzzled, but I believe that those who think that reciprocity is going to bring all the prosperity to Canada are mistaken and those who believe it will bring utter ruin are in the same box. Canada has reached a point where she can hold her own. I think that reciprocity is not necessary. It is not necessary for us to have the American market, nor is it necessary to open our market to the United States."[66]

On August 27, Bourassa took the battle to Sainte-Julienne, where the audience that greeted him and a host of other speakers was much larger (close to eight thousand) than the one that had welcomed Wilfrid Laurier just days before. "Like you, I once admired M. Laurier," Bourassa exclaimed. "I gave him my work and my devotion. But since Mr. Laurier comes today to make arguments out of his white hair, I say that it is in the interest of the people to reject him before his white hair gets wet. If the people note that Laurier has misled them, they must defeat him before the bandits that surround him make him drown in crap ['crotte']. I've said it and I repeat it."[67]

On reciprocity, Bourassa again predicted uneven results. "I don't think reciprocity will produce the expected effects," he told the audience. "Even after the adoption of this measure I think the farmers will still have to work ten hours a day and dinner will not be served on a silver platter. I think that in those years where the harvest will be poor in the United States, reciprocity will be good for Canada, but that when the opposite happens, it will be fatal for Canada." On the Imperial Conference,

Bourassa argued that Laurier had "refused the right for Canada to be consulted on the treaties that concern it. In other words, on one hand he refuses the privilege of nationhood [to be consulted on war] and on the other hand he imposes on us the most serious responsibility of a nation: naval armaments." Finally, Bourassa attacked Laurier's notion of the navy as a self-defence mechanism: "I want to mention, in passing, Mr. Laurier's ridiculous argument. His cause must really be weak for him to raise such arguments. Mr. Laurier tells us: just as cities need a police, we need a navy. Undoubtedly cities need police, but if you pay for your own police in Joliette it is not to send it to Saint-Jerôme. Our navy is not for us."[68]

The *nationaliste* rally in Nicolet on August 30 to support Paul-Émile Lamarche gathered over two thousand people but was distinguished by the fact that four former Liberals gathered on the hustings to denounce the naval service law. Lamarche himself hammered the issue of the navy, calling the issue of reciprocity a smokescreen designed to blind the electorate about the realities of the naval bill.[69] Bourassa then travelled to the small town of Sainte-Scholastique to support André Fauteux. J.A.C. Éthier, the fiery Liberal incumbent, insisted on being heard, and the thousand people who had gathered to hear the *nationaliste* leader were soon treated to a full-fledged debate. "If Mr. Bourassa is a champion of ideas, Mr. Laurier is a champion of action," Éthier declared.[70]

Bourassa followed his path along the Ottawa River, stopping first at Saint-André-Avellin and then in Buckingham, both parts of the riding of Labelle, which he once represented in the House of Commons. Three thousand people gathered in Buckingham to hear him speak for over two hours on reciprocity and the naval question. The trip wound up in Hull, across the river from the national capital, where Bourassa was joined by Charles Cahan to speak to no less than eight thousand people. As in Deux-Montagnes with Éthier, the Liberal candidate Charles Devlin announced himself, along with a noisy contingent of about three hundred supporters that included, in the words of *Le Devoir*'s reporter, "a dozen tough-guys, cigars in their beaks, their caps pulled over one eye, who would venture, now and then, a 'hurrah for Laurier.'"[71]

Bourassa then headed back to Montreal, stopping in Sainte Rose (in what is now part of Laval), where an audience of over four thousand heard him speak in favour of Emile Léonard. Until the last two weeks, Bourassa (like Laurier) had avoided Montreal. On September 8, Bourassa appeared at the Monument-National, where he finally, and perhaps a little reluctantly, shared the stage with Charles Cahan and local candidates Olivar Asselin and J.A. Masse, the *nationaliste* candidate in Sainte-Marie who claimed to speak for workers.[72] Gustave Francq, the general secretary of the labour party in Quebec, however, took a different view. He was in favour of reciprocity. "The labour class," he assured journalists who were covering the Calgary Labour Congress that took place a week before the election, "are voting practically all in favour of reciprocity," and assured them that Laurier would win Quebec.[73]

As Bourassa's campaign gathered momentum, interruptions and violent outbreaks became frequent. There was commotion when Bourassa spoke at a giant rally that gathered over five thousand people on Sunday September 10 at La Prairie. At Verchères on September 12, where he spoke in support of Joseph Rainville, the Liberal incumbent Victor Geoffrion and a few others loudly demanded to be heard, but were turned away. After a brief swing in Sudbury, Ontario, Bourassa returned to the province a day later and produced himself at Victoriaville, where a crowd of eight thousand greeted him and Arthur Gilbert. The riding of Drummond-Arthabaska had assumed an iconic place in federal politics in less than ten months, and Bourassa wanted to make sure the *nationaliste* candidate would be re-elected. That was followed by the climax of the campaign in Montreal, which took place on September 19, where fifteen thousand people heard him and Monk summarize their campaign.

In the final act of his campaign, Bourassa spent the last night of the election where he started it, in Saint-Hyacinthe. Arrangements had been made to meet with *nationaliste* sympathizers at the Hotel Yamaska, where he would give a speech. This time, no large train delegation from Montreal was arranged, and Bourassa was treated roughly by Liberal partisans as he arrived in the hall. A man actually climbed on stage and threatened to kill him before a "friend" delivered a punch to the would-be assailant's jaw and immediately ended the menace. Not a window in the front of Perrault Hall was left intact. A Mrs. Malo, who was staying at the hotel, was struck in the face with a large rock and was rushed to hospital. For two hours the *nationaliste* speakers delivered their addresses to the accompaniment of howls and jeers, punctuated by the thunder of flying rocks against the walls of the building and the crash of falling glass. Many of the stones came though into the hall, and several in the audience were struck by them. Windows were hastily barricaded with tables, and the stage's backdrop was torn down to serve the same purpose. In spite of the improvised fortification, however, many of the stones still showered in, and these were gathered up and placed on the table in front of the speakers, almost as trophies. The audience started to panic as people crowded to the doors only to move back quickly to avert a new volley of stones. The *nationaliste* speakers continued to address them, but few thought of anything but their own safety. They crouched in their chairs or stood huddled together along the wall, out of range of the stones which now and then came hurling through the windows. Bourassa's friends held a lengthy consultation on the platform, trying to devise a means of placating the mob outside.

Finally, shortly after midnight, a truce was declared and it was announced from outside that everybody would be allowed to leave the hall unmolested, except Bourassa and his lieutenants. The audience very quickly deserted the speakers and made for safety. One or two of Bourassa's followers attempted to leave with the crowd, but they were recognized and forced to rush back behind the barricaded windows.

Meanwhile, a second big mob surrounded the train station and watched in case Bourassa escaped the besieged hall. Suddenly, a rumour that Bourassa had reached the railway station flew through the crowd and a large number of those present started down the street. Bourassa and his friends, taking advantage of this opportunity, escaped the building by a back entrance and succeeded in reaching a nearby house where one his lieutenants resided. Here he remained until three o'clock, at which time he was led over the fields out of town. He walked about half a mile down the railway track, where his train picked him up while a big crowd continued to watch for him at the hall and at the station. At daybreak there were still a few who did not believe Bourassa had escaped, and they continued waiting patiently in hopes of capturing him.[74]

Emotions heated to a boil in the last week of the campaign. *Le Nationaliste* denounced Fielding as the "apostle of Nova Scotia separatism," who argued in favour of annexation as early as 1886: "He is a false patriot, an anti-Canadian, an annexationist and [using a colourful expression that defies translation] a *mange canayen*."[75] Louis-Philippe Brodeur was called "a public liar," as was Laurier.[76] Laurier was denounced as "anti-Canadian" for opening Western lands to East European immigrants and other newcomers with "no idea of our aspirations and ideals" or to Great Britain's criminal class.[77] "Laurier has promised ships and fodder in times of war," *Le Nationaliste* argued, "and Fielding has warned us that we will have to fight whether the wars are just or unjust. Voting for Laurier is voting for this."[78]

Laurier was accused of having betrayed the Constitution and Canadian traditions by limiting French-language rights in the creation of Saskatchewan and Alberta. He was supposed to defend Canada against imperialism; instead he had delivered Canada to imperialism. "We want to be something other than cannon fodder," wrote *Le Nationaliste* in the last days of the campaign.[79] Laurier had killed democracy: "We no longer reason, we no longer discuss, we no longer think, eyes closed, ears plugged, but with a mouth open to sing his glories, we have followed him like a dog follows his master."[80] The only solution was to defeat the Liberals and its policies before they took root. "Laurier will die, but his works will stay if we ratify it and our children will suffer the consequences. Let's take back our liberty, renew our dignity as free men, let us stand tall, head high, let's break the whip and affirm our rights, let us break the idol and vote against Laurier and for free men."[81]

The campaign in Quebec thus ended in acrimony and violence. Both Laurier and Bourassa were physically assaulted; both were harshly criticized for their policies, for their character, and for their visions of Canada. The race showed a remarkably even battle. Laurier and the Liberals engaged their adversaries at every turn. The prime minister was tireless in campaigning, easily speaking to at least 120,000 people, and being seen by at least the same. Bourassa's campaign was equally vigorous, carefully tailing Laurier's crusade, hoping to correct the situation and propose alternatives while positions were still fresh in the minds of the voters.

Laurier had demonstrated that his Liberalism was not content in resting on its record in government since 1896. He did not deny that difficult decisions had been made, but argued in favour of a Canada that took its place in the Empire. He argued for a politics of realism, where French Canada had to abide by some of the wishes of English Canada, within the limits of what he saw was an even compromise. Bourassa's vision was no less pan-Canadian, but where Laurier argued for pragmatism and realism, Bourassa saw nothing but high principles. The campaign in Quebec was about two radically different visions for the province. On the morning of the election of September 21, the men of Quebec had to mark an "x" next to the vision that compelled them the most.

CHAPTER 10

THE DAY OF JUDGMENT:
GRITS, TORIES, AND SWITCHERS

We must admit that we did not expect such a turn:
but a number of factors showed that the regime was nearing its end.
— *LE NATIONALISTE*, SEPTEMBER 24, 1911

"Election day at last — O fateful day! This night will tell us 'Which Flag' [will prevail]," the poet Wilson MacDonald confided to his diary on September 21. He cast his vote for Sir George Foster in Toronto, against reciprocity, and for the ideal of a British Canada. "In all my life I never knew the affairs of state to grant me such an hour of sheer ecstasy," he wrote after standing in a crowd outside the offices of *The Evening News*. "It was a sight little short of sublime when I read across the great sea of upturned faces the words 'Our flag, not our pocket books, our country, not our treasury.'" For MacDonald and many other Canadians the choice had not been made for economic reasons. Indeed, for an election supposedly focused on reciprocity, their vote was cast for reasons altogether different. The young poet searched for the right metaphor:

> [S]urely it was the hand of God that urged the pencil of
> the patriot this day. I will sleep little this night for love
> of my country. I stand like a lover who has just been

accepted of his sweetheart, like a sailor who touches the firm earth after a voyage of great hazard, like a soldier who hears the enemy sound the battle call of retreat. O my country — I am most proud of thee. Hereafter it shall be the proudest of privileges to boast a citizenship in a land that refused to sell her birthright — that even spurned the mess of potage from the world's lowest civilization.[1]

Canadian men aged twenty-one and over went to the polls on September 21, 1911, on a typical day of mixed weather. Out of a population of 7,204,527 there were 1,820,742 Canadians on the voters list. About 72 percent of eligible voters (the same turnout rate as in 1908), 1,307,550 people, cast their votes that day; 132,819 more than three years before and more than at any other federal election in Canadian history until that time. The *Saint John Globe* explained that the record-breaking vote, at least locally, came from the "deep and widespread interest in the issues before the country [which] has aroused many indifferent voters and caused them to go to the polls."[2] Polling stations were busy from the moment they opened. In Toronto, "motor cars and carriages were dashing about hither and thither, each one carrying one, two, or three men, who, in many cases appeared unaccustomed to riding in such a state. Needless to say they were members of the electorate."[3] The campaign of 1911 was the last Canadian political event where the presence of automobiles was newsworthy.

There was remarkably little controversy about the fact that women and the indigenous peoples of Canada were not enfranchised. The political map of Canada of the time showed vast expanses of land inhabited by First Nations that were not represented in Parliament. The responsibility to determine who had the right to vote belonged to the provinces, but the federal government did contribute surprising rules through the criminal code. Section 233, for instance, stated: "Individuals who had not lived in the riding for at least six months could not bear arms the day before the election," and that no one at all could come within a mile of a polling station "armed with offensive weapons of any kind." Section 234 proscribed the use of an "ensign, standard or set of colour or any other flag" during the last eight days of the campaign or on election day. Section 235 outlawed the wearing of ribbons and specified that "favours are not to be furnished or worn." Section 236 stated: "No spirituous or fermented liquors or strong drinks shall be sold or given at any hotel, tavern, shop or any place within the limits of any polling division during the whole of the polling day." The penalty for that offence was jail for up to six months and a hundred-dollar fine.

Those rules were observed on election day, 1911, save for a few minor mishaps. At one poll a Liberal voter showed up to find that someone else had voted for him; at another one person tried to vote twice but was prevented from doing so.[4] There were "rumours of impersonation" at other polling stations across the country, and more serious allegations of bribery and fraud arose in the Sunbury-Queen's riding in New Brunswick after a very close vote elected Colonel Hugh McLean, a Liberal, over the Conservative incumbent.[5] In Winnipeg there were allegations that the Liberals added hundreds of bogus names to the voting list.[6] Naturally, there were also a few delays and demands for recounts in very close races (many electors in four ridings did not actually vote until a few days after the results were known!). There was some fighting between Liberal and Conservative supporters in New Brunswick, and in Campbellton one man died from his wound after being jabbed in the eye by an umbrella. The *Halifax Herald* later suggested that the argument that led to the murder "occupied less than a minute, it is said that it could not have been the result of any heated election argument as at first reported."[7] In Toronto, a few bricks were thrown through windows at the *Globe* and other offices.[8] Otherwise, there were relatively few reports of disturbances, vandalism, or violence.

As soon as the polls closed, the candidates, party workers, and voters gathered to await the results. Like several other newspapers, the *Saint John Globe* posted election update bulletins outside its office and a large crowd gathered to watch the polling returns. Many in the crowd were Conservative women who were "wildly enthusiastic — uncommonly so for Saint John." As there were so many close races, including William Pugsley's in Saint John, the crowd stayed until almost midnight.[9] In Halifax, partisan crowds formed outside the offices of *The Morning Chronicle* and *Halifax Herald* and at the Conservative headquarters.

The *Herald* estimated a crowd of ten thousand ready to celebrate the Conservative victory.[10]

In Montreal, large crowds stood outside the offices of their favourite newspapers. *La Patrie* (like many newspapers across the country) used a calcium light to project results from an office window onto a sheet outside to inform the thirty thousand spectators who had gathered despite a heavy rain. In Toronto, where it also rained for most of the night, J.S. Willison stood on the balcony of *The Evening News* office and addressed the crowd that had gathered there;[11] but few in his audience knew of his role in the Conservative win. Similar scenes were repeated at the offices of the other leading newspapers and at Conservative riding offices.

An outsized crowd — estimated at over one hundred thousand — filled Toronto's Yonge Street from Front to Queen and from Church to York Streets. At the *Globe*'s office on Melinda Street, thousands cheered when it was announced that some *nationaliste* candidates had been defeated in Montreal. As the returns revealed a Conservative sweep of the city, "Toronto and Toryism broke into riotous jubilation, and it was hats off to Mr. Borden or get out." Farther north on Yonge, Sir George Foster stood on a table in his campaign office to speak to the crowd and claimed victory for Canada and the British Empire. At Queen's Park, Premier Whitney and Frank Cochrane quietly toasted the win with a smaller group of Conservatives.[12]

In other parts of the city and across the province there were bands, torches, impromptu parades, and speeches — cheering both the winners and the losers. In some rural areas that elected Conservatives, mock funerals were reportedly staged to mourn the demise of reciprocity. In Winnipeg there was a great celebration at Conservative headquarters for Alexander Haggart, the victorious candidate. He and several other Conservatives were lifted up and urged to make speeches from the shoulders of their supporters.[13] Farther west, in Regina, approximately three thousand people — a "mass of seething humanity" — organized a torchlight procession once the results were known.[14]

Elsewhere on the Prairies, three future prime ministers experienced the night in their own separate ways. In Portage la Prairie, Arthur Meighen, who had fought against reciprocity in an area of the province where it was popular, was given an election-night parade, with a drum and fife band playing "The British Grenadiers."[15] R.B. Bennett was among the thousands who gathered around the Calgary *Herald* building, where an elaborate system of bulletin boards was built. The results started coming in at 5:00 p.m., and within an hour the crowd at the corner of Centre and Seventh Streets was so large that both streets were blocked. This was a lonely crowd of Conservatives in Alberta, but a boisterous one that broke out in song and cheer with every bit of news announcing Conservative success. Once his landslide victory was declared, the crowd hoisted Bennett into a chair and carried him from the *Herald* office to a nearby rink to escape from the snow which had turned into drizzling sleet.[16] John Diefenbaker, who was still not old enough to vote, even though he claimed to have attended "all the meetings in Saskatoon," knew that he was on the losing side in the election. His father — indeed most of Saskatchewan — was Liberal, but the young John was already something of a renegade, believing that reciprocity would lead to the absorption of Canada into the United States. This night and the fight against reciprocity, he later wrote, was the moment that "more than anything else made me Conservative."[17]

In Halifax the mood was equally jubilant, where the new prime minister–elect, Robert Borden, spoke to his supporters after midnight. "The people have given the answer to those who desired to force the reciprocity compact through Parliament," he said. "She has wisely determined that for her there shall be no parting of the ways, but that she will continue in the old path of Canadianism, truly Canadian nationhood and British connection." Then, as he gave his first speech as prime minister–elect, he shifted into quiet damage control in dealing with the United States, given that it would now be *his* government's responsibility. "The verdict has been given in no spirit of unfriendliness or hostility to the United States," Borden said, "and no such spirit exists, but Canada desires and elects to be mistress of her destinies and to work out those destinies as an autonomous nation within the British Empire."[18]

Early on the day of the vote, Laurier left his suite in the Château Frontenac and did the rounds of a few local Liberal riding offices in town. He had lunch in the home of a local organizer, and returned in the early afternoon to the Château, where a private wire had been installed so he could read telegrams reporting the returns. He had a quiet dinner alone, eating a sandwich as he read telegrams reporting the defeats in Nova Scotia. Every now and then he would step outside and inform reporters. "Toronto does not seem to favour reciprocity," he noted dryly. He left the hotel at around 8:00 p.m. to share the rest of the results with a few hundred sympathizers in the Marché Saint-Pierre in his own riding. The smoke-filled, dimly lit hall grew quieter with every moment that passed. Laurier sat at a table with two of his key organizers, Charles Devlin, a minister in the Quebec government, and Philippe Paradis.

By 9:30 p.m. the results were fairly clear, and Laurier rose to acknowledge the sinking reality. "We have fallen in a high and honorable cause," he told the crowd. "We have received a check, but we shall come back again to the ring. I thank you for what you have done for me for thirty years, today. We have lost, but our cause shall prevail." He bowed slightly, and the room was silent. Then one person clapped and soon the small hall was filled with cheers led by Devlin. The defeated prime minister left the hall a few minutes later, stepping into a cold, dark night accompanied by Devlin and Paradis, who took him back to the Château Frontenac. "What about the chief? How's he taking it?" reporters asked. "The chief? He is taking it like a chief," was the answer.[19]

Laurier greeted the results with grim expressions of gratitude and resolve. He knew it would take several days for the vote count to be finalized, but he was sorely aware of what had transpired. A Toronto Star reporter, who watched Laurier's concession speech, wrote: "It was one of the big moments of a nation's history, and the man on whom every eye was fixed was the nation's biggest man. It was more than the fall of a government; it was the checking of an idea, the end of a tradition; the turning of the tide. Men have died for a lesser thing."[20] There was considerable speculation — it was the "money kings" that defeated Laurier, announced the Halifax Morning Chronicle; across town, the Herald insinuated that the Liberals lost because they ran out of money and could not buy enough votes.[21] Others argued that it was President Taft and all the silly American statements that undermined the cause of reciprocity, or that Laurier had no one to blame but himself; he was old and tired, and it was time for his government to go.[22]

One Quebec supporter wired Laurier a short seven-word note giving his views: "Orange ignorance and Catholic fanaticism defeated you."[23] What was clear, however, especially to westerners, was that reciprocity was done. "It was a square stand-up fight," John Dafoe wrote in Winnipeg, "the first in a generation — between two ideals of national development."[24]

———•◦•———

The results were barely in before the long process of sifting through the numbers, assessing the issues, and weighing the strengths and weaknesses of both parties began. For most Canadians the results were clear, but understanding the vote and assessing the ramifications of the election decision continued for many years. What did it all mean?

That the Borden Conservative party won the election, there was no doubt. This was the biggest landslide in Canadian history since 1891, when Laurier first lost to Macdonald, and remained the biggest upset until John Diefenbaker's victory in 1958. The big cities all voted Conservative. Three Conservatives (if Monk is included) were elected in Montreal, four were elected in Toronto. Vancouver, Calgary, Winnipeg, Halifax all voted mostly Conservative. Seven of Laurier's cabinet ministers were defeated, including those who had been the principal defenders of the Liberal platform. William Fielding and William Paterson, the negotiators of the Reciprocity Agreement, lost their seats, as did Sydney Fisher, the minister of agriculture. The other defeated ministers were Nova Scotia's Frederick Borden, the minister of militia, and from Ontario, George Graham, minister of railways and canals, and William Lyon Mackenzie King, minister of labour. In British Columbia, William Templeman also lost his bid for re-election.

In the end, 42,563 more Canadians voted for Robert Borden and the Conservatives and *nationalistes* than for the Laurier Liberals. If strict party labels are to be considered, Borden increased his party's share of the popular vote by 4 percent from 1908 (rising from 46.9 percent to 50.9 percent), but this relatively small shift had translated into a decisive victory in terms of a parliamentary majority. If the figures for the *nationaliste* candidates are broken out, the picture changes somewhat, with the Tories earning 42,344 fewer votes than the Liberals. As

Table 10.1 (page 280) demonstrates, the *nationaliste* movement boosted the Borden cause considerably by bringing it 84,907 votes. It was a deceptively tight race, with the Tories winning with only 3.2 percent more votes than the Liberals. Had 21,261 people decided to vote Liberal instead of Conservative or *nationaliste*, Laurier might theoretically have won the election, and reciprocity would have shaped Canada's economic future. In 1908, the Liberals had won such a tight contest, but by a slightly more comfortable margin of 3.5 percent. The Liberals won more votes in Alberta and Saskatchewan in 1911 than they had in 1908. The Conservatives took away votes from the Liberals but also from third parties, who fared poorly in the 1911 election. In 1908, 2.7 percent of the vote had gone to protest parties — an assortment of independents, labour party militants, and local characters. Three years later, the Borden-Laurier contest polarized the electorate a great deal more and third-party votes dropped by almost half, or 1.4 percent of the total ballots cast (17,900). The Conservative Party won the battlefields of Ontario and British Columbia hands down. It also beat the Liberals in key ridings in the Yukon, Manitoba, Quebec, New Brunswick, and Nova Scotia.

The House of Commons had 221 seats representing 218 ridings (three ridings, Halifax, Queen's [PEI], and Ottawa, had two MPs), so 111 seats were needed to form a government. The new House of Commons would seat 134 Conservatives comfortably on the government side (including a bloc of 13 *nationalistes*). The loyal Opposition would be constituted of 87 Liberals. It was a near-exact reversal of the results of 1908, when it was the Conservatives who had won 85 seats and the Liberals 135. There was little need to move desks in the House of Commons — it was as if the parties had simply swapped sides in equal proportions. Of the 221 men who sat in the 11th Parliament (1909–1911), 130 were returned, with both Manitoba and Saskatchewan particularly showing little inclination to change their representation (in both cases, eight of the ten deputies were returned). The greatest turnover occurred in Quebec, where only 52 percent of the MPs were returned.

Many local races were bitterly fought. In all, 71 seats — one third of all the seats — were so close that they were decided by less than a 5 percent plurality. Interestingly, the ridings that were close in 1908 did not necessarily become "swing" ridings in 1911. Some of the ridings that had been handily won in 1908 became unpredictable three years later: 36 of those were in Ontario and 18 were in Quebec. Half the seats in Prince Edward Island, New Brunswick, and Manitoba were won by less than 5 percent, and 10 of the 17 ridings in Nova Scotia were taken by similar margins.

In other words, there was no giant tide of changing partisanship, but a subtle shift in opinion that had a disproportionate effect on the riding count. The official report on the results of the twelfth General Election shows that the Conservatives won 45 seats by margins of less than 5 percent, and 29 of them were taken from the Liberals (the other 16 seats had voted Conservative with slim pluralities in 1908 also).[25] It was those ridings — most of which were actually won with slim pluralities of less than 3 percent — that determined the result of this election. Had the Liberals held on to 24 of those seats, they would have retained power. That possibility was within reach, but lost as a result of a host of factors. In part, it was due to real bungling at the local level that split the Liberal vote. In many ridings, particularly in Ontario, the superior organization of Conservatives clearly made a difference. In other areas the result can be explained through the mysterious processes of demography, socio-economic conditions, and political convictions that changed the minds of relatively few Canadian men. A regional breakdown of the results, focusing especially on the seats that were won by less than 5 percent margins, and particularly the ridings that switched sides, reveals how the Borden Conservatives won, and how the Laurier Liberals lost.

—·•·—

Politics in Nova Scotia was always tough on both parties and 1911 was no different as six of the seventeen ridings (the riding of Halifax had two seats) were narrowly won. In his home province, Borden finally had a breakthrough, although he was still edged in popular votes by the Liberals (50.8 to 48.8). The Conservatives kept four ridings and added five more: Annapolis, Kings, Hants, Lunenburg, and Shelburne-Queens. The Liberals were re-elected in seven ridings and captured two new seats. The political map [see Map 1] shows that the hotly contested seats were located in the southern part of the province and in the northeast and that the Conservatives won most of those [see Map 2] and that most of the "switches" also happened in the southern half of the province [see Map 3].

Annapolis was the tightest race, with the Conservative candidate beating the Liberal incumbent by only thirteen votes. Both parties scored big wins in the polls of their respective 1908 strongholds in the riding, but things changed the most in the towns of Middleton, Belleisle, Nictaux Falls, Lequille, and Round Hill. Solid improvements in turning out the Conservative vote in those five polls (compared to 1908) collectively gave them the slight edge. By maintaining their support in the rest of the riding, they managed to steal it from the Liberals.

The tough race in Hants showed a difference between big polling stations and smaller ones. Even though the Liberals won some polls in this riding that had over 200 votes (the poll in Forks gave 195 votes to the Liberal Party and 39 to the Conservatives, for instance), the Conservatives made sufficient gains in Windsor and Shubenacadie to win the riding by 86 votes.

In the riding of Kings, Frederick Borden was narrowly defeated by Arthur Foster, a twenty-one-year-old student. Borden had won the seat by 491 votes in 1908, but lost it by 151 in 1911. As in 1908, the Conservatives scored lopsided victories in the Berwick and Millville polling stations. The differences in 1911 came in traditionally tight polls such as Cambridge, which went from a virtual tie in 1908 to a 37-vote win for the Tories in 1911. The Conservative vote in Kentville went from 129 in 1908 to 230 in 1911. Even though the riding held one of the highest participation rates in the country in 1908 (79 percent), even more men turned out in 1911 (80 percent). An extra 324 voters participated, clearly sufficient to defeat Borden, who had held the seat (with the exception of one term) since the Alexander Mackenzie victory of 1874. Borden later attributed his defeat to the fact that the factory owners in his constituency had urged their workers to vote against reciprocity, but his prolonged absence from the race (he sat idly, and in vain, for the posting of High Commissioner to the Court of St. James) probably cost him more.

The race in Shelburne-Queens, William Fielding's seat, was evenly divided along geographical lines. Queens (with 17 polls) was a Conservative area and most of the polls were won by the party with relative ease. The Liberals made a stronger showing in the Shelburne part of the riding, except for the towns of Shelburne (2 polls), Gunning Cove, and Centreville, which delivered even bigger wins for the Conservatives than they had in 1908. "We were up against a stiff proposition," the Conservative candidate Fleming McCurdy wrote. "In the first place Shelburne-Queens is largely a fishing county which has always done and is doing a large amount of business with the States; during the past fifteen years extraordinary expenditures have been made on wharves and breakwaters; a contract for a $175,000 breakwater was closed about thirty days ago, and the contractor was in charge of the campaign against us."[26] Notwithstanding the defeat in some of the polling stations near fishing villages, the big Conservative victories in the landlocked polling stations closed the margin of victory in and allowed McCurdy to take the riding away from William Fielding with 170 votes.

The Liberals took two seats from the Conservatives: one of the two Halifax seats and Cape Breton South. The latter was won by the narrow margin of 104 votes using a most unusual political arsenal. James William Maddin had won the riding narrowly in 1908, and the Liberals desperately wanted it back. According to a Maddin supporter, the deputy minister of marine and fisheries, Alexander Johnson, used his own Sydney Record to attack the Conservative incumbent and support William F. Carroll. Maddin's defeat was due to four causes, according to one of the Conservative organizers. One of the big local employers, the Dominion Coal Company, campaigned in favour of reciprocity. A second factor was the spread of "anti-Orangism" among local Catholics. A third weapon was the "great outlay of money and rum by the Liberals" that was matched with effective slogans of cheaper food and cheaper garments. The final aspect was more surprising: "Over confidence on the part of the Conservatives."[27] The other Liberal victory was in the double-seat riding of Halifax. This time, Borden won the first seat with 25.5 percent of the vote, just edging out the Liberal, Alexander MacLean, who took the second seat with 25.1 percent. In

1908, two Tories (including Robert Borden) had been elected to represent the city.

With five new wins, the Conservatives now had pulled up even with the Liberals in Nova Scotia, earning nine of the eighteen seats. More than that, two of the most eminent Liberal ministers who had occupied headline portfolios — Finance and Militia — had gone down in flames. Most people voted the same way as they had in 1908, ignoring the grand plans and accusations hurled by the party leaders. It was the local politics which made the difference in turning out Conservatives in larger numbers in some areas, or in bolstering Liberal support in Cape Breton South and Halifax.

The Conservatives ran their 1911 campaign in New Brunswick with a vengeance after winning only one seat in the province in 1908. They were somewhat rewarded, picking up four new seats in the eastern part of the province and gathering 3 percent more votes than they had in 1908. The Liberals still eked a majority of votes (50.8 percent) in this tightly contested province, but were able to translate that slight edge of 1.6 percent into eight of thirteen seats, including re-election in seven seats.

In 1911, seven ridings were won by tiny margins, and five of those (Carleton, Charlotte, City and County of Saint John, City of Saint John, and Sunbury-Queen's) were as hotly contested as in 1908 [see Map 1]. Liberal Frank Carvell kept his seat of Carleton by beating Benjamin Smith by a mere 11 votes. Hugh McLean beat back his Conservative opponent and kept Sunbury-Queen's by 10 votes. The two former premiers of New Brunswick held their own, but only barely: William Pugsley convinced the riding City of Saint John to switch to the Liberals by 65 votes and Henry Emmerson, the former minister of railways and canals, won Westmoreland by even less: 64 votes. Judging by the political map, it is interesting to note that the tight ridings were in the east of the province, with many of them bordering the Bay of Fundy, and that most of those went to the Tories.

Five ridings switched sides [see Map 3]. In the Acadian riding of Kent, Liberal MP Olivier LeBlanc chose not to seek re-election. This opened the door for Ferdinand Robidoux, the Conservative candidate he had easily beaten in 1908. The Conservatives ran a remarkably strong campaign and managed to close the gap in all the areas of the riding. The keys were the towns of Wellington, Welford, and St. Mary's, who switched from being strong Liberal bases in 1908 to Conservative strongholds in 1911, and that was sufficient to turn the tide. This was a bitter loss for the Liberals, as Acadians tended to give Liberals a slight advantage. In 1911, the English strongholds in the riding made the difference.

Similar to Kent, the Conservative candidate won Kings and Albert on his second try. This was a growing riding — there were 334 more voters in 1911 than in 1908. The riding was almost a perfect switch as the Conservative turned a loss by 352 votes in 1908 into a win by 322 votes in 1911. The issues in Kent were broadly similar to the rest of the country, but according to one observer, there was also suspicion that the riding had lost faith in the Liberal government because it had not delivered on its railway policy.[28] The Liberal defeat was centralized in the growing towns of Hampton and Norton as electors there switched their votes. Clearly, the new voters in that area disproportionately voted for George Fowler, the Conservative Party candidate.

The Liberals recaptured the riding of Charlotte, which traditionally voted Conservative, because of Thomas Hartt's strong campaign. They also won the City of Saint John riding as William Pugsley adopted it. (The riding he abandoned, City and County of Saint John, meanwhile, switched to the Tories). Pugsley took his new seat through small gains made across the riding's 44 polls. Interestingly, the riding recorded a high number of rejected (154) and spoiled ballots (166), leaving the result open to speculation that there was tampering with the votes.

———·•·———

Prince Edward Island's three ridings were represented by four seats in the House of Commons. The vote was also almost equally split, with the Liberals taking 50.4 percent and the Tories 49.6 [see Map 1]. Two of P.E.I.'s ridings — King's and Prince — continued to offer the most intense battles. In 1911, the Liberals won Prince by 115 votes (they had won it by 164 votes in 1908) and took King's in the east by 14 votes (the Conservatives had won it by 182 votes in 1908) [see Map 3]. Queen's, the riding in the middle of the island, was dominated by Charlottetown and had two seats. Both were taken by the Conservatives as they trounced the Liberal pair by 769 votes. (In 1908, the Liberals had won the two seats by a collective margin of 228 votes).

Prince Edward Island thus offered an interesting political sandwich, with the Tories in the more urban middle, and the Liberals on both the east and west coasts [see Map 2]. It is not clear that the reciprocity issue was all that decisive in the final result, as Islanders were traditionally divided. Clearly, there was an economic risk, for reciprocity meant that their markets in the East would be opened to the Americans. That being said, there was also some conviction that potato growers in the province would benefit enormously from more exposure to the U.S. markets. Finally, there was a third issue on the island: the idea of building a tunnel to the mainland. The Liberals had supported the idea, but done nothing to pursue it, and many on the Island voted for the Conservatives in the hope that they would deliver on the longstanding promise.[29]

The situation in Quebec was also a scene of reversal. The Liberals still dominated Quebec in 1911, but their lead in the polls was shrunk by 6.5 percent (to 50.2 percent) and that translated into dramatically fewer seats: only 37 would sit with Sir Wilfrid after the election — down from 54 seats. The Tories improved their showing considerably from 11 seats to an official number of 27, taking 21.9 percent of the vote and 14 seats on their own, with 13 seats taken by *nationalistes* under the Conservative and other banners [see Table 10.1]. In terms of the popular vote, the *nationalistes* clearly had an impact, taking 26.7 of the vote, and 40 percent of the ridings in which they ran. In Quebec, 21 constituencies switched parties [see Map 5]. One seat went to the Labour candidate in Maisonneuve, Alphonse Verville, who was re-elected (the Liberals did not run a candidate against him, and for all intents and purposes considered Verville one of their own. He was recognized as a Liberal (and is listed among them in Table 10.1).

In Quebec, thirty ridings were won by margins of 5 percent or less [see Map 6]. The Conservatives won twelve by margins of less than 3.8 percent of the vote, and some of the very small margins made losses doubly hard to take for the Liberals. Their worst news was that Sydney Fisher, a man even Henri Bourassa had called the most honest, courageous, and prudent man in the cabinet, was defeated.[30] Solicitor General Jacques Bureau won Trois-Rivières and St-Maurice, barely escaping on the strength of nine votes. There was a significant increase in voter turnout in 1911 in this riding, but most of it went to the Conservatives. Most remarkable were the results attained in the traditionally solid Liberal parish of Sainte-Flore, which suddenly shared its vote, and Saint-Barnabé, which swung Conservative.

The other ministers fared better. Laurier was acclaimed in Québec-Est and won in Soulanges also (he would represent the two ridings in the twelfth Parliament). Rodolphe Lemieux, the minister responsible for the navy, was easily re-elected in Rouville, the seat just vacated by Louis-Philippe Brodeur (who had been acclaimed in 1908). But there was a consequence to the win. Lemieux had kept his old seat of Gaspé, no doubt thinking that he could be defeated in a delayed election (the vast riding of Gaspé took longer to organize electorally and much of it tended to vote after results were announced in the rest of the country). Lemieux had won Gaspé in 1908 by taking almost 80 percent of the cast ballots. With the Borden win on September 21, Gaspé voted *nationaliste*. The fifth minister from Quebec, Henri Béland, the Postmaster General since early August, was elected in his own riding of the Beauce but was convincingly defeated in Montmagny (like Laurier and Lemieux, he also ran in two ridings).

There were other consolations for the Liberals. Nine seats were won by over 15 percent pluralities, five were won by 10 percent margins or more, and six were won by 5 percent or more. The Grits took fifteen seats by margins of 5 percent or less of the votes, indicating what a tough contest the election of 1911 was for them in Quebec.

The Liberals actually took four seats from their adversaries. First was Drummond-Arthabaska, which had been lost ten months earlier to the *nationalistes* but had now been reclaimed by the Liberal Ovide Brouillard by 266 votes. William Power defeated the Conservative William Price in Quebec West with only 90 votes to spare. The Liberals also snatched the riding of Sherbrooke — one of only three ridings visited by Borden — by less than 40 votes. The riding of Sherbrooke was an even urban/rural split, with the town Sherbrooke taking up 19 of the 34 polls in the riding. These 19 polls were split into the North, South, East, and Centre wards. The North ward did not change in 1911, as the Conservatives scored another big victory, but the East and South ward turned Liberal and swung the riding. The fourth and final seat taken from the Conservatives was actually a bit of a dirty trick. As noted above, Laurier ran twice in this election. Acclaimed in his riding of Quebec East, he nonetheless ran against the Conservative incumbent Joseph-Arthur Lortie in Soulanges. Laurier defeated him handily, and would represent the two ridings until 1917.

The real story in Quebec, however, was the surge in support for Conservatives and *nationalistes*. The Conservative campaign made big gains, including four victories taken by substantial majorities, the biggest of which was Herbert Ames, who was re-elected in Saint-Antoine in Montreal by a margin of over 27 percent. Seven more seats were won with more than 10 percent advantages, showing strong resilience against prestigious Liberal challengers. Pierre-Edouard Blondin, for instance, increased his margin of victory in Champlain, and Rodolphe Forget (one of the wealthiest businessmen in the province) successfully fought off Lucien Cannon in Charlevoix. (Forget also won

Wilfrid Laurier in Montcalm County, August 1911.

Courtesy LAC, C-022828.

Montmorency and would represent two ridings, like Laurier, in the twelfth Parliament.)

Three Conservative wins were the result of Liberal infighting. The Borden team won Pontiac because two candidates ran under Liberal banners against Gerald Brabazon. Had the Liberals united, they would have won the riding by over 10 percent. The same thing happened in Berthier, where the Conservative Joseph Barrette narrowly beat the incumbent Liberal Joseph Écrement by 26 votes because an independent, Jean Denis, took away the Liberal advantage. Écrement, long suspected of corruption, had been targeted by Godfroy Langlois and the progressive wing of the Quebec Liberals. The voter turnout in Berthier was similar in both elections, and despite only increasing their total votes by 16, the Conservatives won the riding in the 1911 election after losing it by 265 ballots in 1908. What had previously been tightly contested polls in Lavaltrie and Saint-Zénon, for instance, now became key Conservative victories because of a solid showing by the independent. Denis received only 383 votes (fairly distributed across the riding), but many of them evidently came from former Liberal supporters. Last but not least was the ridiculous situation in Chicoutimi-Saguenay, where Joseph Girard — the Laurier candidate at the beginning of the campaign — won as an "independent conservative." The vote in Chicoutimi-Saguenay took place a week after September 21 (like Gaspé). Girard adopted the *nationaliste* platform and was able to win because no less than three Liberals ran against him and split the vote. The people of the Lac Saint-Jean area voted to be with the government.

The Conservative wave drowned Sydney Fisher also. He had made a strong showing in the riding of Brome in 1908, winning the election by 441 votes by dominating in the towns of Brome, Patton, and Farnham specifically. The story changed drastically in 1911, as the Liberals kept the towns of Brome and Patton but lost Farnham, and that was enough to make all the difference. The population change in the riding was slight and the voter participation between the two elections was almost identical. Clearly, the many visits paid by Bourassa (and Borden) to Farnham during the course of the election had a great impact. Sydney Fisher, Laurier's steady minister of agriculture since 1896, lost the riding to a twenty-two-year-old lawyer, George Baker, by 24 votes.

The composition of the riding of Compton, its polls spread widely, lent itself well to the Conservative organization. In 1908, the vote had been evenly split among most of the 52 polls. The Liberals, however, had won the election by scoring big in a few key polls, specifically Moss School House, Saint-Romain Winslow, and Westburg East, which each gave double the votes they gave the Conservatives. In 1911, however, the Conservatives closed the gap in all three of those polls and took big wins in Sainte-Cécile, Linda (county of Westburg), and Cookshire East and West.

The Tories captured Montmorency in a close race. The small riding had only 19 polls and the population was smaller than most other ridings in the province. The Conservatives managed to narrow the lead in every poll that the Liberals relied on to win in 1908. What made the difference in 1911 was the poll in the town of Saint-Tite, which swung Conservative, and that made the difference to elect the wealthy financier Rodolphe Forget.

Yamaska, the sixth riding that switched from Liberal to Conservative, was a divided riding, as areas swung to both parties in different parts of the district. Several towns had multiple polls; with a few villages having only one — this was unusual in Canada's rural ridings. This also made the larger villages more strategically important. In 1908, Yamaska was won in a tight race by the Liberals by 93 votes, but 1911 was a perfect switch, with the Conservatives winning by 88 votes. Saint-Francois-du-Lac (three polls) was the primary village that switched and helped swing the election. There was no doubt that *nationaliste* sentiment played a role in this race (and the Liberal candidate, Oscar Gladu, was a fierce critic of Bourassa), but Albéric Mondou always insisted on being a Conservative and never hesitated to underline the fact that Henri Bourassa had not helped him at all.[31]

The *nationalistes* ran in thirty four ridings across the province, and won thirteen: David L'Espérance (Montmagny), Octave Guilbault (Joliette), Louis-Philippe Pelletier (Quebec County), Paul-Emile

Lamarche (Nicolet), Joseph Lavallée (Bellechasse), Joseph Rainville (Chambly-Verchères), Albert Sevigny (Dorchester), Louis Coderre (Hochelaga), Honoré Achim (Labelle), Frederick Monk (Saint-Jacques Montréal), Joseph Girard (Chicoutimi-Saguenay), Adélard Bellemare (Maskinongé), and Louis-Philippe Gauthier (Gaspé). They took twelve of those thirteen seats from the Liberals (Monk was re-elected in Saint-Jacques). Dorchester, Hochelaga, Montmagny, Gaspé, and Saint-Jacques were won handily, while Bellechasse, Chambly-Verchères, Joliette, Labelle, Maskinongé, Nicolet, Chicoutimi-Saguenay, and Quebec County were won in very close contests.

Bellechasse was a good example of how the Liberals lost support in Quebec. After winning the 1908 election with 76 percent of the vote, the Liberal incumbent, Ernest Talbot, lost his seat by 46 votes. He received 292 fewer votes than in the past election, but that by itself was not enough to lose the riding. The biggest difference was the 823 more *nationaliste* voters in the 1911 election, despite there being only 263 newly eligible voters. These new votes swung almost exclusively to Lavallée, the *nationaliste* candidate.

In Chambly-Verchères, Liberal incumbent Victor Geoffrion's 824-vote victory in 1908 changed to a 136-vote loss in 1911. The 960-vote swing was mostly a result of a massive increase in voter turnout. More than a thousand more citizens showed up to the Chambly-Verchères polls despite there being only about 206 extra eligible voters. The Liberals actually gained total votes between elections (95 votes), indicating that it was not a case of losing support among former partisans. It does show that almost 92 percent of the new voters supported the *nationaliste* Joseph Rainville. Beyond the political motivations that drove voters to the polls, the result also exemplified organizer ability to reach previously inactive voters.

Joliette, visited by both Laurier and Bourassa, was one of the more polarized ridings in Canada across its 29 voting stations, and gave a very narrow victory to the *nationalistes*. Both the Liberal incumbent and his Conservative-Nationalist adversary (it was never clear to what degree Octave Guilbault was *a nationaliste*, but because Bourassa spoke in his favour often, he should be considered as one) scored big victories in polls across the riding. Joliette featured some very large polls at the time, with an average of 35 more people per poll than the average across Canada. The Liberals won big in Saint-Paul, Saint-Thomas, and Sainte-Elisabeth, while the *nationalistes* took Joliette, Saint-Alphonse, Sainte-Béatrice, and Saint-Félix-de-Valois. In the end, the big wins for the *nationalistes* in a few polls made the difference, and they were able to come away with a 66-vote differential in their favour.

Labelle, once Henri Bourassa's riding, swung to the *nationalistes* as an additional 1,145 voters made their way to the polls (an increase of 25 percent). The Liberals still managed to lean on parts of their base and score big wins in Blake, Robertson, and L'Ange-Gardien, but were unable to overcome the groundswell of *nationaliste* support fed by a visit from Bourassa. This was a dramatic reversal of the 1908 result when the Liberals had won Labelle by the substantial margin of 1,327 votes.

The riding of Maskinongé saw another switch where the *nationalistes* made important gains in discrete areas. The two polls of Saint-Léon voted overwhelmingly Liberal in 1908, but in 1911 the Laurier party fell short there by 75 votes. This swing represented a gain of 140 votes for the *nationalistes* in just two polls — enough to make the difference.

Nicolet's votes were spread out across 59 polls. Interestingly, the population of the riding was quite high at the time of the election (36,055) yet there was still just an average amount of total eligible voters (6,909). It is probably safe to suggest there were a significant number of children in the riding, perhaps making voters more attentive to Bourassa's claims that war and conscription were imminent. Nicolet, which had given the Liberals a margin of victory of 666 votes in 1908, handed instead the *nationalistes* a win by 84 votes, with almost every polling station showing better results for the latter.

The riding of Quebec County had an interesting mix of large and small polls. The small polling stations were typically won by the Liberals, and in 1908 the party still managed a good showing in the denser areas. The *nationalistes* struggled in the sparsely populated areas in 1911, but managed to score consistent victories in Saint-Grégoire and in the third polling station in Sillery. These gains allowed the party to take the riding by 48 votes in 1911.

The *nationalistes* won most of their ridings by small margins in the belt that surrounded Montreal. The Liberal campaign, for all its faults, was not a complete failure. It lost relatively few votes: it was the clever Bourassa campaign that focused its punches on the soft flanks of the Liberal vote that made the difference. By invoking conscription, by speaking to the fathers and mothers of young children, and by emphasizing the risk Laurier was taking in catering to imperialists, Bourassa struck sensitive chords and brought out voters who might have stayed home on election day. For their part, the Liberals were aggressive in taking their fight to Bourassa, and beat him in his home ground of Saint-Hyacinthe and in Drummond-Arthabaska, and they kept what they had of French Montreal (Monk's riding and Hochelaga being the exception), thus limiting Bourassa's influence.

----·•·----

An even greater political earthquake shook Ontario. While the Conservatives had taken 51 percent of the vote in 1908, that lead was increased to 56.2 in 1911. Translated into seats, this meant that the Tories went from 48 seats to 73: a dramatic gain [see Map 7]. Almost 40 percent of the Ontario MPs heading for Ottawa after the election would be new. Support for the Conservatives swelled across the province. It was most pronounced in urban areas, but also showed in rural parts of the province. Writing upon his re-election for the riding of Ontario North, Samuel Sharpe noted that "my majority has been increased from 200 to 600 and this is an agricultural constituency, there being no manufacturing towns in it. Owing to our organization, our educational campaign, our splendid leader and the magnificent issue, there was only one result to be expected, namely, victory."[32]

The fortunes of the Liberal Party in Ontario told much of the story of the 1911 election. In 1896, Laurier had won 40.2 percent of the votes, but that was enough to earn him 43 seats — the same as the Conservatives. He improved his record dramatically in 1900 by getting 48.5 percent of the vote, but the Liberals ironically lost six seats. In 1904, his record improved yet again, albeit marginally. With 49.5 percent of the votes, he was within striking distance of matching the Conservative Party's 50.3 percent. But the riding distribution did not show encouraging results: only one seat was gained, giving the Liberals a total of 38. Laurier's popularity in some areas of Ontario proved enduring, but the results of 1908 betrayed a deteriorating situation. Popular support declined to 47.2 percent of the votes, and 37 seats, the same as in 1900. In 1911 another 4 percent of the voters abandoned the Liberals, but the loss translated itself into a devastating riding count. The Liberals had gone from 43 seats in 1896 to 13 in 1911 — most of them in the east and in the southern peninsula, where agriculture was a dominant activity and many Catholics lived.

One Conservative was acclaimed in Thunder Bay/Rainy River, as the election was held on October 12, long after the Borden victory. Three Tories were elected with more than 70 percent of the vote, 18 were elected with more than 60 percent of the vote, and 14 were elected with more than 55 percent of the vote. The other 37 seats were taken with more than 50 percent of the vote. Every region of the province voted Conservative, the rural and the urban, the areas closest to the borders and the most remote. The Conservatives won with huge margins in all the Toronto and Ottawa seats.

The Liberals held on to 13 seats, one earned with over 60 percent of the vote: the Franco-Ontarian stronghold of Prescott. The ridings around Ottawa also tended to vote Liberal. Only one Liberal candidate, William German in Welland, was acclaimed (he had won 53.9 percent of the vote in 1908).

Otherwise, the Liberals were thoroughly routed in Ontario, but the numbers told only part of the story. In 1911, 25 of 85 ridings were taken with less than a 5 percent plurality, far fewer than in 1908, when 36 of the 85 seats were tight races. In 1911, 7 of those seats remained Conservative; 4 remained Liberal, 13 switched from Liberal to Conservative, while one switched from Conservative to Liberal [see Map 8].

The 14 ridings that switched sides cut a wide swath across the province's rural middle and shed light on the dynamics of the election [see Map 9]: Brant, Brockville, Grey South, Huron South, Middlesex North, Northumberland West, Oxford South, Perth South, Peterborough West, Stormont, Waterloo North, Wellington North, and York North went Conservative. The one riding that switched to

Liberal in a tight contest was Norfolk, the agricultural riding on Lake Erie where Laurier had launched his campaign. It was won by William Charlton, a businessman, who beat the incumbent Conservative MP Alexander McCall by 118 votes. Clearly, Laurier had made a difference with his speech in Simcoe.

The narrow Liberal losses affected the three cabinet ministers representing the province: Paterson lost Brant by 129 votes; George Graham lost his Brockville seat by 111 votes; and William Lyon Mackenzie King lost North Waterloo by 315 votes. In Brant, William Paterson lost by what could only be called a political infection. The new 374 votes for the Conservatives were earned across Brant, and benefitted particularly by strong showings in the Onondaga Township and Paris polls. Paterson was defeated by the strong Conservative machine next door. Indeed, the nearby town of Brantford, situated just beside Brant, also swung hard for the Conservatives in 1911. The two ridings were neighbours (they were later united into a single federal riding), which offered an opportunity for Conservative organizers to maximize canvassing efforts.

In Brockville, George Graham sought re-election after winning by only 144 votes in 1908. The key to his victory were the three polls of Front of Yonge Township that had guaranteed his success in 1908 with an 85-vote plurality in this area. Those same three polls were his downfall in 1911. Graham received a similar total number of votes in 1911, but the Conservatives bettered their turnout and reduced the difference to 66. These polls alone did not represent a large change, but they exemplified a theme across the riding. His steady showing (Graham earned 2,144 votes in 1908 and 2,140 in 1911) was not enough as the Conservatives pulled out their vote, increasing their 1908 total of 2,000 to 2,251 votes in 1911. The trend exemplified in Front of Yonge Township carried across the 35 polls, as better Conservative organization led to the defeat of the liberals by 111 votes. The change in vote was slight. One speculation why this was so was the rising price of cheese in Canada (and the Brockville area produced much cheese), and the fear that American competition would undermine profits.[33]

In Grey South, Liberal incumbent Henry Horton Miller faced Robert James Ball, the same Conservative candidate he had defeated in

1908 by only 87 votes. Like many other districts of rural Ontario, Grey South saw a population decrease between the two elections that in turn led to fewer voters. Both parties lost votes in the 1911 election but the Conservatives managed to bring their support out to the voting booths, losing only 41 votes while the Liberals lost 176. Specifically, it was the townships of Sullivan and Hanover that were key to the Conservative success. In Sullivan, the Conservatives improved their turnout, making a town that had split in the previous election swing decidedly toward Robert Borden's Tories. In Hanover, Conservative losses in the Liberal stronghold were minimized through another example of pulling the vote through regional organization.

In Huron South, the vote was fairly evenly distributed among the riding's ten regions. Interestingly, many towns that were tightly contested had individual polls that leaned heavily to a specific party. The Liberals, for instance, won poll 15 in McKillop by 79 votes, but did not take the town by much more. Similarly the Conservatives won poll 46 in Usborne by 67 votes, but lost two of the other three polls in the town to the Liberals. In the end, the Conservatives were able to pull more votes across all 47 polls and unseat the Liberal incumbent candidate.

Middlesex North was a polarized riding. The electoral district itself featured six townships with five polls or more and another three polls dedicated to small areas within the riding. Biddulph and Lobo were particularly at odds as the Conservatives took Biddulph by 129 votes and the Liberals won Lobo by 171 votes. Despite the strong Liberal showing in Lobo, and a solid party turnout in Williams, consistent Conservative showings in Adelaide, McGillvray, and Park Hill were enough to offset the local Liberal wins. Middlesex North was another Northern Ontario riding were Conservative organization seemed to make a key difference.

The Northumberland West result looked remarkably similar to the 1908 election; the Liberal candidate was up for re-election and faced off against the same Conservative opponent. The election in 1908 was narrowly won by the Liberals, who took the riding by only 130 votes. The Liberals made a similar showing in 1911, getting all but 18 of the votes they received in the previous election. The Conservative ability to pull the vote in rural Ontario continued in Northumberland West and it would be enough to unseat another Liberal parliamentarian. After a recount, the Conservatives won one of the tightest ridings in the election by only 6 votes (0.2 percent difference).

Oxford South was another Ontario riding that saw the two parties fighting for fewer votes than the 1908 election. The vote distribution in the riding has two distinct stories: the Liberals won 17 of the first 19 polls in the riding; the Conservatives took 19 of the last 22. This regional difference showed in the final tally, as the Conservatives won a tight contest by 24 votes. Tillsonburg proved to be the most important town, as the Conservatives swept its three polls and won the town by 99 votes.

Perth South saw a decrease in population between the two elections and a decrease in votes for both parties. The 1911 poll distribution trended in similar ways to the 1908 election; however, in 1911 the Liberal Party candidate, Gilbert McIntyre, the Deputy Speaker and Chair of Committees of the Whole of the House of Commons, lost 190 votes compared to the 1908 showing. The Conservatives also lost votes from their past showing (73 votes) but proved to be much better at damage control, reaching the citizens who had stayed in the riding.

In 1911, the Liberals knew they had a tough race in Peterborough West. They had taken the riding three years before by 333 votes, and, given that the Conservative candidate was the same man, could expect a similar race. Since 1908, however, the riding saw an important increase in population. What was remarkable was that the Conservatives increased their total votes by 426, drawing many of those in the city of Peterborough. Although the Liberals did very well in the surrounding areas, it was the city vote that gave the Conservative Party the riding.

Stormont looked very different in 1911 compared to the 1908 election. Two factors contributed to the new reality. The race in 1908 saw an independent receive 658 votes, thereby conceivably splitting the Conservative vote in a tight race that was ultimately won by the Liberal candidate by the thin margin of 350 votes. In 1911, Liberal MP Robert Smith did not seek re-election and no independents ran. The Conservative candidate capitalized on these factors in an interesting manner. Both the Borden and the Laurier teams won the same number of polls, and both parties did a good job of playing to their base in this riding; however, the lack of a third candidate allowed the Conservatives to close the gap in Liberal strongholds of Cornwall and Roxborough. The Conservatives increased their total votes by 506 despite there being only 127 more votes in the riding. The Liberals also increased their total votes, although only by 25, indicating that the independent vote turned Conservative in 1911, and swung the riding.

Future prime minister Mackenzie King was unable to stop the Conservative tide in North Waterloo, and, as he had long feared, he too lost his seat. After winning the riding by 263 votes in 1908, King put up a similar number of votes in 1911. Waterloo, however, saw a sizeable increase in population between elections of almost 6,500. This only translated into another 492 eligible male voters, but that small amount was enough for the Conservative candidate to increase his total votes by 568. It can be speculated that, as in Peterborough West or in Brant, most of these new Conservative votes came from newcomers to the town, attracted by a growing manufacturing sector. Had Waterloo North stayed the same, King could have very well won the election.

Wellington North was another tight victory for the Conservatives, after losing by only 84 votes in 1908. This time, Conservative candidate William Clarke beat the Liberal incumbent by 25 votes. Most of the riding's polls were hotly contested, with Liberals holding the slight edge. It was the small town of Palmerston that made the difference in this election: It gave the Tories 298 of its 374 votes. This 222-vote edge was enough to cover the balance of the other 48 polls in the ridings, in which the Liberals held a 197-vote edge.

York North saw a familiar candidate run, but not the one that may have been expected. Liberal minister Allen Aylesworth, who had won the riding by 306 votes in 1908, retired from politics. Many of the polls in the 1911 race were close, and none was won by more than 50 votes. The big difference this time was Newmarket, which had gone Liberal by more than 100 votes in 1908. In 1911, its five polls gave the Tories a plurality of 28 votes — enough to rob the Liberals of another seat.

The Conservatives won big in Ontario. In larger cities, such as Ottawa, Toronto, and Hamilton, in smaller towns such as Barrie, Peterborough, and Kingston, and in the broad middle of the province the Borden team dominated. The races were considerably tighter in southern Ontario, but even there many Liberal wins were hotly contested. The cartoonist Newton McConnell published a biting piece following the campaign that depicted a man "in the year 2211" examining bone specimens under a jar labelled "Ontario Liberal: This species is supposed to have become extinct about the year 1911" at the office of the Canadian Archives in Ottawa. Clearly, that fate was averted. The Liberal Party under Laurier lived a wrenching decade in the 1910s, but eventually recovered and became the most successful political party at the federal level in the province.

"In the year 2211." The future of the Liberal Party?

The Liberals and the Tories split the West, but in Manitoba, practically nothing changed. The Conservatives took 51.9 percent of the votes, but 80 percent of the seats (eight of the ten seats) just as they had in 1908 [see Map 10]. The Liberals, who took 44.8 percent of the votes, certainly could find a little satisfaction in keeping Provencher, the southeastern riding, and in having reached the voters in farming communities across the province. They acquired bragging rights in Glenlyon Campbell's victory over the Conservative Theodore Burrows in Dauphin, but little else could make them smile.

The distribution of districts in Manitoba worked against them as in no other province. The Liberal win in Dauphin was offset by the loss of Clifford Sifton's old riding of Brandon, which went to the Conservatives by a margin of over 10 percent of the vote. Sifton's political star had been eclipsed — he had narrowly won the riding for the Liberals in 1908. The rising figure in Manitoba politics was now Arthur Meighen, the thirty-seven-year-old Member re-elected for Portage la Prairie, who won this time with a commanding 11.6 percent margin.

As in 1908, half of the ten ridings were taken by small margins [see Map 11]. Lisgar (as in 1908) was won narrowly by the Conservatives, as were the ridings of Macdonald, Marquette, Selkirk, and Souris. In some cases, the Conservatives were helped by the gains made by third parties, who earned 3.3 percent of the vote. This likely hit the Liberals hard. In Selkirk, for instance, the race was narrowly lost by the Liberals because "independent" Wasil Holowacky garnered 3.7 percent of the vote. In Winnipeg, however, the Socialist Party candidacy made no difference as the Conservative Alexander Haggart trounced his collective opposition by more than 10 percent of the vote.

———•◦•———

The election campaign in Saskatchewan was fairly quiet. The Conservatives, as expected, did poorly, taking only one of the ten seats, even though they had 39 percent of the vote, while Liberal support climbed to 59.4 percent, thrashing the Conservatives by 20.4 percent. Saskatchewan strongly supported Laurier, even though it was not represented in cabinet. In 1908, it had awarded the Liberals the same percentage of its votes (just 0.1 percent shy of the Liberal record in Quebec) and nine of its ten seats. The margins of victory in individual ridings were crushing. Two of the ridings were taken by the Liberals with over 70 percent of the vote; another three with over 60 percent. James McKay won a relatively tight race in Prince Albert for the

Conservatives, beating his Liberal opponent by more than 5 percent. It was bittersweet defeat for William Rutan, the Liberal who had held the riding going into the election.

The consolation for the Liberals was the fierce contest in the riding of Qu'Appelle, where Levi Thompson challenged the incumbent Richard Lake, who had won the riding in 1908 by only 52 votes. The Commissioner of the Royal Northwest Police was told that "there is a probability that liquor and other undue influences may be in evidence at certain polls on election day," and so dispatched officers to "maintain peace and good order" at a number of polling booths in the area just east of Regina.[34] In the end, Thompson beat Lake by just over 5 percent of the vote. "Yes, I am among the defeated," reported Lake: "But it was by the Americans, Germans, Hungarians & French. From the older settlements & especially those of chiefly British descent I had a good majority. The local government took a very strong hand against me, while we had to think of our own fight without assistance from the outside."[35]

Alberta responded to the Liberal Party with the same verve as Saskatchewan. In 1911, the Liberals took two more seats for a total of six, and raised their popular vote to 53.3 percent. In 1908, the Liberals had taken 50.2 of the vote and four of the seven seats. Indeed, Alberta gave the Liberals the second highest plurality after Saskatchewan, and 3.1 percent more than in 1908. The Liberals took a seat from the Conservatives, and regained the "Liberal-Conservative" seat of MacLeod. Frank Oliver, the minister of the Interior, who was concerned that the allegations that he had personally profited by awarding land holdings to railways jeopardized his chances, was elected easily in Edmonton with almost 57 percent of the vote, although his 1908 lead was cut by almost half. For their part, the Conservatives who had managed to win three seats in 1908 could only hold on to one in 1911. It was R.B. Bennett, who crushed his Liberal opponent by a commanding 21.7 percent plurality in Calgary.

British Columbia also delivered a lopsided result, but in the opposite direction. It was a situation similar to Manitoba, but worse. Even though they earned 37.5 of the vote, the Liberals were shut out of the seven seats.

The Conservative sweep in British Columbia was a complete revolution over the results of the election of 1904, when Laurier had swept all seven seats with almost 50 percent of the popular vote. In 1908, however, British Columbia showed a cold shoulder and only returned three seats to the Liberals — the result of a sharp reaction against the Liberal government's immigration policies. Three years later, the disdain for the Liberal program was screaming. The first victim was William Templeman, Laurier's minister of Inland Revenue, who lost Victoria City. The second was Ralph Smith, the popular former miner who had strong ties to the Labour movement, who was trounced by his Conservative adversary by an almost 17 percent margin in Nanaimo.

The third loss was in Comox-Atlin, where William Sloan had been acclaimed in 1908, but did not run in 1911. The riding was taken by Herbert Clements, a Conservative, who won by a margin of 5.4 percent. Comox-Atlin was the tightest race, while the Liberal defeats elsewhere in the province were humiliating. In New Westminster and Yale-Cariboo, the Tories beat the Liberal candidate by over 30 percent of the vote, which was no surprise to Laurier, who had predicted defeat there.[36] In New Westminster it was thought that a critical element of Liberal support depended on patronage. One Liberal supplier to the local federal penitentiary demanded guarantees that the Liberal government purchase from its friends. "If we are to have a fighting chance here in the present General Election, we must have from your department an immediate explanation of the matters complained of, with assurance of a different policy with regard to Penitentiary patronage in the future, and also assurance of a very early increase in salaries of Penitentiary employees as long petitioned for and virtually promised."[37] No offer was made by the Laurier Liberals. The Tories took that riding by a 31.4 percent margin.

For the Conservatives, British Columbia was a triumph. Henry Herbert Stevens, the future leader of the Reconstruction Party, made his entrance into federal politics by defeating his Liberal adversary,

John Senkler, by a 26.4 percent margin in Vancouver. The Conservative tide extended to the Yukon, although its vote was cast under very unusual circumstances — two weeks after the September 21 election. The Conservative candidate, Alfred Thompson, won 60.8 percent of the vote — a remarkable turnaround for a party that had garnered barely 10 percent of the vote only three years earlier. Yukoners liked to be represented in the government, no matter the party in power, and voted accordingly.

The West was thus a story of extremes. In Alberta and Saskatchewan, the Laurier Liberals were popular, mostly on account of their support for reciprocity and the promise of higher prices for their goods and cheaper costs for their supplies. That call did not ring true in Manitoba and British Columbia. Borden's trip to the West a few months before the election had probably had an impact in Manitoba, but it is doubtful that his influence had gone much farther. In British Columbia, Premier McBride's years of angry denunciations of the Laurier government had finally taken their toll. That Laurier could not prove stronger allegiance to the Empire mattered a great deal in the province, but only in the sense that it aggravated the perception of his policies in other areas. Where the Liberals were at least competitive in all the provinces, they did not win; in British Columbia, they scored their lowest popularity ratings by far, at 37.5 percent.

———·•·———

The Conservatives won the 1911 election by taking 39 seats from the Liberals, most of these by margins of less than 5 percent. In other words, Canadians were divided, but what made the difference were very local changes of mind. What prompted the few thousand voting men to change their votes? Since September 22, 1911, the explanations have animated debates in families, parties, and history classrooms.

The protagonists themselves, of course, were quick to introduce their own theories to explain the results. In his postmortem account to his cabinet a few days after the defeat, Laurier pointed to hardened attitudes among anglo-protestants and theorized that a French Catholic would never again be elected prime minister (a view shared by Rodolphe Lemieux, who privately renounced any ambition of leading the Liberal Party). He would have liked the explanation offered in New York City that "the men of Ontario are more English than the English themselves, and they are certainly more Scotch than the Irish, and, like all Scotchmen, are very reluctant to give anything they possess."[38] Laurier considered that the *Ne Temere* decree and the 1909 Eucharist Congress in Montreal "worked quietly" to embitter the Protestant attitude against the Liberals. Laurier and his colleagues also blamed the business community for bankrolling the Conservative Party's stance against reciprocity. "I have nothing to regret," Laurier told his cabinet on September 30. "If I had to do the whole thing again I would. If we had not accepted that offer [of reciprocity] we would have been disgraced." Laurier stood up, according to Mackenzie King who recorded the event in his diary, and walked to the fire. He turned again to his colleagues to emphasize his view: "I say again I have nothing to regret. We could not have refused that offer and be true to ourselves. We have been beaten but we can keep our heads erect."

Some pointed out, with disappointment, that the farmers had turned away from the party. Others attributed the loss to the Taft speech on the "Parting of the Ways" and Champ Clark's remarks on annexing Canada. Mackenzie King even noted in his diary (which had only received one entry since the Reciprocity Agreement was tabled in the Commons in late January) that many in the defeated cabinet "felt that the women moved much on this side & exerted a real influence." Outside cabinet discussions, many blamed William Fielding for not doing a better job of organizing the campaign in Nova Scotia. Mackenzie King, for his part, considered that the defeat was the product of "the evil genius," Clifford Sifton.[39] Laurier never did comment on his enormous losses in Quebec (except to blame a few priests) or British Columbia, although he suspected that the government views on Asian immigration were not popular on the West Coast. Regardless, he did not go beyond generalities.

Robert Borden attributed his success to a campaign on reciprocity, barely acknowledging that his alliance with Henri Bourassa had contributed to at least a quarter of his gains. Others blamed the Liberal defeat on the *Naval Service Act*. The *Calgary Daily Herald* argued that the "great and all powerful sentiment which led to the defeat of the Laurier government ... was patriotism."[40]

Historians long accepted those explanations, adding that Laurier was ultimately defeated by the enemies of each and every compromise he had crafted since 1896. The *nationalistes* did not forgive him the Canadian involvement in the South African War, the limited rights of francophones in Alberta and Saskatchewan, and the *Naval Service Act*. The new Canadian nationalists, the imperialists, could not forgive him not doing enough for the Empire, and also resented his compromises to ensure French-language instruction in the West. There was also merit in the notion that the Laurier government had been aging fast, and often seemed overwhelmingly opportunistic and patronage-ridden. For some voters, it had come to the end of its natural life cycle and had to end. But this possibility explained little. Laurier was still the most popular politician in the land, and those ministers that were suspected of corruption (Oliver and Pugsley) were re-elected.

In the 1960s, new interpretations by young historians focused on campaign organization. One argued that it was Conservative organization, particularly in Ontario, that explained the monster gains collected by the Borden team.[41] Another demonstrated the reverse, that it was in fact the collapse of the Liberal machine that explained the result — not so much argument and platform, but simply the ability to turn out the vote.[42]

In the 1980s, economists sought to measure the self-interest of voters to explain the results of the 1911 election. The first attempts were made to understand why some agricultural areas voted Conservative, while others did not, but were inconclusive as to what factors mattered most.[43] A few years later, another team looked at a larger variety of economic variables, observing that labelling the 1911 election as merely about reciprocity was misleading. They concluded that a variety of economic self-interests played a role, along with other factors.[44] More recently, a pair of economists sharpened the economic models to account for the result. Pointing to populations likely to be involved in pork production, they argued that farmers who depended on meat packers to process their product — such as in Ontario — were directly threatened by reciprocity (in that American processors would pay them far less for their goods) and thus they were very likely to vote Conservative. It followed that farmers who processed their own meats

— such as in Quebec — had no reason to fear reciprocity, and yet voted against the Laurier Liberals. In other words, reciprocity could explain much in terms of Ontario, but not across Canada. If people voted Conservative, or more particularly *nationaliste*, it had to be for reasons other than reciprocity.[45]

All these hypotheses hold kernels of truth. There is no doubt that Laurier's cautious policy in supporting the British naval plans angered many anglophile voters, but it is equally clear that many of them were also sympathetic to the Liberal stance. Money played a role, but the Liberals were not innocents in the game of using friends in industry to "buy" votes. Laurier's defeat can only be explained by a perfect storm of opposing winds. In Quebec, Henri Bourassa and Armand Lavergne were at their peaks of energy and political engagement. There was, in many parts of the province, an audience that wanted to hear their message: younger male voters, and men and women with large families who feared the possibility of sacrificing their children on the altar of British defence urged the voters in their families not to support Laurier. In Ontario, the growing sense of power and the feeling that Canada had grown economically to the point where it could help Britain vigorously might have gained hold among younger voters, recent immigrants from Britain, and men in the cities. In the countryside, the arguments that prices for commodities would fall in the wake of a free trade agreement with the United States rang loudly. In other parts, where competition with the Americans was not an issue, or where the benefits of reciprocity outweighed its costs, Liberals held their own.

And yet, for all the arguments and explanations, there were few routs. This is why a micro approach to the switch ridings can be enlightening. Borden won this election by convincing a few dozen, sometimes hundreds, of people in small towns scattered across Canada that the Laurier magic could no longer cure their ills. The slight swing in votes in Manitoba and in the Maritimes was felt most acutely in the ridings which were won with less than a 5 percent margin, and Canada's evolution in this regard was remarkable. That phenomenon was less evident in the westernmost provinces, where all the contests, with one exception, were won with pluralities greater than 5 percent.

In Saskatchewan, nothing changed. The Liberals won nine seats, and the Conservatives held their single seat in Prince Albert.

The truth was that most Canadians were unmoved by the arguments of politicians. Most Conservatives stayed Tories; most Liberals stayed Grits. As most Canadians were not willing to risk changing their votes, it was a small minority that made that decision, and they voted, to borrow Rudyard Kipling's phrase, not to risk Canada's soul. They may have been convinced by the arguments made by Robert Borden that their personal livelihoods would be jeopardized. Perhaps their change of votes was attributable to local political entrepreneurs, and maybe, as Laurier suspected, some "priests" had again convinced some of their flock to vote against the Liberals. The upshot of decisions made at kitchen tables in small places like Gunning Cove in Nova Scotia, Hampton in New Brunswick, and Paris in Ontario, was clear: there was to be no reciprocity deal with the United States, and the relations with Great Britain would continue to evolve in favour of the Empire. In places like Sainte-Cécile and Saint-Léon in Quebec, however, people changed their minds, but for different reasons. Perhaps it was for economic reasons; more likely it was because the idea of a rapprochement with the Empire in the manner Laurier proposed was toxic. Irony of ironies, they cast their votes against the Liberals, thus favouring the party that sought exactly what they feared the most.

Spurred on by appeals of patriotism and the cry that reciprocity was the penetrating wedge for annexation, the Conservatives swept many areas, but most critically made inroads in the soft areas of Liberal support. They argued against the economic advantages of reciprocity and emphasized sentimental considerations, insisting that the eventual result of reciprocity would lead Canada from Great Britain to the United States. The *nationalistes* did the opposite, but the result was the same. In the end, the vast, quasi existentialist debates about Canada and the Empire and Canada and reciprocity had changed the minds of only a few thousand men, but on an electoral map such as Canada's in 1911, that was enough to set the course for the next century.

TABLE 10.1 RESULTS OF THE 1911 ELECTION

	Seats	Candidates				Elected						Popular Votes								Total
		C.	L.	N.	O.	C.	%	L.	%	N.	%	C.	%	L.	%	N.	%	O.	%	
Nova Scotia	18	18	18	–	2	9	50.0	9	50.0	–	–	55,209	48.8	57,462	50.8	–	–	351	0.3	113,022
New Brunswick	13	13	13	–	–	5	38.5	8	61.5	–	–	38,880	49.2	40,192	50.8	–	–	–	–	79,072
Prince Edward Island	4	4	4	–	–	2	50.0	2	50.0	–	–	14,638	51.1	13,998	48.9	–	–	–	–	28,636
Quebec	65	29	65	34	6	14	21.5	38	58.4	13	20	70,915	21.9	162,711	50.2	84,907	26.7	5,528	1.7	324,061
Ontario	86	85	85	–	4	73	84.9	13	15.1	–	–	269,930	56.2	207,078	43.1	–	–	3,564	0.7	480,572
Manitoba	10	10	10	–	2	8	80.0	2	20.0	–	–	40,356	51.9	34,781	44.8	–	–	2,559	3.3	77,696
Saskatchewan	10	10	10	–	2	1	10.0	9	90.0	–	–	34,700	39.0	52,924	59.4	–	–	1,419	1.6	89,043
Alberta	7	7	7	–	4	1	14.9	6	85.7	–	–	29,675	42.5	37,208	53.3	–	–	2,892	4.1	69,775
British Columbia	7	7	7	–	3	7	100.0	–	–	–	–	25,622	58.8	16,350	37.5	–	–	1,587	3.6	43,559
Yukon	1	1	1	–	–	1	100.0	–	–	–	–	1,285	60.8	829	39.2	–	–	–	–	2,114
Total	221	184	220	34	23	121	54.8	87	39.4	13	5.9	581,210	44.6	623,554	47.7	84,907	6.5	17,900	1.4	1,307,550

Elected by acclamation: Liberal: Quebec (2) Ontario (1)

Conservative: Ontario (1)

"Others" (Votes Polled): Nova Scotia: Independent (2) 351

Quebec : Liberal–Independent (1) 1,166; Labour (1) 100; Socialist (1) 359; Independent (3) 3,909

Ontario: Independent (1) 2,281; Labour (3) 1,283

Manitoba: Independent (1) 234; Socialist (1) 2,325

Saskatchewan: Independent (2) 1,419

Alberta: Independent (4) 2,892

British Columbia: Socialist (3) 1,587

Adapted from J. Murray Beck, Pendulum of Power (Toronto: Prentice Hall, 1968), 135.

EPILOGUE

Now the Cabinet making begins — in the papers at the Clubs. B. keeps
to his house and sees those he calls for. No communication.
— SIR GEORGE FOSTER[1]

As the summer of 1911 ended and the meaning of the election
was debated from coast to coast, the protagonists reflected on
their fates. Premier Whitney sent a message to Borden that reflected
the Conservative mood, and claimed that "no such good work was
ever done in British America before, and having regard to its effect
on the future of the Empire I doubt if any one day's work in England
in modern times ever signified as much."[2] Across the country, in
Winnipeg, the frustrated Laurier loyalist John Dafoe was more
resigned: "It is better that [the government] should fall on a big
issue," he wrote, "which covers its defeat with a tragic dignity, than
just that it should have died of old age and incapacity."[3]

Clifford Sifton, basking in success, expressed his own satisfaction
to Dafoe: "The question has been before the people and has been settled
decisively. Moreover it was not a sectional vote. There were only two
provinces where the Opposition did not make substantial gains. These
two provinces are largely settled by people who have no education in
what may be called the Canadian National view."[4]

In Toronto, J.S. Willison, who had long lost his faith in the Liberal Party, was harsher, to the point of bitterness. "When the Liberal Party came into office in 1896 I was trusting, hopeful and enthusiastic," he wrote George Wrong at the University of Toronto. "I looked forward for a period of honest administration and decent electoral methods. I found instead that when the Liberal politicians could not get enough votes to elect candidates they opened ballot boxes, took out Conservative ballots and substituted Liberal ballots." At the centre of his dismay was the Liberal leader. "I know that Sir Wilfrid Laurier cares little or nothing for public morals and that he is an absolute opportunist. What can one expect from the Liberal Party while he is its leader? Charm of manner is not enough." To underline his point he added: "I was inside and I know."[5]

There would never be complete agreement between the different factions as to what exactly happened in September 1911, and, as demonstrated in Chapter 10, several different interpretations have been offered to explain why Canadians voted as they did. There was no doubt, however, that the election helped set the future direction of not just Robert Borden's Conservative government, but of the whole country. Canadians did not all know it then, but 1911 was a turning point in the shaping of their country.

——————

Both party leaders returned to Ottawa within a few days of the election to begin their new careers. Things needed to be sorted out and, in the case of the Liberals, wrapped up. Laurier went home to his wife Zoë for some rest before initiating the formal process of handing over the government. Most reports noted that his spirits were good and that he maintained a positive attitude — he accepted defeat with "imperturbable courage and cheerfulness," wrote Lord Grey[6] — but he must have been greatly saddened by the outcome of the election. His public statements reflected a calm acceptance of the results and he looked forward to a welcome — if unexpected — rest from the pressures of public life. Privately, his dismay was more evident. "Ontario has proved a great disappointment," he wrote one Liberal. "Manitoba does not disappoint me because it is always the same in that province. It always shouts one way and votes the other."[7] To John Dafoe in Winnipeg, he added a list of those aligned against him: "We have had to fight all these elements which you mention: the railroads, corporations, banks, manufacturers, conservatives, the Church, the Imperialists and the Nationalists. Yet, personally, I have nothing to regret, nor do I believe that, politically, we should have acted otherwise. We stood by sound principles and principles which must eventually triumph."[8]

Allen Aylesworth found the prime minister "downhearted over the result," and wrote that the "worst of it is that he cannot be persuaded out of the idea that it is largely because he is himself a Frenchman and a Catholic." Aylesworth wrote that the real reasons for the defeat in Ontario were the Opposition's "unlimited money" and "distrust and dislike towards the Yankees,"[9] conveniently ignoring his own role in allowing the Liberal machine to rot in the field. Alexander Smith, a long-time organizer for the party, was blunter: "It was not religion or race that did in the Liberals," he wrote Laurier, "we had nobody in charge. It was like playing marbles with marbles made out of mud.... The two main causes of your defeat were ... fifteen years in power and ... no organization."[10]

In Berlin, Mackenzie King, another defeated cabinet minister, saw the defeat as a repudiation of Laurier, blaming "largely the Anti-Catholic and Anti-French prejudice" for the defeat in Ontario. "Reciprocity may have been laid low, Liberalism is not," he wrote an old friend in consolation, adding that "economic conditions on this continent have become such that the Americans need what we have to sell, and we need to sell what they need to buy. I think we both stand to gain."[11] In a letter to the American consul-general, he added: "We have concluded a campaign in which prejudice and misrepresentations, fostered by vast resources from selfish interests have done their work to the full."[12] One of the defeated Liberals in Peterborough was less charitable, writing to King that with "the well known and usual activity of manufacturers when they get their Irish up, with an unintelligent rural body, and with the working men being controlled by the manufacturers, what use is there attempting to legislate for the working man or farmer?"[13]

Others blamed the Liberal platform on reciprocity — both the agreement, which proved so unpopular in urban Canada, and the decision to fight an early election on it. Historians have debated the reasons for Laurier's defeat ever since. Did the prime minister really have reason to be optimistic about his party's chances? Did he have a choice, or was his dare a colossal mistake?

Laurier often spoke and wrote as if he was hesitant or reluctant to have an election on reciprocity, but that his hand had been forced by the Opposition's obstructionist tactics in Parliament. If the agreement had passed Parliament, he could have stayed in office another year or two before going to the people for re-election, presumably on the success — or failure — of the agreement. In many ways, however, he was clever to seize on the issue of reciprocity and to make it the focus of his election campaign, especially in English Canada. Without a new policy, a "big" project to propose to voters, to rally his supporters, and to win over new converts, how could he have realistically expected to reverse the electoral trend set by the 1908 result, let alone maintain or increase his seats, especially in Ontario, Manitoba, or British Columbia?

A campaign on reciprocity was a bold alternative. Free trade was a defining characteristic of Canadian Liberalism and it, more than any other policy, distinguished the Liberal from the Conservative brand in 1911 Canada. Indeed, along with the naval debate, it was one of only a few clear national distinctions between the two parties. "During the six years I have been here," wrote the governor general in a private letter to the Colonial Office, other than free trade "I have never been able to discover any distinguishing mark between Liberals and Conservatives."[14] A campaign on reciprocity would sharpen the distinction between the parties and give Canadians a clear choice. It presented a new idea, a cause to fight for, an opportunity to further Canada's economic gains, and a reason to forget the petty scandals that had marked the administration and the many party divisions in Quebec, and in parts of Ontario and the Maritimes. In the West it could preempt the formation of a splinter farmers' party to fight both Liberals and Conservatives on the tariff issue; in the Maritimes the promise of reciprocity could offer a little hope to sweep away the years of disappointment and disadvantage brought on by Confederation; and in Ontario it just might convince enough rural voters to halt the erosion of Liberal support in that province. Even in Quebec, reciprocity had the potential to help voters forget the *Naval Service Act*. If Quebec could be held, then victory was a theoretical possibility.

Without reciprocity, Laurier would have had to run on his naval policy or on his record, neither of which stood to win him many votes in either French or English Canada. Though it accomplished much, his government had aged since 1908, and without reciprocity it was susceptible to opposition calls of "time for a change," and many Canadians, particularly in Ontario, would have agreed. The chances of any government or leader in a democracy being able to win successfully five majority governments and to remain in office for more than fifteen consecutive years were very slim to begin with. Laurier's government, despite its many accomplishments in the short 1908–11 mandate (in the areas of trade, defence, labour legislation, conservation, and civil service reform) was looking for a new direction. Like any time-enduring leader, Laurier lost many of his most talented colleagues; but by 1911, two of them — Clifford Sifton and Henri Bourassa — had not retired to their dotage to write their memoirs but, rather, remained in politics and had actively campaigned against him for at least two years.

Moreover, his government's vision for the future was continental at a time when many in English Canada still clung heartily to their British allegiance. Richard McBride of British Columbia was not alone in belittling the "tin pot navy" Laurier had created, and the prime minister's politics in London in June 1911 only seemed to confirm in the minds of many that he was not the man to lead Canada at a time when the Empire needed help to counter the growing threat of Germany. Finally, there were nagging issues, such as a few unforgotten procurement scandals, and a range of local concerns (the handling of Asian immigration in British Columbia, for instance) that tested the Laurier government's flexibility and principles.

Without reciprocity, many Canadians had less reason to vote for Laurier in 1911 than they had at any other time since 1896. Seen this way, Laurier's decision to fight his campaign on the reciprocity issue was not a political mistake. It was the one viable opportunity he had. Reciprocity probably helped bolster Liberal support in several areas of the country; it just was not enough in the end. He failed in 1911, therefore, not because he called the election too soon and chose to make reciprocity *the* issue of the campaign, and not because the opposition to reciprocity rose up to defeat him; it was more a case of reciprocity failing him and his attempt to *save* his government and his party from a likely, if not certain, defeat. The same could be said on the issue of the navy in Quebec. Laurier clearly blundered in handling this issue by insisting on retaining the government's right to deploy the navy through an order-in-council, and not consulting the House of Commons, and also in refusing to match Borden's promise of consulting the people before implementing naval policy.

Conversely, why did the Conservatives win? Focusing their unified message on loyalty to the Empire and fear of annexation was an effective strategy that furnished Robert Borden with the opportunity to apply his thoroughness, intelligence, and debating skills to good effect. He grew as a communicator during the campaign and proved himself an able salesman for the cause. The 1911 election campaign was the culmination of years of determined work, organization, negotiation, and dogged willingness to accept compromise, disharmony, and even humiliation from his own party. It may not have been pretty, but the credit for the success of the campaign in tight ridings in Ontario, Manitoba, New Brunswick, and Nova Scotia was largely his.

Liberal organizational weakness and ineptness in a number of ridings and Conservative organizational strength were both factors, but the Conservatives had other advantages, as well. One great reward was the active support they received from individuals and groups outside the formal party. Henri Bourassa and the *nationalistes*, of course, gave life to Conservative chances in Quebec, and in English Canada there were allies such as Clifford Sifton, the members of the Toronto Eighteen and a handful of other influential supporters, the Canadian National League, the Canadian Home Market Association, the Anti-Reciprocity League, the business and railroad interests, and the provincial premiers and their organizations. The Liberals had no equivalent allies working for them.

Ultimately, reciprocity with the United States was not an easy idea to sell Canadians in 1911, because many of them believed that the agreement was unnecessary. Canada had experienced more than a decade of prosperity and significant economic growth over the thirty years since the implementation of the National Policy. If it had proven itself successful, why tear it down? Part of the thinking here was that the country was much different — larger, more developed and self-sufficient — than in the 1870s. Reciprocity may have made sense then, but in 1911 it was considered by many as unnecessary and potentially dangerous if it disturbed the prosperity that Canadians had worked so hard to achieve. If nothing else, the National Policy tariff gave a sense of certainty and stability to Canadian economic life; throwing it over for a deal with the Americans was very risky, especially as the Americans could walk away from it or amend it at their own discretion.

In a risky political move, the Conservatives presented reciprocity as an assault on imperial loyalty and a direct challenge to the whole thrust of the National Policy. Sir John A.'s vision of the country, they argued, was of a transcontinental British nation founded on an east–west transportation network and strong inter-provincial trade. Under reciprocity, Canadian trade would succumb to geography, and east–west trade would start flowing north–south. In other words, there was an element of nation-building in the protective tariff that reciprocity would destroy.

Such a possibility guaranteed the hostility of the railway companies and the eastern Canadian business community. Fingers were pointed at the tens of thousands of American immigrants who had moved into Western Canada and were thought to be behind these calls for reciprocity. Was this to be another Texas, where Americans move in and then demand to be brought into the Union? This line of reasoning — however irrational — drove some of the resentment expressed by eastern business leaders who felt that they had worked to open the West, and now felt a lack of appreciation from the westerners.

It is easy to be critical of businessmen and railway promoters such as Walker, White, Flavelle, Van Horne, and others for acting in such an obviously self-interested way, and they might have been the first to agree. But it was more than that, and it is important not to underestimate the profound identification that these business leaders made between their industries, the National Policy, and the concept of Canada as a nation. It was evident, they would argue, that the National Policy protected their companies, but it also helped to create businesses, which in turn created thousands of jobs, kept at home thousands of Canadians who might otherwise have been tempted to leave the country for the

United States, and made the country and Empire stronger.[15] In this way of thinking, Canada needed a national policy for national development, and support for the National Policy not only made economic sense, it was a patriotic act of faith.

The loyalty question increasingly played more easily for Borden and the Conservatives than Laurier and the Liberals. The degree of imperialist and patriotic thinking in English Canada was primed since the dreadnought scare of 1909, and mixed with the powerful fuel of anxiety — anxiety over Canada's role in the Empire; anxiety over the looming influence and power of the United States (and all those American immigrants flooding into Canada); and anxiety, especially in Ontario, over the threat of a rapidly growing French-speaking population (which would soon spark an angry debate over language and religious educational rights as regulations in Ontario outlawed the use of French in schools). The Conservatives could play on these anxieties and turn the debate on a trade agreement into one about loyalty and the very survival of their country.

Loyalty is very hard to prove and disloyalty only needs to be suspected, so all the Conservatives had to do was raise some doubt about the Liberal Party's patriotism and dedication to the Empire. In 1911 English Canada, given that Laurier was a Franco-Catholic from Quebec, it was relatively simple to do. For too many English-speaking Protestant Canadians, concern over the spread of the French language and religious education was very high, and it was easier to have confidence in Robert Borden than in Wilfrid Laurier, and to suspect the true intentions of the Liberals.

Whether it was English or French Canada, Conservatives could argue that Laurier had changed. His push toward closer trade with the United States and his reticence to support the British navy directly showed that his vision was incompatible with the newly intensified allegiance to Britain and the Empire. In French Canada, the argument was also that Laurier had changed, in that his past defence of Canadian autonomy had given way to an accommodation with imperial interests.

It would be easy to believe that Laurier's compromises pleased no one, but that would be wrong. Laurier and the Liberals still carried many Canadians all across the country. It was the few in selected pockets of the country who could no longer support him. At the start of the campaign, Laurier predicted to the governor general that the Liberals might lose a few seats in Quebec, pick up a few in Ontario, and do the same or better than in 1908 in Alberta, Saskatchewan, Prince Edward Island, British Columbia, Nova Scotia, and Manitoba.[16] His confidence might have been misplaced but, other than Ontario, his predictions were not far off the mark. What he had not counted on was how few votes in particular towns and villages it would take to make the difference between victory and defeat. Canadians voted for many different reasons, including economic self-interest, political ideology, party loyalty, for God, country, and Empire, the appeal of the candidates, and for a variety of personal reasons. In the end, Laurier lost and Borden won the election because of the choices made by those few Canadians.

—·•·—

The cabinet met on September 26, but several ministers were absent; William Paterson was home in bed, suffering from the "sting of defeat,"[17] and Frank Oliver and William Templeman were still in transit from the West. Eventually they all arrived, and over the next twelve days several more meetings were held. There was relatively little to do other than the formalities, although the cabinet did agree on officially fixing a date for Thanksgiving.[18] It must have been a strange moment. "We are nearing the close of the Laurier Administration," Mackenzie King wrote in his diary, "and one feels just a slight regret at the thought that possibly in another 24 hours we will have separated forever."[19] For the younger ministers, or those who had won their seats, there was always tomorrow; the defeated veterans must have wondered if it was the end.

For several it was. Sir Richard Cartwright, who had been with Laurier for thirty-seven years, remained in the Senate for a short time but died a few months later, in 1912. Both William Paterson and William Templeman retired and died in 1914. Sir Frederick Borden was out of politics for good and died in 1917. Sydney Fisher, who lost his seat in 1911 and was defeated again in a 1913 by-election, retired to Ottawa, where he died in 1921. Ironically, Allen Aylesworth, who declined to run in 1911 for health reasons, outlived them all, serving in the Senate from 1923 until his death in 1952. Two other ministers who won their seats remained in politics for only a short period: Frank Oliver sat in the House with Sir Wilfrid until defeated in the 1917 election and eventually was appointed to the Board of Railway Commissioners (1923–28), and William Pugsley sat in opposition for a few years before being appointed lieutenant-governor of New Brunswick (1917–23).

The exception to the rule may have been William Fielding, who lost his seat in Nova Scotia and was blamed by many Liberals for the defeat of the government. Fielding moved to Montreal and became an editor at different Montreal newspapers, and in December 1917 was elected as a Unionist, although he did not serve in Borden's wartime cabinet. His support for conscription likely destroyed any possibility that he would replace Laurier as Liberal leader, but in 1919 he ran for the leadership of the Liberal Party. Defeated by Mackenzie King and a new generation of Liberals, Fielding was not yet content to be "yesterday's man," and he served as King's finance minister until 1925. Two younger Quebecers from 1911, Jacques Bureau (solicitor general) and Henri Severin Béland (postmaster general), also served in King's government in the 1920s, and both ultimately received Senate appointments.

Charles Murphy and George Graham remained in politics and helped rebuild the party. Graham in particular was seen as leadership material — including by Laurier — and a seat in Parliament was soon found for him. He never became leader, but served in cabinet in the 1920s, and ultimately was appointed to the Senate in 1926. Much was made of the lack of organization and funding in the 1911 election and Murphy subsequently played an important role in revamping the party organization. A Central Information Office was established to act as a clearinghouse for information for the Liberal Party and, in 1921, almost exactly ten years after the 1911 disaster, the National Liberal Organization Committee was created, with a leader and nine vice presidents, one from each province, and, as members, all provincial Liberal leaders.[20]

Mackenzie King's future was less certain. He was offered a position at the Toronto *Star* and considered becoming leader of the Ontario Liberals, but neither position interested him. He thought of writing a biography of Laurier, or taking a professorship at McGill, which "might prove attractive," or of becoming president of a college. He ruled out a job in the business world because "the making of money has no attractions for me." But one thing was clear to him during those last cabinet meetings: "I feel I should seek to become married."[21] He stayed out of politics during the war, but then returned. As an English-speaking Liberal, and someone who had never deserted Laurier, he was acceptable to both the anglophone and francophone wings of the party. He became leader and served as prime minister for twenty-two years, but never married.

The greatest uncertainty in September 1911 was the future of the prime minister. Laurier won two seats in the election, but had expressed a desire to retire if the party lost, turning the leadership over to Graham or one of the younger Liberals. He told the governor general that he planned for a long, restful winter in California to "enjoy his well-earned repose with his books, amid the flowers and sunshine of that happy land."[22] He was being disingenuous; within four days of the election he told Mackenzie King that he was going to stay on as leader. "The party was so badly shattered," he told King, that he would have to stay and "get it together."[23] There was reason to hope that Borden's uneasy combination of supporters might not last and there was a real chance of a Liberal resurgence. That might have been true until 1913, but events did not unfold well for Laurier or his party. The outbreak of the First World War changed everything and by 1917 Laurier found himself on the defensive, with his party split on linguistic lines over the conscription issue. He never got another chance, and died in 1919.

That was all in the future on October 6, 1911, when the cabinet met for the last time in the same small room in the East Block where in July they had so optimistically decided to call the election. King recorded the moment in his diary: "At about 1:30, after telling us that he had arranged to see His Excellency at three that it might be as well to be in our offices in case anything wd. come up which wd. require further action, he said while leaning on the back of the chair, raising himself erect & without looking at anyone in particular 'Well gentlemen that is all.' The last three words were less audible than the first two, he turned & walked quickly head erect and like one victorious to the little door which goes into the anteroom, and without further ceremony he had parted from his colleagues for ever."[24]

It was over, at least for the Liberal government; for Borden and the Conservatives it was just beginning.

———•◦•———

Borden arrived in Ottawa on September 24, after a few days' rest in his hometown of Grand Pré, Nova Scotia. He was immediately immersed in the task of cabinet-making, with people of all sorts appearing before him with their proposals, requests, and lists of suggested names. Some he had to speak with; others he avoided. "My impression is that nearly every member of his Party thinks himself qualified for a Cabinet position," was the verdict of the governor general.[25] But there weren't enough positions for everyone, and Borden had some difficult choices to make.

Every prime minister selects cabinet members based on a consideration of region/province, language, religion, experience, talent, and political expediency. Added to that mix, Borden had debts to pay — to a party long in opposition and eager for the reins of power, to those, like Sam Hughes, who had stood by him through the long difficult years, and, of course, to all those outside the party whom he had recruited and relied on for his victory in September. "What a salad!" Laurier probably muttered again to himself over the next two weeks as Borden tried to balance all these seemingly antagonistic forces, including the provincial Conservative premiers, the Toronto businessmen, Bourassa and the Quebec *nationalistes*, and former Liberals like Clifford Sifton. Borden had put together a loose coalition of forces opposed to Laurier, which he grafted onto the existing Conservative Party. It was not always a comfortable fit, but it worked extremely well during the election, as each group was separate, usually far apart, and on their own to campaign. But he had not changed the party significantly, and there was little common ideology shared by these disparate elements.[26] Now it was time to fit all the loose ends together.

Borden offered a cabinet seat to each of the four Conservative premiers who had helped so much during the campaign. Of the four, only New Brunswick's J.D. Hazen accepted, and he was given the marine, fisheries, and naval services ministry. McBride in British Columbia,

Roblin in Manitoba, and Whitney in Ontario all declined for their own reasons, but each recommended to Borden another to go in his place. Frank Cochrane, one of Whitney's close colleagues and an important organizer during the campaign, was made minister of railways and canals; Robert Rogers, the political organizer from Manitoba (who also had the support of Sifton and Willison), was given the interior portfolio; and Martin Burrell — "McBride's man" — was appointed minister of agriculture.[27]

The Toronto Liberals who had broken with Laurier were also rewarded for their help. As he had promised earlier in the year, Borden consulted with Sifton, J.S. Willison, and, through them, with Sir Edmund Walker and Zebulon Lash of the Toronto Eighteen (businessman Joseph Flavelle also volunteered his views) on suitable candidates.[28] They agreed on Thomas White of the Toronto Eighteen, who had vigorously campaigned for the Conservatives but had not sought a seat for himself, as minister of finance. "It is well known that White is Flavelle's creature," Mackenzie King wrote in his diary, and he "is of that group & Sifton Willison Walker & Flavelle & Lash have united to insist on him going in."[29]

Not everyone was happy; Sir George Foster, for one, hoped to return to the finance portfolio he had carried under John A. Macdonald, and was disappointed with the selection of White, the former Liberal.

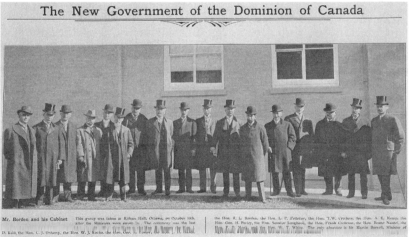

The Borden Cabinet, October 1911.

Foster had supporters in the party, but Borden was not one of them; the Conservative leader earlier credited Foster with "the political sense of a turnip."[30] After several days of waiting, Foster accepted trade and commerce.[31] Another Torontonian, A.E. Kemp, was appointed minister without portfolio.

The most delicate decisions were made concerning Quebec. Tradition dictated that the English community have representation, and Borden chose two anglophone Quebeckers: George Perley, a Protestant, as minister without portfolio, and the Irish-Catholic Charles Doherty as minister of justice. Frederick Monk as Conservative leader in Quebec was an obvious choice, and he was appointed minister of public works, but the other francophone representatives were more of a problem. Bourassa and Lavergne both stayed on the sidelines, but they insisted on a strong *nationaliste* presence in the cabinet. Among English Canadians outside Quebec, feelings were mixed, but concern was generally muted because of the size of Borden's victory, and the incoming prime minister was reminded that he had won enough seats that he could govern "freed from the domination of Quebec in its political affairs."[32] Sifton, for example, seemed nonchalant, even dismissive, about who the francophone ministers should be; his list for Borden of potential cabinet members included under Quebec simply: "Doherty — Perley — 2 French."[33]

Whether Borden accepted Monk's recommendations or made the Quebec-membership decisions on his own was an issue of considerable subsequent debate, but Borden announced the appointment of two staunch Quebec Conservatives who had campaigned as *nationalistes*: Louis Philippe Pelletier as postmaster general and Wilfrid Bruno Nantel as minister of inland revenue.[34] Bourassa, under no illusion, wrote to Charles Cahan that "none of Mr. Borden's colleagues are, or ever have been leaders of the *nationaliste* group." Speaking of Pelletier and Nantel, he noted that "all that can be said is that, in fighting Laurier's navy bill and also in opposing Mr. Borden's previous attitude, they have espoused the *nationaliste* program, and, in consequence, received the support of the *nationaliste* group."[35] For many of Borden's anglo-imperialist supporters, this was rather a fine distinction.[36]

Finally, there was a mixture of old friends and regional appointments to the cabinet, including Sam Hughes as minister of militia and defence, John D. Reid as minister of customs, the Ontarian Thomas Crothers as minister of labour, William James Roche from Manitoba as secretary of state, and, representing Alberta, Senator James Lougheed, the government leader in the senate and minister without portfolio.

Three younger westerners with bright futures were overlooked: Arthur Meighen, H.H. Stevens, and R.B. Bennett. In 1913, Meighen entered the cabinet as solicitor general and ultimately followed Borden as leader and prime minister. Stevens left British Columbia, where he had been a thorn in McBride's side, for Ottawa, where he did much the same for R.B. Bennett in the 1930s. Bennett, however, remained outside the cabinet after 1911, and "Bonfire Bennett" was "hurt and resentful" at being overlooked, especially since he was the only Conservative elected in Alberta and had paid for his own campaign.[37] He would have to bide his time.

In the end the cabinet reflected the outcome of the election. Not surprisingly, ministers were chosen from where the Conservatives were strong: the West received four members, which was relatively high; Ontario received the most and Toronto in particular was the big winner, with Kemp, Foster, and White in key positions. These selections reflected the importance of Toronto and the anti-reciprocity Liberals who helped Borden win, but they also reflected the growing shift in financial power from Montreal to Toronto — so much so that Montreal business interests expressed their concern to Borden. There were no representatives from Prince Edward Island and Saskatchewan, and only one from Alberta (Lougheed). There were four Catholics and, among the Protestants, there were seven Anglicans, six Methodists, and one Baptist. Interestingly, four of the members (White, Rogers, Cochrane, and Hazen) did not have seats in Parliament but, with the help of Senate and other appointments, ridings were opened up for them.[38]

The First Borden Cabinet — 1911

Robert Borden	prime minister
Martin Burrell	minister of agriculture
Frank Cochrane	minister of railways and canals
Thomas Crothers	minister of labour
Charles Doherty	minister of justice
George Foster	minister of trade and commerce
J.D. Hazen	minister of marine, fisheries and naval services
Sam Hughes	minister of militia and defence
A. E. Kemp	minister without portfolio
Senator James Lougheed	minister without portfolio, government leader in the Senate
Frederick Monk	minister of public works
W.B. Nantel	minister of inland revenue
L.P. Pelletier	postmaster general
George Perley	minister without portfolio
John D. Reid	minister of customs
William James Roche	secretary of state
Robert Rogers	minister of the interior
Thomas White	minister of finance

Noticeable, if only by their absence, were, of course, Clifford Sifton, Henri Bourassa, and Armand Lavergne. Sir Clifford as of 1915, Sifton never ran for public office again and had no desire for a cabinet position in Borden's government. He remained chair of the Canadian Commission of Conservation until 1918, and during the war he supported conscription and organized pro-conscription Liberals in the West. He died in New York City in 1929. Lavergne continued his long personal political odyssey from Liberal to *nationaliste* to Conservative and, in 1930, was re-elected to the House of Commons and served as deputy speaker during the Bennett government. Bourassa continued as editor of *Le Devoir* for many years and also returned to the House of Commons in 1925. He lived long enough to see his fears over conscription come true — twice — but he probably derived little satisfaction from having been proven right.

In Ontario, Premier Whitney took advantage of the Conservative momentum and called a provincial election, in which he went on to a sweeping victory. The provincial Liberals floundered: "We had no money, no anything," observed Mackenzie King. "The outlook was hopeless and there was little to criticize in the Government save inaction, and indifference."[39] Newton Rowell, who had worked so hard for the federal Liberals in Ontario in 1911, went on to lead the Ontario provincial opposition, but in 1917 he split with Laurier and joined Borden's government. The others — Walker, Lash, Willison, and Flavelle — lived happily and perhaps more comfortably with an Ontario-dominated Conservative government in Ottawa that more clearly reflected their world view. Their friends and colleagues who controlled the railways now could turn to Borden for financial support and loan guarantees for their expansion plans. And they all could sleep easily at night, knowing that the National Policy was safe and that a man much more sympathetic to the Empire sat in the prime minister's office.

All of these people, both Conservative and Liberal, went forward from 1911 blissfully unaware of the cataclysm that awaited them in August 1914, with the outbreak of the First World War. It was one of the legacies of the 1911 election that it saw the coming together of several groups of Canadians who shared relatively little except their disdain for the Laurier Liberals and the desire to see the government defeated. Their goal was achieved on election night, but almost immediately cracks began to appear. In 1912, Borden turned his back on his promise to hold a plebiscite on the navy and decided to make a direct contribution to the Royal Navy. Frederick Monk immediately resigned from the cabinet, and died two years later. Nantel and Pelletier submitted their resignations in 1914. These resignations weakened the government, and by then it was evident that the Borden government was a government of, and for, English Canada. In addition, Borden's Naval Aid Bill stalled in the Liberal-dominated Senate, and when he refused to call an election on the issue, it was allowed to die. As a result, when the war broke out in 1914 the government was almost three years into its first mandate, it was weakened and divided, had few friends in French Canada, and it had neither built on Laurier's navy nor made strides toward Borden's idea of a naval force. It was not just that Borden's government was unprepared for the war, the fallout from 1911 meant that the voice of one of the two linguistic groups was not heard in the government, and many of the decisions made during the war were made with English Canada in mind. The fracturing of the country along linguistic lines, symbolized by the formation of the Union government and the introduction of conscription, was made possible by the 1911 election.

The election of 1911 shaped the outlines of Canadian politics for much of the twentieth century. This was the first Canadian election that was fought on issues of foreign policy — trade with the United States and support for the British Empire. It had a lasting legacy on Canadian-American relations, on the rapport between English and French Canada, on the relationship between rural and urban centres, and between the West and the financial capitals of Toronto and Montreal. It crystallized political forces that would shape national debates to our day.

For many people, the defeat of reciprocity in 1911 was a dramatic and permanent end to a long chapter in Canadian-American relations. "Canada rejected reciprocity in pride rather than in fear," John Dafoe wrote. "Whether the decision was right or wrong, prudent or rash, vainglorious or self-regarding, it settled for a generation and perhaps for a century all possibility of a mutual agreement for freedom of exchange in trade between these two countries. It is impossible to imagine a recurrence of the favourable conditions which made such an arrangement seem practicable in 1911."[40]

James Bryce, the British ambassador in Washington, was similarly concerned about the impact of the election on Canadian-American relations. "The language used in the recent campaign against the U.S. and in particular against the President produced a very unfortunate impression here," he wrote Grey in Ottawa. "It is to be hoped that people will set it down to campaign methods and not as an indication of real hatred and bitterness on your side of the line towards this country."[41]

There was a great deal of exaggeration in those early predictions. The defeat of reciprocity was neither dramatic nor permanent, in that its demise did not seriously damage Canadian-American relations. Canadians, from Borden and the governor general on down, were quick to remind anyone who cared to listen that Canadians did not vote against reciprocity because they disliked the United States or were unfriendly to Americans, it was more a vote for loyalty and the British connection.[42] The new government made it clear that it would not act in an unnecessarily antagonistic fashion regarding the United States. Indeed, there was little that could be considered anti-American in the Borden administration, although that fact alone cannot be construed as a tacit acknowledgement that all the anti-American rhetoric of the campaign was just that — rhetoric. It was more that Borden had not campaigned on any policy respecting the United States — he was opposed to reciprocity but he and the Conservative Party offered no alternative. Once in power they maintained the status quo as far as possible, and a new direction in Canadian-American relations did not appear, at least before the outbreak of the First World War.

On the other hand, the Conservatives did nothing to stop the growing Americanization of Canada and the increasing economic, cultural, and social connections between the two countries. Even without reciprocity the two countries were becoming more alike. As the American consul-general in Toronto reported just months after the election, the "trade of this region is so intimately connected with the United States and the needs and interests of the two countries so identical that it seems unnecessary to give any more detailed description of conditions here or to attempt any general suggestions for bettering our trade."[43]

Fidelity to the Empire resonated well on the campaign trail, but love of Empire was hardly a sufficiently strong barrier to withstand the influx of American goods, American investment, American ideas, and ... Americans. All the action of Borden and the Conservatives during the campaign was directed at preserving Canadian independence and the imperial connection, but stopping reciprocity was their only accomplishment and the Americanization of Canada continued.[44] Under Borden's watch, Canada became even more closely tied to the

United States and, ironically, much more autonomous in its relations with the Empire. It was an inevitable development perhaps, but only in hindsight.

In the United States, the Republicans were out of office in little more than a year, and for most Americans reciprocity with Canada was not a burning issue. Most probably were never aware of the extent of the anti-American rhetoric espoused during the campaign, and the demise of reciprocity was hardly mourned at all. In 1913, the new lower-tariff Congress and Democratic President Woodrow Wilson supported the passage of the Underwood Tariff, which dramatically reduced American tariffs on foodstuffs, steel products, and on many manufactured goods. Ironically, this Underwood tariff gave the Canadians much of what they were offered — and rejected — under reciprocity, but few in the Canadian business community seemed to mind this unilateral lowering of American tariffs, and no Canadian campaign was launched, as Van Horne put it, to "bust the damned thing." Canadians merely continued to trade more and more with the Americans and, unintentionally, relatively less and less with the British.

As John Dafoe predicted, reciprocity or free trade agreements with the United States were off the agenda for a generation, and it was not until the 1930s that the two countries, mired in depression, turned once again to mutual trading arrangements. In 1937–38, trade negotiations produced a series of agreements between Canada, the United States, and Great Britain, but war broke out before they could have much effect. After the war, Mackenzie King oversaw the secret negotiation of a free trade agreement, but at the last minute — haunted by the spectre of ending his career like his beloved hero Sir Wilfrid Laurier — scuttled the deal. From that moment, trade negotiations of a different and multilateral sort continued, via the General Agreement on Tariffs and Trade. It was another generation — and with a different party in office — before the two sides were back at the table.

It was only in the 1980s that free trade returned, and in 1988 Canadians found themselves once again facing a general election dominated by the single issue of free trade with the United States. The parallels with 1911 were striking in that much of the debate focused on what the agreement *meant* rather than what it *said*. For many

Canadians, the 1980s version of free trade seemed like an attack on Canadian nationhood and they expressed their fears for the future of the country. There was the "thin edge of the wedge," the "slippery slope," the disappearing border, and questions of what free trade would do to the Canadian identity and, perhaps, even the survival of the country. The ghosts of Sir Robert Borden and Sir Wilfrid Laurier would have understood this debate very well.

Even though the parties to the debate were reversed in 1988, with the Conservatives supporting the agreement and the Liberals opposed, there was a strange parallel here as well, with a Conservative leader who had brought together a somewhat uncomfortable alliance between western Conservatives, the business community, and Quebec nationalists to defeat a Liberal government that had been led for many years by a French-Canadian prime minister who was losing popularity. And, like Borden's Conservatives, the Mulroney Conservatives soon were divided amongst themselves and ultimately almost destroyed from within. Borden knew all about these kinds of things, too, and if there were parallels between 1911 and 1988, there were parallels between the Conservative Party debacles of 1921 and 1993 as well. For his part, Laurier may have found some comfort in knowing that the triumph of free trade in 1988 did not lead, as many of his adversaries had warned in 1911, to the submergence or destruction of Canada, its values, and its way of life.

There were, of course, great differences between 1911 and 1988, not least of which was the fact that the forces supporting free trade won in the latter contest. The 1988 agreement was much longer and even less read by Canadians, and the thought of exempting "cultural industries" from the agreement would never have crossed the minds of W.S. Fielding or President Taft in 1911. It also was important that in 1988 the Canadian business community — more mature and self-confident — was on the other side and supporting free trade.[45] Even more important, in 1988 there were three parties in the election campaign, with two (the Liberals and New Democrats) opposed to the agreement. This triangular race enabled the Mulroney Conservatives to win the most seats even though more Canadians voted for parties opposed to the agreement. A final difference, and one that was barely acknowledged in 1988, was how little the connection to Great Britain (let alone the Empire) was a factor in the election campaign. What for most English Canadians resonated at the very heart of their identity in 1911 mattered little in 1988, when nobody talked about it and nobody cared.

———•·•———

The anger was greatest in parts of the agricultural community where the defeat of reciprocity was seen as a blow inflicted on rural Canada by urban Canada and, more generally, by central Canada on Western Canada. Toronto and Montreal financiers put an end to a policy desired by the West; city businessmen and their workers, especially in Toronto, had defeated a policy meant to help the farmers and natural producers. It was a test of political strength, and urban central Canada won. Western Canadian anger was palpable, not just at the Conservatives for orchestrating the defeat of reciprocity, but at central Canada and against both of the old parties. From that time, there would be less trust of the East and traditional politics; conversely, it gave an enormous boost for the creation of regional, rural, and sectional third parties. The defeat of reciprocity in 1911 was, effectively, "the first act in the agrarian revolt of Western Canada."[46]

The politics of agrarianism would be an important feature in Canada in the following years as farmers' movements grew in importance. Ernest Drury, who did not run in the 1911 election but, as secretary of the Canadian Council of Agriculture, spoke in favour of reciprocity during the campaign, soon started to work on the idea of building a political party based on farmer discontent.[47] He was successful, and the United Farmers of Ontario formed a government in Ontario within less than a decade. The farmers' movement also formed a government in Alberta, where it shaped much of the progressive movement in Western Canada and was undeniably important in the creation of the Co-operative Commonwealth Federation.

The 1911 election also precipitated a distinct political force of Quebec nationalism. Until 1911, the expressions of nationalism were calmly literary and symbolic and Quebeckers were content to divide their votes between the Liberal and Conservative candidates. The Bourassa movement against Laurier and his plans for a Canadian navy, however, crystallized the fear that Canada was moving in a direction in which not all Quebeckers were comfortable. Bourassa's purpose in the 1911 election was twofold: first, to destroy Laurier's grip on Quebec politics, and second, to ensure that a block of Quebec votes could not be automatically assumed to support a majority party. That Borden only included one *nationaliste* in his cabinet (who barely stayed for a year) indicated how isolated that block really was.

Quebec's position in Parliament one hundred years later shows eerily similar features. In 1942, another bloc was founded by young Quebeckers to argue against conscription during the national plebiscite, and one year later, three Liberal MPs from Quebec, led by Maxime Raymond, crossed the floor of the House of Commons to form the Bloc Populaire Canadien and fight against the Mackenzie King government's plans for forced military service. In the 1945 federal election, the Bloc fielded thirty-five candidates (thirty-four in Quebec and one in Ontario), but only two were elected.

The Liberals, in particular, learned hard lessons from the 1911 election that were not lost on Laurier's successors. King, St. Laurent, Pearson, and Trudeau worked diligently in different ways to absorb much of Quebec's nationalist perspective into their policies. St. Laurent even indicated that one of the key tests of Canadian foreign policy was its ability to maintain and strengthen national unity.

It was domestic policy that again triggered the creation of the Bloc Québécois in 1990, in the wake of the defeat of the Meech Lake Accord. This time, as it was in Borden's time, the *nationalistes* bolted openly. Strengthened by an ideology of defence of Quebec interests in federal matters, the Bloc Québécois remained a feature of parliamentary life for the next twenty years.

Looking back a century later, the election of 1911 appears as a turning point in Canadian history. The election did not spark the birth of a new Canada, but it does stand out as a moment marking the transition from an older political culture to a more modern one. In this way, the 1911 election can be seen as the fulcrum between two Canadas and a testament to the fact that Canadians were indeed at "a parting of the ways," although of a different kind than suggested by President Taft. There was the Canada of the Age of Laurier, with its disputes over religion and denominational education, and with western settlement and railway expansion at the heart of its national development policies. This was an age when the memory of Sir John A. could still be raised to good political effect, when government correspondence and foreign affairs could be administered via the prime minister's jacket pockets, when the tensions unleashed by the execution of Louis Riel were understood in religious and linguistic terms rather than regional and aboriginal ones, when there was still some doubt about the future development of the West as an English-speaking region, and when to be called an "imperialist" could still be meant as a compliment.

After 1911, the problems facing Canada were very much of the twentieth century: industrialization, government planning, and all the associated problems of urban life — poverty, health, housing, welfare, education, to name but the most obvious. Before, Canada was British and defended itself against the encroachments of the United States; after was the beginning of the "American Century," when Canadians fought on foreign battlefields, not for the Empire, but for themselves.

Laurier's government had done much to create this new Canada, but was less equipped to respond to it. It was a new era of organization — by business, farmers, workers, women, and others — and government needed to act in response. Laurier had made some progress with the introduction of arbitration rules for labour disputes, the establishment of some industrial standards, and various other government regulations, but his government maintained a largely non-interventionist approach to government, business, and society that seemed increasingly anachronistic in the era of the First World War.[48] The government's critics demanded action to "ease the transition from an agricultural to an industrial age."[49] But after fifteen years in office, Sir Wilfrid Laurier — the nineteenth-century liberal free trader and aging *rouge* — had only one bold policy to offer the country: reciprocity.

By 1911 it was not enough. Laurier never lost his charm and charisma, or the respect and admiration of the people of Canada, and his vision of the country as a tolerant nation where people of different languages can coexist and prosper has not been lost on subsequent generations of Canadians. But a majority had spoken, and it was time to go, and time for Robert Borden and his new government to take on the challenge of governing this increasingly urban, industrial, and divided country.

The election of 1911 is still with us a hundred years later. The characters that gave it life and who fought the battle are long gone, and, regrettably, mostly forgotten. Laurier is immortalized in bronze on the east lawn of Parliament Hill. Borden faces in the opposite direction from the west side. They fought face to face, but face immortality with their backs to each other. Still, the battle of 1911 left a legacy that continues to shape our politics.

On the surface, the 1911 election can seem to be another world. Women did not vote, the "media" consisted primarily of daily newspapers and a few magazines, and Canadians did not criss-cross the continent in jets but, rather, followed railway tracks. But 1911 is still with us. One hundred years later we still discuss the economic impact of the United States and fear cultural annexation. We think about Canada's role in the world as our great grandparents wondered about Canada's role in the Empire. The place of Quebec in Canadian politics remains high on the national agenda.

Canadian politics until 1911 were dominated by big projects, infrastructure building, and a growing sense of power. Laurier hoped that the old ways still worked, and merrily promised more growth through trade and the building of what amounted to a new infrastructure — this time one for national (and imperial) defence. But 1911 changed all that. Canada — both in English and in French — richer than it ever had been, was in a darker mood. The result of the 1911 election was the sum of all fears: fear of not doing enough for the Empire, fear of commitments to the Empire that would necessarily lead to the conscription of young men, fear of the rise of French Canada, and fear of the United States. Clearly, this fear was not felt in every heart, but a sufficient number of Canadians were sensitive enough to it to turn away from Laurier and to embrace, instead, Borden's uncertain vision. A hard choice was made, a choice that shaped the country for the rest of the century.

APPENDIX I

THE WINNERS OF THE 1911 ELECTION

C-Conservative
L-Liberal
N-Nationaliste

Ontario

1. Algoma-East (Smyth–C)
2. Algoma-West (Boyce–C)
3. Brant (Fisher–C)
4. Brantford (Cockshutt–C)
5. Brockville (Webster–C)
6. North Bruce (Clark–C)
7. South Bruce (Donnelly–C)
8. Carleton (Kidd–C)
9. Dufferin (Best–C)
10. Dundas (Broder–C)
11. Durham (Thornton–C)
12. Elgin-East (Marshall–C)
13. Elgin-West (Crothers–C)
14. Essex-North (Wilcox–C)
15. Essex-South (Clarke–L)
16. Frontenac (Edwards–C)
17. Glengarry (McMillan–L)
18. Grenville (Reid–C)
19. Grey-South (Ball–C)
20. Grey-North (Middlebro–C)
21. Grey-East (Sproule–C)
22. Haldimand (Lalor–C)
23. Halton (Henderson–C)
24. Hamilton-East (Barker–C)
25. Hamilton West (Stewart–C)
26. Hastings-West (Poerter–C)
27. Hastings-East (Northrup–C)
28. Huron-East (Bowan–C)
29. Huron-West (Lewis–C)
30. Huron-South (Merner–C)
31. Kent-East (Gordon–L)
32. Kent-West (McCoig–L)
33. Kingston (Nickle–C)
34. Lambton-East (Armstrong–C)
35. Lambton-West (Pardee–L)
36. Lanark-North (Thoburn–C)
37. Lanark-South (Haggart–C)
38. Leeds (Taylor–C)
39. Lennox & Addington (Paul–C)
40. Lincoln (Lancaster–C)
41. London (Beattie–C)
42. Middlesex-North (Elliot–C)
43. Middlesex-East (Elson–C)

44. Middlesex-West (Ross–L)
45. Muskoka (Wright–C)
46. Nipissing (Gordon–C)
47. Norfolk (Charlton–L)
48. Northumberland-East (Walker–C)
49. Northumberland-West (Munson–C)
50. Ontario-North (Sharpe–C)
51. Ontario-South (Smith–C)
52. Ottawa (2 seats) (Fripp–C; Chabot–C)
53. Oxford-North (Nesbitt–L)
54. Oxford-South (Sutherland–C)
55. Parry Sound (Arthurs–C)
56. Peel (Blain–C)
57. Perth-North (Morphy–C)
58. Perth-South (Steele–C)
59. Peterborough-East (Sexsmith–C)
60. Peterborough-West (Burnham–C)
61. Prescott (Proulx–L)
62. Prince Edward (Hepburn–C)
63. Renfrew-North (White–C)
64. Renfrew-South (Low–L)
65. Russell (Murphy–L)
66. Simcoe-North (Currie–C)

67. Simcoe-South (Lennox–C)
68. Simcoe-East (Bennett–C)
69. Stormont (Alguire–C)
70. Thunder Bay and Rainy River (Carrick–C)
71. Toronto-East (Kemp–C)
72. Toronto-West (Osler–C)
73. Toronto-Centre (Bristol–C)
74. Toronto-North (Foster–C)
75. Toronto-South (MacDonnell–C)
76. Victoria & Halliburton (Hughes–C)
77. Waterloo-North (Weichel–C)
78. Waterloo-South (Clare–C)
79. Welland (German–L)
80. Wellington-North (Clarke–C)
81. Wellinton-South (Guthrie–L)
82. Wentworth (Wilson–C)
83. York-North (Armstrong–C)
84. York-Centre (Wallace–C)
85. York-South (Maclean–C)

Quebec
86. Argenteuil (Perley–C)

87. Bagot (Marcile–L)
88. Beauce (Béland–L)
89. Beauharnois (Papineau–L)
90. Bellechasse (Lavallée–N)
91. Berthier (Barette–C)
92. Bonaventure (Marcil–L)
93. Brome (Baker–C)
94. Chambly-Vercheres (Rainville–N)
95. Champlain (Blondin–C)
96. Charlevoix (Forget–C)
97. Chateauguay (Brown–L)
98. Chicoutimi-Saguenay (Girard–N)
99. Compton (Cromwell–C)
100. Dorchester (Sévigny–N)
101. Drummond-Arthbaska (Brouillard–L)
102. Gaspé (Gauthier–N)
103. Hochelaga (Coderre–N)
104. Huntingdon (Robb–L)
105. Jacques Cartier (Monk–N)
106. Joliette (Guilbault–N)
107. Kamouraska (Lapointe–L)
108. Labelle (Achim–N)
109. Laprairie-Napierville (Lanctot–L)

110. L'Assomption
     (Séguin–L)
111. Laval (Wilson–L)
112. Lévis (Boutin-
     Bourassa–L)
113. L'Islet (Paquet–C)
114. Lotbinière
     (Fortier–L)
115. Maisonneuve
     (Verville–L-L)
116. Maskinongé
     (Bellemare–N)
117. Mégantic
     (Pacaud–L)
118. Missisquoi (Kay–L)
119. Montcalm
     (Lafortune–L)
120. Montmagny
     (L'Espérance–N)
121. Montmorency
     (Forget–C)
122. Montréal-St. Anne
     (Doherty–C)
123. Montreal-St.
     Antoine (Ames–C)
124. Montreal-St. Mary
     (Martin–L)
125. Montreal-St.
     Lawrence
     (Bickerdicke–L)
126. Montreal-St. James
     (Lapointe–N)
127. Nicolet
     (Lamarche–N)
128. Pontiac
     (Brabazon–C)
129. Portneuf
     (Delisle–L)
130. Québec-Centre
     (Lachance–L)
131. Québec-Est
     (Laurier–L)
132. Québec-West
     (Power–L)

133. Quebec County
     (Pelletier–N)
134. Richelieu
     (Cardin–L)
135. Richmond & Wolfe
     (Tobin–L)
136. Rimouski
     (Boulay–C)
137. Rouville
     (Lemieux–L)
138. Shefford (Boivin–L)
139. Sherbrooke
     (McCrea–L)
140. Soulanges
     (Laurier–L)
141. Stanstead
     (Lovell–L)
142. St. Hyacinthe
     (Gauthier–L)
143. St. Jean-Iberville
     (Demers–L)
144. Témiscouata
     (Gauvreau–L)
145. Terrebonne
     (Nantel–L)
146. Three Rivers
     & St. Maurice
     (Bureau–L)
147. Two Mountains
     (Ethier–L)
148. Vaudreuil (Boyer–L)
149. Wright (Devlin–L)
150. Yamaska
     (Mondou–C)

Maritime Provinces

Nova Scotia

151. Annapolis
     (Davidson–C)
152. Antigonish
     (Chisholm–L)

153. Cape Breton-
     North & Victoria
     (Mckenzie–L)
154. Cape Breton-South
     (Carroll–L)
155. Colchester
     (Stanfield–C)
156. Cumberland
     (Rhodes–C)
157. Digby (Jameson–C)
158. Guysborough
     (Sinclair–L)
159. Halifax (2 seats)
     (Borden–C;
     McLean–L)
160. Hants (Tremain–C)
161. Iverness
     (Chisholm–L)
162. Kings (Foster–C)
163. Lunenburg
     (Stewart–C)
164. Pictou
     (MacDonald–L)
165. Richmond (Kyte–L)
166. Shelburne & Queen's
     (McCurdy–C)
167. Yarmouth (Law–L)

New Brunswick

168. Carleton
     (Carvell–L)
169. Charlotte (Hartt–C)
170. Gloucester
     (Turgeon–L)
171. Kent (Robidoux–C)
172. Kings & Albert
     (Fowler–C)
173. Northumberland
     (Loggie–L)
174. Restigouche
     (Reid–L)
175. Saint John City
     (Pugsley–L)

176. Sunbury-Queen's
(McLean–L)
177. St. John City &
County (Daniel–C)
178. Victoria
(Michaud–L)
179. Westmorland
(Emmerson–L)
180. York (Crocket–C)

Prince Edward Island

181. King's (Hughes–L)
182. Prince (Richard–L)
183. Queen's (2 seats)
(McLean–C;
Nicholson–C)

Western Canada

British Columbia

184. Comox-Atlin
(Clements–C)
185. Kootenay
(Goodeve–C)
186. Nanaimo
(Shepherd–C)
187. New Westminster
(Taylor–C)
188. Vancouver
(Stevens–C)
189. Victoria
(Bernard–C)
190. Yale-Cariboo
(Burrell–C)

Manitoba

191. Brandon (Akins–C)
192. Dauphin
(Cruise–L)
193. Lisgar (Sharpe–C)

194. Macdonald
(Staples–C)
195. Marquette
(Roche–C)
196. Portage La Prairie
(Meighen–C)
197. Provencher
(Molloy–L)
198. Selkirk
(Bradbury–C)
199. Souris (Schaffner–C)
200. Winnipeg
(Haggart–C)

Alberta

201. Macleod
(Warnock–L)
202. Medicine Hat
(Buchanan–L)
203. Calgary (Bennett–C)
204. Red Deer (Clark–L)
205. Strathcona
(Douglas–L)
206. Edmonton
(Oliver–L)
207. Victoria (White–L)

Saskatchewan

208. Battleford
(Champagne–L)
209. Moose Jaw
(Knowles–L)
210. Regina (Martin–L)
211. Assiniboia
(Turriff–L)
212. Qu'Appelle
(Thomson–L)
213. Saltcoats
(MacNutt–L)
214. Mackenzie (Cash–L)
215. Humboldt
(Neeley–L)

216. Saskatoon
(McCraney–L)
217. Prince Albert
(McKay–C)

Yukon

218. Yukon
(Thompson–C)

APPENDIX II

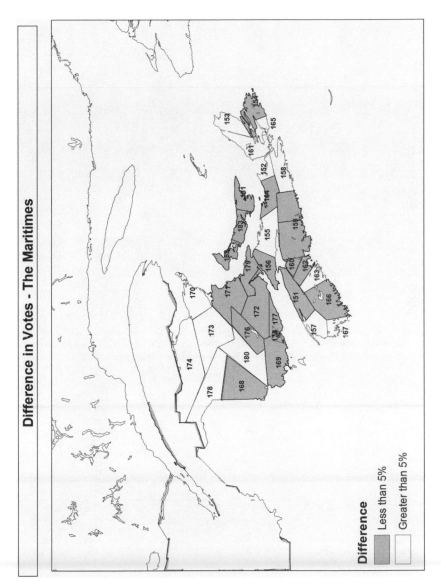

Map 1

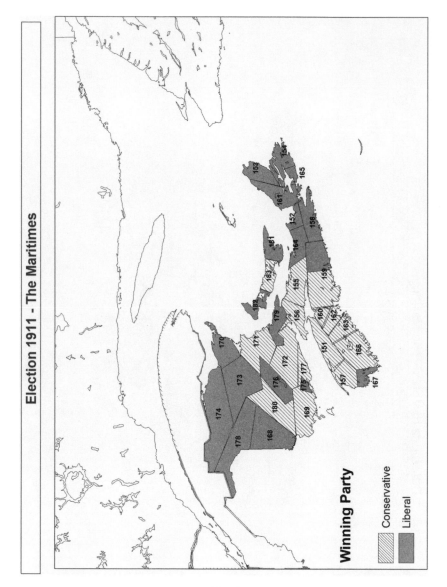

Map 2

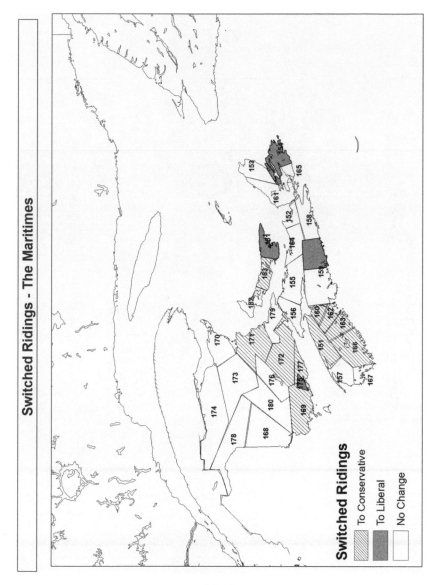

Map 3

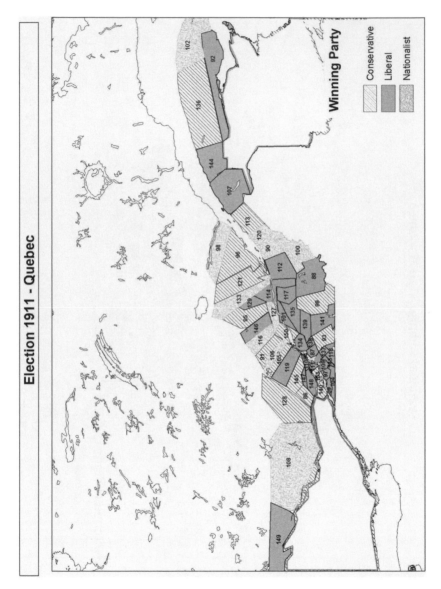

Map 4

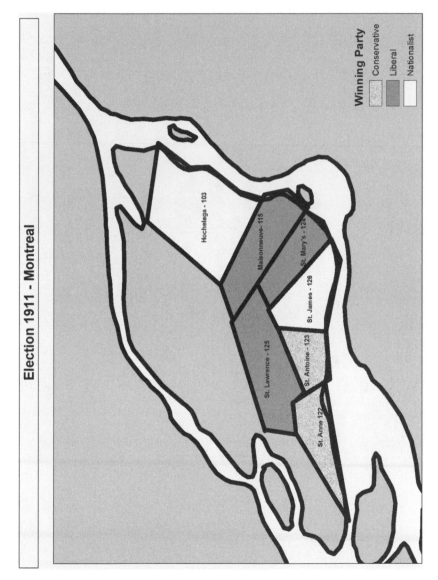

Map 4.1

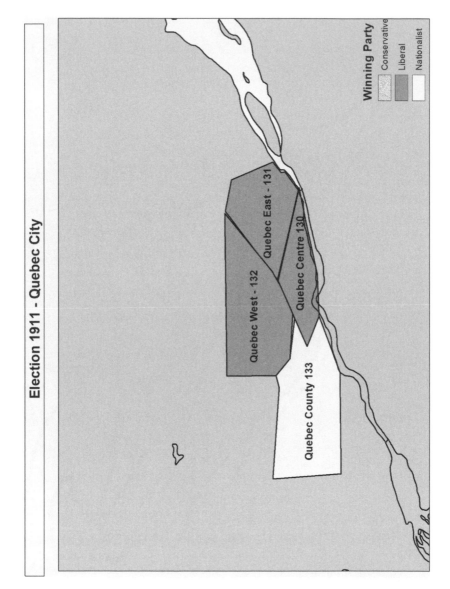

Map 4.2

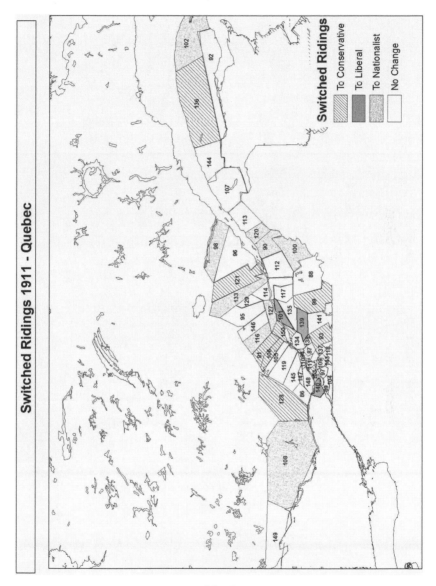

Map 5

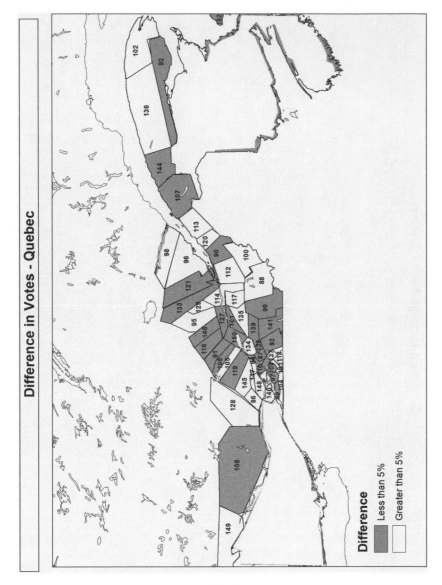

Map 6

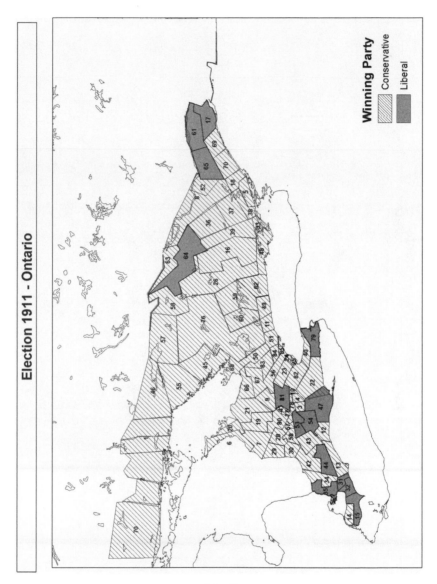

Map 7

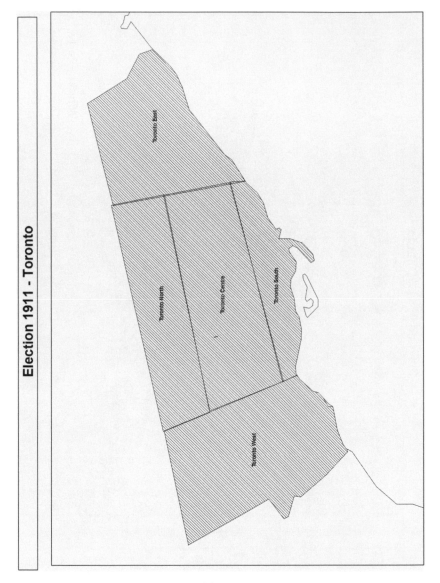

Map 7.1

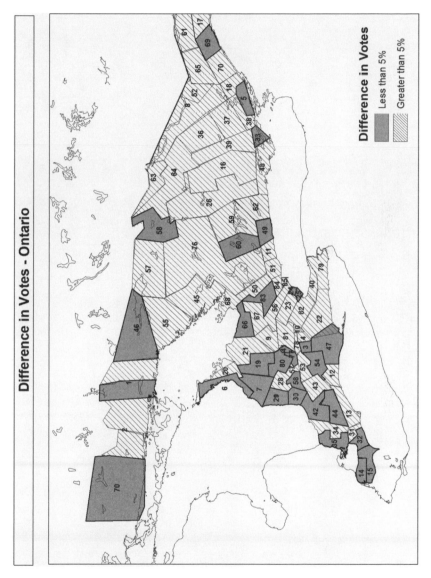

Map 8

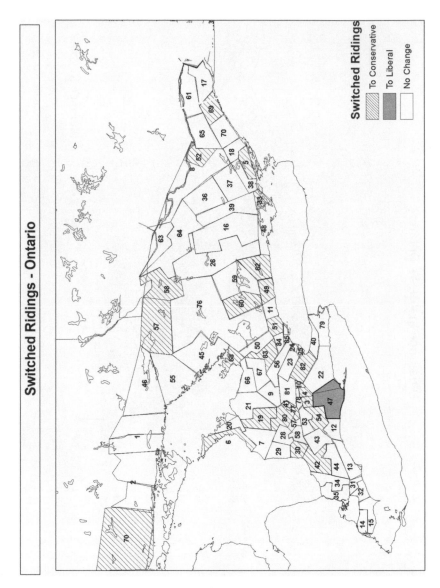

Map 9

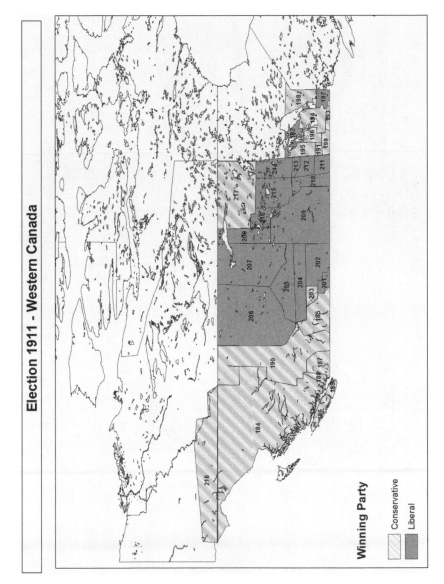

Map 10

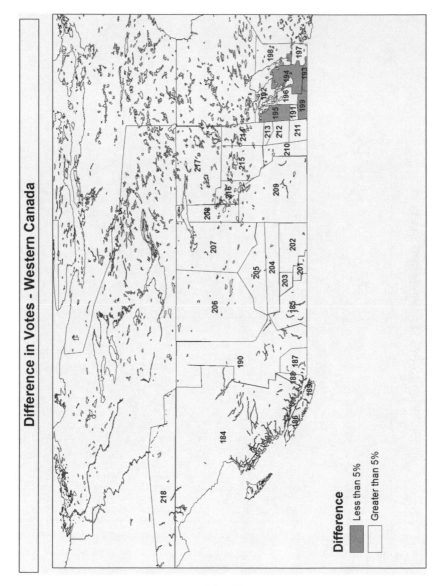

Map 11

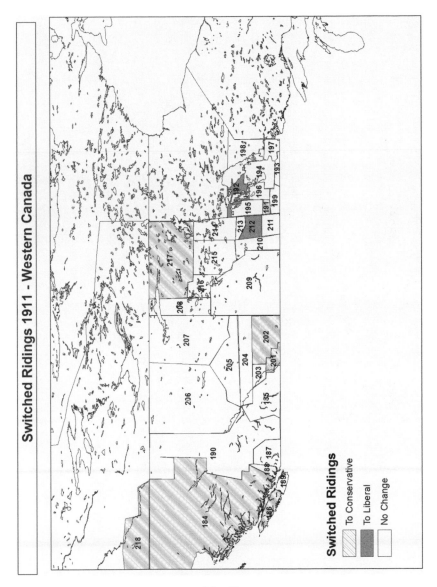

Map 12

NOTES

Chapter 1

1. Theodore was already known informally as Laurier Avenue. "Laurier House" became the home of William Lyon Mackenzie in the 1920s, and is now a historic site.
2. Now the town of St-Lin-Laurentides. The home is now a historic site: *www.pc.gc.ca/laurier.*
3. The home is now a museum, see *www.museelaurier.com/eng/a_accueil.html.*
4. See Oscar Douglas Skelton, *Life and Letters of Sir Wilfrid Laurier, Vol. 1* (Oxford University Press, 1922): 149.
5. *Ibid.,* 314.
6. Montreal *Gazette,* June 9, 1887, cited in Paul Stevens, "Wilfrid Laurier: Politician," in Marcel Hamelin (ed.) *The Political Ideas of the Prime Ministers of Canada* (Ottawa: Editions de l'Université d'Ottawa, 1969): 70.
7. The journalist M.O. Hammond noted traces of Laurier's French accent well into the 1900s. See Paul Bilkey, *Persons, Papers and Things* (Ryerson, 1940).
8. Augustus Bridle, *The Masques of Ottawa* (Macmillan, 1921).
9. Oscar Douglas Skelton, *Life and Letters of Sir Wilfrid Laurier, Vol. 2* (Oxford University Press, 1922): 162.
10. See Carman Miller, "Sir Frederick Borden and Military Reform, 1896–1911," *Canadian Historical Review* 50, No. 3, 1969.

11. J.L. Granatstein and Norman Hillmer, *Prime Ministers: Ranking Canada's Leaders* (Toronto: HarperCollins, 2000): 55.

12. Joseph Schull, *Laurier: The First Canadian* (Toronto: Macmillan, 1965): 412. He quotes Robert Rumilly's *Histoire de la Province de Québec Vol X* (Montreal: Valiquette, 1942): 162.

13. Most of this information is drawn from Robert Craig Brown, *Robert Laird Borden: A Biography, Volume I, 1854–1914* (Toronto: Macmillan, 1975), Chapters 1 and 2.

14. Borden, *Memoirs, Vol. 1, 1854–1915* (Toronto: Macmillan, 1938): 18.

15. O.D. Skelton, *The Life and Letters of Sir Wilfrid Laurier, Vol. 2*, 386.

16. *Ibid.*, 387.

17. *Ibid.*, 257.

18. Brown, *Robert Laird Borden*, 36.

19. *Ibid.*

20. Schull, 428.

21. Arthur Meighen, "Introduction" in Borden's *Memoirs, Vol. 1*, viii.

22. Library and Archives Canada (LAC), J.S. Willison Papers, Clifford Sifton to J.S. Willison, August 27, 1907, cited in Paul Stevens, *op. cit.*, 73–74.

23. LAC, J.S. Willison Papers, Frederick Hamilton to J.S. Willison, July 3, 1908.

24. J. Murray Beck, *Pendulum of Power: Canada's Federal Elections* (Toronto: Prentice Hall, 1968): 107.

25. LAC, J.S. Willison Papers, Frederick Hamilton to J.S. Willison, November 3, 1908.

26. See Juliet Nicolson, *The Perfect Summer: England in 1911* (Toronto: McArthur, 2007).

27. *La Patrie*, July 11, 1911: 1.

28. The *Globe*, July 28, 1911: 1.

29. LAC, Wilfrid Laurier Papers, C-906, 18,315, Laurier to E.H. Lemay, August 1, 1911.

30. Castell Hopkins, ed., *Canadian Annual Review, 1911* (Toronto, 1912): 371. All the statistics that follow were taken from pages 371–401.

CHAPTER 2

1. For a summary of the "panic" of 1909 in Great Britain, see Robert K. Massie, *Dreadnought: Britain, Germany and the Coming of the Great War* (New York: Random House, 1991) Chapter 33.

2. The Montreal *Star*, March 19, 1909, cited in Donald Gordon, *The Dominion Partnership in Imperial Defense, 1870–1914* (Baltimore: Johns Hopkins Press, 1965): 227.

3. The *Globe*, editorial, March 24, 1909.

4. *Ibid.*

5. LAC, J.S. Willison Papers, F. Hamilton to Willison, March 23, 1909.

6. *House of Commons Debates*, First session, 11th Parliament, March 29, 1909: 5.

7. *Ibid.*, 7.

8. LAC, Willison Papers, F. Hamilton to Willison, March 25, 1909.

9. LAC, L.P. Brodeur Papers, reel H-1017, extract of Colonial Conference 1907 proceedings.

10. *House of Commons Debates*, cited in C.P. Stacey, *Canada and the Age of Conflict: A History of Canadian External Policies Volume 1: 1867–1921* (Toronto: Macmillan of Canada, 1977): 129.

11. *Ibid.*, 131.

12. *Ibid.*, March 30, 1909 telegram.

13. LAC, Armand Lavergne Papers, Notes for speech "La légende du Laurierisme," May 16, 1924: 4.

14. LAC, Lord Grey Papers, Grey to Laurier, March 30, 1909.

15. *Ibid.*, Grey to Laurier, March 30, 1909 (ii).

16. *Ibid.*, Grey to Laurier, April 17, 1909.

17. *Ibid.*, Grey to Laurier, April 18, 1909.

18. *Ibid.*, Grey to Laurier, July 26, 1909.

19. *Ibid.*, Laurier to Grey, July 28, 1900.

20. LAC, Willison Papers, F. Hamilton to Willison, October 15, 1909.

21. LAC, F.D. Monk Papers, vol. 1, File 1, Grey to Monk, May 20, 1909.

22. Stephen Leacock, "Canada and the Monroe Doctrine," *University Magazine*, October 1909: 352.

23. *Ibid.*, 374.

24. C. Frederick Hamilton, "Shall Canada Have a Navy," *University Magazine*, October 1909: 396.

25. LAC, Willison Papers, F. Hamilton to Willison, December 4, 1909.

26. *Ibid.*, Hamilton to Willison, November 30, 1909.

27. LAC, F.D. Monk Papers, vol. 1, File 1, Lavergne to Monk, November 10, 1909.

28. LAC, Willison Papers, F. Hamilton to Willison, November 25, 1909.

29. *Ibid.*, December 3, 1909.

30. Henry Borden (editor) *Robert Laird Borden: His Memoirs, Vol. 1* (Toronto: Macmillan Company, 1938): 263.

31. Cited in Stacey, *op. cit.,* 134.

32. *Ibid.*, 135.

33. Quoted in *Robert Laird Borden: His Memoirs, Vol. 1*: 272–73.

34. LAC, Willison Papers, F. Hamilton to Willison, March 1, 1910.

35. *Ibid.*, F. Hamilton to Willison, March 1, 1910.

36. *Robert Laird Borden: His Memoirs, Vol. 1*: 285.

37. LAC, Willison Papers, F. Hamilton to Willison, March 4, 1910.

38. *Ibid.*, F. Hamilton to Willison, March 8, 1910.

39. *Ibid.*, F. Hamilton to Willison, April 5, 1910.

40. LAC, George Foster papers, Vol. 294, 2(2), 172,623–27, W. Burrelle to Sir Robert, October 17, 1932.

41. *Ibid.*, 139.

42. Armand Lavergne Papers, Notes for speech "La légende du Laurierisme," May 16, 1924: 3bis.

43. Willison Papers, F. Hamilton to Willison, July 8, 1910.

44. *Le Devoir*, editorial, January 17, 1910.

45. The text of the resolution was published in *Le Devoir*, July 16, 1910: 1.

46. *Ibid.*

47. LAC, Laurier Papers, C-872, Béique to Laurier, February 2, 1909. For more detail on this episode, see Patrice Dutil, *Devil's Advocate: Godfroy Langlois and the Politics of Liberal Progressivism in Laurier's Quebec* (Montreal: Robert Davies Publishing, 1994), Chapter 10.

48. *Ibid.*

49. *Ibid.*

50. Laurier Papers, C-880, Dandurand to Langlois, September 12, 1909.

51. *Le Pays*, January 15, 1910, editorial.

52. *La Patrie*, October 11, 1910: 1.

53. *Ibid.*

54. LAC, Armand Lavergne Papers, Napoléon Garceau to Lavergne, September 23, 1910.

55. Willison Papers, F. Hamilton to Willison, October 26, 1910.

56. *Ibid.*, F. Hamilton to Willison, October 27, 1910.

57. L.P. Brodeur Papers, Brodeur to Grey, October 31, 1910.

58. Laurier Papers, C-880, Béland to Laurier, October 26, 1910.

59. *Ibid.*, C-880, Béland to Laurier, October 29, 1910.

60. *Ibid.*, C-880, Laurier to Béland, October 30, 1910.

61. *Le Devoir*, September 12, 1911: 1.

62. *Le Pays*, November 6, 1910.

63. Laurier Papers, C-906, 188156-57, A. Cantin to Laurier, July 27, 1911.

64. Brodeur Papers, Brodeur to Simon Sénécal, November 28, 1910.

65. *Le Devoir*, November 4, 1910: editorial.

66. Willison Papers, F. Hamilton to Willison, November 25, 1910.

67. Willison Papers, F. Hamilton to Willison, November 27, 1910.

68. L.P. Brodeur Papers, reel H-1018, "Cost of Canadian Navy When Completed," and "Annual Expenditure on Upkeep of Canadian Navy."

69. *Ibid.*, reel H-1018, Address by the Honourable L.P. Brodeur, Minister of Marine and Fisheries and of Naval Defense, "On the Occasion of the Arrival at Halifax of the First Canadian Cruiser, the *Niobe*."

70. *Ibid.*, reel H-1018, Brodeur to Mrs. Denison, "Saturday Night," November 3, 1910.

71. Willison Papers, F. Hamilton to Willison, October 27, 1910.

72. *Ibid.*, F. Hamilton to Willison, March 8, 1910.

73. *Ibid.*, F. Hamilton to Willison, June 8, 1909.

74. See Willison Papers, F. Hamilton to Willison, May 25, 1910: "Borden had a nasty escape from typhoid, pneumonia or something of the sort. He caught cold through overheating himself while working about his grounds, & puzzled his doctor — high fever and lower pulse. The doctor said he must be working some

poison yet. Perhaps he was paying for the strain of the session. He has not come out yet & will have to be careful in his picnic tour."

75. Willison Papers, F. Hamilton to Willison, May 20, 1909.

76. *Halifax Herald*, August 31, 1910, editorial.

77. *Ibid.*

78. *Ibid.*

79. Brodeur Papers, Brodeur to D.A. Lafortune, December 30, 1910.

CHAPTER 3

1. John Hilliker, *Canada's Department of External Affairs, Volume 1, The Early Years, 1909–1946* (Montreal: McGill-Queen's University Press, 1990): 30–56.

2. See D.C. Masters, *The Reciprocity Treaty of 1854* (Toronto: McClelland and Stewart, 1963).

3. For the evolution of the reciprocity debate, see D.C. Masters, *Reciprocity, 1846–1911* (Ottawa: Canadian Historical Association, 1983); J.L. Granatstein, "Free Trade Between Canada and the United States: The Issue That Will Not Go Away," in *The Politics of Canada's Economic Relationship with the United States*, edited by Denis Stairs and Gilbert Winham (Toronto: 1985): 11–54; Paul Stevens, "Reciprocity 1911: The Canadian Perspective," in *Canadian-American Free Trade: Historical, Political and Economic Dimensions*, edited by A.R. Riggs and Tom Velk (Halifax: Institute for Research on Public Policy, 1987): 9–21, and Michael Hart, *A Trading Nation: Canadian Trade Policy from Colonialism to Globalization* (Vancouver: University of British Columbia Press, 2002): 45–84.

4. Frank H. Underhill, *The Image of Confederation* (Toronto: CBC, 1964): 22. Interestingly, as a young man Underhill cast his first federal vote in 1911, not for the National Policy but for reciprocity and the Liberals. Later that same day he left Canada for Oxford University. See R. Douglas Francis, *Frank H. Underhill: Intellectual Provocateur* (Toronto: University of Toronto Press, 1986): 20.

5. Laurier quoted in John W. Dafoe, *Clifford Sifton in Relation to His Times* (Toronto: Macmillan, 1931): 355–56.

6. Hart, *A Trading Nation*, 68, 96.

7. Stephen Scheinberg, "Invitation to Empire: Tariffs and American Economic Expansion in Canada," *Business History Review* 47 (1973): 236; see also Gordon Stewart, "'A Special Contiguous Country Economic Regime': An Overview of America's Canadian Policy," *Diplomatic History* 6, No. 4 (Fall 1982): 339–57.

8. Taft quoted in Robert E. Hannigan, "Reciprocity 1911: Continentalism and American Weltpolitik," *Diplomatic History* 4, No. 1 (Winter 1980): 17.

9. Hannigan, "Reciprocity 1911": 6; Scheinberg, "Invitation to Empire": 226. See also L. Ethan Ellis, *Reciprocity 1911: A Study in Canadian-American Relations* (New Haven: Yale University Press, 1939): 191–92.

10. *Documents on Canadian External Relations, Vol. 1: 1909–1918* (Ottawa 1967) (*DCER* hereafter), document 899, Lord Grey to James Bryce, March 17, 1910.

11. *DCER*, document 892, Fielding memo, December 1, 1909.

12. Taft quoted in Hannigan, 14.

13. Oscar Douglas Skelton, *Life and Letters of Sir Wilfrid Laurier, Volume II* (Toronto: Oxford University Press, 1921): 366.

14. *DCER*, document 904, Knox to Fielding, March 26, 1910.

15. LAC, Laurier Papers, reel C-892, 172,934, Laurier to Aylesworth, July 7, 1910.

16. *Ibid.*, reel C-893, 173,818, Laurier to Lemieux, August 19, 1910.

17. LAC, George Foster Papers, vol. 108, Roblin to Foster, July 22, 1910.

18. Provincial Archives of British Columbia, Sir Richard McBride Papers, Private 1910 (accessed in Robert Craig Brown Papers, University of Toronto Archives), Burrell to McBride, September 18, 1910.

19. Laurier LaPierre, *Sir Wilfrid Laurier and the Romance of Canada* (Toronto: Stoddart, 1996): 320–21.

20. David MacKenzie, *Arthur Irwin: A Biography* (Toronto: University of Toronto Press, 1993): 15.

21. John G. Diefenbaker, *One Canada: Memoirs of the Right Honourable John G. Diefenbaker, Vol. 1, The Crusading Years 1895–1956* (Toronto: Macmillan, 1975): 75–76.

22. LAC, Laurier Papers, reel C-893, 174,000–01, Secretary of Victoria TLC to Laurier, August 18, 1910.

23. *Ibid.*, reel C-892, 172,739–41, Statement of the Manitoba Grain Growers' Association, July 18, 1910.

24. *Ibid.*, reel C-893, 173,611–12, Liberal Association of Edmonton to Laurier, August 6, 1910.

25. *DCER*, document 919, Lord Grey to Colonial Secretary, November 30, 1910.

26. *Grain Growers' Guide* (December 21, 1910): 4; Louis Aubrey Wood, *A History of Farmers' Movements in Canada* (Toronto: University of Toronto Press, 1975): 264–65.

27. LAC, Laurier Papers, reel C-898, 179,980, Canadian Manufacturers' Association to Laurier, n.d.

28. *Ibid.*, reel C-892, 172,586, R. McLaughlin to J. Macdonald, June 27, 1910.

29. *Canadian Annual Review, 1911* (*CAR* hereafter): 34–35.

30. LAC, Laurier Papers, reel C-898, 179,334–35, McMullen to Laurier, January 6, 1911.

31. NARA, RG84, Records of Foreign Service Posts, Consular Posts, Vancouver, B.C., Canada, vol. 087, David Wilber to Secretary of State, November 15, 1910.

32. *Ibid.*, Consular Posts, Toronto, Ontario, Canada, vol. 033, Chilton to Secretary of State, November 8, 1910.

33. *DCER*, document 926, Bryce to Foreign Secretary, January 19, 1911; and document 928, Canadian Delegation to US Secretary of State, January 21, 1911.

34. C.P. Stacey, *Canada and the Age of Conflict: A History of Canadian External Policies Volume I: 1867–1921* (Toronto: University of Toronto Press, 1984): 145.

35. PRO, Colonial Office Records, CO42 /951, Bryce to Sir Edward Grey, January 22, 1911.

36. Taft to T. Roosevelt, January 10, 1911, quoted in Hannigan, 16–17.

37. LAC, Laurier Papers, reel C-899, 180,321, Fielding to Laurier, January 20, 1911.

38. LAC, Mackenzie King Diary, January 18, 1911.

CHAPTER 4

1. LAC, Mackenzie King Diary, January 18, 1911.
2. John Dafoe, *Clifford Sifton in Relation to His Times* (Toronto: Macmillan, 1931): 359.
3. Quoted in *Canadian Annual Review, 1911* (*CAR* hereafter) (Toronto: Annual Review Publishing Co., 1912): 30.
4. Henry Borden, ed., *Robert Laird Borden: His Memoirs, Vol. 1* (Toronto: Macmillan, 1938): 303.
5. LAC, Borden Papers, C-4199, 532–33, Whitney to Borden, January 27, 1911.
6. John English, *The Decline of Politics: The Conservatives and the Party System, 1901–20* (Toronto: University of Toronto Press, 1977): 56–57.
7. LAC, Borden Papers, reel C-4354, 70,831, Hughes to MacArthur, March 23, 1911.
8. LAC, Grey Papers, reel C-1361, 004488, Grey to Harcourt, April 8, 1911.
9. LAC, Borden Papers, reel C-4380, 97,283, Borden to Kemp, January 30, 1911.
10. Foster, quoted in Stevens, *The 1911 General Election*, 23.
11. *CAR*, 38.
12. Toronto *Star*, March 8, 1911: 1.
13. *CAR*, 37–41.
14. Montreal *Daily Star*, February 4, 1911: 1.
15. *CAR*, 54.
16. Quoted in Valerie Knowles, *From Telegrapher to Titan: The Life of William C. Van Horne* (Toronto: Dundurn Press, 2004): 411.
17. LAC, Borden Papers, reel C-4199, 541, Borden to Whitney, February 24, 1911.
18. PRO, CO 42/946, 387–88, Grey to Harcourt, March 2, 1911.
19. LAC, Laurier Papers, reel C-899, 180,837–38, F.S. Spence to Laurier, February 2, 1911.
20. D.J. Hall, *Clifford Sifton: Volume II: A Lonely Eminence, 1901–1929* (Vancouver: UBC Press, 1985): 224; Dafoe, *Clifford Sifton*, 356–58.
21. LAC, Laurier Papers, reel C-899, 180,773–74, Sifton, Harris, et al., to Laurier, February 1, 1911.

22. Hall, *Clifford Sifton*, 225.

23. English, *Decline of Politics*, 55–56. For example, a year earlier Sam Hughes informed Borden that, thanks to Laurier's imperial and naval policies, many prominent Ontario Liberals were ready to jump to the Conservatives. LAC, Borden Papers, reel C-4354, 70,813, Hughes to Borden, March 23, 1910.

24. LAC, Laurier Papers, reel C-899, 180,930, Lash to Laurier, February 3, 1911.

25. *Ibid.*, 180,932, Laurier to Lash, February 6, 1911.

26. *Ibid.*, 180,937, Lash to Laurier, February 10, 1911.

27. Quoted in Toronto *Star*, February 16, 1911: 1.

28. Quoted in *CAR*, 40.

29. W.M. Baker, "A Case Study of Anti-Americanism in English-Speaking Canada: The Election Campaign of 1911," *Canadian Historical Review* 51, No. 4 (December 1970): 436–37; See also G.P. de T. Glazebrook, *Sir Edmund Walker* (Toronto: Oxford University Press, 1933): 109–10; and James Eayrs, "The Round Table Movement in Canada, 1909–1920," *Canadian Historical Review* 38, No. 1 (March 1957): 1–20.

30. *CAR*, 47.

31. LAC, Laurier Papers, reel C-900, 181,778–79, Ryan to Laurier, February 18, 1911.

32. *Ibid.*, 181,988, Larkin to Laurier, February 23, 1911.

33. *Ibid.*, 181,680, Laurier to Bowman, February 18, 1911.

34. *Ibid.*, 181,772, Laurier to W.D. Gregory, February 20, 1911.

35. Fisher Rare Book Library, University of Toronto, Sir Edmund Walker Papers, box 9, file: 2, Flavelle to Walker, February 2, 1911.

36. Kemp quoted in Robert D. Cuff, "The Toronto Eighteen and the Election of 1911," *Ontario History* (December 1965): 173.

37. LAC, Borden Papers, reel C-4380, 97,283, memo attached, Kemp to Borden, May 23, 1911.

38. OA, Whitney Papers, container B273276, Borden to Whitney, February 14, 1911.

39. Fisher Library, Walker Papers, box 21, file: 43, Walker to Sifton, February 18, 1911.

40. Quoted in Henry James Morgan, ed., *The Canadian Men and Women of the Time* (Toronto: William Briggs, 1912): 236.

41. LAC, Laurier Papers, reel C-900, 181,989–90, unsigned memo, n.d.

42. LAC, King Papers, reel C-1916, 16,848, King to Sims, March 10, 1911.

43. Fisher Library, Walker Papers, box 9, file: 24, Sifton to Walker, February 20, 1911.

44. LAC, Laurier Papers, reel C-900, 181,817, Sifton to Laurier, February 20, 1911.

45. Montreal, *The Gazette*, March 1, 1911: 1.

46. Hall, *Clifford Sifton*, 230.

47. PRO, CO42 /946, Grey to Colonial Secretary, March 2, 1911.

48. Sifton quoted in Stevens, *The 1911 General Election*, 38–46.

49. LAC, J.S. Willison Papers, vol. 37, file: 286, Sifton to Willison, February 23, 1911; LAC, Sifton Papers, reel C-591, 157,061, Lash to Sifton, February 25, 1911.

50. Fisher Library, Walker Papers, box 21, file: 47, Walker to Sifton, February 23, 1911.

51. Richard Clippingdale, "Willison, Sir John Stephen," *Dictionary of Canadian Biography* (accessed online).

52. English, *Decline of Politics*, 60.

53. LAC, Willison Papers, vol. 52, file: "Politics-General, Vol. 4," 38,488–92, Willison memo, n.d. A few years later Lloyd Harris gave his recollection: "He had broken with Laurier on the issue [reciprocity], and then found that the Conservatives were afraid to oppose the issue under Borden's leadership. He went to Borden and found Borden afraid of the division in his own following, and disinclined to fight, a meeting of recalcitrant Liberals was held, and later they met Borden. Sir John Willison has the minutes of that meeting. The result was a well planned opposition to Reciprocity." Queen's University Archives, Norman Lambert Papers, Box 9, *Personal Diaries 1912–1939*, Lambert diary entry February 9, 1919.

54. Borden, *Memoirs, Vol. 1*: 308.

55. Robert Craig Brown, *Robert Laird Borden: A Biography, Volume I: 1854–1914* (Toronto: Macmillan, 1975): 179.

56. LAC, Borden Papers, reel C-4430, 150,602–03, Borden to Dafoe, December 17, 1931.

57. LAC, Willison Papers, vol. 19, file: 140, 14,233, Hamilton to Willison, March 27, 1911.

58. Borden, *Memoirs, Vol. 1*, 309.

59. *Ibid.*, 308.

CHAPTER 5

1. LAC, Wilson MacDonald Papers, vol. 6, Diary 1911, diary entry, April 25, 1911.

2. John W. Garvin, ed., *Canadian Poets* (Toronto: McClelland and Stewart, 1926): 432.

3. LAC, MacDonald Papers, vol. 6, Diary 1911, diary entry, April 25, 1911.

4. PRO, CO42 /946, Grey to Secretary of State for Colonies, March 14, 1911.

5. Quoted in *Canadian Annual Review, 1911* (*CAR* hereafter): 255.

6. Similarly, the letterhead of the Anti-Reciprocity League noted that it was "free from all political parties."

7. Robert Craig Brown, *Robert Laird Borden: A Biography, Volume I: 1854–1914* (Toronto: Macmillan, 1975): 190–91.

8. Arthur Hawkes, "Sir Clifford Sifton and the Reciprocity Election of 1911," reprinted in Stevens, *The 1911 General Election*, 71–72.

9. Brown, *Borden, Vol. I*, 190; Michael Bliss, *A Living Profit: Studies in the Social History of Canadian Business, 1883–1911* (Toronto: McClelland and Stewart, 1974): 112; and L. Ethan Ellis, "Canada's Rejection of Reciprocity in 1911," *Report of the Annual Meeting of the Canadian Historical Association* 18, No. 1 (1939): 102.

10. Brown, *Borden, Vol. I*, 189.

11. LAC, Willison Papers, vol. 19, file: 40, 14,236, Hamilton to Willison, March 31, 1911.

12. W.T.R. Preston, *My Generation of Politics and Politicians* (Toronto: D.A. Rose, 1927): 323.

13. Quoted in Paul Stevens, "Laurier and the Liberal Party in Ontario, 1887–1911," PhD thesis, University of Toronto, 1966: 397.

14. LAC, Graham Papers, vol. 24, file: 216, Fielding to Graham, May 24, 1911.
15. A copy can be found in Fisher Library, Walker Papers, box 32, file: 1.
16. Toronto *Globe*, March 10, 1911: 1.
17. Toronto *Star*, March 10, 1911: 7.
18. Montreal *Gazette*, March 10, 1911: 1.
19. LAC, Sifton Papers, reel C-591, 156,927, A.K.S. Hemming to Sifton, March 16, 1911.
20. Toronto *Globe*, March 21, 1911: 4.
21. Montreal *Gazette*, March 21, 1911: 1.
22. Leacock brought the reciprocity election to Mariposa in his classic *Sunshine Sketches of a Little Town*, published the following year. As the Liberal incumbent asked, "[W]hy not have fought the thing out on whether I spent too much money on the town wharf or the post-office? What better issues could a man want? Let them claim that I am crooked, and let me claim that I'm not. Surely that was good enough without dragging in the tariff." During the campaign, the local bar demonstrated its loyalty by replacing its sign for "American drinks" with one that read "British Beers at all Hours," while Jeff Thorpe, the local barber, went "home to his dinner, the first day reciprocity was talked of, and said to Mrs. Thorpe that it would simply kill business in the country and introduce a cheap, shoddy, American form of hair-cut that would render true loyalty impossible." The Conservative and winning candidate "of course, said nothing. He didn't have to — not for four years — and he knew it."
23. LAC, Laurier Papers, reel C-902, 183,630–31, Cameron to Fielding, March 21, 1911.
24. Quoted in the Toronto *Star*, March 21, 1911: 3. For another view of the meeting, see LAC, Willison Papers, vol. 19, file 140, 14,226, Hamilton to Willison, March 22, 1911.
25. Toronto *Star*, March 9, 1911: 8.
26. For a commentary on a Liberal meeting at Montreal's Windsor Hotel, see LAC, Sifton Papers, reel C-591, 156,929, Hemming to Sifton, March 26, 1911.

27. Queen's University Archives, John G. Foster Papers, Box 1, General Correspondence, file: Correspondence (1909–1926), nos. 1–41, Foster to Charles Pepper (Washington), March 15, 1911.

28. Montreal *Gazette*, February 23, 1911: 1.

29. Borden, *Memoirs, Vol. 2*, 311–13.

30. AO, Whitney Papers, container B273277, Borden to Whitney, March 22, 1911.

31. *Ibid.*, Whitney to Borden, March 23, 1911.

32. *CAR*, 88.

33. PRO, CO42 /946, Grey to Secretary of State for the Colonies, March 14, 1911.

34. LAC, Borden Papers, reel C-4354, 71,073, Borden to Aitken, May 24, 1911.

35. *Ibid.*, 71,068, Borden to Aitken, April 5, 1911.

36. Gregory P. Marchildon, *Profits and Politics: Beaverbrook and the Gilded Age of Canadian Finance* (Toronto: University of Toronto Press, 1996): 208–16.

37. *Ibid.*, 222–24.

38. LAC, Laurier Papers, reel C-902, 184,413, Fleming to Laurier, April 5, 1911.

39. *Ibid.*, 184,415, Laurier to Mackenzie King, April 14, 1911.

40. The whole affair is examined in Marchildon, *Profits and Politics*, 224–25.

41. *Ibid.*, 229–31.

42. Brown, *Borden, Vol. I*, 185; Marchildon, *Profits and Politics*, 225.

43. *Saturday Night*, May 27, 1911: 3.

44. For a few examples, see LAC, Laurier Papers, reel C-902, 183,546–47, Edgar to Laurier, March 20, 1911; 183,571–74, Fowler (Winnipeg Liberal Association) to Laurier, March 20, 1911.

45. LAC, Laurier Papers, reel C-901, 182,487, Fortin to Laurier, March 3, 1911.

46. *Ibid.*, 182,767, Burnett to Laurier, March 8. 1911.

47. *Ibid.*, 182,769, Laurier to Burnett, March 14, 1911. The day after his resignation speech the Toronto *Star* ran a story under the heading: "Sifton Has Been a Burden," March 1, 1911: 1.

48. PRO, CO42 /947, Grey to Secretary of State for Colonies, March 28, 1911.
49. For example, see Ellis, *Reciprocity 1911*, 142.
50. Laurier quoted in A.H.U. Colquhoun, *Press, Politics and People: The Life and Letters of Sir John Willison* (Toronto: Macmillan, 1935): 175.

CHAPTER 6

1. *House of Commons Debates*, July 24, 1911: 10,020.
2. Emma Albani published her memoirs, *Forty Years of Song* (Toronto: Copp, Clark) in 1911.
3. Lord Minto "Interview with Laurier, Secret, 28 January 1902," cited in Paul Stevens and John Saywell (eds.) *Lord Minto's Canadian Papers* (Toronto: The Champlain Society, 1983): 116.
4. Laurier Papers, Laurier to Willison, April 14, 1902: 64,356. Cited in Donald C. Gordon, *The Dominion Partnership in Imperial Defense, 1870–1914* (Baltimore, MD: Johns Hopkins Press, 1965): 155.
5. Minto "Memorandum, 3 June 1902," in Paul Stevens and John Saywell, 167.
6. Lord Minto, "Journal Entry, 13 July 1902," in Paul Stevens and John Saywell, 174.
7. See Skelton, *Life and Letters of Sir Wilfrid Laurier, Vol. II*, 342.
8. The *Globe*, May 23, 1911: 1.
9. John George Findlay, *The Imperial Conference of 1911* (London, 1912): 27.
10. *Ibid.*, 30.
11. Imperial Conference, 1911, London, England (London: His Majesty's Stationary, 1911): 29.
12. *Ibid.*, 84.
13. *Ibid.*, 85.
14. *Ibid.*, 84.
15. *Ibid.*, 86.
16. *Ibid.*, 41.
17. *Ibid.*, 252.
18. *Ibid.*, 262.

19. On the subject of imperial citizenship, see Daniel Gorman, *Imperial Citizenship: Empire and the Question of Belonging* (Manchester: Manchester University Press, 2006).

20. Laurier is cited in C.P. Stacey, *Canada and the Age of Conflict: A History of Canadian External Policies, Vol 1: 1867–1921* (Toronto: Macmillan of Canada, 1977): 140.

21. *Ibid.*

22. *Ibid.*

23. *Ibid.*, 141.

24. Imperial Conference, 1911, London, England, 117.

25. *Saturday Night*, June 17, 1911: 1.

26. Laurier Papers, reel C- 905, 186,889, W.D. Gregory to Laurier, June 9, 1911.

27. Laurier Papers, C-905, 187,091, Laurier to Sydney Fisher, June 6, 1911.

28. *Saturday Night*, July 1, 1911, "London Letter," 5.

29. Imperial Conference, 1911, London, England (London: His Majesty's Stationary, 1911): 335.

30. *Ibid.*, 340.

31. Laurier Papers, reel C- 905, 186,891, Laurier to Gregory, June 21, 1911.

32. *Saturday Night*, June 17, 1911: 1.

33. The articles were published from July 6 to 25 and reprinted in a pamphlet, *La conférence impériale et le rôle de M. Laurier* (Montreal: Imprimerie *Le Devoir*, 1911), 80 pages.

34. *Ibid.*, 5

35. Reported in *Saturday Night*, July 29, 1911: 3.

36. Bourassa, *op cit.*, 17.

37. *Ibid.*, 72.

38. *Ibid.*, 19.

39. *Ibid.*, 75.

40. *Ibid.*, 76.

41. *Ibid.*, 39–40.

42. Lord Grey of Howick Papers, reel C-1358, 1,555–56, Grey to Laurier, July 29, 1911.

43. *Saturday Night*, July 1, 1911: 3.

44. *Saturday Night*, July 22, 1911, "The Man with Borden."

45. Toronto *Daily Star*, July 10, 1911: 1.

46. The *Globe*, July 15, 1911: 1.

47. Laurier Papers, C906, Telegram J. Carroll (acting prime minister of New Zealand) to Laurier, August 4, 1911.

48. *Ibid.*, Telegram, Laurier to Carroll, August 7, 1911.

49. Toronto *Star*, July 10, 1911.

50. *Globe*, July 12, 1911: 1.

51. *Star*, July 12, 1911: 1.

52. Henry Gordon, ed., *Robert Laird Borden: His Memoirs, Vol.1* (Toronto: Macmillan, 1938): 322.

53. *Globe*, July 19, 1911: 1.

54. *House of Commons Debates*, July 19, 1911: 9,710.

55. *Ibid.*, 9,719.

56. *Ibid.*, 9,766.

57. *Ibid.*, 9,835.

58. *Ibid.*, 9,885.

59. *Ibid.*, 9,886.

60. *Ibid.*, 10,003.

61. *Ibid.*, July 24, 1911: 10,010.

62. *Globe*, July 26, 1911.

63. *Ottawa Citizen*, July 26, 1911.

64. *Globe*, July 26, 1911.

65. *House of Commons Debates*, 10,352.

66. *Ibid.*, 10,354.

67. *Ibid.*, 10,590.

68. *Halifax Herald*, August 5, 1911: 1.

69. *Globe*, July 31, 1911: 1.

70. Borden Papers, 16, Borden to Whitney, July 31, 1911, No. 3749. Quoted in Robert Craig Brown, *Robert Laird Borden: A Biography, Volume I, 1854–1914* (Toronto: Macmillan, 1975): 183.

71. Laurier Papers, reel C- 906, 188407, Laurier to M.M. Cowan, August 2, 1911.

CHAPTER 7

1. LAC, Laurier Papers, reel C-903, 185550, John Oliver to Laurier,

April 29, 1911; 185554, Oliver to Laurier, May 14, 1911; reel C-902, 183,594, Andrew Grant to Laurier, March 21, 1911; see also reel C-901, 182,440, Laurier to H.H. Miller, February 28, 1911.

2. *Ibid.*, reel C-903, 185,556, Laurier to Oliver, June 26, 1911.

3. *Ibid.*, 185,553, Laurier to Oliver, May 6, 1911.

4. *Ibid.*, reel 906, 188,156–57, Cantin to Laurier, July 27, 1911.

5. *Ibid.*, 188,280–82, C.C. Paradis to Laurier, July 30, 1911.

6. *Ibid.*, 188,179, J.J. Hughes to Laurier, July 27, 1911.

7. *Ibid.*, reel C-901, 182,700, J.B. MacKay to Laurier, March 6, 1911.

8. *Ibid.*, reel C-902, 183,595, Laurier to Grant, March 23, 1911.

9. *Ibid.*, reel C-897, 178,277, J. J. Stratton to Laurier, December 17, 1910.

10. *Ibid.*, reel C-906, 188,694, D. O'Connell to Laurier, August 8, 1911; reel C-906, 188,828, Father M.F. Fitzpatrick to Laurier, August 10, 1911.

11. *Ibid.*, reel C-906, 188,700, Laurier to D. O'Connell, August 11, 1911.

12. Quoted in Paul Stevens, "Laurier and the Liberal Party in Ontario, 1887–1911," PhD thesis, University of Toronto, 1966: 401.

13. LAC, Laurier Papers, reel C-906, 188,335, Laurier to G.D. Grant, August 1, 1911.

14. *Ibid.*, 188,181–83, McCarthy to Laurier, July 27, 1911.

15. *Ibid.*, 188,658–60, Alfred Clarke to Laurier, July 29, 1911.

16. *Ibid.*, 188,261, Laurier to Clarke, August 1, 1911.

17. *Ibid.*, 188,428, Laurier to Manley Chew, August 2, 1911.

18. *Ibid.*, 188,453, Laurier to Ward, August 2, 1911.

19. See the correspondence in *ibid.*, reel C-906.

20. See Stevens, "Laurier and the Liberal Party in Ontario, 1887–1911," 407–09; for the slow decline of the Ontario Liberals, see Chapter 7.

21. Paul Stevens, "Laurier, Aylesworth, and the Decline of the Liberal Party," Canadian Historical Association, *Historical Papers* (1968): 100–05.

22. For example, see the correspondence between Laurier and J.A. Macdonald of the *Globe* in LAC, Laurier Papers, reel C-892, 172,237–39; 172,896–901.

23. Queen's University Archives, Kingston, Allen B. Aylesworth Papers, vol. 1, Political Correspondence, file: Letters from Sir

Wilfrid Laurier, Laurier to Aylesworth, August 16, 1911.

24. See Margaret A. Ormsby, *British Columbia: A History* (Toronto: Macmillan, 1958): 349–53; W.L. Morton, *Manitoba: A History* (Toronto: University of Toronto Press, 1967): 323–24.

25. See Robert Craig Brown, *Borden: A Biography, Volume I*, 129–35; John English, *The Decline of Politics: The Conservatives and the Party System, 1901–20* (Toronto: University of Toronto Press, 1977): 53–55.

26. Christopher Armstrong, *The Politics of Federalism: Ontario's Relations with the Federal Government, 1867–1942* (Toronto: University of Toronto Press, 1981): 121–23; Charles W. Humphries, *"Honest Enough to Be Bold": The Life and Times of Sir James Pliny Whitney* (Toronto: University of Toronto Press, 1985): 180–85.

27. See the correspondence in AO, Whitney Papers, container B273277, Whitney to Borden, April 12, 1911; Borden to Whitney, April 13, 1911; Whitney to Borden, April 15, 1911.

28. LAC, Kemp Papers, vol. 3, file: 50, J. S. Carstairs, "Memorandum Concerning the Organization in Ontario," May 18, 1912.

29. Scott Young and Astrid Young, *Silent Frank Cochrane: The North's First Great Politician* (Toronto: Macmillan, 1973): 115–17.

30. Robert Cuff, "The Conservative Party Machine and the Election of 1911 in Ontario," *Ontario History* (September 1965): 149–56.

31. LAC, Kemp Papers, vol. 3, file: 50, J. S. Carstairs, "Memorandum Concerning the Organization in Ontario," May 18, 1912.

32. See, for example, LAC, Sifton Papers, reel C-590, 156,343, Sifton to Cochrane, August 15, 1911; 156,345, Sifton to Cochrane, August 15, 1911; reel C-591, 156,841, C.F. Hamilton to Sifton, April 19, 1911; 156,851, Sifton to Hamilton, April 22, 1911.

33. *Calgary Eye Opener*, August 12, 1911: 1.

34. Halifax, *The Morning Chronicle*, September 20, 1911: 4.

35. *Saint John Globe*, August 30, 1911: 5.

36. LAC, Sifton Papers, reel C-590, 156,348, Sifton to Cochrane, August 18, 1911. Ramsay Cook suggests that Dafoe convinced Sifton that to not support reciprocity would damage the paper economically and harm its reputation. Ramsay Cook, *The Politics of John W. Dafoe and the Free Press* (Toronto: University of Toronto

Press, 1963): 49.

37. LAC, Dafoe Papers, reel M-73, Borden to Sifton, September 22, 1911.

38. Quoted in *The Canadian Men and Women of the Time* (Toronto: William Briggs, 1912): 1,162.

39. See *Canadian Annual Review, 1911* (*CAR* hereafter): 201–03.

40. *Saint John Globe*, September 12, 1911: 6.

41. See Fisher Rare Book Library, Walker Papers, Box 9, file: 32, George Perley to Walker, April 3, 1911; G.P. de T. Glazebrook, *Sir Edmund Walker* (Toronto: Oxford University Press, 1933): 111.

42. LAC, Sifton Papers, reel C-591, 157,066, Lash to Sifton, August 3, 1911.

43. *Halifax Herald*, August 5, 1911: 1. The *Herald* and *The Morning Chronicle* both claimed circulations over 200,000. For more on these newspapers, see A. Gordon Brown, "Nova Scotia and the Reciprocity Election of 1911," MA thesis, Dalhousie University, 1971.

44. Halifax, *The Morning Chronicle*, July 6, 1911: 6.

45. *Manitoba Free Press*, August 28, 1911: 4.

46. *The Morning Chronicle*, July 27, 1911: 3.

47. Toronto *Star*, September 14, 1911: 13; see also September 8, 1911: 8.

48. *Halifax Herald*, September 8, 1911: 1.

49. Quoted in the Montreal *Gazette*, September 9, 1911: 1.

50. Stevens, "Laurier and the Liberal Party in Ontario," 341–49.

51. Stevens, "Laurier and the Liberal Party in Ontario," 351. See also Charles Humphries, "The Sources of Ontario 'Progressive' Conservatism, 1900–1914," Canadian Historical Association *Historical Papers* (1967): 119.

52. See Susan Mann Trofimenkoff, "Henri Bourassa and the "Woman Question," in *The Neglected Majority: Essays in Canadian Women's History*, edited by Susan Mann Trofimenkoff and Alison Prentice (Toronto: McClelland and Stewart, 1977): 104–15.

53. Catherine Cleverdon, *The Woman Suffrage Movement in Canada* (Toronto: University of Toronto Press, 1974): 111; on the nineteenth-century women's movement, see Alison Prentice et al., *Canadian Women: A History* (Toronto: Harcourt Brace Jovanovich,

1988): 189–203.

54. *Ibid.*, reel C-907, 189,294–96, Margaret McAlpine to Laurier, September 8, 1911; Laurier to McAlpine, September 12, 1911.

55. Toronto *Star*, September 6, 1911: 1.

56. Montreal *Gazette*, September 13, 1911: 1.

57. *Saint John Globe*, September 14, 1911: 2.

58. *Manitoba Free Press*, September 22, 1911: 15.

59. For the fullest account of the passage of the bill in the United States, see Ellis, *Reciprocity: 1911*, 88–140.

60. The classic text is Albert K. Weinberg, *Manifest Destiny: A Study of Nationalist Expansionism in American History* (Chicago: Quadrangle Books, 1963): 368–81. See also Kendrick A. Clements, "Manifest Destiny and Canadian Reciprocity in 1911," *Pacific Historical Review* 42 (1973): 32–52.

61. NARA, RG84, Records of Foreign Service Posts, Consular Posts, Toronto, Ontario, Canada, vol. 033, R.S. Chilton to Secretary of State, February 24, 1911.

62. Taft quoted in *CAR*, 72.

63. AO, Whitney Papers, container B273277, Borden to Whitney, May 9, 1911.

64. Quoted in *CAR*, 62.

65. Quoted in *ibid.*, 63–65.

66. Quoted in *ibid.*, 65–67.

67. *Ibid.*, 222–24.

68. Clipping attached to NARA, RG 84, Records of Foreign Service Posts, Consular Posts, Vancouver, B.C., Canada, vol. 089, David Wilber to Secretary of State, September 13, 1911.

69. *Ibid.*, Wilber to Secretary of State, June 23, 1911.

70. LAC, Grey Papers, reel C-1359, Bryce to Grey, September 8, 1911.

71. PRO, CO 42/955, t. 198, Bryce to Sir Edward Grey, September 14, 1911.

CHAPTER 8

1. *Saturday Night*, August 19, 1911: 3.

2. *The Morning Chronicle*, August 4, 1911: 1.

3. AO, Whitney Papers, container B 273277, Borden to Whitney, July

31, 1911.

4. *Canadian Annual Review 1911(CAR* hereafter): 161–62.

5. *The Huron Expositor*, August 18, 1911: 1.

6. *Ottawa Citizen*, August 16, 1911: 1.

7. *The Huron Expositor*, September 1, 1911: 5.

8. Borden, *Memoirs, Vol. 1*, 322–25.

9. LAC, Foster Papers, vol. 4, Diaries. For Foster in action in the Maritimes, see *Halifax Herald*, September 6, 1911: 1.

10. For Borden's itinerary, see *CAR*, 173–75.

11. Toronto *Star*, August 21, 1911: 3.

12. *Ibid.*, August 22, 1911: 9.

13. *Ibid.*, August 28, 1911: 7.

14. Montreal *Gazette*, August 26, 1911: 1.

15. Toronto *Star*, August 22, 1911: 1.

16. Quoted in Stevens, "Laurier and the Liberal Party in Ontario," 360.

17. AO, Whitney Papers, container B 273277, Whitney to Borden, August 1, 1911.

18. LAC, Graham Papers, vol. 24, file: 216, 012914, Graham to Fielding, September 15, 1911.

19. Toronto *Globe*, September 11, 1911: 1.

20. *Ibid.*, September 8, 1911: 1.

21. Toronto *Star*, September 6, 1911: 9.

22. *CAR*, 231.

23. Margaret Prang, *N.W. Rowell, Ontario Nationalist* (Toronto: University of Toronto Press, 1975): 92–94.

24. Quoted in Prang, *N.W. Rowell*, 98.

25. Michael Bliss, *A Canadian Millionaire: The Life and Business Times of Sir Joseph Flavelle* (Toronto: Macmillan, 1978): 217.

26. R. MacGregor Dawson, *William Lyon Mackenzie King: A Political Biography, 1874–1923* (Toronto: University of Toronto Press, 1958): 214; Terence Crowley, "Mackenzie King and the 1911 Election," *Ontario History* 61, No. 4 (December 1969): 184–87.

27. LAC, King Papers, reel C-1916, 16,925–28, King to Sims, July 30, 1911; Dawson, *King*, 221; F.A. McGregor, *The Fall & Rise of Mackenzie King: 1911–1919* (Toronto: Macmillan, 1962): 44.

28. Ulrich Frisse, "The Missing Link: Mackenzie King and Canada's

'German Capital,'" in *Mackenzie King: Citizenship and Community*, edited by John English, Kenneth McLaughlin, and P. Whitney Lackenbauer (Toronto: Robin Brass, 2002): 28–29.

29. Dawson, *King*, 209–12; Crowley, "King and the 1911 Election," 182–86. On the railway strike, see Henry Ferns and Bernard Ostry, *The Age of Mackenzie King* (Toronto: James Lorimer, 1976): 99–145.

30. See LAC, Graham Papers, vol. 35, file: 322, King to Graham, June 26, 1911; Graham also felt that the railway strike and the bank failure adversely affected his campaign, see LAC, Laurier Papers, reel C-906, 188,473, Graham to Laurier, August 3, 1911.

31. *Halifax Herald*, September 2, 1911: 17.

32. Frisse, "Missing Link," 29–30, McGregor, *The Fall & Rise of King*, 45.

33. LAC, Grey Papers, reel C-1358, 001,570, Laurier to Grey, August 23, 1911.

34. Brown, "Nova Scotia and the Reciprocity Election of 1911," 47–56.

35. *CAR*, 164–66.

36. Toronto *Star*, September 1, 1911: 3.

37. *Saint John Globe*, August 28, 1911: 1.

38. *The Morning Chronicle*, August 29, 1911: 1.

39. *Saint John Globe*, August 30, 1911: 8.

40. *The Morning Chronicle*, August 30, 1911: 2.

41. *Halifax Herald*, August 31, 1911: 1.

42. *The Morning Chronicle*, September 2, 1911: 1.

43. Toronto *Star*, August 31, 1911: 2.

44. See, for example, *The Morning Chronicle*, August 30, 1911: 2.

45. *Halifax Herald*, September 9, 1911: 1.

46. *Ibid.*, September 11, 1911: 1.

47. Montreal *Gazette*, September 15, 1911: 1.

48. *CAR*, 175–77.

49. *Saint John Globe*, September 6, 1911: 3.

50. *The Morning Chronicle*, July 26, 1911: 4.

51. See LAC, Laurier Papers, reel C-906, 188,352–53, D. McAlister to Laurier, July 31, 1911.

52. *The Morning Chronicle*, September 19, 1911: 1.

53. Brown, *Borden: A Biography, Vol. I*, 186.
54. *The Morning Chronicle*, September 1, 1911: 1.
55. Montreal *Gazette*, September 5, 1911: 1.
56. See Brown, "Nova Scotia and Reciprocity," 227–61.
57. See "Farmers' Organizations are Unanimous in Favor of the Reciprocity Agreement," Toronto *Star*, September 8, 1911: 5.
58. *Saturday Night*, June 10, 1911: 3; *CAR*, 248–49.
59. *Manitoba Free Press*, August 2, 1911: 4.
60. Richard Wilbur, *H.H. Stevens 1878–1973* (Toronto: University of Toronto Press, 1977): 17–18.
61. LAC, Laurier Papers, reel C-906, 188,444, R.L. Drury to Laurier, August 2, 1911.
62. Jean Barman, *The West Beyond the West: A History of British Columbia* (Toronto: University of Toronto Press, 1991): 147; *CAR*, 249.
63. See "Haultain Tries to Explain His Attitude on Reciprocity," *Manitoba Free Press*, September 7, 1911: 16.
64. Regina, *The Morning Leader*, August 1, 1911: 1.
65. See, for example, Toronto *Globe*, September 9, 1911: 20.
66. Regina, *The Morning Leader*, September 18, 1911: 1.
67. See LAC, Laurier Papers, reel C-906, 188,575–78, Laurier to Arthur Sifton, August 7, 1911; and 188,578, Oliver to Laurier, August 5, 1911; for more on the campaign in Alberta, see *CAR*, 245–47.
68. James H. Gray, *R.B. Bennett: The Calgary Years* (Toronto: University of Toronto Press, 1991): 115.
69. LAC, Laurier Papers, reel C-906, 188,649, Jess Dorman to Laurier, August 7, 1911.
70. Toronto *Globe*, September 16, 1911: 20.
71. *Calgary Eye Opener*, August 12, 1911: 1. For more on Bennett's election victory, see Gray, *Bennett*, 122, and John Boyko, *Bennett: The Rebel Who Challenged and Changed a Nation* (Toronto: Key Porter, 2010): 73–79.
72. Regina, *The Morning Leader*, August 1, 1911: 1.
73. Roger Graham, *Arthur Meighen: A Biography, Vol. 1: The Door of Opportunity* (Toronto: Clarke, Irwin, 1960): 65–66; for one interruption that led to a rebuke, see "Mr. Meighen and the Faked

Telegram," *Manitoba Free Press*, September 19, 1911: 4.

74. Quoted in *CAR*, 240.

75. *Manitoba Free Press*, August 29, 1911: 1.

76. See Ramsay Cook, *The Politics of John W. Dafoe and the Free Press* (Toronto: University of Toronto Press, 1963): 44–49; See also Murray Donnelly, *Dafoe of the Free Press* (Toronto: Macmillan, 1968): 62–68.

77. *Manitoba Free Press*, September 20, 1911: 4.

78. *Ibid.*, August 22, 1911: 4.

79. *Saturday Night*, September 16, 1911: 1.

80. *Ibid.*, 3.

81. Gregory P. Marchildon, *Profits and Politics: Beaverbrook and the Gilded Age of Canadian Finance* (Toronto: University of Toronto Press, 1996): 227.

82. Quoted in Heath Macquarrie, "Robert Borden and the Election of 1911," *The Canadian Journal of Economics and Political Science* 25, No. 3 (August 1959): 284.

83. Marchildon, *Profits and Politics*, 227.

84. O.D. Skelton, *Life and Letters of Sir Wilfrid Laurier, Vol. II*, 376.

85. *Saint John Globe*, September 8, 1911: 4.

86. Montreal *Gazette*, September 16, 1911: 1.

87. *Ottawa Citizen*, September 20, 1911: 6.

CHAPTER 9

1. Laurier Papers, C-906, 188396, W. Laurier to H.H. Dewart, August 2, 1911.

2. Laurier Papers, C-906, 188331, Telegram W. Laurier to H.S. Béland, July 29, 1911.

3. LAC, Henri Bourassa Papers, H. Bourassa to C.H. Cahan, January 25, 1912.

4. *Le Devoir*, August 30, 1911: 5.

5. *Le Devoir*, August 30, 1911: 1.

6. *La Patrie*, September 14, 1911: 14; see also September 18, 1911: 14.

7. *La Patrie*, August 24, 1911: 6.

8. *La Patrie*, September 8, 1911: 12.

9. See *Saturday Night*, September 16, 1911: 1.
10. *La Patrie*, September 18, 1911: editorial, 4.
11. *La Patrie*, September 16, 1911: 6.
12. *La Patrie*, September 22, 1911: 16.
13. *La Patrie*, September 6, 1911: 1.
14. *La Patrie*, September 19, 1911: 11.
15. Translated by the London *Sunday Times*, August 6, 1911: 5.
16. See Laurier Papers, C-906, 189107, Gustave Durant to W. Laurier, August 23, 1911, and 189,119, Eugene Roberge to Laurier, August 24, 1911. Laurier gives his response to Durant in a letter dated August 20, 1911, 189,113d.
17. LAC, Armand Lavergne Papers, Henri Bourassa to Armand Lavergne, July 27, 1911.
18. That Girard was a Nationaliste left no doubt, see LAC, Cameron Nish Papers, letter from D Maltais to Henri Bourassa, September 4, 1911. On the Liberal confusion, see Laurier Papers, C-906, 188,934, P.L.M. Vézina to Laurier, August 14, 1911 and Laetare Roy to Laurier, August 14, 1911, 189,117. Laurier's response is in his letter to Vézina, August 17, 1911, 188,936.
19. See *Le Devoir*, August 28, 1911, 6a; *Le Devoir*, August 24, 1911: editorial, 1.
20. Henri Bourassa Papers, Bourassa to Tom Chase Casgrain, May 31, 1913.
21. LAC, Laurier Papers reel C106, 188,447–48, J.A.C. Ethier to Laurier, August 2, 1911.
22. *Ibid.*, 188,449, Laurier to Ethier, August 7, 1911.
23. LAC, Cameron Nish Papers, O. Asselin to Bourassa, September 5, 1911, No. 513. Asselin's campaign in Saint-Jacques is described in detail in Hélène Pelletier-Ballargeon, *Olivar Asselin et son temps: Le militant* (Montreal: Fides, 1996), Chapter 24.
24. *Ibid.*, Cauchon to Bourassa, September 7, 1911, No. 514.
25. Toronto *Star*, August 28, 1911: 7b.
26. LAC Armand Lavergne Papers, Henri Bourassa to Lavergne, August 8, 1911.
27. See Frank Myron Guttman, *The Devil from Saint-Hyacinthe: Senator Télésphore-Damien Bouchard* (New York: iUniverse, 2007),

Chapter 4.

28. *Le Nationaliste*, August 13, 1911: 1.

29. *Le Devoir*, June 27, 1911: editorial.

30. LAC, J.S. Willison Papers, Frederick Hamilton to Willison, January 22, 1908.

31. *Quebec Chronicle*, August 14, 1911: 1, cited in René Castonguay, *Rodolphe Lemieux et le Parti libéral, 1866–1937* (Québec : Presses de l'Université Laval, 2000): 126.

32. Bouchard, *op cit.*, 258.

33. René Castonguay argues that Lemieux held his own in this debate in his *Rodolphe Lemieux et le Parti libéral, 1866–1937* (Québec: Presses de l'Université Laval, 2000): 126–28. Robert Rumilly, who profoundly admired Bourassa and Lavergne, devotes many colourful pages to the debate in his *Henri Bourassa: La vie publique d'un grand canadien* (Montreal, Editions Chantecler, 1953): 417–21. This book was republished by Les Editions de l'homme, but no date is indicated for that edition.

34. *Le Devoir*, September 19, 1911: front page editorial.

35. Laurier Papers, C-906, 188431, Laurier to Sir Francois Langelier, August 7, 1911.

36. See LAC, Armand Lavergne Papers, letter from Henri Béland to Armand Lavergne, December 7, 1910.

37. LAC Armand Lavergne Papers, Henri Bourassa to Armand Lavergne, July 27, 1911.

38. Montreal *Witness*, August 22, 1911: 1.

39. *Le Devoir*, August 18, 1911: 3.

40. *Le Devoir*, August 18, 1911: 3.

41. *Saturday Night*, September 9, 1911: 3.

42. *Le Devoir*, August 22, 1911: 2.

43. See *La Patrie*, August 23, 1911: 1, and *Le Devoir* (same date): 2.

44. *Le Devoir*, August 23, 2011: 2.

45. Quoted in the Toronto *Star*, August 23, 1911: 3b.

46. Laurier Papers, C-906, 188280, C.O Paradis to Laurier, July 30, 1911. Laurier manifested his support in a letter dated August 1, 1911: 188, 284.

47. Laurier Papers, C-906, Adélard Lanctôt to Wilfrid Laurier, August

7, 1911, 188,622–23 and August 10, 1911: 188,856–57. In terms of correspondence, this was without a doubt the riding that gave Laurier the most trouble.

48. *La Patrie*, August 24, 1911, 1; Laurier warned him to fall into rank in a letter dated August 8, 1911: 188,868.

49. *Le Devoir*, August 25, 1911: 2.

50. *Le Devoir*, August 26, 1911: 6.

51. *Saturday Night*, June 19, 1911.

52. Toronto *Star*, August 28, 1911: 7b.

53. See Laurier Papers, C-906, 188,797, Laurier to Hector Laferté, August 12, 1911.

54. *La Presse*, September 12, 1911: 1.

55. *Morning Leader*, September 12, 1911.

56. See Norman Ward (ed.) *A Party Politician: The Memoirs of Chubby Power* (Toronto: Macmillan, 1966): 30.

57. *New York Times*, September 19, 1911.

58. *Globe*, September 18, 1911: 1.

59. See J.C. McGee, *Histoire politique de Québec-Est* (Quebec: Belisle éditeur, 1948): 144–47.

60. The size of the audience varies widely. The *Star* wrote that ten thousand attended, while *La Presse* counted twenty-five thousand.

61. Toronto *Star*, September 20, 1911: 3a.

62. Toronto *Star*, September 20, 1911: 3b.

63. T.D. Bouchard writes that the students called for Laurier to be assassinated. See his *Memoirs, Vol. II*, 262.

64. *La Patrie*, August 24, 1911: 1.

65. Winnipeg *Tribune*, September 19, 1911.

66. Toronto *Star*, August 19, 1911: 5.

67. *Le Devoir*, August 28, 1911: 6b. This was not the first time Bourassa held these words against Laurier; he used them in the Drummond-Arthabaska by-election in 1910, also. See T.D. Bouchard, *Mémoires, Vol. II, Gravissant la colline* (Montreal: Éditions Beauchemin, 1960): 232.

68. *Ibid*.

69. *Le Devoir*, August 30, 1911: 1.

70. *Le Devoir*, August 31, 1911: 1.

71. *Le Devoir*, September 2, 1911: 1.
72. Asselin was clearly worried that he needed Bourassa's support and asked that Bourassa again share the stage with him. LAC, Cameron Nish Papers, O. Asselin to Henri Bourassa, September 13, 1911.
73. Winnipeg *Tribune*, September 8, 1911. Francq did not play an important role in this election, which is surprising. His biographer only devotes a few lines to the campaign. See Éric Leroux, *Gustave Francq: Figure marquante du syndicalisme et précurseur de la FTQ* (Montreal: VLB Editeur, 2001).
74. Toronto *Star*, September 21, 1911: 1.
75. *Le Nationaliste*, September 17, 1911: 6.
76. *Le Nationaliste*, September 17, 1911: 1.
77. *Le Nationaliste*, September 17, 1911: 17.
78. *Le Nationaliste*, September 17, 1911: 3.
79. *Le Nationaliste*, September 17, 1911:.1.
80. *Le Nationaliste*, September 17, 1911: 1.
81. *Ibid.*

CHAPTER 10

1. LAC, MG30 D279, Wilson MacDonald Papers, vol. 6, Diary, Thursday, September 21, 1911.
2. *Saint John Globe*, September 21, 1911: 1.
3. Toronto *Star*, September 21, 1911: 1.
4. *Saint John Globe*, September 21, 1911: 1.
5. Montreal *Gazette*, September 29, 1911: 1.
6. *Manitoba Free Press*, September 22, 1911: 4.
7. *Halifax Herald*, September 25, 1911: 1.
8. Toronto *Globe*, September 22, 1911: 13.
9. *Saint John Globe*, September 22, 1911: 8.
10. *Halifax Herald*, September 22, 1911: 1.
11. A.H.U. Colquhoun, *Press, Politics and People: The Life and Letters of Sir John Willison* (Toronto: Macmillan, 1935): 181.
12. Toronto *Globe*, September 22, 1911: 1, 13; Scott Young and Astrid Young, *Silent Frank Cochrane: The North's First Great Politician* (Toronto: Macmillan, 1973): 124.
13. Montreal *Gazette*, September 23, 1911: 5; *Manitoba Free Press*,

September 22, 1911: 15.

14. Regina, *The Morning Leader*, September 22, 1911: 1.

15. Roger Graham, *Arthur Meighen: A Biography, Vol. 1: The Door of Opportunity* (Toronto: Clarke, Irwin, 1960): 67.

16. James H. Gray, *R.B. Bennett: The Calgary Years* (Toronto: University of Toronto Press, 1991): 123.

17. John G. Diefenbaker, *One Canada: Memoirs of the Right Honourable John G. Diefenbaker, Vol. 1: The Crusading Years, 1895–1956* (Toronto: Macmillan, 1975): 75–76; Denis Smith, *Rogue Conservative: The Life and Legend of John G. Diefenbaker* (Toronto: Macfarlane Walter & Ross, 1995): 41–42.

18. Montreal *Gazette*, September 22, 1911: 1.

19. Toronto *Star*, September 22, 1911: 1.

20. Toronto *Star*, September 22, 1911: 1.

21. *The Morning Chronicle*, September 22, 1911: 1; *Halifax Herald*, September 25, 1911: 6.

22. See Toronto *Star*, September 22, 1911: 1; Montreal *Gazette*, September 25, 1911: 1.

23. LAC, Laurier Papers, reel C-907, 189,463, A.A. Durocher to Laurier, September 22, 1911.

24. *Manitoba Free Press*, September 22, 1911: 4.

25. *12th General Election 1911, Report of the Clerk of the Crown in Chancery for Canada, Sessional Paper No. 18*, 1912.

26. LAC, George Foster Papers, FB McCurdy to Foster, September 25, 1911.

27. George Foster Papers, NG27 II D7, vol. 107, William Tobin to Foster, September 27, 1911 (Glace Bay, NS).

28. See Laurier Papers, C-906, 188,317–19, C.J. Ouman to George Graham, July 31, 1911: 188,317–19.

29. *Saturday Night*, September 2, 1911: 3.

30. *Le Devoir*, May 11, 1911: editorial.

31. Robert Rumilly, *Henri Bourassa*, 438.

32. LAC, Foster Papers, Sam Sharpe to Foster, September 23, 1911 (Uxbridge Station).

33. *Victoria Times-Colonist*, September 2, 1911: 1.

34. LAC, RCMP Files (1911) RG 18 File 459, Arthur Roberts to

Commissioner RNWM Police, September 15, 1911. See the reports: J.R. Tubby to J.D. Moody, Officer Commanding RNWM Police, Regina District, September 23, 1911; Wheatly to J.D. Moody, September 23, 1911; Warnock to Moody, September 23, 1911; Bossange to Moodie, September 22, 1911.

35. George Foster Papers, vol. 107, Richard S. Lake to Foster, September 28, 1911.

36. Laurier Papers, C-906, 188,445, Laurier to R.L. Drury, August 5, 1911.

37. *Ibid.*, 188,270–71, New Westminster Liberal Association to A. Aylesworth, July 28, 1911. (Weart dropped out of the Liberal race after receiving the nomination in early August.)

38. J.E. McLean, President of the Canadian Club in New York City, cited in the *New York Times*, September 22, 1911: 6.

39. These views were articulated by members of the Laurier cabinet. See LAC, Mackenzie King Diaries, September 25, 26, 30, 1911.

40. *Calgary Daily Herald*, September 22, 1911: 1.

41. Robert Cuff, "The Conservative Party Machine and the Election of 1911 in Ontario" *Ontario History* 57 (1965): 149–56.

42. P.D. Stevens, "Laurier, Aylesworth, and the Decline of the Liberal Party in Ontario" *Historical Papers/Communications historiques*, March 1, 1968: 94–113.

43. Richard Johnston and Michael Percy, "Reciprocity, Imperial Sentiment, and Party Politics in the 1911 Election" *Canadian Journal of Political Science*, 13 (April 1980): 711–29.

44. M.B. Percy, K.H. Norrie, and R.G. Johnston, "Reciprocity and the Canadian General Election of 1911," *Explorations in Economic History* 19 (1982): 409–34.

45. Eugene Beaulieu and J.C. Herbert Emery, "Pork Packers, Reciprocity and Laurier's Defeat in the 1911 Canadian General Election," *Journal of Economic History* 62 (April 2001): 1,083–1,101.

Epilogue

1. LAC, George Foster Papers, vol. 4, Diary, September 25, 1911.

2. AO, Whitney Papers, container B273277, Whitney to Borden,

September 22, 1911.

3. LAC, Dafoe Papers, reel M-73, Dafoe to George Iles, September 27, 1911.

4. *Ibid.*, Sifton to Dafoe, September 26, 1911.

5. UTA, George Wrong Papers, B2003-0005/005, box 5, Willison to Wrong, October 24, 1913.

6. PRO, CO 42 /948, Grey to Harcourt, September 29, 1911.

7. LAC, Laurier Papers, reel C-907, 189,466, Laurier to J.H. King, September 23, 1911.

8. LAC, Dafoe Papers, reel M-73, Laurier to Dafoe, September 27, 1911.

9. Queen's University Archives, Aylesworth Papers, Box 3, Letter Book n. 19, September 5–October 9, 1911, Aylesworth to Cane, September 25, 1911.

10. Quoted in Joseph Schull, *Laurier: The First Canadian* (Toronto: Macmillan, 1965): 537–38.

11. King quoted in Charles Humphries, "Mackenzie King Looks at Two 1911 Elections," *Ontario History* 56, No. 3 (September 1964): 205.

12. Queen's University Archives, John G. Foster Papers, Box 1, General Correspondence, file: Correspondence (1909–1926), nos. 1–41, King to Foster, September 24, 1911.

13. LAC, King Papers, reel C-1916, 17,050, Stratton to King, October 7, 1911.

14. LAC, Grey Papers, reel C-1361, 004,432, Grey to Harcourt, January 30, 1911.

15. Michael Bliss, *A Living Profit: Studies in the Social History of Canadian Business, 1883–1911* (Toronto: McClelland and Stewart, 1974): 102–03.

16. LAC, Grey Papers, reel C-1358, 001,537–38, Grey memo, July 26, 1911.

17. Montreal *Gazette*, September 27, 1911: 1.

18. R. MacGregor Dawson, *William Lyon Mackenzie King: A Political Biography, 1874–1923* (Toronto: University of Toronto Press, 1958): 221.

19. LAC, King Papers, Diary, October 4, 1911.

20. Reginald Whitaker, *The Government Party: Organizing and*

Financing the Liberal Party of Canada 1930–58 (Toronto: University of Toronto Press, 1977): 6–8. See also Margaret Prang, "Mackenzie King Woos Ontario, 1919–1921," *Ontario History* 58, No. 3 (March 1966): 17.

21. LAC, King Papers, Diary, September 24–25, 1911.

22. LAC, Grey Papers, reel C-1359, 002,967, Grey to Bryce, September 26, 1911.

23. LAC, King Papers, Diary, September 25, 1911. Laurier told the governor general the same thing. See PRO, CO 42 /948, Grey to Lewis Harcourt, September 29, 1911.

24. LAC, King Papers, Diary, October 6, 1911.

25. LAC, Grey Papers, reel C-1359, 002,973, Grey to Bryce, September 26, 1911. For a selection of letters concerning cabinet appointments, see LAC, Borden Papers, reel C-4364, 81,819, Cahan to Borden, October 1, 1911; LAC, Willison Papers, vol. 19, file: 140, Hamilton to Willison, October 2, 1911; AO, Whitney Papers, container B 273277, Crothers to Whitney, September 23, 1911; LAC, Bennett Papers, reel M-907, 770, Bennett to E.W. Beatty, n.d.

26. English, *The Decline of Politics*, 69.

27. See Robert Craig Brown, *Robert Laird Borden: A Biography, Volume I: 1854–1914* (Toronto: Macmillan, 1975): 199–200.

28. See Heath N. Macquarrie, "The Formation of Borden's First Cabinet," *The Canadian Journal of Economics and Political Science* 23, No. 1 (February 1957): 94–95.

29. LAC, King Papers, Diary, October 6, 1911.

30. Quoted in John English, *Borden: His Life and World* (Toronto: McGraw-Hill Ryerson, 1977): 62.

31. For Foster's efforts see LAC, Foster Papers, vol. 107, file: Cabinet Formation, 1911, and vol. 4, Diaries, September–October 1911.

32. *Saturday Night*, September 30, 1911: 1.

33. Roger Graham, "The Cabinet of 1911," in *Cabinet Formation and Bicultural Relations*, edited by Frederick Gibson (Ottawa: Queen's Printer, 1970): 53.

34. See Graham, "Cabinet of 1911," 55–57, and Macquarrie, "Borden's First Cabinet," 103–04.

35. LAC, Bourassa Papers, reel M-721, Bourassa to Cahan, January 25,

1912.

36. Graham, "Cabinet of 1911," 60.

37. John Boyko, *Bennett: The Rebel Who Challenged and Changed a Nation* (Toronto: Key Porter, 2010): 78–79.

38. Macquarrie, "Borden's First Cabinet," 99; see also Graham, "Cabinet of 1911," 61.

39. King quoted in Charles Humphries, "Mackenzie King Looks at Two 1911 Elections," *Ontario History* 56, No. 3 (September 1964): 204.

40. Quoted in Dafoe, *Clifford Sifton in Relation to His Times*, 374.

41. LAC, Grey Papers, reel C-1359, 002,964, Bryce to Grey, September 23, 1911.

42. See "A Canadian," "Why Canada Rejected Reciprocity," *Yale Review* 1, No. 2 (January 1912): 173–87. See also O.D. Skelton, "Canada's Rejection of Reciprocity," *The Journal of Political Economy* 19, No. 9 (November 1911): 726–31, and W.L. Grant, "The Canadian Elections," *Queen's Quarterly* 19, No. 2 (October 1911): 170–80.

43. NARA, RG84, Records of Foreign Service Posts, Consular Posts, Toronto, Ontario, Canada, vol. 33, American Consulate, *Annual Report*, March 13, 1912.

44. Kendrick Clements, "Manifest Destiny and Canadian Reciprocity in 1911," *Pacific Historical Review* 42 (1973): 52.

45. Bill Dymond, "Free Trade, 1911 and All of That," *bout de papier* 5, No. 2 (summer 1987): 25.

46. W.L. Morton, *The Progressive Party in Canada* (Toronto: University of Toronto Press, 1950): 26.

47. Charles M. Johnston, *E.C. Drury: Agrarian Idealist* (Toronto: University of Toronto Press, 1986): 34–36.

48. Richard Clippingdale, *Laurier: His Life and World* (Toronto: McGraw-Hill Ryerson, 1979): 144–45.

49. Robert C. Brown and Ramsay Cook, *Canada 1896–1921: A Nation Transformed* (Toronto: McClelland and Stewart, 1974): 186.

BIBLIOGRAPHY

Primary Sources

Archives
Fisher Rare Book Library, Toronto
    Sir Edmund Walker Papers
Library and Archives Canada (LAC), Ottawa
    R.B. Bennett Papers
    Sir Robert Borden Papers
    Henri Bourassa Papers
    Louis-Philippe Brodeur Papers
    John Dafoe Paper
    Sir George Foster Papers
    George Graham Papers
    Lord Grey Papers
    A.E. Kemp Papers
    William Lyon Mackenzie King Papers
    Sir Wilfrid Laurier Papers
    Armand Lavergne Papers
    Wilson MacDonald Papers
    F.D. Monk Papers
    Cameron Nish Papers
    RCMP Papers

Clifford Sifton Papers

J.S. Willison Papers

National Archives and Records Administration (NARA), Washington D.C.

RG84, Records of Foreign Service Posts, Consular Posts, Vancouver, B.C.; Toronto, ON.

Ontario Archives (OA), Toronto

Sir James P. Whitney Papers

Public Records Office (PRO), London

Colonial Office Records CO42

Queen's University Archives, Kingston

Allen B. Aylesworth Papers

John G. Foster Papers

Norman Lambert Papers

University of Toronto Archives (UTA), Toronto

G.M. Wrong Papers

Robert Craig Brown Papers

Newspapers, Magazines

Calgary Eye Opener

Grain Growers' Guide

Halifax Herald

Halifax, *The Morning Chronicle*

The Huron Expositor

La Patrie

La Presse

Le Devoir

Le Nationaliste

Le Pays

Manitoba Free Press

Montreal *Star*

Montreal *Gazette*

Montreal *Witness*

New York Times

Ottawa Citizen

Regina, *The Morning Leader*

Saint John Globe
Saturday Night
Toronto *Star*
Toronto *Globe*
Winnipeg *Tribune*

PUBLISHED SOURCES

Canada, *Documents on Canadian External Relations, Vol. 1: 1909–1918* (Ottawa 1967).
Canada, House of Commons, *Debates*.
Canada, House of Commons, *Sessional Papers. 12th General Election 1911, Report of the Clerk of the Crown in Chancery for Canada*, No. 18, 1912.

SECONDARY SOURCES

Allan, John. "Reciprocity and the Canadian General Election of 1911: A Reexamination of Economic Self-Interest." MA thesis, Queen's University, 1971.
Armstrong, Christopher. *The Politics of Federalism: Ontario's Relations with the Federal Government, 1867–1942*. Toronto: University of Toronto Press, 1981.
Baker, W.M. "A Case Study of Anti-Americanism in English-Speaking Canada: The Election Campaign of 1911." *Canadian Historical Review* 51, No. 4 (December 1970), 426–49.
Barman, Jean. *The West Beyond the West: A History of British Columbia*. Toronto: University of Toronto Press, 1991.
Beaulieu, Eugene, and J.C. Herbert Emery. "Pork Packers, Reciprocity, and Laurier's Defeat in the 1911 Canadian General Election." *The Journal of Economic History* 62, No. 10 (December 2001), 1,083–1,101.
Beck, J Murray. *Pendulum of Power: Canada's Federal Election*. Toronto: Prentice Hall, 1968.
Bilkey, Paul. *Persons, Papers and Things*. Toronto: Ryerson, 1940.

Bliss, Michael. *A Canadian Millionaire: The Life and Business Times of Sir Joseph Flavelle, Bart. 1858–1939*. Toronto: Macmillan, 1978.

_____. *A Living Profit: Studies in the Social History of Canadian Business, 1883–1911*. Toronto: McClelland and Stewart, 1974.

Borden, Robert. *Robert Laird Borden: His Memoirs*, Vol. I, edited by Henry Borden. Toronto: Macmillan, 1938.

Bouchard, T.D. *Mémoires, Vol II, Gravissant la colline*. Montreal: Editions Beauchemin, 1960.

Bourassa, Henri. *La conférence impériale et le rôle de M. Laurier*. Montreal: Imprimerie Le Devoir, 1911.

Boyko, John. *Bennett: The Rebel Who Challenged and Changed a Nation*. Toronto: Key Porter, 2010.

Bridle, Augustus. *The Masques of Ottawa*. Toronto: Macmillan, 1921.

Brown, A. Gordon. "Nova Scotia and the Reciprocity Election of 1911." MA thesis, Dalhousie University, 1971.

Brown, Robert C., and Ramsay Cook. *Canada 1896–1921: A Nation Transformed*. Toronto: McClelland and Stewart, 1974.

Brown, Robert Craig. *Robert Laird Borden: A Biography, Volume I: 1854–1914*. Toronto: Macmillan, 1975.

Castonguay, René. *Rodolphe Lemieux et le Parti libéral, 1866–1937*. Quebec: Presses de l'Université Laval, 2000.

Charlesworth, Hector. *More Candid Chronicles*. Toronto: Macmillan Company, 1928.

Clements, Kendrick A. "Manifest Destiny and Canadian Reciprocity in 1911." *Pacific Historical Review* 42 (1973), 32–52.

Cleverdon, Catherine. *The Woman Suffrage Movement in Canada*. Toronto: University of Toronto Press, 1974.

Clippingdale, Richard. *Laurier: His Life and World*. Toronto: McGraw-Hill Ryerson, 1979.

_____. "Willison, Sir John Stephen." *Dictionary of Canadian Biography*. (Accessed online.)

Colquhoun, A.H.U. *Press, Politics and People: The Life and Letters of Sir John Willison*. Toronto: Macmillan, 1935.

Cook, Ramsay. *The Politics of John W. Dafoe and the Free Press*. Toronto: University of Toronto Press, 1963.

Crowley, Terence A. "Mackenzie King and the 1911 Election." *Ontario History* 61, No. 4 (December 1969), 181–96.

Cuff, Robert D. "The Conservative Party Machine and the Election of 1911 in Ontario." *Ontario History* 57, No. 3 (September 1965), 149–56.

_____. "The Toronto Eighteen and the Election of 1911." *Ontario History* 57, No. 4 (December 1965), 169–80.

Dafoe, John W. *Clifford Sifton in Relation to His Times.* Toronto: Macmillan, 1931.

Dawson, R. MacGregor. *William Lyon Mackenzie King: A Political Biography, 1874–1923.* Toronto: University of Toronto Press, 1958.

Diefenbaker, John G. *One Canada: Memoirs of the Right Honourable John G. Diefenbaker,* Vol. 1, *The Crusading Years, 1895–1956.* Toronto: Macmillan, 1975.

Donnelly, Murray. *Dafoe of the Free Press.* Toronto: Macmillan, 1968.

Dutil, Patrice. *Devil's Advocate: Godfroy Langlois and the Politics of Liberal Progressivism in Laurier's Quebec.* Montreal: Robert Davies Publishing, 1994.

Dymond, Bill. "Free Trade, 1911 and All of That." *bout de papier* 5, No. 2 (summer 1987), 22–25.

Eayrs, James. "The Round Table Movement in Canada, 1909–1920." *Canadian Historical Review* 38, No. 1 (March 1957), 1–20.

Ellis, L. Ethan. "Canada's Rejection of Reciprocity in 1911." *Report of the Annual Meeting of the Canadian Historical Association* 18, No. 1 (1939), 99–111.

_____. *Reciprocity 1911: A Study in Canadian-American Relations.* New Haven: Yale University Press, 1939.

English, John. *Borden: His Life and World.* Toronto: McGraw-Hill Ryerson, 1977.

_____. *The Decline of Politics: The Conservatives and the Party System, 1901–20.* Toronto: University of Toronto Press, 1977.

Evans, A. Margaret. *Sir Oliver Mowat.* Toronto: University of Toronto Press, 1992.

Ferns, Henry, and Bernard Ostry. *The Age of Mackenzie King.* Toronto: James Lorimer, 1976.

Findlay, John George. *The Imperial Conference of 1911*. London, 1912.

Francis, R. Douglas. *Frank H. Underhill: Intellectual Provocateur*. Toronto: University of Toronto Press, 1986.

Frisse, Ulrich. "The Missing Link: Mackenzie King and Canada's 'German Capital.'" In *Mackenzie King: Citizenship and Community*, edited by John English, Kenneth McLaughlin, and P. Whitney Lackenbauer. Toronto: Robin Brass, 2002, 18–34.

Garvin, John W., ed. *Canadian Poets*. Toronto: McClelland and Stewart, 1926.

Glazebrook, G.P. de T. *Sir Edmund Walker*. Toronto: Oxford University Press, 1933.

Gordon, Donald. *The Dominion Partnership in Imperial Defense, 1870–1914*. Baltimore: Johns Hopkins Press, 1965.

Gorman, Daniel. *Imperial Citizenship: Empire and the Question of Belonging*. Manchester: Manchester University Press, 2006.

Graham, Roger. *Arthur Meighen: A Biography, Vol. 1: The Door of Opportunity*. Toronto: Clarke, Irwin, 1960.

_____. "The Cabinet of 1911." In *Cabinet Formation and Bicultural Relations*, edited by Frederick W. Gibson, Ottawa: Queen's Printer, 1970, 47–62.

Granatstein, J.L. "Free Trade Between Canada and the United States: The Issue That Will Not Go Away." In *The Politics of Canada's Economic Relationship with the United States*, edited by Denis Stairs and Gilbert R. Winham. Toronto: 1985, 11–54.

_____, and Norman Hillmer. *Prime Ministers: Ranking Canada's Leaders*. Toronto: HarperCollins, 2000.

Gray, James H. *R.B. Bennett: The Calgary Years*. Toronto: University of Toronto Press, 1991.

Guttman, Frank Myron. *The Devil from Saint-Hyacinthe: Senator Télésphore-Damien Bouchard*. New York: iUniverse, 2007.

Hall, D.J. *Clifford Sifton: Volume I: Young Napoleon*. Vancouver: University of British Columbia Press, 1981.

_____. *Clifford Sifton: Volume II: A Lonely Eminence, 1901–1929*. Vancouver: University of British Columbia Press, 1985.

Hamilton, C. Frederick. "Shall Canada Have a Navy." *University Magazine* (October 1909), 396.

Hannigan, Robert E. "Reciprocity 1911: Continentalism and American Weltpolitik." *Diplomatic History* 4, No. 1 (Winter 1980), 1–18.

Hart, Michael. *A Trading Nation: Canadian Trade Policy from Colonialism to Globalization*. Vancouver: University of British Columbia Press, 2002.

Hawkes, Arthur. "Sir Clifford Sifton and the Reciprocity Election of 1911." Reprinted in *The 1911 General Election: A Study in Canadian Politics*, edited by Paul Stevens, Toronto: Copp Clark, 1970, 71–77.

Hilliker, John. *Canada's Department of External Affairs, Volume 1: The Early Years, 1909–1946*. Montreal: McGill-Queen's University Press, 1990.

Hopkins, J. Castell. *The Canadian Annual Review of Public Affairs, 1911*. Toronto: Annual Review Publishing Co., 1912.

Humphries, Charles. *"Honest Enough to Be Bold": The Life and Times of Sir James Pliny Whitney*. Toronto: University of Toronto Press, 1985.

_____. "Mackenzie King Looks at Two 1911 Elections." *Ontario History* 56, No. 3 (September 1964), 203–06.

_____. "The Sources of Ontario 'Progressive' Conservatism, 1900–1914." Canadian Historical Association *Historical Papers* (1967), 118–29.

Johnston, Charles M. *E.C. Drury: Agrarian Idealist*. Toronto: University of Toronto Press, 1986.

Johnston, Richard, and Michael B. Percy. "Reciprocity, Imperial Sentiment, and Party Politics in the 1911 Election." *Canadian Journal of Political Science* 13, No. 4 (December 1980), 711–29.

Knowles, Valerie. *From Telegrapher to Titan: The Life of William C. Van Horne*. Toronto: Dundurn Press, 2004.

LaPierre, Laurier. *Sir Wilfrid Laurier and the Romance of Canada*. Toronto: Stoddart, 1996.

Leacock, Stephen. "Canada and the Monroe Doctrine." *University Magazine* (October 1909), 352.

Leroux, Éric. *Gustave Francq: Figure marquante du syndicalisme et précurseur de la FTQ*. Montreal: VLB Editeur, 2001.

MacKenzie, David. *Arthur Irwin. A Biography*. Toronto. University of Toronto Press, 1993.

Macquarrie, Heath N. "The Formation of Borden's First Cabinet." *The Canadian Journal of Economics and Political Science* 23, No. 1 (February 1957), 90–104.

_____. "Robert Borden and the Election of 1911." *The Canadian Journal of Economics and Political Science* 25, No. 3 (August 1959), 271–86.

Marchildon, Gregory P. *Profits and Politics: Beaverbrook and the Gilded Age of Canadian Finance.* Toronto: University of Toronto Press, 1996.

Massie, Robert K. *Dreadnought: Britain, Germany and the Coming of the Great War.* New York: Random House, 1991.

Masters, Donald C. *Reciprocity, 1846–1911.* Ottawa: Canadian Historical Association, 1983.

_____. *The Reciprocity Treaty of 1854.* Toronto: McClelland and Stewart, 1963.

McGee, J.C. *Histoire politique de Québec-Est.* Quebec: Belisle éditeur, 1948.

McGregor, F.A. *The Fall & Rise of Mackenzie King: 1911–1919.* Toronto: Macmillan, 1962.

Miller, Carman. "Fielding, William Stevens." *Dictionary of Canadian Biography.* (Accessed online).

_____. "Sir Frederick Borden and Military Reform, 1896–1911." *Canadian Historical Review* 50, No. 3 (September 1969), 265–84.

Morgan, Henry James, ed. *The Canadian Men and Women of the Time.* Toronto: William Briggs, 1912.

Morton, W.L. *Manitoba: A History.* Toronto: University of Toronto Press, 1967.

Nicolson, Juliet. *The Perfect Summer: England in 1911.* Toronto: McArthur, 2007.

Ormsby, Margaret A. *British Columbia: A History.* Toronto: Macmillan, 1958.

Percy, M.B., K.H. Norrie, and R.G. Johnston. "Reciprocity and the Canadian General Election of 1911." *Explorations in Economic History* 19 (1982), 409–34.

Prang, Margaret. "Mackenzie King Woos Ontario, 1919–1921." *Ontario History* 58, No. 1 (March 1966), 1–20.

_____. *N.W. Rowell, Ontario Nationalist*. Toronto: University of Toronto Press, 1975.

Prentice, Alison, et al. *Canadian Women: A History*. Toronto: Harcourt Brace Jovanovich, 1988.

Preston, W.T.R. *My Generation of Politics and Politicians*. Toronto: D.A. Rose, 1927.

Rumilly, Robert. *Henri Bourassa: La vie publique d'un grand canadien*. Montreal: Editions Chantecler, 1953.

_____. *Histoire de la Province de Quebec* Vol. X.

Scheinberg, Stephen. "Invitation to Empire: Tariffs and American Economic Expansion in Canada." *Business History Review* 47 (1973), 218–38.

Schull, Joseph. *Laurier: The First Canadian*. Toronto: Macmillan, 1965.

Skelton, Oscar Douglas. *Life and Letters of Sir Wilfrid Laurier*, 2 volumes. Toronto: Oxford University Press, 1921 and 1922.

Smith, Denis. *Rogue Tory: The Life and Legend of John G. Diefenbaker*. Toronto: Macfarlane Walter & Ross, 1995.

Stacey, C.P. *Canada and the Age of Conflict: A History of Canadian External Policies Volume I: 1867–1921*. Toronto: University of Toronto Press, 1984.

Stevens, Paul. "Laurier and the Liberal Party in Ontario, 1887–1911." PhD thesis, University of Toronto, 1966.

_____. "Laurier, Aylesworth, and the Decline of the Liberal Party." Canadian Historical Association, *Historical Papers* (1968), 94–113.

_____. "Reciprocity 1911: The Canadian Perspective." In *Canadian-American Free Trade: Historical, Political and Economic Dimensions*, edited by A.R. Riggs and Tom Velk, Halifax: Institute for Research on Public Policy, 1987, 9–21.

_____. "Wilfrid Laurier: Politician" In *The Political Ideas of the Prime Ministers of Canada*, edited by Marcel Hamelin, Ottawa: Editions de l'Université d'Ottawa, 1969.

_____, ed. *The 1911 General Election: A Study in Canadian Politics*. Toronto: Copp Clark, 1970.

_____, and John Saywell, eds. *Lord Minto's Canadian Papers*. Toronto: The Champlain Society, 1983.

Stewart, Gordon. "'A Special Contiguous Country Economic Regime': An Overview of America's Canadian Policy." *Diplomatic History* 6, No. 4 (Fall 1982), 339–57.

Trofimenkoff, Susan Mann. "Henri Bourassa and the 'Woman Question.'" In *The Neglected Majority: Essays in Canadian Women's History*, edited by Susan Mann Trofimenkoff and Alison Prentice. Toronto: McClelland and Stewart, 1977, 104–15.

Underhill, Frank H. *The Image of Confederation*. Toronto: CBC, 1964.

Velk, Tom, and A.R. Riggs. "Reciprocity 1911: Through American Eyes." In *Canadian-American Free Trade: Historical, Political and Economic Dimensions*, edited by A.R. Riggs and Tom Velk. Halifax: Institute for Research on Public Policy, 1987, 23–31.

Ward, Norman, ed. *A Party Politician: The Memoirs of Chubby Power*. Toronto: Macmillan, 1966.

Weinberg, Albert K. *Manifest Destiny: A Study of Nationalist Expansionism in American History*. Chicago: Quadrangle Books, 1963.

Whitaker, Reginald. *The Government Party: Organizing and Financing the Liberal Party of Canada 1930–58*. Toronto: University of Toronto Press, 1977.

Wilbur, Richard. *H.H. Stevens 1878–1973*. Toronto: University of Toronto Press, 1977.

Wood, Louis Aubrey. *A History of Farmers' Movements in Canada*. Toronto: University of Toronto Press, 1975.

Young, Scott, and Astrid Young. *Silent Frank Cochrane: The North's First Great Politician*. Toronto: Macmillan of Canada, 1973.

INDEX

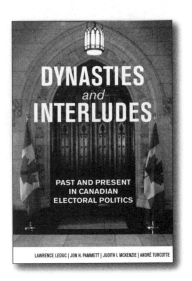

Dynasties and Interludes
Past and Present in Canadian Electoral Politics
by Lawrence LeDuc, Jon H. Pammett,
Judith I. McKenzie, and André Turcotte
978-1554887965 | $35.00

A comprehensive and unique overview of elections and voting in Canada from Confederation to the recent spate of minority governments. This book examines changes in the composition of the electorate, as well as the technology and professionalization of election campaigns.

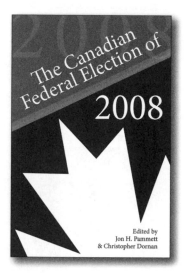

The Canadian Federal Election of 2008
edited by Jon H. Pammett and Christopher Dornan
978-1554884070 | $36.99

A comprehensive analysis of all aspects of the campaign and election outcome. The chapters are written by leading professors of political science, journalism, and communications. They examine the strategies, successes, and failures of the major political parties — the Conservatives (Faron Ellis and Peter Woolstencroft), Liberals (Brooke Jeffrey), New Democrats (Lynda Erickson and David Laycock), Bloc Québécois (Eric Belanger and Richard Nadeau), and Green Party (Susan Harada).

Available at your favourite bookseller.

DUNDURN
www.dundurn.com

What did you think of this book?
Visit www.dundurn.com for reviews, videos, updates, and more!